BEHAVIORAL ANALYSIS
OF SOCIETIES
AND
CULTURAL PRACTICES

The Series in Health Psychology and Behavioral Medicine

Charles D. Spielberger, *Editor-in-Chief*

IN PREPARATION

BEHAVIORAL ANALYSIS OF SOCIETIES AND CULTURAL PRACTICES

Edited by
P. A. Lamal
University of North Carolina
Charlotte, North Carolina

⊙ **HEMISPHERE PUBLISHING CORPORATION**
A member of the Taylor & Francis Group

New York   Washington   Philadelphia   London

BEHAVIORAL ANALYSIS OF SOCIETIES AND CULTURAL PRACTICES

1 2 3 4 5 6 7 8 9 0   B R B R   9 8 7 6 5 4 3 2 1

This book was set in Times Roman by Hemisphere Publishing Corporation. The editors were Dave Weber and S. Michele Nix. The typesetter was Phoebe Carter.
Cover design by Debra Eubanks Riffe.
Braun-Brumfield, Inc. was printer and binder.

A CIP catalog record for this book is available from the British Library.

Library of Congress Cataloging-in-Publication Data

Behavioral analysis of societies and cultural practices / edited by
* P. A. Lamal.*
*   p.   cm.*
* Includes bibliographical references and index.*

* 1. Social psychology.   2. Behavioral assessment.   3. Human*
behavior.   4. Social interaction.   I. Lamal, Peter A.
HM251.B4482   1991
302—dc20   91-13232
                                                                         CIP

ISBN 1-56032-123-7
ISSN 8756-467X

To Polly

Contents

III
THE FUTURE

Contributors

JUDY L. AGNEW, Department of Psychology, University of Victoria, Victoria, BC, Canada

K. ANTHONY EDWARDS, Ph.D., Clinical Services Unit, Green Bay Correctional Institution, P. O. Box 19033, Green Bay, WI 54307

JANET ELLIS, Center for Behavioral Studies, University of North Texas, Denton, TX 76203

SIGRID S. GLENN, Center for Behavioral Studies, University of North Texas, Denton, TX 76203

JOEL GREENSPOON, Center for Behavioral Studies, P. O. Box 13438, University of North Texas, Denton, TX 76203

FRANK HOVELL, Department of Psychology, San Francisco State University, San Francisco, CA 94132

MELBOURNE F. HOVELL, Division of Health and Behavioral Science, School of Public Health, San Diego State University, San Diego, CA 92182-0405

ROBERT KAPLAN, School of Medicine, University of California at San Diego, San Diego, CA 92037

JOHN H. KUNKEL, Department of Sociology, The University of Western Ontario, London, Ontario N6A 5C2, Canada

P. A. LAMAL, Department of Psychology, University of North Carolina, Charlotte, NC 28223

W. DAVID PIERCE, Center for Experimental Sociology, Department of Sociology, The University of Alberta, Edmonton, Alberta T6G 2H4, Canada

RICHARD F. RAKOS, Department of Psychology, Cleveland State University, Cleveland, OH 44115

WILLIAM K. REDMON, Department of Psychology, Western Michigan University, Kalamazoo, MI 49008-5052

LESLIE A. WILK, Center for Entrepreneurial Studies and Development, School of Engineering, West Virginia University, Morgantown, WV 26506

Preface

Other things being equal, theories of wider scope are considered to be superior to theories that encompass a smaller domain. Although behavior analysis is a relatively well-developed discipline, it has, with few exceptions, been limited to a consideration of small groups of individuals in circumscribed and usually controlled settings. This approach has unarguably paid off in the formulation and confirmation of a number of principles of behavior. A major thesis of this book is that the working assumptions, constructs, and methods of behavior analysis can, and should, now be extended to societies and cultural practices. Articles exemplifying this extension have recently appeared, but no single source incorporating the concepts and principles underlying this extension, which also includes examples of the extension, has appeared before this book.

Part I of this book presents the concepts and principles of behavior analysis and societies and cultural practices. As discussed in this section, the foundations of this extension are not considered to be canonical. Rather, refinements of, elaboration of, additions to, and perhaps even rejections of these concepts and principles are accepted as possibilities.

Part II presents diverse examples of behavior analysis of societies and cultural practices. These examples are not intended as catalogues of behavioral interventions. Rather, they describe the contingencies and metacontingencies operating in, and characterizing, various societies and cultural practices. The reader will doubtless think of many other societies and cultural practices amenable to this treatment.

Part III considers the context of behavior analysis of societies and cultural practices within the larger context of behavior analysis. The future of this subdiscipline is also considered.

This book is intended for anyone familiar with the basic concepts and principles of behavior. This audience may include sociologists, economists, and political scientists, as well as those working in public policy, criminal justice, education, business, and therapy and counseling.

The book can be used as a whole. Alternatively, those already familiar with such concepts as metacontingencies and rule-governed behavior may be more drawn to the examples considered in Part II and the views expressed in Part III.

A reassignment of duties for Fall 1990 from the University of North Carolina at Charlotte enabled me to devote more time to this book than would otherwise have been possible. I want to particularly acknowledge the help of Winifred Swinson; her unfailing composure, good will, and efficiency, when presented with emergencies and ASAPs was of great help—and relief. Holly Boye, Betty Cook, Carl Frye, and Sara Good were also of invaluable assistance. Special thanks is extended to George Windholz.

P. A. Lamal

I

PRINCIPLES

1

Behavioral Analysis of Societies and Cultural Practices

P. A. Lamal

INTRODUCTION

The discipline of behavioral analysis is relatively well established. It encompasses a set of principles, techniques, and research methods and a large body of empirical findings. These findings, however, have been obtained in settings and across time periods that have been circumscribed to varying degrees (Kunkel, 1987). Relatively few studies have involved entire organizations as the unit of analysis. Fewer still have been concerned with practices that are found throughout a society. Twenty years ago, a sociologist wrote, "In view of the fact that, after all, psychologists produced the findings of behavioral psychology, it is surprising how little they have done to apply behavioral psychology to the explanation and prediction of social behavior" (Homans, 1969, p. 23). The implied criticism is valid today. An underlying theme of this book is that now is the time for a systematic effort to begin the behavioral analysis of societies and cultural practices. Pennypacker (1986a) has written that "The economies of both the United States and the world are adjusting to the joint perils of expanding population and diminishing natural resources and will not long provide sustenance to an intellectual endeavor that is irrelevant to both" (p. 149). In the present view, the behavioral analysis of societies and cultural practices is the relevant intellectual endeavor.

Indeed, a start in this direction has been made. Since at least 1948, with his publication of *Walden Two*, B. F. Skinner was interested in extrapolating to entire societies principles of behavior that have often been derived from laboratory experiments (Skinner, 1953, 1961, 1969, 1971, 1974, 1981). A few others (e.g., Fraley, 1988; Glenn, 1986, 1988; Malagodi, 1986; Malott, 1988; Rakos, 1983) have shared Skinner's interest in a behavioral analysis of societies. This body of work, however, has dealt primarily with societies in the abstract, or with fictional societies. The behavior analysis of societies and cultural practices is also congenial to and overlaps Marvin Harris's cultural anthropology (Glenn, 1988; Lloyd, 1985; Malagodi & Jackson, 1989; Malott, 1988; Vargas, 1985).

The subdiscipline of behavioral community psychology is clearly relevant to the behavioral analysis of societies and cultural practices. Some of the conclusions

Earlier versions of this chapter were presented at the meeting of the Association for Behavior Analysis, Milwaukee, May 1989, and the Interamerican Congress of Psychology, Buenos Aires, Argentina, June 1989.

I am grateful to Joel Greenspoon for comments on an earlier draft.

3

reached by behavioral community psychologists can be quite useful; for example, the idea that, ". . . typical psychological interventions may be inappropriate for ameliorating complex social problems . . . The psychologist possessing a knowledge base in a number of disciplines could propose, develop, and evaluate reforms for social problems unique to a particular community or indicative of the country as a whole" (Nietzel, Winett, MacDonald, & Davidson, 1977, p. 262). Behavioral community psychologists have also pointed out the importance of considering the larger social systems—economic, political, and sociological—of which individuals are a part (Jason & Glenwick, 1980; Nietzel et al., 1977).

In general, the results of behavioral community psychology constitute a caveat for undue optimism concerning the likelihood of easily bringing about significant change at the societal level (e.g., Winett, 1976). In their discussion of the progress and prospects of behavioral community psychology, Glenwick and Jason (1980) had little to say about behavioral interventions at the level of society, presumably because so little had been done at that level. This is still the case. In addition, Jason and Glenwick (1980) maintain that most behavioral community psychology interventions have not been able to achieve maintenance and generalization of behavior change.

It thus appears that the subdiscipline of behavioral community psychology may be a source of helpful guidelines, but at the same time its results should serve as a warning of the difficulties of bringing about large-scale planned behavior change.

A few behavior analytical studies of actual historical (Kunkel, 1985) and contemporary societies or cultural practices (Kunkel, 1986; Lamal, 1984, (in press); Rakos, 1988; Zifferblatt & Hendricks, 1974) have also appeared, most during the last decade. It does not seem premature to outline a framework for further research in behavioral analysis of societies and cultural practices. However, the framework is tentative, not canonical; it would be surprising if the framework survived completely unchanged for long.

Characteristics of and Questions Concerning Behavioral Analysis of Societies

Presented here are the major characteristics of, and questions about, the subdiscipline of behavioral analysis of societies. One characteristic is that this subdiscipline is derived from applied behavior analysis, the aspects of which were described in the seminal 1968 article of Baer, Wolf, and Risley, and is still prescriptive—and increasingly descriptive of the field in 1987 (Baer, Wolf, & Risley, 1987). At the same time, however, the subdiscipline outlined here leans toward the functional, as opposed to the structural approach. Hayes, Rincover, and Solnick (1980) expressed concern with what they saw as the technical drift of applied behavioral analysis—that is, a premature emphasis on cure-oriented research at the expense of concern with conceptual issues. A structural approach is concerned with changing problem behaviors in their natural settings. The emphasis "is based strictly upon the nature of the subjects, settings, and behavioral topography being studied" (Hayes, Rincover, & Solnick, 1980, p. 281). On the other hand, a functional approach embraces basic and analogue studies, types of studies that may also be of help to the applied worker. Whereas the structural approach emphasizes the importance of the *appearance* of similarity between the research setting and the setting in which the results are used, the functional approach is concerned with the *functional* similarity between the two settings.

A critical question for any discipline concerns its unit(s) of analysis. What is, or are, the unit or units of analysis for the behavioral analysis of societies? A first, seemingly obvious, response is that the unit is the group, rather than the individual. This, for example, is said to be a difference between behavioral analysis and Marvin Harris's cultural materialism (Lloyd, 1985; Vargas, 1985); that is, behavioral analysis, with few exceptions, has not been concerned with large groups. In this respect, then, behavioral analysis of societies would correspond with cultural materialism.

But positing the group as the unit of analysis may, on further reflection, lead us to a set of questions, the answers to which are not self-evident. (I thank Joel Greenspoon for raising these questions.) Among the questions are the following: Would we consider the United States, say, to be a society or many societies? If many societies, how do we specify the characteristics of a society to delineate the different societies in the United States? Is a society differentiated from other societies in terms of the controlling variables? The behavioral differences? Different contingencies? All of these? (J. Greenspoon, personal communication, September 2, 1988). At this early stage of development of the subdiscipline, the question of what or who constitutes the group is probably determined to a great extent by the questions being asked in any particular study. Thus, if the concern is with the health care system of a given country, all of the people in that country constitute the relevant society. Particular attention, however, might be paid to certain segments of that society such as health care providers, insurance companies, legislators, and the chronically ill. If, on the other hand, the concern is with the practice of higher education in that country, attention will be focused on a different set of groups, such as faculty, administrators, legislators (again), and students. Although it is true that individuals, not groups per se, behave, it is also possible and doubtless in many cases useful to investigate *sets* of individuals who behave in "the same way due to some shared functional relation to their environment" (Vargas, 1985, p. 426). Thus we can usefully consider groups as they wage war, vote for presidents, and work productively or not.

A second fundamental question for any discipline is what measurements are to be used. In this respect the behavioral analysis of societies shares with its progenitor the notion of measures of behavior and measures of its products as being the proper (and only possible) measurements.

Baer et al. (1968) wrote about a *society* that might be "willing to consider a technology of its own behavior . . ." (p. 91). One of the defining characteristics of applied behavior analysis is that it is applied. Baer et al. (1968) wrote that the term "applied" referred to the interest that society shows in the problems being studied. Baer et al. (1987) reaffirmed the view that the concern of behavior analysts may be with problems that are society-wide. However, they are also concerned with the other end of the scale (e.g., one client and one therapist). The behavioral analysis of societies is not concerned with this end of the scale.

Almost all articles and books on behavior have dealt with behaviors on a scale smaller than cultural practices. Baer et al. (1987) acknowledge, however, that ". . . the problems of today are not as delimited as those of our beginnings. They are called lifestyles in recognition of their systemic nature" (p. 323). But, as Kunkel (1987) pointed out, behavior analysts still concentrate on relatively simple

problems of children and people in various institutional settings. The actual boundaries of applied behavior analysis have yet to be determined. Among the questions
posed by Kunkel is this one: Are the principles that underlie applied behavior
analysis cross-culturally valid? His answer is "yes." My response is, "Let's continue to demonstrate that they are." As Kunkel (1989) has recently pointed out,
some psychologists have asserted that in the Third World, psychologists do, or
should, employ unique scientific methods and have unique perspectives, and the
inhabitants of the Third World have unique psychological characteristics. That is,
that there are different psychologies. But behaviorists do not maintain that there
are different sets of behavioral concepts and principles corresponding to different
areas of this planet. However, we need more cross-cultural behavioral analysis to
buttress this view.

Another fundamental question raised by Kunkel is the extent to which applied
behavior analysis can be done outside the laboratory and institutional settings. He
also asks whether those who practice applied behavioral analysis must be specially
trained in the use of, and be aware of, behavioral principles. These are among the
relevant questions for the behavioral analysis of societies. The research will usually be done over significantly longer time spans than has usually been true of
applied behavior analysis studies; that is, it will be done over years.

Another question relevant to behavioral analysis of societies concerns social
validity. Social validity has been touted as a measure with which behavior analysts
should be concerned (Wolf, 1978). According to Wolf, two of the aspects of social
validation are: (1) the social significance of the goals, "Are the specific behavioral
goals really what society wants?" (p. 207), and (2) "the social importance of the
effects (italics in original)" (p. 207). That is, are the consumers satisfied with all
the results of behavioral interventions, including unpredicted ones? In my view,
there are problems with the notion of social validity. The earlier two aspects
(significance of goals and consumer satisfaction with the results) can often conflict
in important ways. For example, the desired goal of low taxation may very well
have the eventual, but direct, effect of huge government indebtedness, which may
in turn result in effects on taxpayers that they consider quite aversive. Another
example: support for the goal of a large military buildup may have the effect of tax
increases, or a reduction in the goods and services that people would otherwise
receive from their central government. The question also arises of just how social
validity is determined. Is some kind of vote to be taken? Does a vote of 50% plus 1
of consumers mean that a social practice is socially valid?

According to Wolf (1978), only the consumer can evaluate whether or not a
behavioral treatment program is helpful. He contends that behavior analysts may
give their opinions, and those opinions may be supported with objective behavioral
data, "but it is the participants and other consumers who want to make the final
decision about whether a program helped solve their problems" (p. 210). Wolf
advocates development of measurement systems "that will tell us . . . whether or
not our clients are happy with our efforts and our effects" (p. 213). But program
consumers do not live in isolation from the rest of us. If we design a behavioral
program to help certain populations reduce the likelihood of contracting the HIV
virus, and thus the likelihood of developing AIDS, and we later learn unequivocally that the program is effective in reducing the spread of the HIV virus, do we
then agree to discontinue the program because its consumers do not particularly
like it? Because they rate it unfavorably? Because they do not subjectively believe

that the program is helpful? Wolf (1978) says that "consumer satisfaction ratings are *often* (emphasis added) highly correlated with objective measures of effectiveness . . ." (p. 211). But when they are not highly correlated, we may often have to consider which is more important, social validation or objective measures of effectiveness.

Particularly in the early stages of the development of behavioral analysis of societies, we should expect that the measures we are able to obtain are fewer in number, more incomplete, and farther from the mark than we desire. In a 7-year study of an educational setting, Filipczak and his colleagues (Filipczak, Archer, Neale, & Winett, 1979) found that their dependent measures were constrained in various ways common to programs in natural settings. They obtained data on a maximum of only 120 students in any year. The relative difficulty of collecting data on, say, hundreds of thousands of people is not yet clear. In some cases it may be relatively easy to collect the necessary data, in other cases, impossible.

Another characteristic of behavioral analysis of societies is that it is primarily descriptive, rather than experimental. This is because of necessity, however, not design (no pun originally intended). With doubtless very few exceptions we simply are not able to manipulate cultural practices. As Baer (1987) put it, we are underempowered. In his view we "are merely temporarily and quite variably underempowered" (p. 336). I see no reason to share Baer's apparently optimistic view that behaviorists will in some unspecified time become empowered. Research that indicates the lack of impact of behaviorism on our culture supports this absence of optimism (Lamal, 1989).

There have been behavioral interventions at an intermediate level, that is, at a level narrower in scope than an entire society or even subculture, but wider than the typical small N or classroom study. Fawcett, Mathews, and Fletcher (1980) have pointed out problems with these early behavioral community technologies. Among the problems were these: (1) Many interventions were too expensive for widespread adoption; (2) some required professionals for continued use; (3) some "include such extraordinary detail as to be perceived by community members as inflexible and nonadaptable to slightly divergent situations . . ." (p. 507); and (4) use of the behavior technology ended when the program developers left.

Fawcett et al. (1980) also pointed out that ". . . exclusive attention to behavioral technology may limit the kinds of *problems* (italics in original) selected for analysis and modification" (p. 513)—that is, to those problems amenable to solution by our current methods—as opposed to newly developed methods. In the view of Fawcett et al. (1980), ". . . the potential contributions of behavioral technology to *social change* (italics in original) may be limited to changes at the more microlevels of society" (p. 514). They went on to point out that there had been "a few examples (of behavioral technology) at the organizational, institutional, and community levels and no examples at the level of the broader society . . ." (p. 514). With the exception of the impact of behavioral analysis on special education, this assessment still holds.

According to Fawcett et al. (1980), the contributions of behavioral technology may be limited to what they called first-order changes. Those are ". . . changes within a basic social system that itself remains unchanged" (p. 515). But behavioral technology may not be able to bring about what Fawcett et al. called second-order change—". . . the redistribution of power, wealth, and other resources within the system. Though behavioral principles may contribute to the *analysis* (italics in original) of society and its controlling mechanisms . . . its potential role in changing the social system is less clear" (p. 515). In this respect, it is significant that Geller (1990) has recently noted, and outlined reasons for, the decline of behavioral environmental psychology.

Another characteristic of behavioral analysis of societies is that it will probably have to rely on natural experiments for most, if not all, of its experimental analysis. One thinks of astronomy and earth science as fields in which natural experiments have been very important. An important kind of natural social experiment would be reforms, as Donald Campbell (1969) pointed out over 20 years ago. Such a natural social experiment is now underway in the Soviet Union and was underway in The People's Republic of China, until the events in Tiananmen Square in 1989.

A few years ago, the Association for Behavior Analysis honored a state legislator for his work on adolescent pregnancy legislation (Goldstein, 1986; Pennypacker, 1986b). The relevant data in existence before and after this legislation became law are just the kind that could be amenable to some kind of quasi-experimental analysis. And if behaviorists ever become sufficiently empowered, legislation and its effects would be an obvious area for experimental analysis.

A desired characteristic of the field of behavioral analysis of societies would be the making of predictions that are so sufficiently nonvague that their falsification or support by data would be possible. This characteristic, it seems, is noncontroversial. How many times have we heard that our goals are the prediction and control of behaviors? At the same time, however, published work in applied behavior analysis is virtually devoid of predictions. Perhaps one could respond that when an empirical study is done, the clear implication is that a particular outcome or set of outcomes is implicitly predicted. However, why not make these predictions explicit? We would also need, then, to seriously consider the question of how detailed we are willing to have our predictions be. To paraphrase Paul Meehl, it is one thing to predict that it will rain in June; it is quite something else to predict that it will rain between $1/10$ and $1/8$ of an inch on June 17.

This is not to say that we should never just investigate phenomena to try and determine what is going on. Just "playing around" with relevant materials can be reinforcing and also lead to later advances. There is room for both approaches.

Another characteristic of the behavioral analysis of societies is that it unabashedly borrows from other disciplines. It does not ape other fields, but to the extent that other fields can contribute to the description, prediction, and control of social processes, the assistance is welcomed. It would be surprising if sociology, anthropology, political science, public administration, behavioral economics, and perhaps other disciplines had absolutely nothing of value for the behavioral analysis of societies and cultural practices. Just what that is remains to be seen. There are two examples, however, at hand already—the work of the anthropologist Marvin Harris and the work of such behavioral sociologists as John Kunkel (1975, 1983). Behavioral sociology has a history of at least 20 years (vide Burgess & Bushell, 1969), although it does not seem to be a popular viewpoint (Molm, 1981, and following comments).

John Kunkel has advocated a behavioral approach to societies for some time. He has advanced the notion, among others, that few significant reinforcers will be available, and the links between behavior and its consequences will often be quite weak in some societies (Kunkel, 1975). These are affluent societies ". . . whose citizens subscribe to a belief in immediate gratification and the rights of individuals to a host of material possessions . . ." (p. 68). In such societies there will seldom be strong deprivation, often the prerequisite for significant behavior change. In Kunkel's analysis, very poor and affluent societies are alike: poor societies offer the general population few reinforcers, and in affluent societies few reinforcers will be perceived. In both kinds of societies many people will believe that their activities have few or no positive consequences.

If we move from the description of societies and cultural practices, to their modification, Kunkel (1975) alerts us to likely problems. He contends that the larger the change program, and the more ambitious its design, ". . . the narrower will be the parameters set by the cultural and historical context, and the more severe will be the limitations exerted by conceptions of political acceptability, the conflicts of interests, and compromises required by the heterogeneous character of most nations" (Kunkel, 1975, p. 144). There are two other problems likely to be encountered by any large-scale behavior change program, according to Kunkel (1975): (1) such programs conflict with the psychodynamic models of humans that are cherished by many people; and (2) such programs are likely to be opposed by those who have a vested interest in the continuation of the problem(s) the program is designed to solve. This group includes ". . . those who make a living by analyzing and 'working with' the problem and those who need the problems as a foundation for their political beliefs and programs" (p. 158).

Kunkel maintains, as do I, that the analysis and solution of social problems requires the cooperative efforts of researchers from disciplines outside of behavioral analysis. He has also provided a step-by-step approach to the behavioral analysis of social problems (Kunkel, 1983).

The reverse might also be true: behavioral analysis of societies might contribute to some other disciplines. Lloyd (1985), for example, has listed some behavior analytical methods and concepts potentially useful for anthropology.

Related to the practice of borrowing from other disciplines is the practice of generating and adopting new or foreign concepts, principles, and practices. Such novel concepts, principles, and practices would not be incorporated into the discipline until they clearly assisted with the description, prediction, and control of social processes. It is doubtful that behavior analysis is now complete, but what form new developments will take is beyond present comprehension.

The behavioral analysis of societies is applied to any human society. It transcends space and time. The analysis of past societies and social practices (e.g., Kunkel, 1985) allows us to test the generality of our concepts. So does the analysis of contemporary societies other than our own.

Problems and Prospects

Some problems and prospects with regard to the behavioral analysis of societies should be discussed, if only briefly. Some have been presaged earlier; others may become salient as the subdiscipline develops.

One such problem is that of obtaining sufficient information about societies' cultural practices; this is particularly true of certain societies usually referred to as closed societies. Recently, however, some of these societies seem to be willing to make more information available.

There would seem to be two main sources of information for our endeavor. One source is archival information, which some of us have already tapped in initial studies. The other source is field-based data collection. Perhaps anthropologists could offer some helpful tips to optimize our efforts in that area.

The assumption is made that behavior analysts never have all of the information relevant to any question. That should not prevent us from drawing conclusions. It certainly does not prevent policy makers and others from doing so.

Another problem for the field is that of extrapolating principles and concepts derived from laboratory or other controlled settings of small scope, to large groups of geographically dispersed people. It is a long way from a bar press to peristroika. But one of our goals is to determine the generality of behavior principles and concepts. Another is to generate new ones, as needed. And one way of discovering if we need new notions is to see to what extent our current set can account for the practices of our society and others.

We must always be alert to what Willems (1974) called ". . . the system-like complexity of behavioral phenomena" (p. 154), when he advocated a behavioral ecological orientation. Behavioral ecology emphasizes the system-like interdependencies among environment, organism, and behavior. It calls attention to the widespread possibilities for unintended effects of simple, single interventions.

Initial steps in the behavioral analysis of societies have been taken. A 1970 book by Kunkel applied behavior principles to the topic of economic development. Wiest and Squier (1974) proposed a behavioral approach to controlling population growth. In 1978, Holland maintained that the science of behaviorism provides the means to analyze the structures, the system, and the forms of societal control that produce such problems as alcoholism and crime. Glenn (1986, 1988) has advanced the notion of metacontingencies operative over large segments of societies, and has advanced a behavioral definition of *cultural practice*: ". . . a cultural practice is a set of interlocking contingencies of reinforcement in which the behavior and behavioral products of each participant function as environmental events with which the behavior of other individuals interacts" (1988, p. 167). I have attempted descriptions of contingencies and metacontingencies operating in the People's Republic of China (Lamal, 1984) and in the Soviet Union (in press). Rakos (1988) has provided a comparison of capitalism and socialism in behavioral terms.

There have even been a few behavioral interventions that approach what is being proposed here. For example, Van Houten et al. (1985) assessed the effect of a behavioral intervention in a Canadian and an Israeli city. The same intervention reduced speeding and accidents in both cities.

A few people have gone beyond the level of interventions to establish a behaviorally based community. The community of Los Horcones was established in Mexico in 1973 and continues its evolution as an experimental community (Comunidad Los Horcones, 1989; Los Horcones, 1989).

There is obviously much more to be done. We have barely started to describe cultural practices behaviorally, and we have made very few or no predictions concerning societies and cultural practices. As for behavioral interventions at the level of cultural practices, this is something about which at present we can only dream. But if behavioral analysis of the future is to be comprehensive, it will have to include societies and cultural practices within its domain. We may wish, however, to be guided by Calvino's *Mr. Palomar* (1985):

As long as it is a matter of demonstrating the ills of society and the abuses of those who abuse, he has no hesitations . . . He finds it more difficult to say something about the remedies, because first he would like to make sure that they do not cause worse ills and abuses, and that wisely planned by enlightened reformers, they can be put into practice without harm by their successors: foolish perhaps, perhaps frauds, perhaps frauds and foolish at once (Calvino, 1985, pp. 111 & 112).

REFERENCES

Baer, D. M. (1987). Weak contingencies, strong contingencies, and many behaviors to change. *Journal of Applied Behavior Analysis, 20,* 335–337.

Baer, D. M., Wolf, M. M., & Risley, T. R. (1968). Some current dimensions of applied behavior analysis. *Journal of Applied Behavior Analysis, 1,* 9–97.

Baer, D. M., Wolf, M. M., & Risley, T. R. (1987). Some still-current dimensions of applied behavior analysis. *Journal of Applied Behavior Analysis, 20,* 313–327.

Burgess, R. L., & Bushell, D. (Eds.). (1969). *Behavioral sociology: The experimental analysis of social process.* New York: Columbia University Press.

Calvino, I. (1985). *Mr. Palomar.* San Diego: Harcourt Brace Jovanovich.

Campbell, D. T. (1969). Reforms as experiments. *American Psychologist, 24,* 409–429.

Comunidad Los Horcones. (1989). *Walden Two* and social change: The application of behavior analysis to cultural design. *Behavior Analysis and Social Action, 7,* 35–41.

Fawcett, S. B., Mathews, R. M., & Fletcher, R. F. (1980). Some promising dimensions for behavioral community technology. *Journal of Applied Behavior Analysis, 13,* 505–518.

Filipczak, J., Archer, M. B., Neale, M. S., & Winett, R. A. (1979). Issues in multivariate assessment of a large-scale behavioral program. *Journal of Applied Behavior Analysis, 12,* 593–613.

Fraley, L. E. (1988). Introductory comments: Behaviorology and cultural materialism. *The Behavior Analyst, 11,* 159–160.

Geller, E. S. (1990). Behavior analysis and environmental protection: Where have all the flowers gone? *Journal of Applied Behavior Analysis, 23,* 269–273

Glenn, S. S. (1986). Metacontingencies in *Walden Two. Behavior Analysis and Social Action, 5,* 2–8.

Glenn, S. S. (1988). Contingencies and metacontingencies: Toward a synthesis of behavior analysis and cultural materialism. *The Behavior Analyst, 11,* 161–179.

Glenwick, D., & Jason, L. (Eds.). (1980). *Behavioral community psychology; Progress and prospects.* New York: Praeger.

Goldstein, M. K. (1986). He has acted to save the world: Award to Marlin Schneider, Wisconsin state representative. *The Behavior Analyst, 9,* 193–196.

Hayes, S. C., Rincover, A., & Solnick, J. V. (1980). The technical drift of applied behavior analysis. *Journal of Applied Behavior Analysis, 13,* 275–285.

Holland, J. G. (1978). Behaviorism: Part of the problem or part of the solution? *Journal of Applied Behavior Analysis, 11,* 163–174.

Homans, G. C. (1969). The sociological relevance of behaviorism. In R. L. Burgess & D. Bushell (Eds.), *Behavioral sociology: The experimental analysis of social process* (pp. 1–26). New York: Columbia University Press.

Jason, L., & Glenwick, D. (1980). Introduction to Part V. In D. Glenwick & L. Jason (Eds.), *Behavioral community psychology: Progress and prospects* (pp. 352–359). New York: Praeger.

Kunkel, J. H. (1970). *Society and economic growth.* New York: Oxford University Press.

Kunkel, J. H. (1975). *Behavior, social problems, and change: A social learning approach.* Engelwood Cliffs, NJ: Prentice-Hall.

Kunkel, J. H. (1983). The behavioral-societal approach to social problems. *Behaviorists for Social Action Journal, 4,* 8–11.

Kunkel, J. H. (1985). Vivaldi in Venice: An historical test of psychological propositions. *The Psychological Record, 35,* 445–457.

Kunkel, J. H. (1986). The Vicos project: A cross-cultural test of psychological propositions. *The Psychological Record, 36,* 451–466.

Kunkel, J. H. (1987). The future of *JABA*: A comment. *Journal of Applied Behavior Analysis, 20,* 329–333.

Kunkel, J. H. (1989). How many psychologies are there? *American Psychologist, 44,* 573–574.

Lamal, P. A. (1984). Contingency management in the People's Republic of China. *The Behavior Analyst, 7,* 121–130.

Lamal, P. A. (1989). The impact of behaviorism on our culture: Some evidence and conjectures. *The Psychological Record, 39,* 529–535.

Lamal, P. A. (in press). Three metacontingencies in the preperestroika Soviet Union. *Behavior and Social Issues.*

Lloyd, K. E. (1985). Behavioral anthropology: A review of Marvin Harris' *Cultural Materialism. Journal of the Experimental Analysis of Behavior, 43,* 279–287.

Los Horcones. (1989). Personalized government: A governmental system based on behavior analysis. *Behavior Analysis and Social Action, 7,* 42–47.

Malagodi, E. F. (1986). On radicalizing behaviorism: A call for cultural analysis. *The Behavior Analyst, 9,* 1–17.

Malagodi, E. F., & Jackson, K. (1989). Behavior analysts and cultural analysis: Troubles and issues. *The Behavior Analyst, 12,* 17–33.

Malott, R. W. (1988). Rule-governed behavior and behavioral anthropology. *The Behavior Analyst, 11,* 181–203.

Molm, L. D. (1981). The legitimacy of behavioral theory as a sociological perspective. *The American Sociologist, 16,* 153–166.

Nietzel, N. T., Winett, R. A., MacDonald, M. L., & Davidson, W. S. (1977). *Behavioral approaches to community psychology.* New York: Pergamon.

Pennypacker, H. S. (1986a). The challenge of technology transfer: Buying in without selling out. *The Behavior Analyst, 9,* 147–156.

Pennypacker, H. S. (1986b). The ABA award for outstanding legislative action: Introduction of the presenter. *The Behavior Analyst, 9,* 191.

Rakos, R. F. (1983). Behavior analysis as a framework for a multidisciplinary approach to social change. *Behaviorists for Social Action Journal, 4,* 12–16.

Rakos, R. F. (1988). Capitalism, socialism, and behavioral theory. *Behavior Analysis and Social Action, 6,* 16–22.

Skinner, B. F. (1948). *Walden Two.* New York: Macmillan.

Skinner, B. F. (1953). *Science and human behavior.* New York: Macmillan.

Skinner, B. F. (1961). The design of cultures. *Daedalus.* Summer, 534–546.

Skinner, B. F. (1969). *Contingencies of reinforcement: A theoretical analysis.* New York: Appleton-Century-Crofts.

Skinner, B. F. (1971). *Beyond freedom and dignity.* New York: Knopf.

Skinner, B. F. (1974). *About behaviorism.* New York: Knopf.

Skinner, B. F. (1981). Selection by consequences. *Science, 213,* 501–504.

Van Houten, R., Rolider, A., Nau, P. A., Friedman, R., Becker, M., Chalodovsky, I., & Scherer, M. (1985). Large-scale reductions in speeding and accidents in Canada and Israel: A behavioral ecological perspective. *Journal of Applied Behavior Analysis, 18,* 87–93.

Vargas, E. A. (1985). Cultural contingencies: A review of Marvin Harris's *Cannibals and Kings. Journal of the Experimental Analysis of Behavior, 43,* 419–428.

Wiest, W. M., & Squier, L. H. (1974). Incentives and reinforcement: A behavioral approach to fertility. *Journal of Social Issues, 30,* 235–263.

Willems, E. B. (1974). Behavioral technology and behavioral ecology. *Journal of Applied Behavior Analysis, 7,* 151–165.

Winett, R. A. (1976). Disseminating a behavioral approach to energy conservation. *Professional Psychology, 7,* 222–228.

Wolf, M. M. (1978). Social validity: The case for subjective measurement or how applied behavior analysis is finding its heart. *Journal of Applied Behavior Analysis, 11,* 203–214.

Zifferblatt, S. M., & Hendricks, G. G. (1974). Applied behavioral analysis of societal problems: Population change, a case in point. *American Psychologist, 29,* 750–761.

2

Culture and Society:
The Role of Behavioral Analysis

W. David Pierce

INTRODUCTION

Human behavior occurs in a social environment. Society and culture refer to aspects of the social environment that regulate human conduct. One of the primary tasks of behavioral analysis is to show how individual behavior is acquired, maintained, and changed through interaction with others. An additional problem is to account for the behavioral practices of the group, community, or society that set the contingencies for individual action.

This chapter addresses the role of behavioral analysis as a research methodology and theoretical perspective for the study of society and culture. A major point is that operant methodology may be extended to the analysis of social systems. Behavioral methods may be used to study social behavior at different levels of analysis. These levels include the experimental analysis of human behavior, the study of social processes and social systems, and behavioral analysis of culture and cultural evolution. At each level, behavioral theory offers the concepts of contingency, selection by consequences, and the context of reinforcement. These conceptual relations (and others) allow behaviorists to provide a functional analysis of social systems and culture that is congruent with the principles of behavior at the individual level. The overall enterprise is to develop a unified theory of human behavior based on general behavioral laws and principles.

SCIENCE AND SOCIAL BEHAVIOR

The role of behavioral analysis for the study of social systems was first outlined by B. F. Skinner (1953) in his book *Science and Human Behavior*. In terms of social science, this is perhaps the most important of Skinner's writings because he begins to outline a program of research for the study of society and culture. In this regard, Skinner emphasizes the analysis of social contingencies and the selection of behavior by its consequences. Skinner recognizes that there are well-established disciplines who already address the behavior of people in groups including sociology, political science, anthropology, and economics. Most of these fields address human behavior from circumscribed perspectives. Thus, humans are viewed as social, political, cultural, and economic animals.

A behavioral perspective offers an alternative to the separation of human nature into unique parts. Principles of behavior that describe individual action presumably operate when people act in a political context or in economic circumstances.

It is, therefore, possible to provide a consistent account of human behavior by showing how behavioral laws are expressed in large-scale social systems. Of course, as Skinner recognizes, it is not necessary to express "social facts" in terms of individual behavior. For example, Gresham's law of economics states that bad money drives good money out of circulation, and there is no reference to human behavior. Although social scientists may prefer to state their generalizations at the level of groups or aggregates, behavior analysts may also provide an account of social phenomena in terms of behavioral laws and principles. Eventually, the social laws must be congruent with the behavioral laws since "it is always the individual that behaves, and he behaves with the same body and according to the same processes as in a nonsocial situation" (Skinner, 1953, p. 298).

To begin a behavioral analysis of social processes, it is important to provide a functional definition of social behavior. Throughout this paper, social behavior is defined as "the behavior of two or more people with respect to one another or in concert with respect to a common environment" (Skinner, 1953). Such a definition must apply to examples of human behavior that are commonly regarded as social. Thus, sexual behavior is social because the partners respond "with respect to one another," and cooperation is social because two or more people must coordinate their responses with respect to "a common environment." On the other hand, "brushing one's teeth" to maintain a healthy mouth is a nonsocial response. Although other people may have established this performance, "the behavior of two or more people" is not required.

The social environment is composed of stimuli and consequences arranged by others. The behavior of another person may be necessary to produce an effect on the physical environment. To move a car that is stuck in the snow, the behavior of two or more people must be coordinated and the contingencies of reinforcement require differences in the form of response: one person steers and the other one(s) pushes. Similar contingencies at the societal level may result in a division of labor based on attributes and skills that increase efficiency. The consequences here are probably economic involving changes in rate of production and return in dollars or goods.

When other persons arrange reinforcement through their behavior, the behavior becomes reinforcing in itself. Attention, approval, affection and submission are generalized social reinforcers that regulate a wide range of human behavior. It is important to examine the effectiveness of such reinforcement when delivered by another person or by the common response of group members. Although the approval of a friend or spouse may sustain writing of a paper, the acceptance by one's colleagues is likely to be much more effective. People may join or form groups because of the powerful reinforcing effects that are achieved. In addition, the group expands the sources of reinforcement for an individual. Thus, participation in a strike may bring improvement in wages and reduction in hours that could not be achieved by any single worker.

A functional analysis of social behavior and social systems is based on a systematic extension of behavior theory to more complex settings. The analysis immediately reveals that a group is not equal to the sum of its parts since effects, outcomes, or consequences often cannot be obtained without the coordinated action of many people. Analysis also suggests that emergent forms of interaction may occur that are not specified by the operating contingencies. Finally, behavior principles that regulate social conduct are often the same as those that govern nonsocial behavior.

ANALYSIS OF HUMAN BEHAVIOR

The first role of behavioral analysis is to extend basic principles to human behavior. Since the early work of Herrnstein (1961), there have been numerous experiments with nonhuman subjects showing that the distribution of behavior matches the distribution of reinforcement (de Villiers, 1977). Behavior analysts have designed concurrent-operant experiments for people, and their results generally show that humans also match their responses to relative rate of reinforcement (see reviews by Bradshaw & Szabadi, 1988; Pierce & Epling, 1983).

Failures to Replicate

On the other hand, some principles of behavior do not directly extend to human performance. It is well known that pigeons in choice situations respond to stimuli or events that signal the time to reinforcement on the respective alternatives (Fantino, 1977). Thus, pigeons allocate behavior in terms of relative delay reduction when placed on concurrent-chain schedules of reinforcement. In contrast, Belke, Pierce, and Powell (1989) found that humans were not sensitive to stimuli correlated with delay reduction and behaved in a way that maximized the overall rate of reinforcement. One possibility for this is that the nature of the reinforcers accounted for the performance differences of pigeons and humans. Pigeons responded for food—a reinforcer that was consumed at the moment of presentation. On the other hand, humans responded for monetary reinforcers that were not consumed until some time after the experiment. This procedural difference may have contributed to the discrepancy in performance between pigeons and people.

Preliminary laboratory data (Kwan, Pierce, & Epling, in progress) suggest that the behavioral differences were not a result of this reinforcement factor. Humans failed to show delay reduction even when they were food-deprived and responded for consumable reinforcers dispensed by a vending machine. At the present time, it has not been possible to develop a situation that leads to delay reduction by humans. Overall, the evidence indicates that human choice is closely regulated by the rates of reinforcement from alternatives and is apparently less sensitive to delay-reduction variables.

This research shows that the experimental analysis of human behavior is an important bridge between laboratory research and the study of social behavior. If behavior principles do not directly extend to human performance in controlled experiments, it is unlikely that these principles can be used in the analysis of social behavior. Currently, basic research with humans points to overall and relative rates of reinforcement as important conditions for the regulation social behavior.

ANALYSIS OF SOCIAL BEHAVIOR

Experimental analysis of social behavior is another role for behaviorists who are interested in society and culture. This kind of research may draw on the principles and results of basic research with humans, but may also proceed as an independent area of investigation. A major task is to investigate contingencies of reinforcement and group behavior using well-established operant methods.

The Basic Design

The A-B-A reversal design exemplifies the operant approach to experimentation (Sidman, 1960). The basic idea is to compare an organism's behavior in the treatment phase (B) with the baseline phases (A). Thus, the rate of bar-pressing is compared with and without a food-reinforcement contingency. The general strategy is to relate changes in bar-pressing (dependent variable) to the presence or absence of food reinforcement (independent variable).

Although some investigators define baseline as an experimental phase without planned intervention, other researchers recommend the use of controlled baselines (see Sidman, 1960). In this case, a procedure known to produce behavioral stability is preferred because the effects of the independent variable (B) are more easily detected and interpreted. For example, reinforcement of cooperation on an intermittent schedule may establish a high and steady rate of team responses (i.e., person A followed by person B or vice versa). The cooperation condition may then be used as a baseline to investigate the regulation of social behavior by other variables (e.g., rate of reinforcement and stimulus control).

Experimental analysis requires that the experimenter demonstrate control by the independent variable. In terms of social behavior, this requirement means that the coordinated action of two or more organisms changes with the introduction and removal of an independent variable. Thus, the same team (or group) is observed over all phases of the experiment and changes in social interaction are shown to reliably follow from changes in the experimental conditions.

Research with Animals

Experimental analysis of social relations has been conducted with nonhuman subjects. Skinner (1962) reported the operant conditioning of "synthetic social relations" with laboratory pigeons. Basic procedures of reinforcement, successive approximation, and discrimination were used to establish a repertoire of striking a ping-pong ball. Two pigeons received individual training to peck a ball with sufficient force to send it across the length of a small table. During acquisition, when the ball hit a cross bar it activated a microswitch that operated the bird's food hopper. After training, two birds were allowed to play a game of ping pong. One bird pecked the ball and when it reached the other side of the table the other bird pecked it, returning it to the first pigeon. If a pigeon missed the ball, it entered a trough, which operated the food hopper of the opponent bird. Although the training produced pseudo competition, the birds had trouble with the delays to reinforcement required to "win a point" and neither bird responded to place or pace shots to make the opponent miss. Human competition therefore involves additional contingencies that were not specified in the pigeon research.

In the same report, Skinner (1962) indicated that cooperation could be conditioned by standard laboratory procedures. In this case, two pigeons were individually trained to peck one of three keys for food reinforcement. The birds were then placed in adjacent compartments separated by a plexiglas partition. Both birds pecked their respective keys, but the contingency now required that they strike the keys almost at the same time to activate the two hoppers. Under these conditions, simultaneous pecking of the same keys developed and leader-follower relations emerged from the interaction. Thus, one bird selected the appropriate key (leader), and the other pecked the key that matched (follower). Skinner states that leadership could be controlled by varying food deprivation; the more-deprived bird would initiate key pecking and the less-deprived subject would follow. Unfortunately, a systematic analysis of deprivation and leader-follower relations was not undertaken. Finally, Skinner reports that these contingencies seem to establish generalized imitation—where the behavior of one bird set the occasion for a corresponding response by the other (e.g., drinking from the same cup). The relationship between cooperation and generalized imitation remains unexplored even at the human level.

Animal Models

Behavior analysts have not followed Skinner's example of studying social relations with animals. Laboratory researchers prefer to study basic principles with single organisms, and behaviorists who study humans seldom want to return to animal models. However, research with animals tests our understanding of social behavior at the human level. If contingencies can be arranged that generate complex social behavior by animals (Harlow & Zimmerman, 1959; Seligman & Maier, 1967), then plausible accounts can be given of similar processes in humans. More importantly, animal models may be used to identify social processes that occur in humans but fail to develop in nonhuman organisms. Such failures indicate that social behavior in humans is a result of biological and environmental conditions that are not yet well understood or cannot be replicated at the animal level. Generally, there is a need to develop an interplay between animal models of social relations and experimental studies of social behavior in humans (see Soumi, 1982, for a similar view about clinical psychology).

Experimental Research with Humans

Cooperative Contingencies

At the same time that Skinner was demonstrating social relations in animals, Azrin and Lindsley (1956) conducted social experiments with humans. These researchers used free-operant methods to study the social behavior of two-person teams. The contingencies required each teammate to perform a response and when two responses occurred within a half-second of each other both participants received monetary reinforcement. The contingency of reinforcement required cooperation, and the researchers found that differential reinforcement of cooperation increased the frequency of this team response, whereas extinction weakened cooperative action. Thus, the behavior of teams followed the principles of reinforcement and extinction that were known to regulate individual behavior.

The experimental analysis of social relations has continued to develop, although the rate of progress has been slow. Schmitt (1984) presented an overview of the research on cooperation and competition—two contingencies in which reinforcement is determined by the responses of both participants (Hake & Olvera, 1978; Hake & Vukelich, 1972; Marwell & Schmitt, 1975; Schmitt & Marwell, 1972). Important questions remain in terms of setting events (Miller & Hamblin, 1963; Rosenbaum, 1979; Schmitt, 1981), the stimulus properties of others (Bond & Titus, 1983; Hake, Donaldson, & Hyten, 1983; Hake, Vukelich, & Kaplan, 1973), transitional and steady state performance (Sidman, 1960), and the size of the group (Messick & Brewer, 1983; Schmitt, 1976). Further research is also required to specify the effects of communication and negotiation on interpersonal relations (Deutsch, 1958; Deutsch & Krauss, 1962; Krauss & Deutsch, 1966; Osgood, 1962, 1967).

Emergent Interactions

Patterns of social behavior occur as a by-product of cooperative contingencies. Experiments by Cohen (1962) and Lindsley (1966) found that cooperative contingencies generated leader-follower sequences that were not required for reinforcement. This finding parallels the observations of Skinner (1962) who studied cooperation in pigeons (see earlier discussion). In humans, such emergent interactions were consistently observed during cooperation and were related to the status and power relations outside of the laboratory. People with higher status (e.g., parent or football captain) emerged as leaders and those with lower status (e.g., sibling or fellow student) were followers. This finding has been consistently observed in the literature of social psychology (Moore, 1968, 1969). Presumably, the leader-follower interaction based on prior status occurred because it insured a higher rate of reinforcement for the team.

The researchers inadvertently tested the rate of reinforcement hypothesis by arranging contingencies for cooperation that also specified the leader-follower sequence. When only A followed by B sequences were reinforced, this pattern predominated during cooperation; and when B followed by A sequences were required for reinforcement, the leadership pattern reversed. When status distinctions were present, it took longer for the operating contingencies to gain control, but eventually the high status members relinquished their leadership role. Generally, the prior status and power of team members organizes social interaction only if supported by the operating contingencies.

Many social contingencies do not specify the behavioral sequences that are required for reinforcement, and under these conditions alternative patterns or strategies of interaction emerge on the basis of the contingencies. For example, in a game like chess the "rules of the game" establish the allowable moves and payoffs. Classic strategies of play are well known, and players learn to respond on the basis of the past and current layout of the board. Thus, chess exemplifies the relation between the broad contingencies of the game and the emergent contingencies of moves and countermoves.

The analysis of chess indicates that it is useful to distinguish between contingencies set by the experimenter and those that arise from social interaction (Weingarten & Mechner, 1966). Contingencies that are programmed before the actual interaction of the group members, participants, or partners may be referred to as independent contingencies. The rules of chess describe the independent contingencies established before any specific match. The match involves moves and countermoves that establish emergent contingencies of the game. Generally, we can refer to the contingencies generated by interaction as dependent contingencies. The behavior of each participant, therefore, contributes to the conditions that regulate the behavioral sequences of the opponents. In this view, the independent contingencies are experimental variables manipulated by the researcher, whereas dependent contingencies are the measured effects.

A social contingency is an if-then relation between the behavior of two (or more) persons in a situation or setting. The verbal expression of such a contingency is called a "rule" or norm. Notice that the rule is a description of a social contingency, and this description may be accurate or inaccurate (Skinner, 1969). For example, if people give good things to those that treat them well, and give bad things to those who treat them poorly, then the norm of reciprocity may be stated as "do unto others as you would have them do unto you." The social contingency described by the rule is of great interest in the social sciences. Early work by Sidowski, Wyckoff, and Tabory (1956) showed that reciprocal positive reinforcement or social exchange arises when each person can provide reinforcement and punishment to the other.

Social Exchange

Behavioral sociologists currently use the methods of experimental analysis to study social exchange in the laboratory (Burgess & Nielsen, 1974; Cook & Emerson, 1978; Cook, Emerson, Gillmore, & Yamagishi, 1983; Gray & Tallman, 1987; Molm, 1988, 1990). In this literature, the independent contingencies are called "reward structures." The structure of reward is the availability of reinforcement (positive or negative) over a network of alternative relationships. Reinforcement may be allocated to positions (rather than to people) so that each position has power relative to other statuses. Any person who occupies the position therefore attains some structural power. The researcher manipulates the value of the reinforcement at each position—where value is a function of reinforcement rate and magnitude. Essentially, the more valuable the reinforcement controlled by a position relative to other statuses the greater the structural power.

Experimental analysis involves two experimental subjects who are assigned to interaction panels (i.e., positions) A and B. Both subjects may operate a button to give reinforcement (points exchanged for money) to a partner, but cannot produce reinforcement for themselves. Each subject also has an alternative "exchange partner" that is simulated by a computer program. Person A may give reinforcement to B, an experimental subject, or to C—a computer simulated participant; similarly, subject B may give to A or D, where D is the simulated partner. Over repeated opportunities to choose, interest focuses on the A-B relation and the allocation of giving by the respective participants.

Recent findings by Molm (1990) showed that the allocation of giving (or relative rate of exchange) is a function of the relative reward power of a position. For example, as the relative value of reinforcement from A increased, B's relative rate of giving to A also increased. With each person responding to the relative reinforcement from the alternatives, A's giving to B may be less than B's giving to A, over repeated opportunities. In this case, A is said to have a power advantage over B. This advantage results in inequity where reinforcement given is not equal to reinforcement received.

Exchange and Matching

Although Molm has not tied her research to basic principles, the matching law (Baum, 1974a; Herrnstein, 1961) may be an underlying mechanism of power and social exchange (Sunahara & Pierce, 1982). Behavioral matching requires that the relative rate of giving to others equals the relative rate of reinforcement from others. To illustrate, in a marital relationship each partner provides sexual reinforcement to the other. However, the allocation of sexual favors is regulated by the network of alternatives. If the husband has one (or more) extramarital sexual partners and his wife has none, the matching law requires that the husband be unfaithful (i.e., distribute sexual behavior) and his wife be faithful. The degree of infidelity is regulated by the value of sexual reinforcement in the marital relationship relative to extramarital reinforcement.

Notice the inequity of this situation. Given the contingencies, the matching law necessitates that the wife give all of her sexual reinforcement to her husband, whereas he only give some portion in return. To insure greater fidelity and less inequity, society often arranges legal sanctions for extramarital choices including loss of income, investments, and family. Negative reinforcement arranged by the legal system may increase selection of the socially acceptable alternative (e.g., sexual intercourse with spouse). In many cases, however, legal sanctions are delayed because of the time it takes to detect and prosecute infidelity. Such delays weaken the effectiveness of the legal consequences and insure that sexual choice is usually regulated by the current distribution of sexual reinforcement.

This example illustrates the powerful analysis that follows from an integration of social exchange research with basic behavior principles. Social exchange concepts anchor the analysis to historically relevant social settings, groups, and interactions (e.g., marriage and family). The matching law suggests that social exchange by individuals, or aggregates of individuals, is part of a more general theory of behavioral choice and preference (Baum, 1974b). In this view, power advantages, inequities, and other social regularities characterize interpersonal relationships because choices to exchange are regulated by alternative sources of reinforcement (Sunahara & Pierce, 1982).

BEHAVIORAL ANALYSIS OF SOCIAL SYSTEMS

The behavioral analysis of culture and society also may be extended to larger social systems. These systems usually involve the operant behavior of many people who coordinate their actions with respect to a common environment. An example of a relatively simple social system is the North American family—a mother, father, and several children. A family may be viewed as an exchange system involving many reinforcement domains (see social networks, Cook et al., 1983). The behavior of family members is organized with respect to work and income, food purchase, preparation and consumption, procreation, child care and education, and many other activities. The contingencies in each domain represent concurrent schedules of reinforcement that many operate independently or with some degree of dependence (i.e., interaction of the schedules). For example, contingencies involving work and income may be incompatible with those set by child care and education. Incompatible concurrent schedules of reinforcement may play an important role in social system problems such as conflict, abuse, and divorce. At the present time, little research has been directed to this possibility.

To study the contingencies that regulate social systems, it is necessary to expand the methodology of behavioral analysis. Acceptable methods include: (1) observational techniques that describe the organized behavior of people in terms of setting events, specific discriminative stimuli, and functional consequences; (2) quasiexperimental studies that attempt to isolate the causal variables of a particular social practice; and (3) experimental analysis of behavior in small groups.

Functional Analysis and Observational Research

Participant Observation

A behavioral analysis of residential real estate agents by House (1975) illustrates the use of participant observation to study social systems. The data consisted of transcripts of dialogue among agents and descriptions of the broader contingencies that regulated the real estate industry. The agents were paid on a commission basis by a firm in Montreal, Canada. In terms of analysis, House pointed to an agent's role as "middleman" in the larger socioeconomic system of property exchange.

In Canada, houses are bought and sold through private transactions that comprise the residential real estate market. In this market, an agent is a third party whose services are valuable to sellers and buyers who are unfamiliar with the details of the market and the procedures of legal transactions. The behavior of agents involves finding houses for potential buyers, identifying buyers for potential sellers, and negotiating transactions between purchasers and vendors. Commissions are paid by the sellers and are shared between the listing and selling agents. In this system, an agent's income and career success depend on the behavior of acquiring listings and negotiating sales (House, 1974). Based on these contingencies, House found that agents entered into periodic and unpredictable relations with each other, some competitive and others cooperative. The dynamics of daily interactions among colleagues could be understood in terms of the broader contingencies of the real estate industry.

Participant observation of social systems has an advantage over interpretations solely based on laboratory research (see Skinner, 1957, for an example of such an interpretation). This method provides a detailed analysis of the operating contingencies and descriptive evidence about behavioral effects. This means that an account based on laboratory principles can be assessed in terms of empirical results. Although this is an advantage, there are many sources of invalidity in such studies that make it difficult to attribute social behavior and practices to specific functional variables (Campbell & Stanley, 1966). It is often impossible to distinguish a behavioral account based on laws of the single operant (discriminative stimuli and immediacy of consequences) from an interpretation that emphasizes concurrent-operant principles (correlation-based law of effect, matching, and delay reduction).

Ethological Observation

One solution is to use an ethological approach to observation. Clear functional categories are specified for behavioral and environmental events. The task is to show that the behavioral measure covaries with specific setting events, stimuli, and consequences. It is also possible to establish the temporal priority of the presumed cause, and this enhances internal validity.

An example of the ethological approach is provided by Patterson's (1976) work on coercive family systems. Laboratory research in behavioral analysis showed that schedules of reinforcement were important for the regulation of behavior (Ferster & Skinner, 1957). Based on this finding, Patterson and his associates expected that coercive behavior was also regulated by the schedule of consequences. In fact, early observational studies in institutional settings indicated that verbal statements about delinquent behavior received positive consequences by peers about 88% of the time (Buehler, Patterson, & Furniss, 1966). Later research, however, has argued against the importance of reinforcement schedules. For example, a study by Taplin (1975) showed that a child's deviant behavior was reduced at a time when there was an overall increase in positive consequences by parents. Also, a cross-lag correlation analysis showed that changes in deviant behavior and parental consequences were independent of each other. These results and others lead Patterson to conclude that the scheduling of consequences may not be as important as the presentation of specific-functional stimuli. These stimuli set the occasion for coercive behavior—the more presentations the more the occurrence of deviant and aggressive responses (Patterson, 1974).

The importance of Patterson's work is his search for functional events in natural social systems. To do this, reliable coding techniques were developed in terms of facilitating and inhibiting stimuli, classes of coercive behavior, and accelerating and decelerating consequences (Patterson & Cobb, 1973). Later, Patterson (1976) used a sequential analysis of observational data to isolate the conditional probabilities of response and stimulus classes (described further by Gottman & Notarius, 1978; Sackett, 1979). One important finding was that the controlling stimuli for deviant behavior were quite different in the home and the school (Wahler, 1975). It is possible that each social system (family and school) sets up separate but supportive contingencies for the coercive behavior of children. In general, social behavior such as deviance and aggression is regulated often by interlocking sets of contingencies arranged at the cultural, societal, community, and family levels.

Statistical Analysis

The search for sequential events, or contingencies in natural systems raises the old issue of statistical analysis. Skinner (1969) made it clear that behaviorists should eschew actuarial data, and yet it is impossible to conduct observational analyses without statistical interpretation. One way to understand Skinner's objections is to recognize that he was mostly concerned with experimental research. Most psychological experiments use randomized-group experiments where subjects are randomly assigned to treatments. Skinner objected to the analysis of group means, because group functions often obscure order at the individual level (see Sidman, 1960, on this point). In addition, Skinner argued against statistical inference as a method of scientific decision-making. Experimental analysis, he suggested, was based on systematic control of the causal event rather than statistical assessment of its impact.

Although these criticisms remain important, researchers in experimental analysis have not rejected the use of statistics. For example, research on the matching law typically uses linear regression techniques to estimate the form of the function between relative rate of response and relative rate of reinforcement (see Heth, Pierce, Belke, & Hensch, 1989, for a critique). Given this acceptance at the basic level, there appears to be no a priori reason to reject statistical techniques for the analysis of social behavior and social systems. Statistical methods may include time series (Box & Jenkins, 1970), interrupted time-series analysis (Glass, Wilson, & Gottman, 1975), sequential or lag-sequential methods (Gottman & Notarius, 1978; Sackett, 1979), and other relevant techniques. The objective of any statistical method should be to identify and clarify the relations between social behavior and its controlling variables. Given this requirement, each group, organization, or institution should be studied as a distinct social system—statistical methods being applied to the single unit rather than an aggregate of such units.

Functional Analysis and Naturalistic Experiments

Quasiexperimental Research

Statistical techniques should not be confused with adequate research designs. No amount of statistical sophistication can replace the requirement to rule out extraneous variables. Behavioral researchers must strive for designs that eliminate many confounding factors. The use of quasiexperiments such as the nonequivalent groups designs (Campbell & Stanley, 1966; Cook & Campbell, 1979) and interrupted time-series designs (Glass et al., 1975) can greatly strengthen internal validity. Also, these designs may be preferred over true experiments when there is concern for realism and generalization of results (i.e., external validity).

Kunkel (1985) presented a behavioral analysis of historical data that illustrates the use of quasiexperimental research. He analyzed historical data between 1650 and 1800 on the rise and fall of concert-quality musical performances by orphan girls in Venice. The study demonstrates how behavioral researchers may organize historical facts about society, specify independent and dependent variables, stipulate adequate measures, and build in control over extraneous factors. Data were taken from biographers' accounts of the composer Antonio Vivaldi (1678–1741) and historical analyses of Italian music during the 18th century. The objective of the study was to assess the relevance of behavior principles to acquisition, maintenance, and change in musical performances.

The experimental group consisted of the four best known orphanages for girls in Venice. During the historical period, schools and conservatories of music developed within these institutions, and by 1710 they were known as music centers. Kunkel also identified other orphanages within Venice and other towns in Italy who were not known for musical expertise—these served as the control group. Experimental procedures consisted of changes in contingencies arranged by boards of governors of the four orphanages.

Generally, the reinforcement system involved increasing benefits that were tied to musical skill and performance. Special privileges (e.g., extra fire wood) and monetary incentives were given to girls who became members of the orchestras and choirs, and selection to these groups was based on musical competence. Thus, girls who worked hard at their music were most likely to reap the benefits of the system. In addition, the best performers were allowed to teach music. As music teachers, these girls received tuition fees and opportunities to meet wealthy patrons. All of these more immediate outcomes were supplemented by longer term consequences for high achievement—including the possibility of a good marriage, and the chances of a successful music career. Finally, those who were too young to give public concerts actively pursued music because they observed the privileges and rewards that accrued to older, more accomplished students.

None of these contingencies were arranged in the orphanages that served as the control group. Also, by the mid 1750s, Venice experienced an economic decline that directly reversed the contingencies supporting musical performance in the four experimental institutions. The economic collapse meant that there was little money to support concert music and the music programs of these orphanages. Because of this, privileges and monetary incentives for musical performance were withdrawn by the governors. The course of historical events therefore created an A-B-A reversal design for the experimental group. The A-phases represented periods where musical performance was not reinforced by the governors, whereas the B-phase was the interval when specific contingencies supported such behavior.

During the period of investigation, there were no systematic changes in musical performance at orphanages in the control group. Kunkel, however, did find behavioral changes in the four experimental institutions. The number of performers at La Pieta (the most famous orphanage) increased from zero before 1650, to 40 by 1703 (when Vivaldi came to teach), and then to 70 in the 1740s. Over the next 50 years, reinforcement of musical performance declined and so did the number of performers. Kunkel states that by 1790 there were "only a handful, and a few years later there were none" (p. 442). A similar pattern of results occurred in terms of the number of concerts. The frequency of concerts increased and peaked between 70–90 a year during the 1750s—a remarkable number given that each concert required extensive preparation and practice of new pieces of music (there was no established repertoire). By 1800, however, there were few concerts, and these were only given on special occasions. Finally, the quality of concerts improved over time and "were among the very best in Europe, better than most professional organizations . . . [however] the quality of concerts declined after 1760, and in subsequent years an increasing number of visitors expressed their disappointment" (p. 453).

Limitations to Quasiexperiments

I have spent some time describing Kunkel's (1985) historical experiment because the study illustrates how creative use of archival data can further the behavioral analysis of social systems. Also, I suspect that quasiexperiments will make an important contribution to the behavioral analysis of culture and society. Behaviorists may use historical data to study social systems of the past or they may generate data based on contemporary society. In either case, thoughtful design will be an important ingredient for acceptability and credibility of behavioral results and interpretations.

Behavior analysts who use quasiexperimental methods should be aware of possible pitfalls. Although this kind of natural experiment rules out many sources of invalidity, it does not eliminate all extraneous influences. For example, Kunkel indicates that the economy of Venice was changing at the same time as the contingencies that supported music within the orphanages. The study does not rule out the possibility that changes in the broader economy contributed to the level and quality of musical performances independent of the reward system within the orphanages.

Another limitation of naturalistic experiments is imprecise specification of the independent variable. Kunkel's study does not provide a fine-grain analysis of the contingencies and is therefore weak in terms of experimental analysis. It is difficult to tell which of the many contingencies set by the governors actually regulated the musical performance of students (e.g., privileges, incentives, modeling, etc.). In addition, the study did not clarify the underlying behavioral processes and principles. Although the rise of musical performance may have been a reinforcement process (e.g., law of effect, matching, correlation-based law of effect, Premack principle, etc.) the exact nature of this process is not explored.

There is also some doubt that the demise of concert music was similar to experimental extinction. Kunkel did not report historical accounts of a flourish of musical activity during the 1750s, when support for public concerts waned. This flourish would be expected if the process was analogous to an extinction burst following withdrawal of reinforcement. Also, behavioral variability usually increases during experimental extinction, but Kunkel does not mention greater variation in musical performance during its demise. It is therefore difficult to see the rise and fall of concert music as simply reinforcement and extinction processes. A more complete behavioral account would have to include the interplay of verbal and nonverbal behavior, the interaction of reinforcing events and schedules, the context of reinforcement, and the interrelations among many stimulus-control variables.

Even with these limitations, natural experiments on social systems can play an important role in testing and refining behavioral interpretations. If interaction of reinforcement variables is suspected, quasiexperiments may be designed to detect these effects. When naturalistic evidence and laboratory findings converge, behavioral accounts have more credibility in the broader scientific community. In addition, natural experiments show that behavior principles can operate in uncontrolled settings and at different historical moments. Although most behaviorists accept these assumptions, other researchers have challenged them (Schwartz & Lacy, 1982). Social-system experiments provide information about plausible causation and the generality of behavior theory. Precise details about sources of behavior regulation will, however, require more direct control and manipulation.

Functional Analysis and Small Group Research

Experiments with Small Groups

It is possible to study social systems in laboratory settings with small groups. With an appropriate coding system, the frequency and rates of social behavior can be counted and analyzed (Conger & McLeod, 1977). Three or four people are recruited to join a discussion group and are paid to attend regular sessions. In this context, researchers can observe the development of stable interaction patterns (dependent contingencies) involving divisions of labor, systems of reward (e.g., equity), and distributions of status and power.

The next step is to expose the group to contingencies designed to alter social interaction (Burgess, 1968; Conger & Killeen, 1974; Wiggins, 1966). During the 1970s, I reported an experiment that illustrates this methodology (Pierce, 1975, 1977). The experiment concerned the maintenance and change of social stratification and inequality in groups. Four-person groups were established by bringing together people who were interested in discussing and solving a variety of problems. Communication and prestige responses of the members were monitored until a clearly defined status system emerged from the interaction.

At first, the percentage of speaking-time became different for each group member. Consistent with these differences in conversation, group members allocated different amounts of prestige to the other participants. The person who talked the most received the highest prestige scores, and the individual who talked least received the lowest.

Once a stable system of ranks had developed, I attempted to alter the social system by manipulating contingencies of reinforcement (see also Bavelas, Hastorf,

Gross, & Kite, 1965). One contingency involved reinforcement of talking with points that were later exchanged for money. The highest ranked member received a talk discouragement schedule. This person lost points for speaking and earned points for 20 seconds of silence. In contrast, the person with the least status received a talk encouragement schedule. This member earned points for talking and lost points for every 20 seconds of silence. Other group members (ranked 2nd and 3rd) received reinforcement to maintain their relative level of participation.

The results showed that reinforcement contingencies could alter the communication system of a group—people who spoke a lot reduced participation and those who were usually quiet talked more often. More importantly, the distribution of prestige also changed although not required by the imposed contingencies. Low-status members who increased communication attained higher prestige in the group. On the other hand, high-status members who reduced communication were given less prestige. One reason for the shift in prestige relates to relative rates of reinforcement. If communication was reinforcing to group members, then the experimentally imposed changes in discussion altered the relative rates of reinforcement given to others. This change in relative reinforcement presumably controlled the prestige responses of group members.

I tested this account (Pierce, 1977) by having group members deliver explicit reinforcement to others when they talked. In one condition, talking by low-status members produced monetary outcomes both for them and others in the group. Under these contingencies, the low-ranked member talked more, increased monetary reinforcement allocated to others, and received greater prestige from fellow members. Overall, the experiment showed that status systems in small groups reflect the distribution of reinforcement among the members.

Social inequality in everyday life may also depend on the resources, benefits, and valued activities dispensed by different sectors of society. War and revolution are common ways that people use to reallocate wealth and property; however, these responses seldom guarantee an equal distribution of reinforcement power. Usually, leaders of rebellions and their followers achieve a sudden rise in power to reinforce, whereas the establishment becomes disenfranchised (i.e., a new distribution of reinforcement). In this way, social inequality is shifted from one sector of society to another but is never eliminated. At the present time, there is no experimental evidence to support the assumption that social equality is a possible steady state for social systems.

ANALYSIS OF CULTURE
AND CULTURAL EVOLUTION

The behavioral analysis of social systems is actually part of the more general problem of culture and cultural evolution. A culture has been defined in terms of the ideas and values of a community, but a natural-science approach defines culture as all the conditions, events, and consequences arranged by other people that regulate individual behavior (Skinner, 1953). Thus a culture is composed of social contingencies of reinforcement. When individuals of a community are exposed to commonly arranged social contingencies, they acquire a style of behavior that is characteristic of the group. People who speak English show syntactic and semantic regularities of speech that differ from those who speak French. Also, subtle changes in the verbal contingencies from one location to another provide an account of the differences in dialect within the larger English-speaking community.

Verbal Behavior

The principles and laws of behavior explain how a culture regulates individual behavior. A person in an English-speaking culture learns to speak in accord with the verbal practices of the community. Presumably, the community arranges events and consequences to establish and maintain the complex verbal repertoire of the speaker. On a specific occasion, the community provides reinforcement for a certain "way of speaking" and withholds reinforcement or supplies aversive stimulation for other, unacceptable responses. In this manner, the individual comes to conform to the customary practices of the community and, in so doing, contributes to the perpetuation of the culture.

Although behavior principles provide a reasonable account of how the individual learns from exposure to a culture, most of the analysis has involved interpretations rather than research. This is seen in the field of verbal behavior where Skinner has provided an interpretation of the contingencies that regulate the behavior of speakers (Skinner, 1957). Although Skinner's analysis has generated many additional interpretations and philosophical debates (Lee, 1984), relatively few empirical studies have been conducted. The studies that do exist are suggestive but not conclusive.

Osgood (1953) found that an infant's babbling included all the speech sounds that make up the different languages of the world. This suggests that a child's speech sounds may be shaped toward adult forms by reinforcement of successive approximations. There is, however, no convincing data on this point. Evidence also indicates that a child's distribution of speech sounds becomes increasingly similar to the adults in a community. Speech sounds that occur frequently in the community increase over time, whereas infrequent sounds drop out of the repertoire (Irwin, 1948, 1952). Again, the exact basis of these changes is not yet established. Reinforcement, modeling, or even repeated exposure are possible mechanisms, but evidence is lacking. Other researchers have demonstrated the operant conditioning of speech sounds in infants using an adult's social response as reinforcement (Rheingold, Gewirtz, & Ross, 1959). Also, a substantial amount of literature has accumulated on verbal conditioning of adult-human speech (Kanfer, 1968), although strong challenges have also been presented (Spielberger & DeNike, 1966). These conditioning studies of infant and adult speech indicate that reinforcement contingencies can regulate communication in controlled settings; however, they fail to show that reinforcement processes do govern verbal behavior outside of the laboratory.

Several problems are apparent with the research on verbal behavior. These difficulties also extend to other areas of culture and social learning, although not reviewed here (see Pierce & Epling, 1984). One problem is that a great deal of the research is dated. Behavior analysts simply have not kept pace with theoretical and empirical advances in other fields (e.g., developmental psychology, linguistics, socialization). Another difficulty is that studies have often been demonstrations of behavior control rather than analyses of the controlling variables. Operant researchers have shown that the behavior of a speaker may be modified by reinforcement procedures; however, few studies have focused on the experimental analysis of verbal behavior, as suggested by Skinner (see Oha & Dickinson, 1989, for recent exceptions). In addition, there has been an absence of longitudinal studies that document the natural development of verbal operants and the role of the social environment in this process. Generally, behavior analysts have not generated the empirical evidence to show that culture works through reinforcement processes to affect individual behavior.

Practices and Consequences

Although the analysis of culture and individual behavior remains a priority, a more difficult task is to account for the cultural practices themselves—the social contingencies of reinforcement. Sigrid Glenn (1988, 1989) has proposed a behavioral analysis of culture (Chapter 3) that builds on the works of Skinner (1953, 1969) and anthropologist Marvin Harris (1979). In this view, cultural practices involve the operant behavior of many people who compose the members of a culture. Each person's behavior functions as part of the reinforcement contingencies of others—providing stimulation and consequences. A cultural practice is therefore defined in terms of interlocking (social) contingencies—where the behavior of each member supports the behavior of others. The pattern of operants that comprise the interlocking contingencies is referred to as the form of a cultural practice—or the type of practice.

Cultural practices are functionally similar to operants at the individual level. Both operants and practices may be viewed as behavior classes. An operant such as "opening the door" is composed of various response forms, both verbal and nonverbal, that produce a common environmental effect (an open door). A cultural practice of "making water jars" involves alternative sets of interlocking operants that result in a common outcome, efficient transportation, and storage of water. Forms of this practice may include making and using shells, hollow leaves, or baked-clay containers. The cultural form that predominates (e.g., clay jars) reflects the basic process of selection by consequences. In terms of selection, operants are selected by contingencies of reinforcement, and practices are selected by metacontingencies.

Metacontingencies are specific relations between practices and their effects or outcomes (Glenn, 1988). For example, competence in science is an important concern for people who live in a culture with advanced technology. This is because the scientific competence of the population is correlated with more fundamental outcomes related to survival (i.e., production and reproduction). Different forms of education may produce greater or lesser levels of scientific competence in the population. The effects of greater scientific skills are technological gains for industry (e.g., microchips, efficient electrical products) and benefits in terms of population, such as reduced health risks for disease and improved regulation of environmental pollution.

According to this analysis, a metacontingency exists between educational practices and scientific competence. This contingency implies that there may be an increase in those forms of education that result in more and better trained students of science. However, in complex cultures like the United States and Canada, competing (or concurrent) metacontingencies may mean that the "best" educational practice is not selected. A suboptimal form of education (in terms of teaching science) may prevail for some time because this practice results in a relatively higher rate of production/reproduction outcomes. Thus, cultural practices and their outcomes may show a matching relation: the distribution of a practice (types of education) equals the distribution of its outcomes (production/reproduction consequences). If the relative outcomes of an educational practice resulting in low-scientific competence exceed those of a practice yielding high-scientific achievement, then the less adequate educational practice will predominate in the culture.

Behavioral Research on Culture

The behavioral interpretation of culture and cultural evolution must also be grounded in empirical observation. Most of the methods that I have discussed in terms of social systems may be applied to questions of culture. Thus, it is possible to conduct descriptive-field studies as exemplified by Harris (1966), quantitative observational research that demonstrates serial-dependency between practices and presumed outcomes, quasiexperiments in natural settings (Kunkel, 1986), and small-group experiments with human subjects (Jacobs & Campbell, 1961).

Animals and Culture

In terms of the origins and maintenance of cultural practices, animal models may provide useful information. At the time of writing this paper, I was unable to track down a reference to a classic study about the evolution of a cultural taboo in animals. In fact, I am not sure if this experiment was ever carried out (it should be if it was not). Dr. Donald Heth, Department of Psychology at the University of Alberta (personal communication) provided me with some details.

Apparently, a troop of baboons (or chimpanzees) were kept in a zoo enclosure and were provided with a choice between a preferred food (bananas) and a less appetizing food source (lab chow). Over a period of days, the baboons consistently chose the bananas most of the time.

Following the baseline period, the researchers established a negative reinforcement contingency for eating the less preferred food. Whenever any animal approached the bananas, the entire colony was drenched with water from a fire hose, used to clean the enclosure. After exposure to this contingency, the troop would attack any member that approached the bananas. Eventually, all members of the troop were eating exclusively the less preferred food (chow), and avoiding cold showers. The researchers then removed the reinforcement contingency—approaching and eating the bananas no longer resulted in being soaked with water. As you might expect, the group never tested the operating contingencies and continued to attack any member that went toward the preferred food.

Over time, new infants were born and raised in the colony. These infants had never been present when the original troop was soaked for eating the preferred food. The infants, however, learned to eat the chow rather than the bananas. As previously stated, the troop would attack any member if it went near the preferred food—and this social contingency also applied to new infants. In addition, modeling and imitation were apparently used for social training of the taboo, since all members of the troop selected the chow and rejected the bananas. Thus, social reinforcement and observational learning contributed to the maintenance of the food taboo, even though the original reinforcement contingencies had long since been removed.

This "transmission" of a cultural practice in a troop of baboons may be an analogue for food taboos in humans. For example, Harris (1974) has recounted the history of the Jewish people in terms of their taboo regarding pork. Current evidence suggests that the taboo did not arise simply from avoidance of disease. Many other kinds of meat at that time were also susceptible to trichinosis bacteria. The actual contingencies may have involved the high cost of raising and maintaining pigs in an arid region. A pig consumes about as much food as an adult human. Thus, to keep several pigs, much of the human food supply would be exhausted. The Jewish people faced a social trap involving the immediate benefit of eating tasty pork and the long-term loss of food supplies that resulted from raising pigs. To avoid this trap, it appears that rabbis declared a law against eating pork. Based on this law and religious socialization, the Jewish community has maintained this practice into modern times, even though the original conditions are no longer relevant (see also Sidman, 1989, who notes the persistence of avoidance behavior when the relevant contingencies are withdrawn).

In addition to animal models, naturalistic studies and experiments may provide information about cultural evolution in humans (e.g., Kawamura, 1959). The Japanese macaque troop of Koshima Island is well known for its cultural innovations and their spread. In one example, an infant female called Imo began to wash sweet potatoes to remove the grit. This behavior was later observed in Imo's playmates and her mother who taught it to another offspring. Imo was also among the first to take up swimming and to throw wheat kernels on the water to remove pieces of sand. Both of these practices were eventually adopted by the entire troop (see Jolly, 1985, for more on animal culture).

Although it is clear that novel behavior can spread throughout a troop, the behavioral processes that lead to this practice are less clear. Menzel and Menzel (1979) indicate that "the individuals who detect an object, and those who lead the approach, and those who initially test it out, and those who fool around with it the longest, and those who will best remember its nature and location need not necessarily be the same individuals; and in each of these aspects of group performance there might be transmission of information from one animal to the others" (p. 278). Behavioral research with animals in naturalistic and laboratory settings may build on such observations. Eventually, it may be possible to provide a more precise description of the interlocking contingencies that contribute to the discovery and adoption of innovative behavior.

Social Experiments and Reforms

Throughout this paper I have emphasized the relationship between behavioral analysis of social processes and basic research. This emphasis is important in developing a scientific account of culture and society. However, I want to end this discussion on a more practical note. One of the great strengths of a behavioral approach is its implications for modification. The application of behavior modification to cultural practices is what Skinner has called the "design of a culture" (Skinner, 1953).

Most people think of *Walden Two* as the behaviorists' ideal for cultural design (Skinner, 1948). Using a fictional utopian community, Skinner provides analyses and solutions to economic, political, and social problems of modern life. All of these solutions are based on the application of basic behavior principles to community life. Since the time of this work, at least two real communities have adopted the utopian lifestyle portrayed in Skinner's novel—Twin Oaks and Los Horcones. These communities are interesting social movements, but I have not seen any systematic attempts at experimental analysis. It is likely that the members are more concerned with the daily operation of their group than with an experimental analysis of programs and policies.

In the future, however, it may be possible for applied behavior analysts to work with the planners of behavioral communities to test alternative cultural designs. One interesting problem concerns the transfer of wealth and property from generation to generation. I recently had several intriguing discussions with two graduate students from China. The students were unable to return to their country because of the political climate; we talked about the social system of China and the problem of overpopulation. One of the contingencies that apparently contributes to overpopulation and the division of Chinese society into social classes is the system of inheritance of property and wealth. In Chinese culture, a father's estate is passed on to his son(s)—and there are many rules and laws regulating such transactions. Although the father may have worked hard to achieve such wealth, his sons acquire these possessions only on the basis of kinship.

One implication of this practice is that wealth is transferred from generation to generation—perpetuating social class differences. Another effect is that a preference for male offspring develops since property can only be transferred through this lineage. When population size is a problem, as in China, this preference for male children may lead to a higher number of births, as people continue to have babies until at least one male child is born. Finally, since property and lineage have been tied together throughout Chinese history, a father (and the family of which he is the head) works hard to acquire property and wealth that will be passed on to future generations.

In an experimental community, it may be possible to analyze the implications of inheritance laws for labor and productivity, procreation and birth control, and the division of society by social class. Once an inheritance system is operating in the community, the planners could change the system by implementing new laws and policies. Based on principles such as successive approximation, it should be possible to gradually withdraw the father-to-son inheritance to a point where the state (or community) takes back most of the wealth. This will, of course, equalize the wealth among social groups and presumably reduce social inequality.

One possibility, however, is that the state will squander its newly acquired resources and contribute to programs that result in greater inefficiency (however measured). Questions about the productivity of fathers and sons after the removal of the estate system will also remain. What happens to fathers (and their families) who lose the incentive of passing on acquired property? Do they become "indifferent and apathetic" (see Chapter 12)? What about a system where each person can work to accumulate as much wealth as possible during a lifetime, but this is not passed on over generations (a compromise between capitalism and socialism)? How does the family of the deceased survive within such a system? Such questions are of great practical relevance but have never been systematically explored.

Although this kind of social experiment is not beyond possibility, it is also not very likely. Behavioral communities will probably not opt for planned interventions by applied behavior analysis. Assuming this is the case, a more limited and piecemeal approach to cultural design will be required. Such an approach is currently seen in the literature of behavioral-community psychology (Glenwick & Jason, 1980), although the role of the behavior analyst is often to "cure" individuals rather than to design improvements in the social system (Holland, 1978). In a democratic society, behaviorists could develop a role similar to economists who advise the government about planning and policy. In addition to offering consultation in terms of government programs, behavior analysts may also provide valuable information in terms of assessment and evaluation. So-called representative communities could be used to evaluate government programs and policies before they are implemented on a more massive scale.

Many governments throughout the world are faced with mounting population and declining food and resources. Economists, demographers, and other social scientists are hired by government agencies to develop programs that curb population growth. These consultants formulate plans of action based on assumptions of rational choice or naive psychology. Because their analyses are faulty, the programs are usually ineffective (Hernandez, 1981). In contrast, behavior analysts are skilled at specifying the behavioral classes that underlie population growth and the contingencies that support such behavior. Behaviorists can, therefore, play a vital role in the regulation of human fertility (or other social problems) by providing analyses and research on controlling variables and designing new systems of reinforcement.

In fact, a behavioral approach to human fertility has already been developed. Wiest and Squier (1974) reported a reinforcement analysis of this problem. This article is probably not well known to behavior analysts, since it was published in the *Journal of Social Issues,* rather than in a behavioral journal. In this paper, the authors provide a component analysis of birth control methods, the time of use relative to coitus, the frequency of use for each method, and the sex of the user. They note that "contraceptive performances that are coitus-dependent are difficult to measure directly simply because heterosexual behavior always occurs in private" (Wiest & Squier, 1974, pp. 251–252). One solution, suggested by Wiest and Squier, is to target behavior that is reliably correlated with contraceptive behavior. For example, research may show that talking about the negative consequences of unwanted pregnancies and the long-term advantages of a small family is correlated with contraceptive use. Reinforcement contingencies applied to these verbal responses could indirectly increase requisite behavior (e.g., Lovaas, 1961).

Wiest and Squier provide an analysis of the contingencies that regulate contraceptive behavior. Their analysis separates those who are "strongly motivated to avoid pregnancy" from people who "want too many" children. The researchers argue that little reinforcement is required to contact family planning agencies if pregnancy is more aversive than positively reinforcing. In these cases, deficits in the behavioral repertoire of effective contraceptive use may be the problem, and techniques of modeling and providing instructions could be employed.

On the other hand, it may be more difficult to alter the behavior of those who are positively reinforced by pregnancy and children. One solution is "a government might pay each female a monthly sum, beginning at fecundity, until a birth occurs. The amount would increase as pregnancy risk became greater in early womanhood, and drop as the woman aged. This would regularly reward the successfully nonpregnant, and focus attention on the cost to a woman of bearing a child" (Wiest & Squier, 1974, p. 252). Although the authors do not mention it, a similar contingency could be applied to males given the advances in genetic matching for paternity. In this way, neither women nor men would "want" to have children.

It is apparent that a behavioral analysis of fertility (and other social problems) is an important contribution to culture and society. Behavior analysts are clearly capable of designing socially important programs and policies. Unfortunately, less effective methods are accepted and used because behavioral analysis challenges the cultural values of freedom and dignity (Lamal, 1989; Skinner, 1971). Behavioral analysis also is unacceptable because it directs the problem to the social system rather than to the individual. To avoid scrutiny of its practices, our culture trains people to reject any technology or scientific view that "externalizes" the regulation of human behavior. Based on this training, people in North America usually are opposed to behavioral technology.

It may be possible to design contingencies that reinforce the adoption of behavioral technology, but to date this has not been a successful strategy. Another plan is to find societies and governments that are predisposed to the concepts and methods of cultural design. Given the rapidly changing world in which we live, and the shift away from communism in Europe and the Soviet Union, it should not be too hard to identify societies that are interested in behavioral technology. One way to make initial contact with governments is to have prominent members of The Association for Behavior Analysis visit different countries and speak to government officials about behavioral analysis and society. Further, the Association could combine with the Cambridge Centre for Behavioral Studies to bring together a core of behavior analysts interested in cultural design. These researchers could be hired by governments and interest groups to plan and assess changes in the system of reinforcement for individual behavior and the metacontingencies that regulate cultural practices. If the design of culture proves useful and cost effective, then widescale adoption may follow. At this point, the application of behavioral analysis to society and culture will have both practical and basic importance.

CONCLUSION

There is a clear role for behavioral analysis in the study of society and culture. Behavior analysts should tackle analytical problems at both the basic and applied levels. Laboratory research with humans contributes to the systematic extension of behavior principles, but other areas of research are needed. One area concerns the experimental analysis of social relations. Experiments on social processes such as cooperation, competition, and exchange help to bridge the gap between principles of individual behavior and the analysis of social systems. Behavioral research is also needed on large-scale social systems. Additional methods are required to study these systems, including statistical analysis, observational studies, quasiexperimental research, and experiments in small-group contexts. In each case, the objective is to analyze the system of reinforcement formed by a network of interlocking contingencies.

Finally, a scientific account of human behavior will require a detailed analysis of culture and cultural evolution. This analysis must go beyond behavioral interpretations. Empirical research is needed on the transmission of cultural practices from generation to generation, and the metacontingencies that regulate such practices. There is also a need for applied research. Currently, the evaluation of government programs is conducted by economists and other social scientists. These consultants are not familiar with contingency management, and their programs are often inefficient and ineffective. Given this situation, many of the world governments may be interested in applied behavioral analysis. Behavior analysts who design government programs as social experiments will contribute to the science of human behavior and to the long-term survival of humankind.

REFERENCES

Azrin, N. H., & Lindsley, O. R. (1956). The reinforcement of cooperation between children. *Journal of Abnormal Psychology, 52,* 100–102.

Baum, W. M. (1974a). On two types of deviation from the matching law: Bias and undermatching. *Journal of the Experimental Analysis of Behavior, 22,* 231–242.

Baum, W. M. (1974b). Choice in free ranging wild pigeons. *Science, 185,* 78–79.

Bavelas, A., Hastorf, R. H., Gross, A. E., & Kite, W. R. (1965). Experiments on the alteration of group structure. *Journal of Experimental Social Psychology, 1,* 55–70.

Belke, T. W., Pierce, W. D., & Powell, R. A. (1989). Determinants of choice for pigeons and humans on concurrent-chains schedules of reinforcement. *Journal of the Experimental Analysis of Behavior, 52*(2), 97–109.

Bond, C. F., Jr., & Titus, L. J. (1983). Social facilitation: A meta-analysis of 241 studies. *Psychological Bulletin, 94,* 265–292.

Box, G. E. P., & Jenkins, G. M. (1970). *Time series analysis forecasting and control.* San Francisco, CA: Holden-Day.

Bradshaw, C. M., & Szabadi, E. (1988). Quantitative analysis of human operant behavior. In G. Davey & C. Cullen (Eds.), *Human operant conditioning and behavior modification* (pp. 225–259). London: John Wiley & Sons.

Buehler, R. E., Patterson, G. R., & Furniss, J. M. (1966). The reinforcement of behavior in institutional settings. *Behavior Research and Therapy, 4,* 157–167.

Burgess, R. L. (1968). Communication networks: An experimental re-evaluation. *Journal of Experimental Social Psychology, 4,* 324–337.

Burgess, R. L., & Nielsen, J. M. (1974). An experimental analysis of some structural determinants of equitable and inequitable exchange relations. *American Sociological Review, 39,* 427–443.

Campbell, D. T., & Stanley, J. C. (1966). *Experimental and quasi-experimental designs for research.* Chicago: Rand McNally.

Cohen, D. J. (1962). Justin and his peers: An experimental analysis of a child's social world. *Child Development, 33,* 697–717.

Conger, R., & Killeen, P. (1974). Use of concurrent operants in small group research. *Pacific Sociological Review, 17,* 399–416.

Conger, R. D., & McLeod, D. (1977). Describing behavior in small groups with the Datamyte event recorder. *Behavioral Research Methods & Instrumentation, 9*(5), 418–424.

Cook, K. S., & Emerson, R. M. (1978). Power, equity and commitment in exchange networks. *American Sociological Review, 43,* 721–739.

Cook, K. S., Emerson, R. M., Gillmore, M. R., & Yamagishi, T. (1983). The distribution of power in exchange networks: Theory and experimental results. *American Journal of Sociology, 89,* 275–305.

Cook, T. D., & Campbell, D. T. (1979). *Quasi-experimentation: Design and analysis issues for field settings.* Chicago: Rand McNally.

de Villiers, P. A. (1977). Choice in concurrent schedules and a quantitative formulation of the law of effect. In W. K. Honig & J. E. R. Staddon (Eds.), *Handbook of operant behavior* (pp. 233–287). Englewood Cliffs, NJ: Prentice-Hall.

Deutsch, M. (1958). Trust and suspicion. *Journal of Conflict Resolution, 2,* 265–279.

Deutsch, M., & Krauss, R. M. (1962). Studies of interpersonal bargaining. *Journal of Conflict Resolution, 6,* 52–76.

Fantino, E. (1977). Conditioned reinforcement: Choice and information. In W. K. Honig & J. E. R. Staddon (Eds.), *Handbook of operant behavior* (pp. 313–339). Englewood Cliffs, NJ: Prentice-Hall.

Ferster, C. B., & Skinner, B. F. (1957). *Schedules of reinforcement.* New York: Appleton-Century-Crofts.

Glass, G. V., Wilson, V. L., & Gottman, J. M. (1975). *Design and analysis of time-series experiments.* Boulder, CO: Colorado Associated University Press.

Glenn, S. S. (1988). Contingencies and metacontingencies: Toward a synthesis of behavior analysis and cultural materialism. *The Behavior Analyst, 11,* 161–179.

Glenn, S. S. (1989). Verbal behavior and cultural practices. *Behavior Analysis and Social Action, 7,* 10–15.

Glenwick, D., & Jason, L. (1980). *Behavioral community psychology: Progress and prospects.* New York: Praeger.

Gottman, J. M., & Notarius, C. (1978). The sequential analysis of observational data. In M. Lamb, S. Soumi, & G. Stephenson (Eds.), *Single subject research.* Madison, WI: University of Wisconsin Press.

Gray, L. N., & Tallman, I. (1987). Theories of choice: Contingent reward and punishment applications. *Social Psychology Quarterly, 50,* 16–23.

Hake, D. F., Donaldson, T., & Hyten, C. (1983). Analysis of discriminative control by social behavioral stimuli. *Journal of the Experimental Analysis of Behavior, 39,* 7–23.

Hake, D. F., & Olvera, D. (1978). Cooperation, competition, and related social phenomena. In A. C. Catania & T. A. Brigham (Eds.), *Handbook of applied behavior analysis* (pp. 208–245). New York: Irvington.

Hake, D. F., & Vukelich, R. (1972). A classification and review of cooperation procedures. *Journal of the Experimental Analysis of Behavior, 18,* 333–343.

Hake, D. F., Vukelich, R., & Kaplan, S. J. (1973). Audit responses: Responses maintained by access to existing self and coactor scores during nonsocial, parallel work, and cooperation procedures. *Journal of the Experimental Analysis of Behavior, 19,* 409–423.

Harlow, H. F., & Zimmerman, R. R. (1959). Affectional responses in the infant monkey. *Science, 130,* 421–432.

Harris, M. (1966). The cultural ecology of India's sacred cattle. *Current Anthropology, 7,* 51–59.

Harris, M. (1974). *Cows, pigs, wars and witches.* New York: Vintage Books.

Harris, M. (1979). *Cultural materialism.* New York: Random House.

Hernandez, D. (1981). The impact of family planning programs on fertility in developing countries: A critical evaluation. *Social Science Research, 10,* 32–66.

Herrnstein, R. J. (1961). Relative and absolute response strength as a function of frequency of reinforcement. *Journal of the Experimental Analysis of Behavior, 4,* 267–272.

Heth, D. C., Pierce, W. D., Belke, T. W., & Hensch, S. A. (1989). The effects of logarithmic transformation on estimating the parameters of the generalized matching law. *Journal of the Experimental Analysis of Behavior, 52,* 65–76.

Holland, J. G. (1978). Behaviorism: Part of the problem or part of the solution? *Journal of Applied Behavior Analysis, 11,* 163–174.

House, J. D. (1974). Entrepreneurial career patterns of residential real estate agents in Montreal. *Canadian Review of Sociology and Anthropology, 11,* 110–124.

House, J. D. (1975). Structured forms of social behaviour: Colleague relations in the real estate business. *Canadian Journal of Behavioural Science, 7*(3), 201–215.

Irwin, O. C. (1948). Infant speech: Development of vowel sounds. *Journal of Speech and Hearing, 13,* 31–34.

Irwin, O. C. (1952). Speech development in the young child: 2. Some factors related to the speech development of the infant and the young child. *Journal of Speech and Hearing, 17,* 209–279.

Jacobs, R. D., & Campbell, D. T. (1961). The perpetuation of an arbitrary tradition through several generations of a laboratory microculture. *Journal of Abnormal and Social Psychology, 62,* 649–658.

Jolly, A. (1985). *The evolution of primate behavior* (2nd ed.). New York: Macmillan Publishing.

Kanfer, F. H. (1968). Verbal conditioning: A review of its current status. In T. R. Dixon & D. L. Horton (Eds.), *Verbal behavior and general behavior theory* (pp. 254–290). Englewood Cliffs, NJ: Prentice-Hall.

Kawamura, S. (1959). The process of sub-culture propagation among Japanese macaques. *Primates, 2,* 43–60.

Krauss, R. M., & Deutsch, M. (1966). Communication in interpersonal bargaining. *Journal of Personality and Social Psychology, 4,* 572–577.

Kunkel, J. H. (1985). Vivaldi in Venice: A historical test of psychological propositions. *The Psychological Record, 35,* 445–457.

Kunkel, J. H. (1986). The Vicos project: A cross-cultural test of psychological propositions. *The Psychological Record, 36,* 451–466.

Kwan, T., Pierce, W. D., & Epling, W. F. (in progress). *Human performance on concurrent-chain schedules of reinforcement: Effects of consumable and non-consumable reinforcement.*

Lamal, P. A. (1989). The impact of behaviorism on our culture: Some evidence and conjectures. *The Psychological Record, 39,* 529–535.

Lee, V. L. (1984). Some notes on the subject matter of Skinner's *Verbal Behavior. Behaviorism, 12*(1), 29–40.

Lindsley, O. R. (1966). Experimental analysis of cooperation and competition. In T. Verhave (Ed.), *The experimental analysis of behavior* (pp. 470–501). New York: Appleton-Century-Crofts.

Lovaas, I. O. (1961). Interaction between verbal and nonverbal behavior. *Child Development, 32,* 329–336.

Marwell, G., & Schmitt, D. R. (1975). *Cooperation: An experimental analysis.* New York: Academic Press.

Menzel, E. W., & Menzel, C. R. (1979). Cognitive developmental and social aspects of responsiveness to novel objects in a family group of marmosets (*Saguinus fuscicollis*). *Behaviour, 70,* 251–279.

Messick, D. M., & Brewer, M. B. (1983). Solving social dilemmas: A review. In L. Wheeler & P. Shaver (Eds.), *Review of personality and social psychology* (pp. 11–44). Beverly Hills: Sage.

Miller, L. K., & Hamblin, R. L. (1963). Interdependence, differential rewarding, and productivity. *American Sociological Review, 28,* 768–778.

Molm, L. D. (1988). The structure and use of power: A comparison of reward and punishment power. *Social Psychological Quarterly, 51,* 108–122.

Molm, L. D. (1990). Structure, action, and outcomes: The dynamics of power in social exchange. *American Sociological Review, 55,* 427–447.

Moore, J. C., Jr. (1968). Status and influence in small group interaction. *Sociometry, 31,* 47–63.

Moore, J. C., Jr. (1969). Social status and social influences: Process considerations. *Sociometry, 32,* 145–168.

Oha, S., & Dickinson, A. M. (1989). A review of empirical studies of verbal behavior. *The Analysis of Verbal Behavior, 7,* 32–40.

Osgood, C. E. (1953). *Method and theory in experimental psychology.* New York: Oxford University Press.

Osgood, C. E. (1962). *An alternative to war or surrender.* Urbana, IL: University of Illinois Press.

Osgood, C. E. (1967). Escalation and de-escalation as political strategies. *Phi Kappa Phi Journal, 47,* 3–18.

Patterson, G. R. (1974). A basis for identifying stimuli which control behaviors in natural settings. *Child Development, 45,* 900–911.

Patterson, G. R. (1976). The aggressive child: Victim and architect of a coercive system. In E. J. Mash, L. A. Hamerlynck, & L. C. Handy (Eds.), *Behavior modification and families* (pp. 267–316). New York: Brunner-Mazel.

Patterson, G. R., & Cobb, J. A. (1973). Stimulus control for classes of noxious behaviors. In J. F. Knutson (Ed.), *The control of aggression: Implications from basic research* (pp. 145–199). Chicago: Aldine.

Pierce, W. D. (1975). *Altering a status order: Contingencies of reinforcement controlling group structure.* Unpublished doctoral dissertation, York University, Department of Sociology, Toronto, Canada.

Pierce, W. D. (1977). Rank consensus and experimentally induced changes in interpersonal evaluations. *Psychological Reports, 41,* 1331–1338.

Pierce, W. D., & Epling, W. F. (1983). Choice, matching, and human behavior. *The Behavior Analyst, 6*(1), 57–76.

Pierce, W. D., & Epling, W. F. (1984). On the persistence of cognitive explanation: Implications for behavior analysis. *Behaviorism, 12,* 15–17.

Rheingold, H. L., Gewirtz, J. L., & Ross, H. W. (1959). Social conditioning of vocalizations in the infant. *Journal of Comparative and Physiological Psychology, 52,* 68–73.

Rosenbaum, M. E. (1979). Cooperation and competition. In P. Paulus (Ed.), *Psychology of group influence* (pp. 291–331). Hillsdale, NJ: Erlbaum.

Sackett, G. P. (1979). The lag sequential analysis of contingency and cyclicity in behavioral interaction research. In J. Osofsky (Ed.), *Handbook of infant development* (pp. 623–649). New York: John Wiley & Sons.

Schmitt, D. R. (1976). Some conditions affecting the choice to cooperate or compete. *Journal of the Experimental Analysis of Behavior, 25,* 165–178.

Schmitt, D. R. (1981). Performance under cooperation and competition. *American Behavioral Scientist, 24,* 649–679.

Schmitt, D. R. (1984). Interpersonal relations: Cooperation and competition. *Journal of the Experimental Analysis of Behavior, 42*(3), 377–384.

Schmitt, D. R., & Marwell, G. (1972). Withdrawal and reward allocation as responses to inequity. *Journal of Experimental Social Psychology, 8*, 207–221.

Schwartz, B., & Lacy, H. (1982). *Behaviorism, science, and human nature.* New York: W. W. Norton.

Seligman, M. E. P., & Maier, S. F. (1967). Failure to escape traumatic shock. *Journal of Experimental Psychology, 74*, 1–9.

Sidman, M. (1989). *Coercion and Its Fallout.* Boston, MA: Authors Cooperative.

Sidman, M. (1960). *Tactics of scientific research.* New York: Basic Books.

Sidowski, J. B., Wyckoff, L. B., & Tabory, L. (1956). The influence of reinforcement and punishment in a minimal social situation. *Journal of Abnormal and Social Psychology, 52*, 115–119.

Skinner, B. F. (1948). *Walden Two.* New York: Macmillan.

Skinner, B. F. (1953). *Science and human behavior.* New York: The Free Press.

Skinner, B. F. (1957). *Verbal behavior.* New York: Appleton-Century-Crofts.

Skinner, B. F. (1962). Two "synthetic social relations." *Journal of the Experimental Analysis of Behavior, 5*, 531–533.

Skinner, B. F. (1969). *Contingencies of reinforcement: A theoretical analysis* New York: Appleton-Century-Crofts.

Skinner, B. F. (1971). *Beyond freedom and dignity.* New York: Alfred Knopf.

Soumi, S. (1982). Relevance of animal models for clinical psychology. In P. C. Kendell & J. N. Butcher (Eds.), *Handbook of research methods in clinical psychology* (pp. 249–271). New York: John Wiley & Sons.

Spielberger, C. D., & DeNike, L. D. (1966). Descriptive behaviorism versus cognitive theory in verbal operant conditioning. *Psychological Review, 73*, 306–326.

Sunahara, D., & Pierce, W. D. (1982). The matching law and bias in a social exchange involving choice between alternatives. *Canadian Journal of Sociology, 7*, 145–165.

Taplin, P. (1975). Changes in parent consequating behavior as an outcome measure in the evaluation of a social reprogramming approach to the treatment of aggressive boys. *Dissertation Abstracts International, 36*, 1B–982B.

Wahler, R. G. (1975). Some structural aspects of deviant child behavior. *Journal of Applied Behavior Analysis, 8*, 27–42.

Weingarten, K., & Mechner, F. (1966). The contingency as an independent variable of social interaction. In T. Verhave (Ed.), *The experimental analysis of behavior* (pp. 447–470). New York: Appleton-Century-Crofts.

Wiest, W. M., & Squier, L. H. (1974). Incentives and reinforcement: A behavioral approach to fertility. *Journal of Social Issues, 30*, 235–263.

Wiggins, J. A. (1966). Status differentiation, external consequences, and alternative reward distributions. *Sociometry, 29*, 89–103.

3

Contingencies and Metacontingencies: Relations Among Behavioral, Cultural, and Biological Evolution

Sigrid S. Glenn

INTRODUCTION

This chapter is about behavioral processes and cultural processes, how they are related to one another, and how both are related to biological evolution. The increasing number of newspapers, books, and periodicals that spell out the consequences of overpopulation, nuclear war, pollution, crime, and inadequate education suggests there is a growing recognition of those dangers; and some individuals act in small but important ways to do what they personally can do to avert these large-scale threats.

Many of us, however, are quite unaware that our own behavior contributes to the overall situation; it is difficult to discern how our individual and quite legal actions relate, for example, to an increase in crime rates. Many of us who recognize our own contributions to our society's problems also recognize that even if we behave differently, social problems cannot be alleviated until many other people's behavior changes, too. In short, we are all caught up in a larger system that seems impervious to our small efforts. Yet, dramatic changes do occur—in societies and in individuals. We need to understand how this happens. In other words, we need to know how individual behavior works, how social systems work, and how they are related. Then we can begin to specify the actions most likely to deter and reverse calamitous trends and the conditions under which individuals take such action. By arranging such conditions, lawmakers and judges, employers and employees, educators, chief executive officers, and parents can improve our chances of averting the threats that face us.

James Lovelock (1988) gives a scientific account of the earth and everything on it as part of a single, unified system in which all its parts affect all other parts, directly or indirectly. Lovelock portrays the earth as a living entity, one small

Preparation of this chapter was made possible by support in the form of developmental leave from the University of North Texas. I am indebted to Marc Branch, Bryan Byrne, Janet Ellis, Joel Greenspoon, Irene Grote, Marvin Harris, William A. Luker, E. F. Malagodi, and Francis Mechner for their valuable suggestions and comments on earlier versions of the paper. In addition, the chapter has benefitted from the many astute comments of graduate students and faculty in the Experimental Analysis of Behavior seminar, Fall 1990, at the University of Florida. I thank Philip N. Hineline and Timothy Hackenberg for directing me to references I might otherwise have missed as well as for valuable commentary.

(albeit potent) part of which is human life. All parts of the earth evolve in the context of all other parts, each providing successive environments that function to select change in the other parts. In short, Lovelock broadens the bootstrapping operation of biological evolution to cover biological and nonbiological features of the earth. From a different perspective, but along similar lines, Ervin Laszlo (1987) suggested that, for the first time in history, a scientific paradigm may exist to provide a framework for all natural processes, including social systems. This paradigm is the evolutionary paradigm. Although the theory of biological evolution provided the impetus for "evolutionary thinking," it now may be considered as one example of evolutionary thinking. It is the thesis of this chapter that evolution occurs at biological, behavioral, and cultural levels through different mechanisms. As a result, phenomena at successive levels of organization emerge as products of mechanisms occurring at historically earlier level(s) of organization.

We need, then, to review briefly the evolutionary processes that account for the emergence of behavioral processes, which in turn account for the emergence of cultural processes. Although our main interest here is in human behavior and social systems, satisfactory scientific comprehension of behavioral and cultural processes rests on our understanding of the biological origins of "our kind," as Marvin Harris spells out in his recent book of that title (Harris, 1989). Fortunately, there is a rather widely understood body of knowledge to draw on regarding biological evolution. However, the evolution of behavior during the lifetime of individuals is not widely understood, even though considerable scientific progress has been made. Even scientists who vigorously oppose invoking a plan or a purpose to account for biological, chemical, or physical phenomena see no problem in invoking plans and purposes to account for human behavior. B. F. Skinner (1981/86, 1990) isolated the critical issue as one of origins and suggested that parallel processes of "selection by consequences" occur in biological, behavioral, and cultural evolution. Even as natural selection obviates the need for positing prior design to account for complex organisms, behavioral selection obviates the need for positing prior design to account for complex human activity, and cultural selection obviates the need for wise geniuses to have planned and spearheaded changes in cultural practices. (The four writers referenced in the first four paragraphs of this chapter each write from a perspective consistent with his specialty. Although some, or all, of them may not see the relevance of the work of all the others, I believe that the important ideas of all four are thoroughly integratable, and I believe this chapter, although certainly only scratching the surface of their work, is not inconsistent with the main thrust of the work of each of them.)

Many people find it difficult to view the entire human enterprise as just another part of the natural universe because they have prior commitments to alternative views about humankind. We have been so taken by the apparent differences between ourselves and the rest of the animal kingdom that we have sometimes compared ourselves to angels (Irvine, 1955). (Irvine succinctly discloses this fantasy with the following quotation from a speech by Benjamin Disraeli: "What is the question now placed before society with a glib assurance the most astounding? The question is this: Is man an ape or an angel? My Lord, I am on the side of the angels.") Reporting recent work of evolutionary anthropologists, Edey and Johanson (1989) note that molecular evidence discloses that an overwhelming proportion of the DNA constituting human genetic structure is perfectly matched with the DNA of chimpanzees, our nearest living relatives. The DNA evidence strongly supports the fossil evidence that chimp and human evolutionary lines split fewer than 7 million years ago, a tiny fraction of the time during which biological evolution has been occurring. In terms of DNA sequences specifying their genetic characteristics, chimpanzees are more like humans than they are like any other living species.

Despite the structural similarities we have with our primate cousins, we are confronted by vast differences in the kinds of things we do and the resulting products. By the evolutionary standards of survival and reproduction, we must admit the unbridled success of our own species. At least this is the case so far, we should add, since the earth is peppered with fossil remains of highly successful species that no longer exist.

"Success," in evolutionary calculus, involves an equation in which the biological characteristics of a species remain fitted to the characteristics of the environment that function as selection filters. In the human case, this equation has an immense number of factors on both sides. The factors on the environment side of the equation have been (and are) changing at an accelerating rate, whereas the biological characteristics of our species appear to have changed little during the past 85–90,000 years or more. How has humankind remained fitted to its environment when its environment is continuously and rapidly changing? Where does human achievement originate if not in the human mind? Have the seeds of our own destruction been sewn in our evolutionary success? If that is so, can those seeds be uprooted? I believe those questions will begin to be answered only if we understand the nature of human behavior and the cultural processes in which it is embedded. For it is behavior that keeps the evolutionary equation balanced and, paradoxically, it is human behavior that causes the environment to change so rapidly, threatening catastrophic imbalance in the equation. And it is cultural practices in which behavior patterns are preserved long enough to produce cumulative change in the environments that sustain the human species. It is also through cultural practices that behavior patterns are preserved long enough to threaten the survival of the whole earth and all living things. So we will discuss these topics after a brief review of the context in which behavioral and cultural processes have emerged in world history.

BIOLOGICAL EVOLUTION

As mentioned earlier, the continuing existence of a species depends on a continuing "fit" of the biological characteristics of its members with the characteristics of the environment in which the species exists. The "matching" process is ongoing and dynamic, not static and once-and-for-all. Changes in characteristics of a species are always occurring, usually on a small scale, because of heritable variations in genetic characteristics of its members. These changes comprise the variation that provides the raw material for selection. Selection occurs when inherited characteristics of the new generation are sufficiently fitted to the requirements imposed by their environment to allow survival and reproduction of those characteristics in yet another generation. Important to note is that the characteristics inherited by each generation were selected by the environment in which its ancestors lived. To the extent that the critical characteristics of the environment of offspring differ from the environmental characteristics of their ancestors, some progeny may be ill-prepared to survive and reproduce. If inherited characteristics of some individuals are so mismatched with a changing environment that they do not survive and reproduce their genes in progeny, their genetic characteristics are less represented in the gene pool of the species. This "winnowing" process may eventuate in modification of species characteristics or in extinction of the entire species.

Natural selection also produces entirely new species, new kinds of organisms. Many biologists and historians consider Darwin's most important and original contribution to be natural selection as a key process in accounting for the origin of species. Important as selection may be in maintaining the existence of species, it has a more interesting role in shaping changes in species characteristics, particularly when those changes result in the emergence of new species. In this capacity, selection has a creative function, even though it works without foresight or plan. The reason for the term "creative" is that natural selection produced increasing degrees of complexity in biological organization during the course of our planet's history. Richard Dawkins (1987) explains how natural selection, without plan or foresight, can result in increasingly complex biological entities. Complexity in structure and function often allows subtler fits with complex environments that serve as filters for the next generation of genes, organisms, or species.

One way in which living things have become more complex is in their behavioral repertoires. Among the more interesting (at least from the human perspective) of evolutionary innovations are behavioral processes that result in behavior change that occurs during the lifespan of individual organisms. Such ontogenic evolution has been especially important in the emergence and preeminence of our own species.

BEHAVIOR

Living things engage in an amazing range of activities. They walk, swim, fly, crawl, brachiate, and slither. They sit, lie, hang, scratch, spin webs, build dams, and make honeycombs. They cry, whine, howl, screech, peep, sing, and chatter. This is just a "starter list" but is enough to make the point that different kinds of animals do different kinds of things.

Many of the specific things that most animals do have been built into their genetic programs, which are passed from generation to generation through reproduction. Such genetically specified behavior patterns are evident when, generation after generation, members of a species engage in the same forms of behavior. However, some animals engage in highly individualized forms of behavior within and across generations; this great variety, most notable in humans, requires explanation.

Virtually all scientists interested in such explanation believe that natural selection and other processes of biological evolution ultimately account for the species characteristics of humans, but this does not require that biological evolutionary processes bear the entire explanatory burden.

There are at least two reasons why a wide range of highly specified and complex behavior patterns in a single species would be difficult to establish in the evolution of a species. First, as has been pointed out by Skinner (1974), natural selection is able to build highly specified behavioral repertoires into the genetic structure of species only with respect to environmental features that remain relatively stable across generations. Biological evolution occurs across (not within) generations; selection occurring with respect to one generation results in the next generation's inheriting the characteristics that were fitted to the previous generation's environment. Thus, natural selection can result in adaptation only if the environment does not change radically from one generation to the next. In this case, natural selection is hampered by the time required to produce change in species characteristics across generations. A second hindrance to increasing size and complexity of behavioral repertoires has to do with the amount of genetic space that would be required if thousands (even tens of thousands) of possible behavioral relations were to be precisely specified in DNA. Indeed, even though there are only small differences in DNA of chimpanzees and humans, vast differences are evident in their behavioral repertoires. Biologist Richard Dawkins (1976) suggested that cultural replicators, which he dubbed "memes," account for the complexity of human activity. As it turns out, nature, as usual, preceded human imagination, but replication at the cultural level requires understanding of replication at the behavioral level first.

The instability of local environments and what might be considered a limit on behavioral complexity in genetic programs appears to have given rise to a less cumbersome and more rapid sort of variation and selection. Instead of building thousands of complex behavioral relations into DNA, evolution built a few programs for behavioral processes that allowed changing environments to build behavioral repertoires "as needed" during the lifetime of individuals. A relatively small change in a bit of DNA could result in profound changes in the possibilities for ontogenic adaptability if that change involved a gene for a behavioral process. All that was required as a first step was genetically uncommitted activity and susceptibility of that activity to selection by behavioral consequences (Skinner, 1969). A small change in DNA affects morphology in a similar way when small genetic changes "produce large effects on form because they alter early stages of development with cascading effects upon subsequent growth" (Gould, 1985, p. 372). [Glen Sizemore suggested to me the similarity of Gould's point regarding cascading change to my point (based on Skinner, 1969)]. Skinner's point is about the effect of a small genetic change on behavioral processes, or function, and Gould's point is about the effect of a small genetic change on structure.

Behavioral Processes

By behavioral processes, I mean those processes that produce and maintain specific behavior in the repertoires of individual organisms during each organism's lifetime. Natural selection accounts for the presence of behavioral processes as part of the genetic inheritance of some species and these processes, in turn, account for behavioral repertoires of individual members of those species. Such "freeing" of behavioral content from genetic specification (most notable in humans) is in contrast to the tight specification of behavioral content by natural selection in many species.

Behavioral processes (as here defined) have been the focus of scientific study for less than 100 years. In fact, there is widespread ignorance of their existence and some tendency among those vaguely aware of their existence to discount their importance in favor of reductionistic and organismic explanations of behavior, particularly human behavior.

A reductionistic explanation accounts for a phenomenon in terms of principles developed to account for phenomena at a "lower level" of organization. Using principles of Newtonian mechanics to account for behavior of molecules in an expanding gas, and using principles of evolutionary theory to account for the behavioral content of individual humans are examples of reductionistic theorizing. An organismic explanation involves using the way the brain works to account for the occurrence of a particular behavior at a particular time. Behavioral scientists do not doubt that neurophysiological explanations will be given for what is happening inside the organism when behavior is acquired and when it is later emitted. We will still need behavioral processes, however, to account for the existence of behavioral repertoires because they describe how new behavioral content emerges at the interface between organism and environment. The relation between neurophysiology and behavioral processes is similar to that between biochemistry and processes of biological evolution. No matter how much we know about DNA, we will still need evolutionary processes (genetic replication, variation, natural selection) to account for the existence of species.

B. F. Skinner (1984) reviewed several kinds of behavioral processes, many of which have been the object of intense scientific scrutiny, and suggested the general order in which they may have appeared during the evolution of species. The present paper will focus on the process of behavioral selection, which accounts for behavior called "voluntary" in everyday language, and which scientists call operant behavior. It is the behavior involved in most human action. Because operant behavior is a necessary condition for the emergence of cultures as we know them, we will concentrate on behavioral selection and other operant processes.

Another major category of behavioral processes has to do with behavior generally called "respondent." The categories of operant and respondent behavioral relations may ultimately involve only one set of behavioral processes, as suggested by Schoenfeld and Cole (1972, Chapter 6), but most writers view them as different in fundamental ways. For example, Hineline and Wanchisen (1989) characterize respondent relations as "open loop" and operant relations as "closed loop." For an excellent summary of behavioral processes (operant and respondent) and the procedures by which the processes are distinguished, refer to Michael (1984).

There are several reasons for our focus on operant behavior. First, natural selection appears to have provided behavioral processes more latitude in operant behavior than in any other kind of behavioral process. Operant processes (sometimes in conjunction with other behavioral processes) produce entirely novel forms of behavior during a single individual's lifetime. Second, operant behavior is directly responsible for the emergence of cultural systems. Third, cultural practices are entities that provide the environmental context in which operant repertoires emerge in individual humans.

Operant behavior has evolutionary import because it operates on the environment, thereby producing change in that environment (Skinner, 1953). Because behavior has been taken by some scientists to be identified solely in terms of movement—the organismic part of the relation—Lee (1988) suggested that the term action be used instead of behavior "in order to see action as a subject matter in its own right" (p. 42). Although the problem Lee identified is real, the solution of substituting "action" for "behavior" probably won't solve it, since seeing action as a subject matter is just as difficult as seeing behavior as a subject matter.

Even so, Lee's book presents a good case for behavior (or action) as a scientific subject matter of practical and theoretical importance.

A given instance of operant behavior cannot be identified without considering both what an organism's parts are doing and those dimensions or portions of the environment that are functionally related to the activity of those parts. The events are "functionally related" in two different senses of this term. First, the activity has a function when it changes the environment and the environment has a function when it evokes or selects behavior. Second, behavior and environment are related to each other like two sides of an equation: changes in the environmental side of an operant relation are correlated with changes in the activity side and vice versa (cf. Baum, 1989).

It is this reciprocal relation that makes behavioral evolution possible. Operant behavior is an evolving interface between organism and environment. Operant processes produce novel forms of behavior, just as evolutionary processes produce novel forms of organisms. Further, the vehicle for producing both kinds of novel forms is selection (Campbell, 1956; Skinner, 1953, 1981/86). But different kinds of selection processes occur in biological evolution and in behavioral evolution. Natural selection accounts for novel kinds of organisms and gene combinations; behavioral selection accounts for novel behavioral units in individual organisms. In both cases, the respective units (biological or behavioral) sometimes exist in a kind of steady state, wherein the characteristics of the species (or operant) match to the environment and for some time both the environment and the species (or operant) remain relatively unchanged with respect to one another. The functional relations between steady state behavior and environment are quantified in molar behavioral theories (Baum, 1989). Although little experimental work has been done on transition states, Mechner (1990) has suggested an experimental preparation for studying transition.

Behavioral Selection

Behavioral selection is a process that typically builds ever-increasing complexity in operant repertoires of individuals. As in the case of natural selection, behavioral selection works with other processes at its own level of integration. For selection of any kind to operate, there must be variation among entities available for selection. This variation provides the raw material on which selection can operate. In the case of behavioral selection, the variation is among instances of action with respect to particular attributes of the environment. [In this paper, I discuss behavioral and biological evolution in language that seems to me to be consistent with standard views in each of those fields. Alternative accounts exist in both cases, some of which have been rejected, at least temporarily, by the majority and some of which are new and have not yet been given a scientific hearing. Among the latter are quite original points (Mechner, 1990) that reformulate the way in which reinforcement works in behavioral evolution.]

Behavioral selection has been studied in terms of three subprocesses: reinforcement, extinction, and punishment. We call behavioral selection reinforcement when some activity of an organism occurs and is followed by a change in the environment, which has the effect of making similar activity more likely in the future. Imagine a young child who squeezes his rubber duck for the first time and it squeaks. This is an example of some activity of an organism followed by a change in the environment. If the child then squeezes the duck (makes it squeak) repeatedly during the next several days and weeks, reinforcement has occurred. (Marc Branch suggested that the duck-squeezing example may be misleading because the rate of squeezing rubber ducks often decreases after a child has produced the squeak repeatedly. On the other hand, the reinforcement value of many behavioral consequences changes over time, perhaps as other consequences acquire reinforcing value and additional behavioral content is acquired. It is doubtful, however, that the squeak loses all reinforcement value as may be witnessed by the number of adults who can be observed to produce squeaks by squeezing rubber toys that happen to be in their vicinity.) Notice that the structure of this process is similar to the structure of natural selection. Something occurs, or has temporal existence (organisms and instances of activity) and operates with respect to an environment. The operation either fits or does not fit the environmental context in which it occurs. The outcome of a fit is the replication of dimensions of the entity in succeeding occurrences. Such selection produces historical entities that evolve over time. The unit that evolves in biological evolution is the species (Hull, 1981/84) and the unit that evolves in behavioral evolution is the operant (Skinner, 1969).

Extinction in behavioral evolution operates in a fashion that is parallel with extinction in the evolution of species. Some activity of an organism occurs (usually an activity that has produced a change in the past) and no change occurs in the environment. For example, after a few weeks (when the squeaker is worn out), the child squeezes the duck and no squeak occurs. This will not result in the immediate disappearance of the duck-squeezing any more than the failure of one member (organism) of a species to survive and reproduce in its environment results in the immediate disappearance of the species. But if the environment fails repeatedly to reciprocate, the activity (squeezing the duck) ceases to occur, just as the species ceases to occur after its members have failed to meet the demands of a fickle environment. The species disappears from the earth when organisms of which it is composed seldom or never make it through the environmental filter (their genes are not replicated). Similarly, the behavior disappears from the repertoire when instances of the activity are seldom or never reinforced.

Punishment in behavioral selection appears to be less straightforward. Sometimes an activity of an organism occurs (having been selected previously either by natural selection during the history of the species or by reinforcement during the lifetime of the organism) and a change occurs that has the effect of making the behavior less likely. For example, the child squeezes his rubber duck and his hand is sharply pricked by a cocklebur stuck to its surface. The child may not squeeze his duck again for a long time—maybe never. But the punished behavior is not extinct—that is, it can be reproduced, under certain conditions, without further reinforcement. The punishment process involves the suppression of behavior, not its extinction.

The Behavioral Environment

The environment in which organisms exist changes over time. Many of those changes result from the organisms' existence in that environment. Many of the characteristics of an organism's locale have no direct effect on its survival or reproduction, whereas those same characteristics may be important to the survival of others. Attributes of the environment important to the survival of a species acquire their importance by way of earlier operation of natural selection. For example, the color of the objects in a bat's world are irrelevant, whereas the color of certain objects in a bee's world are very important to its survival.

Natural selection has outfitted humans with receptors that are sensitive to certain environmental events (e.g., several dimensions of light and of sound). But we come into the world with very little specific behavioral content with respect to the world around us (reflexes being the main exception). Put another way, the world around us has very little specific effect on our behavior at first; objects and events must acquire behavioral function. This does not mean that all objects and events have equal likelihood of acquiring behavioral function; nor does it mean that all possible behavioral relations have equal potential. For example, Garcia and Koelling (1966) found that rats avoided drinking water accompanied by light and noise after their paws were shocked when they drank water accompanied by light and noise; but they did not avoid drinking "noisy water" if it had been previously accompanied by irradiation that later made them ill. Conversely, the rats avoided sweetened water if it previously had been accompanied by irradiation but not if previously accompanied by shock to the paws. Thus, distal stimuli and shock (but not flavor and shock) could be made functionally interchangeable. In cases like this, it may be said that natural selection pre-adapts organisms to respond to certain combinations of environmental events as functionally interchangeable. Even so, the noise (and the flavor) had to acquire a function with respect to (avoidance) behavior in the rats; those environmental dimensions originally had no behavioral function.

Operant Units

Throughout this chapter behavioral evolution has been compared to biological evolution, behavioral selection to natural selection. In both evolutionary biology and what might be called "evolutionary behaviorology," scientists have had difficulty in identifying the units involved in the selection process. Biology has had the advantage of an 80-year headstart and the further advantage of having a starting point in entities (organisms) that are tangible over extended periods of time. Even so, biologists still do not agree regarding the unit of selection or the conceptual status of species.

There appears to be growing recognition that a given species might best be considered an existing entity, the parts of which are distributed across time (Ghiselin, 1974; Mayr, 1982, Chapter 6). Species are what evolve, not organisms, because the variation on which selection acts is variation among instances (organisms and their genes). Thus, species are the units of analysis in evolutionary biology (but not necessarily the units of selection). Members (or parts) of a particular species unit make contact with the environment and the environment grants passage into the future of some genes. An important point to remember is that selection is not pointing toward a particular future because future environments are unknown; selection merely passes certain characteristics of presently existing organisms on to the future. To the extent future environments are like past environments, those characteristics will continue to be selected (passed on to the future). If future environments change, the variation built into the species unit sometimes allows the later environment to select some of those variations.

The recent characterization among biologists of a species as an historical entity distributed across time is consistent with Skinner's (1969) comparison of the concepts of species and operants. Operants are what evolve and they are comprised of members (instances of activity) that make contact with some part of the environment. Instances of activity vary among themselves on a variety of dimensions (squeezing a duck with varying pressures or with varying grips). Some of the variations produce a particular change in the environment, which ensures that characteristics of that activity are more likely to occur in the future (i.e., they are reinforced); if no variations (or too few) are reinforced, the operant undergoes extinction (all variations of the activity cease to exist). The notion of a behavioral unit as being distributed across time does not lend itself to easy understanding. As Hineline & Wanchisen (1989) noted, "The core concept of behavior analysis has a subtlety and abstractness that often goes unrecognized. The operant . . . is impalpable through its dispersion" (p. 228).

The evolution of biological units (species, made up of individual organisms) proceeded from very simple forms of living things to extremely complex forms. Natural selection, in concert with other evolutionary processes (e.g., genetic replication and variation) built more and more complex organisms and species units. These organisms and species are parts of a vast and complex ecological system—the biological universe. As the reader might guess, there is a behavioral parallel. It requires us to shift our focus from an ecosystem of biological entities to the behavioral repertoire of a specific individual human. A human repertoire exists as an integrated system with respect to a unique behavioral environment—that is, no two humans are the same with respect to the specific behavioral relations that comprise their repertoires.

For each individual, the repertoire and the environment together comprise a behavioral ecosystem. A behavioral ecosystem is comprised of all behavioral units (simple and complex) in a particular human repertoire together with all the environmental events that have behavioral functions in that repertoire. One might conceive of each human being as the locus of a unique behavioral universe. What accounts for similarities in the repertoires of some people are (1) the constraints imposed by characteristics of the species (e.g., two arms and no wings); (2) similarities in the physical environment, which has or acquires various behavioral functions (e.g., visual and auditory stimulation); and (3) similarities in socially constructed environments, the elements of which acquire behavioral functions in human repertoires (e.g., digging tools, books).

A behavioral ecosystem begins with activity that is relatively undifferentiated with respect to the environment. Predisposed by inherited characteristics of receptors, effectors, and nervous system components, certain dimensions of the world in which infant activity occurs function as reinforcers. By way of various inherited behavioral processes, other events acquire behavioral functions and become part of the behavioral ecosystem. (These behavioral functions of the environment will be discussed in the next section.) Simple behavioral units are built very soon after birth, and the simplest units are very soon compounded into more complex units.

Although most laboratory work until recently has been done with fairly discrete behavioral units (e.g., pressing a lever), applied researchers have built very complex repertoires by carefully arranging contingencies to produce more and more complex behavior (Lovaas & Smith, 1989). Fortunately, most people seem to be able to acquire fairly extensive repertoires with more haphazardly programmed environments. Cursory observation tells us, however, that most of us could benefit from expanding our repertoires in one way or another.

Simple and complex behavioral units (operants and others) are interlinked in multiple ways in a behavioral ecosystem, in a way parallel to the interlinking of species in the biological ecosystem. Simple behavioral units (called "basic behavioral repertoires" by Staats, 1977) become linked in larger units. The linkages among these more complex behavioral units, and between them and environmental events, are detectable in the systematic ways in which an individual responds to a range of situations. For example, if under a variety of pain-producing circumstances, a person goes on about her everyday work and play, we may call her stoic. If another person in such circumstances lashes out at those around her, we may call her aggressive. (To give a label, such as "stoic" or "aggressive" to the cluster of behavioral relations observed makes talking about them easier. Such labels have caused serious problems, though, because we have the tendency to progress to explaining the behavior by invoking the label. "He lashes out because he is aggressive" tells us nothing. Worse, we mistakenly think we explained the behavior and fail to seek the functional relations that account for such clusters of behavioral units.) As Lubinski and Thompson (1986) noted, "aggregates of more basic response units can be analyzed as functional entities in their own right . . ." (p. 281). In other words, in attempting to understand the content of an individual's behavioral repertoire, it is useful to look for clusters of behavioral units that are evoked and are maintained by a range of environmental events with common features.

As a person interacts with the world around him, thousands of environmental objects and events come to have behavioral function. But those that have behavioral function for some do not have behavioral function for others. Or they have a different behavioral function. We intuitively understand this when we say, "Different strokes for different folks." Or "We need to raise the consciousness of women [or blacks, or the poor]." Or "How can he tell those bacteria under the microscope apart . . . they all look alike to me." More often than not, however, we forget (or do not really know) that there are vast and subtle differences in behavioral histories of human individuals. Only because we spend so much time with other humans—because they want to be with us and take the time to teach us to be one of them—are there enough similarities among our behavioral repertoires that we can make sense out of one another at all—can live, work, and play together and can understand the feelings, motivations, and actions of others, or our own. This is so because much of the environment that comes to have behavioral function is the behavior (especially the verbal behavior) of other humans. Other humans provide, directly or indirectly, most of the behavioral contingencies that account for our repertoires.

BEHAVIORAL CONTINGENCIES

When elements of the environment can be shown to have function with respect to the behavior of an individual, the functional relations between behavior and environment are called behavioral contingencies. The environment acquires many functions with respect to operant behavior, and scientists arrange conditions in the behavioral laboratory so that they can study how the environment operates in the origin and maintenance of behavioral units. They pick a simple, easily measured activity (like pressing a button) and make some behavioral consequence (like food) contingent on its occurrence. That is, food is delivered if the behavior meets the contingency established by the experimenter. (This is very much like the world outside the laboratory, where the contingencies are maintained by the natural environment. For example, whereas the child in the laboratory has to press a button to get a piece of cookie, the child in his kitchen has to open the cookie jar.) The contingency set by the experimenter requires that the activity have certain characteristics. For example, the child may have to space presses at least 10 seconds apart, or to press at least one time per second; the child may have to press an average of 20 times for each eating opportunity, or food may be available for a press only after 30 seconds has passed. Furthermore, the button may require a certain amount of pressure to move it sufficiently (and count toward meeting the contingency).

The food functions (if the child is hungry) to select the characteristics of the behavioral unit and the characteristics it selects depend on the contingency in effect. If the contingency is that food is delivered after a press of a certain force and at least 10 seconds or more after the previous press, then presses having those dimensions come to occur more frequently and other presses (and a lot of other behavior) will occur less frequently than before the contingency was in effect. The particular operant unit created by this contingency is composed of repeated instances of button presses distributed across time; the instances will vary in that many will be very near 10 seconds apart, a few will be less than 10 seconds apart and some will be more than 10 seconds apart, with "overshoots" and "undershoots" of varying lengths of time (more of them closer to 10 seconds than departing significantly from 10 seconds). Similarly, most presses will be just forceful enough to depress the button, occasionally one will be too weak, and there will be a declining number of overshoots at successive values above the required force. All of the presses (of this particular child) that actually occur as a result of this contingency comprise a behavioral unit (with historical continuity) in the repertoire of this particular individual. This behavioral entity has been termed a functional operant (Catania, 1973) to distinguish it from the specified behavioral requirements set by the experimenter, which Catania called the descriptive operant. In other words, a descriptive operant is specified by stating relations that are experimentally programmed, and a functional operant is specified by stating the relations that are produced by the contingencies specified in the program.

In the case of both functional and descriptive operants, all of the events entering into the relations can be specified in physical terms, which is the empirical basis of the science. The dimensions of the descriptive operant are specified in advance of the existence of the behavioral unit that actually emerges. The dimensions of a functional operant can only be described after variation and selection have done their work. Smith (1986) in reviewing Sober (1984) pointed out similarities in the conceptual structure of operant theory and evolutionary theory in biology, particularly with respect to the "supervenience" of both independent and dependent variables in behavior analysis. That is, "operant" (like "fitness") is not reducible to any physical characteristics, although every instance of an operant has physical characteristics.

One might think that the child would be better served if there were less "slop" in the system—that is, if the food contingency created a unit in which all presses were exactly 10 seconds apart and of the exact force required (i.e., if the descriptive operant and the functional operant were exactly the same). This would insure maximum amount of food for minimum amount of effort, which would be fine if the child's environment never changed (if all cookie jars were exactly alike).

Recall, however, that the value of behavioral selection to biological evolution is that it allows adaptation to environments that change during the lifetimes of individuals. As in biological evolution, the process that works in concert with selection is variation. Because the behavioral unit varies in its dimensions across instances, the unit can evolve if the contingencies shift, as they often do in the natural environment. As it happens, the amount of "slop," or variation, among instances of an operant unit can itself be selected (Goetz & Baer, 1973; Page & Neuringer, 1985), even though variability is an endogenous characteristic of behavior (Neuringer, 1986).

In addition to accounting for the temporal, spatial, and topographical characteristics of activity comprising a particular operant unit, reinforcement can also imbue particular dimensions of the environment with evocative functions with respect to particular operant units. Imagine the following state of affairs. The child can get pieces of cookie if she presses the button at least 10 seconds after the last press, but only when a high-pitched tone (within the child's hearing range) is on; when a low-pitched tone is on, nothing happens when button presses occur, no matter what their dimensions. Instances of the behavioral unit come to occur only when the high-pitched tone is on; when the low-pitched tone is on, no pressing occurs. This is similar to the child's learning to open the cookie jar when it is on the cabinet top, but not when it is in the pantry (where it sits when it has no cookies in it). The selection processes of reinforcement and extinction together produce a more complicated behavioral unit called a discriminated operant. The name given to the systematic relation between an environmental event and instances of a behavioral unit evoked by that event is stimulus control. Environmental events that acquire evocative functions as the tone did in the previous example are called discriminative stimuli.

Other environmental events can acquire functional control over particular discriminated operants in a similar manner. For example, what if the tone contingencies just described were in effect only when the experimenter was sitting by the child, but when the experimenter was absent, the tones were correlated with exactly opposite contingencies? That is, with the experimenter absent, pressing when the low-pitched tone is on results in food and pressing when the high-pitched tone is on results in nothing. The behavioral unit that emerges under these conditions would involve even more subtle kinds of relations between dimensions of the environment and dimensions of the child's activity. These kind of units are called conditional discriminations and their import is described by Sidman (1986).

Operant relations get more complex in other ways, too. One such way has to do with distributions of behavior when a single kind of consequence enters into two different time-based contingencies concurrently in effect. Consider the following laboratory example. If a person (or a rat) can get food in one of two ways, say pressing button 1 or pressing button 2, and if contingencies are arranged so food is available twice as often for pressing button 1 as for pressing button 2, the person (or rat) will press button 1 close to twice as often as button 2. The mathematical statement that expresses this fact is called the matching law (Herrnstein, 1970; see McDowell, 1988, 1989, for well-written reviews of this research that are comprehensible to the uninitiated). Because people in the everyday world are constantly moving from one activity to another, some researchers have arranged to examine how behavior is distributed over days and even weeks when the contingencies involve different kinds of consequences (Bernstein & Ebbesen, 1978; Brady, in press). Morris (in press) has pointed out that when researchers are interested in what behavior occurs under various circumstances they are interested in behavioral content. Others, Morris points out, are more interested in learning about the kinds of relations that exist between activity and environment. The latter researchers are studying behavioral processes.

When researchers study behavior under concurrent contingencies, they are interested in the distribution of behavioral units already in the repertoire. This is true whether they are trying to find out about processes or content. One process that helps account for the distribution of behavioral units in time involves what has been called "establishing operations" (EOs) (Keller & Schoenfeld, 1950; Michael, 1982). These are motivating conditions that (1) "momentarily alter the reinforcing effectiveness of some event or stimulus" and (2) as a result, "momentarily alter the frequency of [evoke] any behavior that has been reinforced by [that] event or stimulus" (Michael, 1990, pp. 8, 9). For example, if you are in a really interesting conversation with a friend and your alarm clock begins buzzing raucously, you will leave the conversation (stop talking and listening) and turn off the alarm clock. The alarm noise (1) momentarily (as long as it was on) made a return to the prealarm noise level reinforcing and (2) evoked the behavior of turning off the alarm. After you turn off the alarm, you may go back to talking and listening.

But what if you have not had any liquid in a long time? You may detour by way of the kitchen for a drink on your way back to your friend. The absence of liquid over an extended period of time is another EO, which (1) momentarily (until you have drunk) alters the effectiveness of water as a reinforcer and (2) thus evokes behavior that has previously obtained water. Although you may have conversed for another half hour before getting that drink if it had not been for the alarm, the absence of liquid would have eventually taken precedence over the reinforcers that maintained your talking and listening. Thus, establishing operations may involve conditions of the environment that obtain over an extended time period and gradually shift the probability of a behavioral unit (e.g., water deprivation) or conditions of the environment that instantaneously shift behavioral probability (e.g., the alarm).

Although there are many other important ways that environmental events and conditions function in the origin, evolution, and maintenance of behavioral units, we must turn to another topic of great import in understanding human behavior as it enters into cultural practices.

VERBAL BEHAVIOR

One very useful way of thinking about verbal behavior of individual humans is that it emerges in operant units, discriminated operants, conditional discriminations, and so forth through the same processes as does nonverbal behavior (Skinner, 1957; see Peterson, 1978, for an introduction to Skinner's very difficult book). But one big difference between verbal and nonverbal behavior is that the nonhuman environment has no good way of establishing a repertoire of verbal behavior, whereas it can (and does) establish nonverbal repertoires. One reason for this difference is that verbal activity doesn't "make a difference" in the nonhuman world. One cannot shout down mountains, sweet talk one's car into starting, or move tapwater to run by begging for water. Pieces of furniture treat you no differently whether you can specify the "period" of every piece you see or whether you do not know a Renaissance chair from a Goodwill chair. The only part of the world that can play the role of selecting environment in the origin of verbal units is the world of human behavior—not human organisms, human behavior. Behavioral events function as part of the behavioral environment of other humans, and they play an especially important role in the origin of verbal behavior in the repertoires of human infants, children, and adults.

But this appears to pose a "chicken or the egg problem." If the verbal behavior of each person is a function of the behavioral environment provided by other people, how does verbal behavior ever get initiated? If we look closely, we see that there are really two evolutionary phenomena to consider. One has to do with the evolution of verbal behavior in the repertoires of individual humans; the other has to do with the evolution of a living language, which is the systematic behavioral contingencies provided by a community of verbally interacting human beings (see Skinner, 1957). The "chicken or the egg" problem is inherent only in the evolution of languages, which are the products of verbal communities' interactions. This topic will be taken up in the next section. For now, the focus will be on verbal behavior of individuals.

Individual humans are usually born into a verbal community comprised of other humans outfitted with well-developed linguistic repertoires—that is, members of the verbal community have large repertoires of speaking and listening. In other words, the members of an ongoing verbal community are reasonably well prepared to do what needs to be done for new members to acquire the verbal repertoires they need to function in the verbal community. (Members of the verbal community could be a lot better prepared if they had a clearer understanding of the functions of their own behavior in the emergence of the repertoires of others.) Members of the verbal community are also well motivated to do this for reasons that will become clear.

Having acquired linguistic (speaker and listener) repertoires themselves, adult members of human communities often produce changes in their environments by talking. "Pass the salt," they say, and they get the salt; "Put the scissors in the fourth drawer," they say, and then they are able to find the scissors later. These requests and instructions can affect only the human environment, and they can affect that environment only if other people have learned to behave as listeners (responders such as passers of the salt). So those people old enough to have experienced the usefulness of having listeners around find it very much to their advantage to make a listener out of the young. Usually they are not motivated to do so until the infant acquires enough nonlinguistic behavior to be useful as a listener, which may account for the fact that verbal behavior is usually acquired after children can move around. The fact that some children begin acquiring a verbal repertoire much earlier suggests that if more adults were interested in making speakers of the young (not just listeners), children would acquire verbal repertoires sooner. Doris Durrell, in *The Critical Years,* explains some ways of achieving this.

Adults make listeners out of the young by building on a tendency to imitate. First, they provide reinforcement for at least some appropriate listening behavior. For example, when children imitate the listening behavior of others (e.g., they pass items requested when they see their siblings do the same), reinforcement may occur in many forms. The person who received the salt may look pleased, or may say "Thanks." The child may forestall a sibling's elbow to his ribs or a parent's swat on his bottom for "ignoring" an adult. Such consequences need only to occur for some listening behavior (not every instance) to maintain a large repertoire of such action.

If the reader doubts that reinforcement is necessary to generate and maintain instruction following, I invite the reader to observe what happens in a first-grade classroom, for about a 16-week period, when the teacher does not provide differential consequences for following and not following instructions. Even so, readers should not assume that all the content of a listening repertoire is shaped in similarly simple ways. The point is that the verbal environment acquires functions with respect to listening behavior through processes that account also for the relations between behavior and the nonverbal environment. Additional processes may or may not be needed to account for listening repertoires (see Hayes, 1991).

The second general way in which people build a listening repertoire is by providing specific occasions for the inductee to function as a listener. Because people usually do not do this "on purpose," or with the awareness that they are inducting the young into their verbal community, much that is irrelevant is interpolated in the behavioral contingencies, which probably slows down early learning in many cases. Excluding of its nonfunctional elements, an episode of inducting the young into the verbal community goes something like the following. "Bring me your teddy bear," members of the verbal community say to the baby. Then they watch and when the child has approached the bear, they respond. "That's right" (the speech and the smile may function as reinforcement); "Pick it up." If the child looks confused, the adult may pick up the bear and hold it within reach of the child (making it more likely the child will take it). When the child has grasped the bear, the adult may then hold out his hand and say, "Give it to me." Perhaps responding more to the extended hand (which has probably already been learned) than to the verbal request at first, the child may then hand over the bear. "Yeeees, you can do it," the smiling adult says (reinforcing the child's approximation of the desired listening behavior). Such an interchange was observed by the author in an airport. The toddler's mother was uncommonly adept in that she waited for the desired behavior, prompted appropriately, and provided frequent reinforcement. That some parents are considerably more effective than others in providing a range of effective behavioral consequences during language acquisition of children is evident in the extensive analysis by Moerk (1983) of three-term contingency structures in mother-child natural language dyads. Interesting from the present perspective is that the child whose mother most often provided explicit and implicit reinforcement (during 40 hours of recorded interactions) had mean length of utterance (MLU) of 4.0 morphemes at 27 months compared to MLU of 2.0 morphemes at 27 months for a child whose mother rarely provided what Moerk considered "explicit" reinforcement. However, both parents provided a range of responses to their children's utterances.

And so it goes, members of the verbal community mixing nonverbal (already learned) cues and verbal requests to get the early listening repertoire started; then mixing new verbal requests (instructions) with already learned verbal cues to extend it further, all the while selecting appropriate listening behavior by the differing ways they respond to the child's listening behavior.

At other times, adults and older children actively encourage the infant to behave as a speaker by arranging the verbal environment in a variety of ways, as Moerk shows in analyzing language acquisition of two children (Moerk, 1983, 1990).

Again, it is to the advantage of parents and others to provide such conditions for learning. Think how convenient it is to have an appropriately verbal speaker around when you have reason to ask, "Who is at the door?" or "Did you put away the clothes?" or "What is 12 times 9?" or "Where did you put the scissors?" ("Where you told me, in the fourth drawer"). In general, our lives are made easier to the extent that we are effective in arranging a verbal environment that produces maximally effective speaking and listening in our young. But there are many other outcomes of our behavior of inducting the young into the verbal community, whether or not such outcomes help account for our behavior of doing so. In addition to making our life easier, their learning to speak makes their life easier. Speaking also allows them to do vast numbers of things useful to the larger community. Acquiring a verbal repertoire even made it possible for one of them to write *Romeo and Juliet,* and one to pen the formula $E = mc^2$. Together, some produced the Magna Carta and some the description of the DNA code.

We have only scratched the surface here of the ways that verbal operants are embedded in environmental contingencies. As the discerning reader may have deduced from some of the examples, the elements of the environment that enter into verbal contingencies include objects and events in both the verbal and nonverbal environments. Those elements not only include relations among objects and events but also abstract dimensions of them. They include hierarchical relations among verbal relations themselves. Perhaps the critical thing to remember, however, is that the ultimate value of verbal behavior to the survival of a verbal species is that it makes possible effective nonverbal behavior that could otherwise not occur. Without verbal behavior, the miracles of modern life would certainly never have occurred; we probably would still be living in caves. But all the verbal behavior in the world can do nothing in the absence of nonverbal behavior to clothe, feed, warm, cure, or protect us.

TRANSITION TO CULTURES

Recall that behavioral processes were selected during biological evolution because they allowed more flexibility in the behavioral content of individual repertoires. With the emergence of behavioral processes that operated during the lifetime of individuals, natural selection's control over behavioral content diminished. The business of building relations between organisms and their local, rapidly changing environments became the provenance of the "younger generation" of selection processes. But natural selection retains a supervisory function: it continues (at least so far) to give the edge to species who take fullest advantage of behavioral processes; and it endows the environment with critical functions to get behavioral selection started in each human born. The dual processes of behavioral and natural selection work in concert. Behavioral selection, on natural selection's tether, accounts for the matching of the activity of individuals to a kaleidoscope of environmental events with functional possibilities that could only remain untapped in the time frame available to processes of biological evolution.

In terms of the calculus of natural selection, behavioral processes were a stupendously beneficial genetic variation, at least in the evolutionary short run. In the case of humans, behavioral processes have resulted in a formidable range of behavioral content, including linguistic content. (The specific biological equipment that is required for linguistic behavior is not known, but the pharynx seems necessary for human speech.) Whatever the value to humans themselves of their achievements (and we are especially enamored of our verbal achievements) a sobering fact remains: the nonverbal actions of humans threaten the very existence of hundreds of species daily (including large numbers of their own), and the verbal actions of humans aid, abet, and enhance the threat. Natural selection's apprentice, although equally without direction, has been so successful that its handiwork threatens the existence of the whole shop.

The name of the evolutionary game is to generate behavioral content that results in survival and reproduction of genes, organisms, and species; the survival and reproductive success of our kind is disconcertingly evident. The rampant evolutionary success of the human species took more than the innovation of behavioral selection. Behavioral processes have produced order at another level: the behavior of individual humans has become integrated into units that transcend the lifetime of individuals. The same behavioral processes that lead to as many behavioral universes as there are behaving individuals also result in vast webs of interrelations among the behavioral repertoires of individual humans. These are the elements of cultural units. They have been termed "interlocking contingencies" (Glenn, 1988) to call attention to the dual roles that each person's behavior plays in social processes—the role of action and the role of behavioral environment for the action of others.

Biological and Behavioral Prerequisites for Cultures

Cultural processes grow out of and build on behavioral processes in a manner parallel to the way behavioral processes build on the processes of biological evolution. Ontogenically acquired behavioral repertoires were the consequences of the progressive freeing of the behavior of individual organisms from genetic micromanagement. However, behavioral processes are constrained by the requirements of survival and reproduction, thus there are limits to the freeing of behavioral content from genetic specification.

Because natural selection has the last word, humans are built so that events critical to survival have innate behavioral function and take precedence in entering behavioral contingencies. Food, water, sexual contact, and other social contact (e.g., eye contact, touch, auditory signals) remained powerful selection agents in the origin and maintenance of behavioral content of individuals of many species. (Freud recognized this fact and incorporated it into his concept of the *id*; but he subsumed social contact under sexual contact.) If behavioral content was not selected by such primary reinforcers, organisms failed to survive and reproduce, leaving the field to the progeny of those organisms whose behavior was susceptible to those selection agents. Thus, behavior that produced primary reinforcers was necessary for the survival of a species. The power of social and sexual reinforcers also enhanced the likelihood that individuals would spend time near one another. Such proximity in turn provided many occasions for the behavior of each of them to enter into the behavioral contingencies of others.

Human infants are dependent on others of their kind for a much longer time than any other mammal. Whereas other animals assume their adult roles relatively early in their life spans, 20-25% of the human lifespan is spent preparing for a similar level of independence. Most of the preparation involves acquiring the specific behavioral repertoires needed to survive, contribute to the social practices of the community. and integrate the behavior of the young into those practices. This virtually insures that the social environment (behavior of other humans) will be prominent among those features of the environment that enter into behavioral contingencies. Such ontogenically programmed social behavior (unlike the phylogenically programmed social behavior of some insects) can and does take many forms within and between generations. When interlocking behavioral contingencies are replicated across generations through behavioral processes, this marks the beginning of cultures.

Biologists and many anthropologists tend to agree that rudimentary cultures are evident in many extant primate species, and there is fossil evidence that human forebears were engaged in cultural practices (tool making) over 3 million years ago. Since then biological, behavioral, and cultural evolution have continued to occur and account for continuous change in the human condition. But the balance of power appears to have shifted (gradually at first and now at an increasing rate) from change through natural selection to change through behavioral and cultural evolutionary processes. The breakeven point, reached a mere 45–55,000 years ago by homo sapiens, has been called "cultural takeoff" (Harris, 1989). ·

What happened? How did cultural entities emerge from behavioral processes? What are the entities that exist at the level of cultures and what is their relationship to behavioral units? Do cultural units build on themselves, becoming hierarchical systems-within-systems as biological units went from proto-cells to complex organisms and species; and as behavioral units build, during the lifetime of individual humans, from simple units like picking up objects, through actions like planting petunia seeds, to whole gardening repertoires, which in turn are subunits of the entire behavioral repertoire of one person?

To begin answering these questions, we return to behavioral contingencies in which the behavior of other people functions in the role of environment. Consider the following scenario, which is consistent with what we know about human behavior. An infant who has learned to pick up objects, stretches her hand toward a berry, not having yet learned to behave differently toward objects within reach and those out of reach. The berry is out of reach but a juvenile sees the infant reaching. He gives her the berry (having seen others so respond to such infant behavior, and having found it possible in this way to prevent infants from shrieking), and the infant then looks at him contentedly. If no one ever provided the infant with objects out of reach, she would learn to reach only when objects were within reach. If the infant did not cry when lacking the repertoire to obtain berries and such reinforcers, people might be less inclined to notice those early misguided reaches. The infant's built-in (or early acquired) behavior of making eye contact with others may provide additional and perhaps redundant consequences for the juvenile's behavior of mediating between the infant and her environment. With all those elements in place, the juvenile's action reinforces the infant's reaching and the infant's response reinforces the juvenile's action. The behavior of each is becoming part of the behavioral environment of the other.

The behavior of more experienced individuals can enter into the contingencies that shape and sustain budding repertoires of the young only if the behavior of the young has a reciprocal effect. Natural selection endowed our ancestors with the biological equipment that allows environmental events to fashion functional behavioral repertoires from undifferentiated, nonfunctional, movement. But if the process is to occur anew in each newborn, certain critical environmental events (food, cries, perhaps eye contact, the human voice, and touch) must have powerful behavioral functions. These are some of the raw materials out of which human repertoires emerge. By their nature, they rig the game (especially given the long period of helplessness in humans) so that much of the environment that acquires behavioral function is comprised of the behavior of others. Thus the behavioral ecosystem of each individual human is integrated from its inception into a larger system, sometimes termed a "social system," which is comprised of interlocking behavioral contingencies, or social contingencies.

Effect of Social Contingencies

Profound indeed are the effects of the early and sustained enmeshment of the repertoire of each human in an evolving behavioral environment comprised in large measure of the behavior of others. Because the behavior of other humans plays such an important role in the contingencies accounting for the behavior of their young, the young become acutely responsive to subtle differences in the behavior of others. (Consider the ability of many children to detect emotion in slight movements and facial expressions of significant adults.) Further, the mere presence of others acquires behavioral functions; for example, it reinforces behavior that keeps the young in fairly close proximity to adults and juveniles, which in turn allows the youngster opportunities to observe, imitate, and learn new behavior with respect to both the social and the nonsocial environments.

An established history of social relations provides the foundation of a social repertoire, which can then serve effectively as the behavioral environment for others (providing that the others have behavioral histories sufficiently similar). The process, of course, works in both directions so each individual's repertoire increases in size and complexity. At the same time, each individual's behavior becomes more useful in its role as a behavioral environment for others.

Interlocking behavioral repertoires make it difficult, if not impossible, for participating individuals to "go it alone." Also, once the behavior of others is established in the role of behavioral environment, individuals are positioned to operate in a cooperative manner to produce changes in the environment that they cannot produce alone. Although evolutionary contingencies may account for each individual's behaving in ways that maximize his or her chances for survival and reproduction (i.e., selfishly), behavioral processes, in the human case at least, surely increase the survival value of cooperative behavior in humans. Interlocking behavioral units that produce changes beneficial to participants in the social contingencies also provide the basis of cultural selection. However, before discussing cultural selection, we must consider the role of verbal behavior in interlocking contingencies.

Verbal Behavior in Social Contingencies

The importance of interlocking contingencies to the emergence of a new level of order lies in the fact that four hands are better than two. They are more than twice as good as two. The coordinated behavior of two people can produce outcomes that could never be achieved by one, or even by two acting independently.

When each of the two is both a speaker and a listener, that behavior can be coordinated even more effectively. Skinner (1986) provided an extended example of the way in which primitive verbal behavior may have initially entered into the behavioral contingencies of two people working together to catch fish. Any time two people worked together over extended time periods, it seems quite likely that a few simple utterances of each acquired behavioral functions for the other. Those utterances may not have been linguistic at first; a yelp that accompanied a loosening of grip may have preceded A's dropping his end of a heavy carcass. After a couple of carcasses fell on B's foot, B might respond to the yelp as if A were saying "I'm about to drop this." A, observing B's behavior in doing this, might then emit the sound before heavy loads started slipping. After several occasions, the sound might take on a stylized character, something close to a word. Before long, each of the individuals would be emitting that sound under similar conditions. Many dyads may have produced unique primitive language systems, something like "twin language" that is said to develop occasionally between twins.

Both in his classic book on verbal behavior in individuals (Skinner, 1957) and in his more recent work (e.g., 1986), Skinner suggested that among the earliest verbal behavior in individual repertoires and languages are verbal responses he called "mands." Although the mand has a technical definition, verbal responses that would be designated as requests, commands, or demands often meet the definition. Because verbal behavior is a way of producing reinforcement by way of the action of others, requests, commands, or demands seem highly likely to have been among the first forms of human speech. They remain prevalent in everyday human exchanges; for example, Harris (1989) reported that he and his students found (by studying videotapes of everyday behavior of New York families) "that messages exchanged among humans . . . consist largely of requests of one sort or another" (p. 79).

A speaker with a repertoire of mands increases his operant control over the physical environment by enlisting the arms and legs of the listeners in his environment. A more subtle way that verbal behavior strengthens social contingencies involves listeners' enlisting the eyes and ears, and other senses, of speakers. If A can report that she just saw a snake near where you are standing, you may be able to move before you are bitten. Or if B, whose leg is broken, can tell you in which direction he found a stream yesterday, you may get to the water before you (and he) perish. It is not hard to imagine that accurate reports are worth enough to listeners for them to reinforce the behavior of reporting and describing by speakers. Such reporting behavior may often be initiated by mands: "Have you seen any snakes around these bushes?" "Where did you find that water yesterday?" Such mands set the occasion for verbal interchange. At this point, the verbal behavior of each person is serving as part of the other's behavioral environment. This clearly affords opportunities for complex social contingencies to bring more and more dimensions of the world (both social and nonsocial) into the behavioral environments of participating individuals. As the range of environmental dimensions that can enter into behavioral contingencies increases, so does the size of the behavioral repertoire.

Limited verbal interchanges may have arisen repeatedly before a single linguistic environment really got underway. However, at some point at least some dyads of speakers and listeners, scattered here and there, began the transformation to genuine linguistic communities and thus to increasingly complex cultural practices. To the extent that verbal behavior promoted effective nonverbal behavior, it was likely to be incorporated into social contingencies. The next step was the gradual emergence of cultural practices from such unique social contingencies.

CULTURAL PRACTICES

Cultural practices involve repetition of analogous operant behavior across individuals of a single generation and across generations of individuals (Glenn, 1988; Malagodi & Jackson, 1989). Many of the specific activities passed from one generation to the next are acquired by individuals through imitation. Researchers have shown that humans can learn to imitate the behavior of others as a generalized response class (Peterson, 1968). That is, once imitation of several different responses produces reinforcing consequences, new responses can be acquired by imitation in the absence of reinforcement. All that is required is that some instances of imitation be reinforced—a likely eventuality. As pointed out by Skinner (1953), individuals who imitate others are likely to produce the same reinforcers others are producing.

A cultural practice may be carried out by a single individual engaged in a solo performance. Harris (1989) provided the example of a behavioral unit (washing potatoes) that was acquired by a macaque monkey, then imitated by others until it became a standard part of the repertoire of each member of the troop. Each monkey acquired the operant unit (washing potatoes) by way of imitating another's action. Each monkey's behavior was reinforced by its own consequences (more potato taste, less dirt taste). Although the acquisition of each monkey's operant involved another's behavior as part of its behavioral environment, once the behavior was in their repertoires, the practice was carried out by each monkey individually, and each produced consequences for itself. Thus the necessary elements of a cultural practice are: (1) behavioral content acquired during the lifetime of each participant; (2) behavioral environments of one or more participants that include (but are not limited to) the behavior of conspecifics; (3) the repeated acquisition of the behavior within and between generations. Most cultural practices, however, have an additional element: they involve two or more individuals whose interactions produce consequences for each of them individually and whose joint behavior, in addition, produces an aggregate outcome that may or may not have a behavioral effect. When a cultural practice involves such interlocking behavioral contingencies and associated aggregate outcomes, the stage is set for increasing complexity at the cultural level of analysis (Glenn, 1988). The critical difference between the protocultures of humans and other primates and the cultures of humans appears to be the complexity of the interlocking behavioral relations in human cultures. The glue that was necessary to maintain such interlocking relations was verbal behavior (But see Skinner, 1990, for reciprocal roles of modelling and imitation.). Verbal behavior could emerge only in the context of verbal communities, which had to evolve. Like all other evolutionary processes, such evolution begins slowly and increases in rate of change. No wonder 55,000 years or more passed from the emergence of anatomically modern homo sapiens to "cultural take-off" (Harris, 1989).

CULTURAL-LEVEL ENTITIES

Harris (1964) provides a taxonomy of cultural entities on which I base the ideas in this section, with apologies to Harris for what may appear to him as unwarranted departures from the original. The smallest unit in Harris's taxonomy is a bit of behavior. Although behavioral events in and of themselves do not constitute cultural entities, they are a necessary condition for them. This is similar to saying that DNA itself does not constitute organisms; the chemical properties of DNA are a necessary condition for biological evolution to commence. From the present perspective, behavior is transformed into cultural level entities when the interlocking behavior of individuals produces aggregate outcomes that could not be achieved by any individual acting alone.

What Harris called a "scene" establishes the potential for a cultural level unit. A scene involves two or more people interacting at specific space/time coordinates. Sandy's birthday party on August 10, 1980, constituted a scene. The participants and their interactions with one another and with the party items are an "idioclone." If the scene is replicated in the behavior of the same individuals at later times, the people participating and their interrelated behavior comprise, together, a cultural unit called a "nomoclone." A nomoclone, like an operant, is distributed over time.

If participants in the scene change over time (Sandy's brother is born between her 4th and 5th birthdays, two first-grade friends are included on her 6th birthday, her cousin moves away between her 7th and 8th birthdays), the cultural unit is called a "permaclone": a cultural practice comprised of repeated instances of interlocking behavioral contingencies maintained by specific individuals, who are replaced one by one by other individuals while the behavioral contingencies remain relatively stable (or evolve gradually) over time. Notice that each occurrence of the practice has a beginning and an end and the occurrences are distributed across time. The distributed occurrences of nomoclonic or permaclonic interlocking behavior are a cultural unit comparable to the operant unit and the species unit at the behavioral and biological levels, respectively. Permaclones are the source of the power of cultural things. They are the evolving behavioral environments into which successive generations of humans are born and to which they are enculturated.

The replicating entities in the cultural unit are the operants of individual participants. Variability is endogenous in the cultural practice. The interlocking behavioral contingencies that identify a permaclone may gradually change over time as a result of a variety of factors. Changing personnel and a changing physical environment may result in adjustment of the interlocking contingencies to accommodate unique characteristics of the behavior of the newer personnel. Repertoires of regular participants will also be changing over time, as a result of changing contingencies in other parts of their behavioral environment. Because such changes have ramifications on the whole behavioral ecosystem of an individual, these ramifications have some impact on every permaclone in which the individual participates. Most of us are aware, for example, that changes in the work environment may have lasting impact on behavior at home (and vice versa). More precisely, changes in the behavioral contingencies sustaining one's behavior in a work permaclone affect one's behavior as it enters into behavioral contingencies at home. A bidirectional feedback loop could result in considerable change in both permaclones.

The variation endogenous to cultural practices arises directly from the fact that cultural practices involve replication of operant behavior in the context of interlocking behavioral contingencies. Variability also arises from the fact that behavioral evolution in individuals rests on the variability underlying behavioral units themselves; this has an indirect effect on variation in a cultural practice.

In the earliest human cultures, small bands of hunter-gatherers may have engaged in a few practices in which virtually all members of a band were participants. The personnel of the band's permaclones may have been almost entirely overlapping. As in the case of biological and behavioral entities, complex cultures involve the hierarchical organization of the basic units of culture into increasingly complex entities. So it is that interrelated permaclones form permaclonic systems, and they are, in turn, sometimes subsumed in permaclonic supersystems. Today, many people participate in permaclones whose members are distributed all over the globe. It is becoming ever more apparent that our cultural destiny is increasingly linked to that of people everywhere.

We have discussed the units of replication in cultural practices and described some sources of variability. If natural selection is the mechanism that accounts for increasing biological complexity and behavioral selection accounts for increasing behavioral complexity, how does selection operate at the cultural level?

METACONTINGENCIES

Behavioral contingencies account for the evolution and maintenance of behavioral units; metacontingencies account for the evolution and maintenance of evolving cultural units—permaclones, permaclonic systems, and supersystems. Metacontingencies are contingent relations between cultural practices and outcomes of those practices. The term "metacontingencies" (Glenn, 1986, 1988) was coined to call attention to the ways these cultural-level contingencies are related to behavioral contingencies. First, they are conceptually related in that they involve analogous selection processes. Thus, each involves contingencies of selection. Second, the prefix "meta-" implies a substantive and hierarchical relation, and in fact metacontingencies emerge in the evolution of cultures by building on behavioral contingencies. Thus, metacontingencies are functional relations at the cultural level of analysis whose existence derives from but is not equivalent to behavioral contingencies.

Sometimes the term "cultural contingencies" has been used, by myself as well as others, but that term is ambiguous. Cultural contingencies often implies behavioral contingencies, the elements of which are cultural products (either social or material). The contingencies are identified as "cultural" in terms of their content. That is not what I mean by metacontingencies, which is a term that identifies process—specifically, process at the cultural level of analysis. I may be getting at the same point as Vargas (1985) in his use of the term megacontingencies. But the contingencies at the cultural level are not behavioral contingencies writ large, in the sense of more inclusive or more extended in time (as the prefix "mega-" suggests); they involve units the existence of which can only be explained at a different level of analysis from the level at which behavioral relations are understood.

Recall that the behavior of each individual in a set of interlocking behavioral contingencies functions as part of the behavioral environment of the others. Although the examples previously provided have always involved only two interacting individuals, the behavior of any number of individuals may be involved. So long as some level of reinforcement (usually provided by the other participants) keeps each behaver participating, the interlocking contingencies are likely to be repeated across time.

If 2 . . . *n* people repeatedly reenact a particular scene because the behavior of each has become integrated into a repeated pattern through the reinforcement contingencies provided by others, the entire integrated set of contingencies constitutes an instance of a cultural practice. What accounts for the origin of such a unit, its extended survival or its disappearance (lack of behavioral descendants), or its evolution? Variation and selection. As usual, the variation is endogenous (although it may be selected as a characteristic), and selection is exogenous. In the case of cultural practices, the selection agent is the outcome (aggregate effects) produced by the practice (the interlocking behavioral contingencies). The variation is provided by permutations in the behavior of individuals participating in the practice. An extended example follows, accompanied by additional related points.

Our human ancestors were for thousands of years large game hunters. As predators of large game, those ancestors (like ourselves) had serious anatomical and behavioral deficiencies. But animal foods are extraordinarily nutritious (Harris, 1985) and, when available in large numbers (as in the early days of humanity) large game provided the most cost-efficient food that humans could obtain. By acting in concert, our ancestors were able to obtain more food and better variety per capita than even the most proficient among them could obtain acting alone. The outcomes of the conjoint behavior supported by interlocking behavioral contingencies were of several kinds. Individual kills were outcomes of instances of the practice, but they also likely served as direct reinforcement for the behavior of people participating in the scene. Now imagine people participating in such a practice whose numbers become too large for them to hunt together effectively. Some permaclonic participants might split off, creating two different populations engaging in the practice, perhaps one moving on to another area where there was less competition. If a variant of the practice emerged in one of the groups, which increased the level of sustenance for that group, that group may have been favored in at least two ways: their sustenance level may have enhanced their survival as individuals (and as participants in the "improved" practice); and they may have become so proficient that they had more time and inclination to interact in more ways with one another and the physical environment. Such increased levels of interaction could have led to the emergence of additional practices over extended periods of time.

The interlocking behavioral contingencies that could produce cultural products obviously did not emerge overnight. In fact, the archaeological record suggests that thousands of generations were required to reach a point where practices were not limited to those directly related to physical survival. Throughout that time, people were generally better off sticking with one group, because their behavior was more effective when they "grew up with the contingencies," as it were. Thus, their progeny's behavior would become integrated into the interlocking contingencies of a particular group. (There would be a propensity to "identify with their group," which is an effect of cultural practices, not a cause.)

Cultural practices evolved because each new generation of participants benefitted by participating in a practice in which adjustments in the previous pattern of interlocking contingencies led to superior outcomes, which selected the interlocking contingencies. But modification of integrated behavior patterns was not the only legacy of previous generations. Some of the products that resulted from that behavior were less ephemeral than good meals. Tools and containers, clothing, and weapons improved by each generation could be passed on to the next, allowing members of each generation to interact with more complex behavioral environments than members of previous generations.

The interlocking contingencies were, in short, selected by the aggregate changes in the material environment that resulted from the integrated behavior of participants. Such "cultural outcomes" have the same kind of relationship to interlocking behavioral contingencies as behavioral consequences have to operant units. The cultural practice that defines a specific permaclone is the unit at the cultural level that parallels the operant at the behavioral level. It emerges, as an entity comprised of replicated instances, through the selective function of its outcomes (the aggregate results of the interlocking behavior, often distributed across time).

To repeat, behavioral selection and associated behavioral processes (1) emerged as a result of natural selection and (2) account for the content of individual repertoires. Cultural selection and associated cultural processes (1) emerged as a result of behavioral selection and (2) account for the content of cultural practices. Although individual repertoires may differ vastly, the same behavioral processes account for all of them; differences in content are the result of differences in characteristics of the behavioral environment that account for each repertoire (in the context of individual genetic differences). Although the content of different cultural practices may differ vastly, the same processes account for all of the practices; differences in cultural content are the result of differences in characteristics of the environment that account for the practices.

Harris (1979, p. 78) makes a similar distinction regarding analysis at the cultural level. That is, nomothetic explanations "deal with recurrent types of conditions, general causes, and general effects" and idiographic explanations "usually stress the unique sequential thoughts and activities of prominent individuals rather than recurrent causal processes." In these terms, explanation of behavioral relations, per se, in terms of recurrent types of conditions, causes, and effects is nomothetic. Explanation of an individual's behavioral repertoire (content) in terms of specific relations that can be observed to obtain between dimensions of the environment and behavior would be idiographic. (Case studies of behavior change are idiographic research and, ideally, make use of known behavioral principles to inform their analysis. Single-subject experimental analysis of the kinds of relations that are brought about between behavior and the environment are nomothetic research. The nomothetic character of basic behavioral research is hard to understand for scientists who study populations of organisms rather than populations of behavioral instances.)

Recall that metacontingencies are the contingent relationships between cultural practices and outcomes of those practices. The continuing existence of a practice depends on the effectiveness of the practice in producing outcomes that sustain the existence of permaclones through which the replicators operate. In the early stages of cultural evolution, interlocking behavioral patterns may have been supported simply by the continuing existence of the participants as living organisms with behavioral units embedded in interlocking contingencies. But the cultural unit that survives or does not survive in any particular instance is the interlocking behavioral contingencies that produce aggregate outcomes. In complex cultures, the instability of permaclones may be a sign that the entire system is becoming destabilized.

As cultural evolution proceeds, some practices evolve, some remain relatively stable (like modern-day hunter collectors who are presumably behaving in ways similar to hundreds of generations of ancestors), and some disappear. For example, as big game diminished, the practices of some hunter-gatherers probably did not change fast enough to ensure survival. Others may have continued in their old ways, in what amounted to "more of the same" when what was required was a shift to practices that exploited a new niche. As permaclones became extinct, some of their participants may have been incorporated into other communities, where they may have increased variation in the interlocking contingencies of local practices. Sometimes such adjustments led to revised practices, some of which led to outcomes that perpetuated the evolving practice. Ayres (1944/78) attributes a great deal of cultural evolution to the variation and retention that results from bringing together technological practices of differing origins. In any case, horticultural and then agricultural practices eventually emerged.

One might suspect that virtually all permaclones would have at least one member who recognized such outcomes as diminishing food supplies and who proceeded to lead his/her fellows to take remedial action. My guess is that such planned and foresightful adaptation was (and still is) rare. If this sounds counterintuitive, consider the fact that individuals often fail to act in their own self-interest when behavioral contingencies fail to support rational behavior. Even when we can explain the likely effects on our health, we eat foods that clog our arteries, killing large numbers of us; we inhale smoke that gradually destroys our lungs; we remain sedentary even though exercise would prolong our lives; we poison the air we breathe in our homes rather than coexist peacefully with insects. Malott (1989) suggested that the negative consequences of our behavior are too small with regard to each instance of behavior, and their effects accumulate too slowly for these consequences to function as reinforcement. If single individuals often fail to behave in ways that enhance their own survival, even when they have rules that predict such negative outcomes, consider how much more difficult it would be for a cultural practice to change in the face of outcomes whose accumulating damage will not be seriously felt for another two generations (Skinner, 1987). As in biological and behavioral evolution, cultural evolution has occurred as a result of processes that operate without respect to any future. Cultural practices that exist do so because they fit the environment of a previous time, which is to say that they may not continue to exist.

Although the behavior of humans engaging in cultural practices continuously produces cultural outcomes, most of the behaving individuals never come into contact with even a verbal description of those outcomes, let alone the events that comprise the outcomes themselves. Once some outcome has been specified as resulting from a particular cultural practice, people's behavior in the cultural practice may change as a result of following rules that describe the relations between participants' behavior and the outcome. Such rule-governed behavior is explored by Malott (1988). Although such behavior undoubtedly occurs, I believe it has accounted for extremely little of cultural evolution for two reasons. First, the relations between behavior in specific cultural practices and the outcomes of those practices have rarely been specified; thus, rules describing the relations have rarely existed. Practices have existed, produced outcomes, changed, and disappeared while most of us participating in them have had little or no knowledge of this process. Second, individuals, even if they understand that a cultural practice is producing potentially lethal outcomes, can usually make little impact on the practice by taking personal action. The reason that species become extinct, that individuals fail to behave in their own self-interest, and that cultural practices continue despite their overall negative effect is that contingencies of selection can only operate with respect to the present and the characteristics of current entities (biological, behavioral, and cultural) exist in their current form as a result of past environments. Future environments, even when they are the direct outcome of the existence of current organisms, behavior, or cultural practices, can have no effect on the current entities. At the level of natural selection, every currently existing species is a potential candidate for extinction; at the level of behavioral selection, reinforcement processes guarantee neither survival-oriented nor rational behavior in individuals (see Herrnstein, 1990), nor the continuing existence of any particular behavioral content in an individual's repertoire; at the cultural level, the outcomes of practices are not guaranteed to be conducive to survival of the practices, the higher order cultural units that emerge from them, or the individuals who participate in them. In all cases, the changing environment has the last word, even when human cultures provide individuals with the repertoires of predicting and controlling the genes, behavior, or cultural practices of their species. For this reason, it is imperative to understand how the environment operates in selection processes.

STRUCTURE OF CULTURES

The beauty of theories describing functional relations (such as those between biological, behavioral, and cultural entities and dimensions of the environment) is that they account for the emergence of structure at succeeding levels of organization. Biological evolutionary theory accounts for the organization of genes, organisms, and species as hierarchical biological entities (Arnold & Fistrup, 1984). Operant behavioral theory accounts for the organization of operants, traits, and repertoires (Lubinski & Thompson, 1986) and their underlying neural organization. Cultural evolutionary theory accounts for the emergence of cultural practices and their organization in cultures (Harris, 1977). Because human cultures have their origin in human behavioral processes, which in turn have their origin in biological evolution, cultural survival ultimately rests on cultural practices that ensure the survival and reproduction of the carriers of the behavior involved in the interlocking contingencies, and thus in the cultural practices themselves. Such practices comprise what Harris (1979) terms the cultural infrastructure, the first of a hierarchy of cultural practices that emerged in cultural evolution.

Cultural Infrastructure

Archeological evidence suggests that for at least the past 85–90,000 years our ancestors have had essentially the same biological equipment that humans have today. Yet 45–55,000 years or so passed before "cultural take-off" (Harris, 1989). From the present perspective, this is entirely predictable. Evolutionary processes seem to begin slowly and increase in rate of change as they build complexity; complexity breeds complexity. In the case of biological evolution, about a billion years passed before the simplest single-celled organisms acquired a nucleus; in less than $1/145$ of that time, the ancestor we have in common with chimpanzees evolved into homo sapiens.

In a similarly halting manner, simple cultural practices must have emerged very slowly as humans went through variation after variation of interlocking behavioral contingencies, slowly and painfully learning to take an active role in insuring transmission of primitive practices. By fits and starts, verbal interchange may have evolved repeatedly in dyads, triads, and small groups as people learned to say what their elders said in specific circumstances and to provide the behavioral contingencies necessary to get their progeny to do the same. This halting process enhanced survival of those early humans who became better and better able to coordinate their behavior and produce or maintain food, warmth, water, and human contact.

The foundation of cultures was slowly laid down and that foundation was comprised of cultural practices that produced the means of survival—called "production practices" (Harris, 1979). Until their tools were good enough to insure them a modicum of safety in the hunt, to insure they could obtain adequate sustenance, to insure they could defend themselves and their young against predators, to insure they could keep their fire alive, humans seem unlikely to have been in a position to while away their hours painting pictures, carving figurines, or least of all spinning yarns about their origins. In the latter case, they would have needed a great deal more verbal behavior than that likely to have emerged as they went about their business developing their basic tool kit, feeding, and protecting themselves and their young.

However, by about 30,000 B.C., our ancestors had developed technologies that were producing sophisticated versions of tools and weapons such as knives, awls, harpoons, and needles (Harris, 1977, Chapter 2). The success of their practices had brought them to a point where they had time to engage the physical and social environment in ways not directly related to survival. A more mixed blessing that resulted from their ever more sophisticated production practices was increasingly larger populations. According to Harris (1977, Chapter 2), population growth constituted an ongoing threat to the well-being of individuals participating in prehistoric hunter-collector production practices. As local populations grew, local prey were depleted and people moved on. Weather changes and increasing numbers of human predators depleted or sharply reduced big game with the result that humans who survived were those who turned to small game and vegetation (e.g., fish, birds, nuts, legumes, wild grains). Eventually, as their production practices intensified to keep up with population growth, humans turned to cultivation of plants and finally to agriculture (Harris, 1977, Chapter 3).

The purpose of reviewing these changes in production practices was to provide the context for introducing the second general kind of practice of the cultural infrastructure—reproduction practices (Harris, 1979). Dating back to the time that human production practices became so effective as to begin depleting prey—with the result of increased hunger, increased work, and decreased leisure time— (Harris, 1977, Chapter 2), humans began to engage in practices that had the effect of controlling population growth. As a result, a variety of culturally transmitted practices emerged (including various methods of preventing and terminating pregnancies as well as infanticide), which were successful in limiting the number of people to be supplied with food (Harris and Ross, 1987).

As production practices became more complex in a community, several perma-clones were required to jointly produce some outcomes, and division of labor became more complex. For example, some people may have worked together to gather grain, others to hunt big game, and others to fish. If the community became very large, two or more permaclones (sets of interlocking contingencies among specific individuals) may have been involved in any given production practice. Recall that instantiations of the practice involve behavior (of individuals) that functions both as action and behavioral environment for others' actions. Practices changed as a result of changes in the behavior of individuals participating, changes in the personnel (thus in behavioral repertoires of participants), and changes in the physical environment (manmade or not). If one permaclone produced more, par-ticipants in others could learn by observing the more successful, or by participat-ing with that group for awhile, or possibly, at some point in time, by verbal instruction around a campfire. Those permaclones in which such behavior emerged would have been most likely to produce infrastructural outcomes that maintained the existence of the interlocking contingencies. So it is that such behav-ior remains as elements in existing permaclones to this day.

The outcomes of production and reproduction practices can be measured in terms of such variables as the number of people to feed, amount of food produced, number of people per room, average life span, and efficiency of tools. The relent-less and continuous increase in size of human populations has resulted in continu-ous intensification of production practices. Thus, practices that produced more goods faster have always been selected, and those practices became increasingly complex as hunting and gathering gave way to horticulture, agriculture, and indus-trialization. Increasing complexity in production practices required larger commu-nities in which individual people participated in multiple permaclones.

The number of permaclones in which the average person participates is prob-ably a fairly good measure of the complexity of a culture. More complex is not necessarily better, though. As far as the survival criterion goes, bacteria are doing wonderfully well and likely will outlast humans despite the fact that they preceded humans by billions of years.

Cultural practices emerged that had the function of maintaining order among behaving individuals and permaclones. These practices had no direct effect on such outcomes as how many yams were grown, how many bison were slain, or how much water an irrigation system carried. In short, they cannot be considered practices of production or reproduction.

Cultural Structure

The permaclones comprising hundreds, perhaps thousands, of small communi-ties must have involved practices that failed to produce outcomes that sustained the existence of the practice. In some cases, all of the members surely perished; in others, members split off and affiliated with other communities taking elements of their practice with them. The practices of still others changed with a changing environment and were transformed into totally different practices over time. Por-tions of some communities probably split off, going their own way, and if completely separated from the parent group, their practices evolved along a different path than the practices of the larger group that they left behind.

The practices that continued to exist, and those that continued to evolve, did so because the aggregate behavior of participants produced outcomes that sustained the practice. Such outcomes included victory in battle, technological innovation in production and reproduction, domestic and political organization that sustained or enhanced infrastructural practices, and games, myths, or art forms that strengthened the social relations among members of a community participating in infrastructural permaclones.

As the examples just given suggest, communities eventually evolved practices that did not involve behavior that produced sustenance, tools, or weapons—or anything else that was directly related to survival or reproductive practices (Harris, 1979). These were domestic and political practices called "structural practices," the second level of cultural practices. A few examples of structural practices are the ways that family responsibilities are organized and the roles of family members; the ways that people are grouped into castes and classes having different responsibilities and privileges; the ways in which leaders are designated; and the ways in which followers exert countercontrol over the behavior of leaders. These kinds of practices have had farreaching consequences for the behavioral repertoires of individual participants, for the interrelated permaclones that comprise communities, and for the interrelated communities of permaclones that comprise sociocultural systems. Participation in these practices often benefitted some participants more than others (consider differences in adjudication of upper-class delinquents and working-class delinquents or educational opportunities for women as compared to men throughout most of history).

If these practices enhanced infrastructural outcomes, and if infrastructural practices continued meeting the requirements of the physical environment, the structural practices survived. The survival of a structural practice does not suggest that it is the best possible practice. Although practices emerge for whatever reason, they are maintained if they support the infrastructure (or at least do not harm it), but they may be maintained even after they no longer serve a function (like the human appendix).

If structural components of a culture do not change as infrastructural requirements change, misalignment could prove lethal. If structural practices tag along, changing along with the infrastructure, they will continue to be selected along with the infrastructural practices. Of course, structural practices, like other cultural practices and like behavioral units, may have multiple outcomes. And some of those outcomes may, in the long run, weaken cultures by way of consequences with subtle but profound effects on the viability of the system, most critically its infrastructure. A possible example of this is the practice of slavery in the United States. In the 18th and 19th centuries, slavery handsomely supported the infrastructure of the South. However, whites without large amounts of land and blacks, most of whom were slaves, did not have the means by which to acquire extensive repertoires being acquired by many citizens in other parts of the nation. The nation as a whole, and many (by no means all) descendants of those blacks and poor whites, still suffer the consequences when those descendants grow up in verbal communities whose behavioral environments are not as complex as they need to be if the younger people are to acquire the repertoires they need in the current culture. This disadvantage may be especially acute for black descendants because they can less easily infiltrate in permaclones that provide "state-of-the-art" behavioral environments. Chances are the full impact of these delayed outcomes of slavery is not yet manifest. Many thoughtful people believe massive intervention is needed to insure that all people obtain the repertoires they need to sustain infrastructural practices that support the nation.

The multiple, and often delayed, outcomes of complex cultural practices make it difficult to assess the role of any practice in enhancing survival or promoting failure of the cultural infrastructure. The fact that many practices are linked to one another in the warp and woof of the cultural fabric also makes it difficult to know if changes in one practice might unravel too much of the fabric, threatening the integrity of the infrastructure.

Political and domestic practices evolve and continue to survive only if the infrastructure of a culture in which they are embedded survives. Their role in the survival of cultures depends on the support they provide the infrastructure. This has been called the "priority of the infrastructure" or infrastructural determinism (Harris, 1979).

Cultural Superstructure

A third level of practices has outcomes that feed back into both the cultural infrastructure and cultural structure. The cultural superstructure includes those practices involved in sports, the arts, science, literature, and games. They also include myths, ideologies, philosophies, religions, taboos, aesthetic standards, and other practices. This latter group is characterized almost entirely in terms of interlocking verbal contingencies. Often these verbal practices become nearly or entirely divorced from the physical, biological, and behavioral realities from which they arose. These verbal practices are called "emic" by Harris (1979); they are peculiar to the culture in which they evolved. Because emic verbal behavior sometimes takes on a life of its own, supported by interlocking verbal contingencies supplied by a linguistic community, it may be of interest in and of itself but is not considered by many scientists to be useful in shedding light on its own origins or the origins of the cultural practices it purports to explain. Instead, a naturalistic account of the behavioral origins of linguistic behavior, in individuals and verbal communities, is a prerequisite to understanding the existence of emic verbal behavior and the differences between it and what Harris (1979) calls "etics"—verbal behavior that describes relations between cultural practices and the naturalistic events that account for those practices.

Superstructural practices may have the effect, at any time in a culture's history, of supporting the cultural infrastructure and structure, of opposing necessary changes in those cultural components, or of simply running alongside the practices of the infrastructure and structure. The cultural superstructure sometimes supports the infrastructure of modern cultures (as in the case of science-based technology). The cultural superstructure may sometimes oppose infrastructural requirements (as when religions prohibit birth control in the face of overpopulation and dangerous levels of intensification). And the effects of some superstructural practices are opaque (at least to this writer). When superstructural practices "take on a life of their own" and evolve in ways that are destructive to the infrastructure, the social maintenance of the behavior constituting those practices is close to what Ayres (1944/78) calls "ceremonial." The behavioral contingencies that give rise to such behavior have been considered by Glenn (1985, 1986). When superstructural practices remain responsive to changes in infrastructural metacontingencies, they may alert a community of interlocking permaclones to potential disaster and, in some cases, may provide a means of averting Armageddon.

CAN UNDERSTANDING HELP?

The purpose of this chapter is to provide a general scientific framework in which the topics of later chapters can be understood. As Malagodi (1986) noted, we must understand the larger context in which behavior functions, as well as behavior itself. Such understanding requires that we know about both processes and content.

This chapter is an attempt to integrate some of what is known about the processes that account for our existence as organisms, our actions, and our cultural practices. Such knowledge provides a framework within which to order information about the particulars of behavior and cultures, and especially how they relate to one another.

If we are to make use of what we know of processes, we need to have a clear picture of the nature of the products of these processes. We need to be able to specify, at least within a range of feasibilities, the content of behavioral repertoires that is required to sustain the existence of complex cultural practices conducive to survival of the human race. We also need to be able to specify the content of behavioral contingencies necessary to produce those repertoires. And we need to learn how to bring about the necessary changes in behavioral contingencies.

We also need to understand the characteristics of the cultural practices that mold our behavior, individually and collectively. Harris (1981) has made a beginning by documenting the causes and effects of some of the massive changes that have occurred in the United States during the past 50 years or so. We need to know much more. If scientists in biological, behavioral, and cultural fields work together, we may be able to learn exactly what must be done to ensure that planet earth will be able to sustain itself and its living creatures. Others of good will may be able to develop the behavioral technology that will establish the human race as good citizens of the earth rather than people that threaten its very survival and ours. Make no mistake, human behavior is the greatest threat to human survival, and it is also our only salvation.

REFERENCES

Arnold, A. J., & Fistrup, K. (1984). The theory of evolution by natural selection: A hierarchical expansion. In R. N. Brandon & R. M. Burian (Eds.), *Genes, organisms, populations: Controversies over the units of selection* (pp. 292–319). Cambridge, MA: The MIT Press.

Ayres, C. E. (1944/1978). *The theory of economic progress* (3rd ed.). Kalamazoo, MI: New Issues Press.

Baum, W. M. (1989). Quantitative prediction and molar description of the environment. *The Behavior Analyst, 12,* 167–176.

Bernstein, D. J., & Ebbesen, E. B. (1978). Reinforcement and substitution in humans: A multiple-response analysis. *Journal of the Experimental Analysis of Behavior, 30,* 243–253.

Brady, J. V. (in press). Continuously programmed environments and the experimental analysis of behavior. In S. S. Glenn (Ed.), *Progress in behavioral studies: Vol. 3.* Cambridge, MA: Cambridge Center for Behavioral Studies.

Campbell, D. T. (1956). Adaptive behavior from random response. *Behavioral Science, 1,* 105–110.

Catania, A. C. (1973). The concept of the operant in the analysis of behavior. *Behaviorism, 1,* 103–116.

Dawkins, R. (1976). *The selfish gene.* New York & Oxford: Oxford University Press.

Dawkins, R. (1987). *The blind watchmaker.* New York: W. W. Norton.

Durrell, D. (1984). *The critical years: A guide for dedicated parents.* Oakland, CA: New Harbinger.

Edey, M. A., & Johanson, D. C. (1989). *Blueprints: Solving the mystery of evolution.* New York: Penguin Books.

Garcia, J., & Koelling, R. A. (1966). Relation of cue to consequence in avoidance learning. *Psychonomic Science, 4,* 123–124.

Ghiselin, M. (1974). Categories, life, and thinking. *Behavioral and Brain Sciences, 4,* 269–283.

Glenn, S. S. (1985). Some reciprocal roles between behavior analysis and institutional economics in post-Darwinian science. *The Behavior Analyst, 8,* 15–27.

Glenn, S. S. (1986). Metacontingencies in *Walden Two. Behavior Analysis and Social Action, 7,* 1–7.

Glenn, S. S. (1988). Contingencies and metacontingencies: Toward a synthesis of behavior analysis and cultural materialism. *The Behavior Analyst, 11,* 161–179.

Goetz, E. M., & Baer, D. M. (1973). Social control of form diversity and the emergence of new forms in children's blockbuilding. *Journal of Applied Behavior Analysis, 6,* 209–217.

Gould, S. J. (1985). *The flamingo's smile.* New York: W. W. Norton.

Harris, M. (1964). *The nature of cultural things.* New York: Random House.

Harris, M. (1977). *Cannibals and kings.* New York: Random House.

Harris, M. (1979). *Cultural materialism: The struggle for a science of culture.* New York: Random House.

Harris, M. (1981). *Why nothing works.* New York: Simon & Schuster.

Harris, M. (1985). *The sacred cow and the abominable pig.* New York: Simon & Schuster.

Harris, M. (1989). *Our kind.* New York: Harper & Row.

Harris, M., & Ross, E. B. (1987). *Death, sex, and fertility: Population regulation in preindustrial and developing societies.* New York: Columbia University Press.

Hayes, S. C. (1991). A relational control theory of stimulus equivalence. In L. J. Hayes & P. N. Chase (Eds.), *Dialogues on verbal behavior.* Reno, NV: Context Press.

Herrnstein, R. J. (1970). On the law of effect. *Journal of the Experimental Analysis of Behavior, 13,* 243–266.

Herrnstein, R. J. (1990). Behavior, reinforcement, and utility. *Psychological Science, 1,* 217–223.

Hineline, P. N., & Wanchisen, B. A. (1989). Correlated hypothesizing and the distinction between contingency-shaped and rule-governed behavior. In S. C. Hayes (Ed.), *Rule-governed behavior: Cognition, contingencies, and instructional control* (pp. 221–268). New York: Plenum Press.

Hull, D. (1981/84). Units of evolution: A metaphysical essay. In R. N. Brandon & R. M. Burian (Eds.), *Genes, organisms, populations: Controversies over the units of selection* (pp. 142–160). Cambridge, MA: The MIT Press.

Irvine, W. (1955). *Apes, angels, and Victorians.* New York: McGraw-Hill.

Keller, F. S., & Schoenfeld, W. N. (1950). Principles of psychology. New York: Appleton-Century-Crofts.

Laszlo, E. (1987). *Evolution: The grand synthesis.* Boston & London: New Science Library.

Lee, V. L. (1988). *Beyond behaviorism.* Hillsdale, NJ: Lawrence Erlbaum.

Lovelock, J. (1988). *The ages of Gaia.* New York: W. W. Norton

Lovaas, O. I., & Smith, T. (1989). A comprehensive behavioral theory of autistic children: Paradigm for research and treatment. *Journal of Behavior Therapy and Experimental Psychiatry, 20,* 17–29.

Lubinski, D., & Thompson, T. (1986). Functional units of human behavior and their integration: A dispositional analysis. In T. Thompson & M. D. Zeiler (Eds.), *Analysis and integration of behavioral units* (pp. 275–314). Hillsdale, NJ: Lawrence Erlbaum.

Malagodi, E. F. (1986). On radicalizing behaviorism: A call for cultural analysis. *The Behavior Analyst, 9,* 1–17.

Malagodi, E. F., & Jackson, K. (1989). Behavior analysis and cultural analysis: Troubles and issues. *The Behavior Analyst, 12,* 17–33.

Malott, R. W. (1988). Rule-governed behavior and behavioral anthropology. *The Behavior Analyst, 11,* 181–203.

Malott, R. W. (1989). The achievement of evasive goals. In S. C. Hayes (Ed.), *Rule-governed behavior: Cognition, contingencies, and instructional control* (pp. 269–322). New York: Plenum Press.

Mayr, E. (1982). *The growth of biological thought.* Cambridge, MA: Belknap Press of Harvard University Press.

McDowell, J. J. (1988). Matching theory in natural human environments. *The Behavior Analyst, 11,* 95–109.

McDowell, J. J (1989). Two modern developments in matching theory. *The Behavior Analyst, 12,* 153–166.

Mechner, Francis (1990). *The revealed operant: A laboratory model for studying individual occurrences of operant responses, including their durations.* Unpublished manuscript.

Michael, J. L. (1982). Distinguishing between discriminative stimuli and motivational functions of stimuli. *Journal of the Experimental Analysis of Behavior, 37,* 149–155.

Michael, J. L. (1984). Behavior analysis: A radical perspective. In B. L. Hammonds (Ed.), *Psychology and learning: Master lecture series, Vol. 4* (pp. 95–121). Washington, DC: American Psychological Association.

Michael, J. L. (1990). *Concepts and principles of behavior analysis.* Unpublished manuscript.

Moerk, E. L. (1983). A behavioral analysis of controversial topics in first language acquisition: Reinforcements, corrections, modeling, input frequencies, and the three-term contingency pattern. *Journal of Psycholinguistic Research, 12,* 129–155.

Moerk, E. L. (1990). Three-term contingency patterns in mother-child verbal interactions during first-language acquisition. *Journal of the Experimental Analysis of Behavior, 54,* 293–305.

Morris, E. K. (in press). The experimental analysis of behavioral content: A third domain of behavior-analytic research. In S. S. Glenn (Ed.), *Progress in behavioral studies: Vol. 3.* Cambridge, MA: Cambridge Center for Behavioral Studies.

Neuringer, A. (1986). Can people behave "randomly?": The role of feedback. *Journal of Experimental Psychology: General, 115,* 62–75.

Page, S., & Neuringer, A. (1985). Variability is an operant. *Journal of Experimental Psychology: Animal Behavior Processes, 11,* 429–452.

Peterson, N. (1978). *An introduction to verbal behavior.* Grand Rapids, MI: Behavior Associates, Inc.

Peterson, R. F. (1968). Some experiments on the organization of a class of imitative behaviors. *Journal of Applied Behavior Analysis, 1,* 225–235.

Schoenfeld, W. N., & Cole, B. K. (1972). *Stimulus schedules: The t-τ systems.* New York: Harper & Row.

Sidman, M. (1986). Functional analysis of emergent verbal classes. In T. Thompson & M. D. Zeiler (Eds.), *Analysis and integration of behavioral units.* Hillsdale, NJ: Lawrence Erlbaum.

Skinner, B. F. (1953). *Science and human behavior.* New York: Free Press.

Skinner, B. F. (1957). *Verbal behavior.* New York: Appleton-Century-Crofts.

Skinner, B. F. (1969). *Contingencies of reinforcement: A theoretical analysis.* New York: Appleton-Century-Crofts.

Skinner, B. F. (1974). *About behaviorism.* New York: Alfred A. Knopf.

Skinner, B. F. (1984). The evolution of behavior. *Journal of the Experimental Analysis of Behavior, 41,* 217–221.

Skinner, B. F. (1981/86). Selection by consequences. *Science, 213,* 501–504, July 3, 1981. Reprinted in A. C. Catania & S. Harnad (Eds.). *The selection of behavior* (pp. 11–20). Cambridge: Cambridge University Press.

Skinner, B. F. (1986). The evolution of verbal behavior. *Journal of the Experimental Analysis of Behavior, 45,* 115–122.

Skinner, B. F. (1987). Why we are not acting to save the world. Chapter 1 in *Upon Further Reflection.* New York: Prentice-Hall

Skinner, B. F. (1990). Can psychology be a science of mind? *American Psychologist, 45,* 1206–1210.

Smith, T. (1986). Biology as allegory: A review of Elliott Sober's *The Nature of Selection. Journal of the Experimental Analysis of Behavior, 46,* 105–112.

Sober, E. (1984). *The nature of selection: Evolutionary theory in philosophical focus.* Cambridge, MA: The MIT Press.

Staats, A. W. (1977). *Child learning, intelligence, and personality: Principles of a behavioral interaction approach* (Rev. ed.). Kalamazoo, MI: Behaviordelia.

Vargas, E. A. (1985). Cultural contingencies: A review of Marvin Harris's *Cannibals and Kings. Journal of the Experimental Analysis of Behavior, 43,* 419–428.

II

APPLICATIONS

4

Aspects of Some Contingencies and Metacontingencies in the Soviet Union

P. A. Lamal

INTRODUCTION

Anyone who attempts to analyze the dynamics of the Soviet Union today could fairly be characterized as foolhardy. As the leadership tries to solve the perennial problems of that vast and variegated conglomeration of ethnic groups and nationalities, virtually every day brings new reports of changes in plans, policies, laws and in the leadership of the Soviet Union. In many cases it is clear that the leadership, instead of being in the vanguard, is simply trying to catch up with events over which it clearly has no control. The alternative to analyzing current events in the Soviet Union is to wait until they are no longer current. This is a reasonable approach, but not the one taken here. Nevertheless, the pace of change in the Soviet Union since Gorbachev's accession to power, at least in some spheres, has been so swift and dramatic that the analysis presented here may be more historical than contemporary by the time it appears in print.

Background

The present turmoil in the Soviet Union follows a period of what is usually referred to as "stagnation" under Brezhnev, Andropov, and Chernenko. Rather than economic stagnation, however, the evidence indicates that the pre-Gorbachev economy was declining (Lamal, in press). It is now clear, and admitted by both Soviet economists and political leaders, that "the Soviet economy is in a deplorable state . . ." (Nove, 1990, p. 50). Indeed, even bread is in short supply, a situation unheard of for decades. The overarching goal of Gorbachev and his allies is to reverse this decline and to develop a world-class economy. Attainment of this goal will necessitate changing rules (Hayes, 1989), contingencies, and metacontingencies (see Chapter 1), some of which have been operating in the Soviet Union for generations. The obstacles are many and high and the likelihood of success, while at present unclear, is no more than 50-50.

Some changes in the Soviet Union have been enacted, some have only been partially enacted, some have yet to be enacted, and others have been advanced and withdrawn. I have earlier outlined (Lamal, in press) three of the pre-Gorbachev metacontingencies that are responsible in large measure for the staggering problems of the Soviet Union. These metacontingencies are: (1) centralized control of the

77

economy, the *command-administrative system*; (2) increased production as the primary economic goal; (3) maintenance of privilege and power by the *nomenklatura*.

Another set of metacontingencies has also had a deleterious effect on the Soviet economy. The rules responsible for these metacontingencies are found in Marxist ideology, particularly those aspects of Marxism that prescribe state ownership of the means of production and a classless society. The cultural practices envisioned by these prescriptions of Marxism are still attractive to large segments of Soviet society, if only for negative reasons. Many Soviet citizens fear that allowing increased property rights for individuals or small groups will herald the rise of an entrepreneurial class of "speculators" and those who live on "unearned income."

Many Soviet citizens see the ideal of a classless society slipping away if large differentials in income are allowed, even if those with higher incomes earned them in perfectly legitimate ways. Gorbachev and other reformers have recognized for some time the envy of and enmity toward those with high incomes, among the vastly greater number of those with lower incomes. For some time, the reformers have criticized "wage-levellers," and have argued that the correct view is "to each according to his [sic] work."

Although the Soviet Union has never had a classless society—witness the nomenklatura, this has not prevented the mass of its citizens from embracing the wage levelling rule. The nomenklatura have doubtless been considered by most Soviet citizens to be a separate phenomenon about which little or nothing could be done. It is clear, however, that the reinforcers enjoyed by the nomenklatura have been resented, often bitterly, by those who were not in their position (e.g., Vaksberg, 1989).

The metacontingencies of state-owned property and positing of a classless society as the ideal, both part of Marxist ideology, contribute to the present economic debacle that could have been readily predicted from a behavior analytical viewpoint. A fundamental problem is that these two metacontingencies fail to provide for important links between the individual's work and positive reinforcers. Consider the metacontingency of state-owned property. If, at the workplace, the state owns all of the property, little or no incentive exists for the worker to exercise more than minimal care in using and maintaining the property. If equipment is maintained poorly, and thus has a shorter than necessary life-span, the state must replace it. If an individual works on a state farm or collective farm, there is little incentive to be a good steward of the land and to try to produce as much as possible, since wages do not depend on a good harvest. The worker has no property rights in the land and is simply a wage-earner.

This analysis is admittedly somewhat simplistic. I have elsewhere (Lamal, in press) outlined in some detail practices that are part of, and support, some of the Soviet metacontingencies. However, the primary assertation stands: Soviet metacontingencies fail to provide necessary links between the individual's work and important consequences for the individual.

NEW METACONTINGENCIES ENVISIONED
BY REFORMERS

Under the command-administrative system (or metacontingency), production targets for state enterprises and for agricultural units were set by the appropriate ministries. The inputs for the state enterprises and agricultural units were also determined by central authorities. These data constituted the famous 5-year plans under which 1-year plans were subsumed. These plans incorporated an incredibly large number of data and were extremely complex. Thus, it was virtually impossible to modify such plans to meet rapidly changing conditions. The plans were changed frequently, but not in time to accommodate changing circumstances.

A major reform envisioned by Gorbachev and other reformers entails changing this metacontingency of centralized planning to allow more decision-making at lower levels. It should be pointed out that many of the implemented and proposed reforms in all areas of Soviet society are the result of compromise. Aslund (1989) maintains that "the design of economic reform is essentially worked out in strife between reformist academic economists and a conservative Gosplan [State Plan Committee] backed by other central economic organs" (pp. 63, 64). Not surprisingly the central authorities resist surrendering any of their power. An interesting question is to what extent such power is primarily or secondarily reinforcing to individuals.

The central authorities have been remarkably skillful and successful in avoiding erosion of their authority since Gorbachev came to power in 1985. One tactic they have employed is to ignore prescriptions for change. Another has been to implement *pro forma* change. Yet another tactic has been to issue yet more regulations and interpretations that preclude or mitigate the changes that reforms are designed to achieve. According to the eminent Soviet sociologist Tat'iana Zaslavskaia (1989):

> The sham supporters of restructuring in the administrative apparatus . . . present a major danger. While creating the appearance of a high degree of active involvement, and of their real participation in working out guideline documents and instructions, in practice they imperceptibly reduce efforts for change to nothing. (p. 7)

One economic reform was intended to simplify matters by emphasizing only the most important economic plan targets. State enterprises were also to be more independent of their ministries. However, these attempted changes failed to bring about any significant improvement. "One reason may be that ministries ignored the new rules. However, it does not appear a sufficient explanation. It is more likely that ever more complex regulations tied enterprises so much that a partial deregulation did not help" (Aslund, 1989, p. 105).

Another major economic reform has been self-financing. Under self-financing, state farms and enterprises are responsible for their profits and losses. If an enterprise consistently loses money, it will, supposedly, no longer be subsidized by the central authorities. However, according to Aslund (1989), self-financing "was effectively resisted by branch ministries and central economic bodies, since it worked against their interests and reduced their powers" (p. 106).

One way to bring about decentralization is to reduce the percentage of orders placed by the state with enterprises (e.g., Seliunin, 1989). Aslund (1989) says that a goal of the reformers ". . . was to reduce the share of state orders in GNP to 20–30 percent in 1991 (primarily arms), corresponding to the U.S. proportion of state procurement" (p. 125). Not surprisingly, Gosplan wanted to proceed much more slowly in the reduction of state orders.

To expedite decentralization, Gorbachev has replaced those in the highest positions, which has apparently had little impact. It seems that the replacements succumb to the prevailing contingency at the centers of power: "The new officials fend loyally, and more skillfully than their predecessors, for the vested interests of their institutions. The simple truth is that interests are more important than competence or professional background . . ." (Aslund, p. 146).

It may be useful to distinguish between changes in policy and true reforms. Much of what has been done in the past has consisted of changes in policy—that is, attempts to fine-tune the system, tinkering at the margins. These attempts have usually had only minor, if any, effects and those effects have often been short-lived. In the first years after his accession to power Gorbachev seems to have been unwilling to propose real reforms, as opposed to policy changes.

In contrast to policy changes, reforms unmistakably involve the replacement of metacontingencies with other metacontingencies. It now appears, as will be discussed later, that Gorbachev is willing to institute two economic reforms, and that political reforms have recently been instituted.

However, until the economic reforms are functioning, the Soviets operate in an equivocal economic system characterized by a tension between centralized institutions and moves toward decentralization. The present system includes a virtually universal design flaw. The flaw is that, whereas the enterprises have been given more autonomy, the central administrators,

> are expected to do what they have done before . . . guarantee the supply of key products to the economy. That sets up a contradiction between the new rights of enterprises and the continuing rights and responsibilities of higher levels in the hierarchy. (Hewett, 1988, p. 24)

What we have here is a clash of metacontingencies.

Resistance by central administrators and planners to policy changes and reforms can take various forms. Among the most common obstructionist tactics used by central authorities are the following: (1) delaying issuing the necessary implementing decrees for changes, (2) designing the implementing decrees so that they bend the reform in the direction of the old system, and (3) interpreting ". . . whatever regulations have been issued in such a way as to minimize the actual effect of the reforms" (Hewett, 1988, p. 26). The result of these tactics is that ". . . reform decrees take considerable time to implement and are seldom fully implemented as intended" (Hewett, 1988, p. 27; See also Mann, 1990).

Often there is opposition to reforms not only from central authorities but also from managers of enterprises and their workers. At first blush this may seem odd, but on reflection it makes sense from a behavioral point of view. Although enterprises and their workers operate in deficient environments, they have by and large learned how to survive. Enterprise managers have learned to obtain inputs outside of the system by developing relationships with the right people. They have learned how to fulfill plan targets by *storming,* that is, mobilizing workers or peasants to achieve quotas at the end of a month, quarter, or year, and by having their plan targets revised downward (Lamal, in press). Workers, in turn, know that they have virtually guaranteed job security, that they usually do not have to work particularly hard, and that "bonuses" are not contingent on unusual effort. There is little incentive to "earn" more money since there are few, if any, consumer goods to buy and those that are available are of poor quality. Education and health care are free, and housing, although scarce and usually cramped, is easily affordable.

Reforms, on the other hand, would mean not only that managers and workers would have to compete with those of other enterprises, but that they would have to make such unprecedented decisions as to what to produce, in what quantity, and of what quality—fearsome decisions for those who have never had to make them. Particularly when the survival of their jobs, and indeed their "company" would depend on those decisions. Thus it is not surprising that the prospect of such changed contingencies and metacontingencies is not universally welcomed.

Hewett (1988) makes a distinction between the formal economic system and the de facto economic system. He says that reforms of the formal system have little effect unless they interact with the de facto system. It would be a mistake, however, to believe that the de facto system is entirely different from, or runs completely counter to, the formal system. Lack of reliable data hinders study of the de facto system. Nevertheless, we know, for example, that as part of the de facto system ". . . expediters (*tolkachi*) working on behalf of enterprises sell surplus commodities and purchase products the enterprises need [both on the black market]" (Hewett, 1988, p. 155).

This brings us to a consideration of the black market (also called the shadow economy) and the second economy. When behavior cannot be sufficiently reinforced by following official rules, people will often follow other rules that lead to reinforcement. In this case, these latter contingencies comprise the black market and second economy. Anyone who has ever been in a country with a thriving black market knows that you obtain many more tokens (money) by exchanging your U.S. dollars on the black market than on the official market. Many who would characterize themselves as law-abiding, if not model, citizens readily engage in black market transactions when given the opportunity. In the Soviet black market, "Everything is there, and everyone knows it" (Belikova & Shokhin, 1989, p. 27).

So, too, Soviet enterprise managers use a mix of legal and illegal means to meet their targets. The central planners know the managers are doing this:

> *implicitly they expect it of them. An enterprise director would be a fool to 'work according to rule' and fail to fulfill the plan because he chose not to rely on the shadow economy. He would either have to change his ways or lose his position. (Hewett, 1988, p. 178)*

As of this writing, there is still a great deal of central control over enterprises. Detailed management of enterprises by central planners by means of annual plans has been eliminated. Nevertheless, the ministries are still responsible for the performance of their sectors, and they retain effective means of control over their enterprises by the setting of norms, taxes, and prices. Two factors work against decentralization (Hewett, 1988): (1) Some share of industrial output will be subject to high-priority state orders—the larger that share, the less enterprise autonomy; (2) central planners will send control figures (indicators of productive activity and efficiency) to enterprises as part of each 5-year planning cycle. There is concern that the ministries and central planners will use those figures to retain control over enterprise operations, although the figures are not supposed to be obligatory.

GOALS AND OBSTACLES

The specific goals of perestroika are unclear. This constitutes a major problem, for as every behavior analyst knows, clear goals are a *sine qua non* of any effective change program. However, there does seem to be a consensus (but not total agreement) about general goals. There is agreement that decentralization of economic decision-making is necessary, concomitant with increased decision-making authority for enterprises. There is general agreement that consumer demand should play a much greater role in determining what goods are produced, in what quantities, and in what quality. With respect to agriculture, the consensus is to replace state ownership of land, livestock, and machinery, with increased property rights of individuals or small groups of individuals. Private enterprise ("cooperatives") is now seen as a necessary part of the economy. A fundamental reform that is increasingly seen as an underpinning for all of these reforms is a reform of the price system. Any and all of the previously mentioned changes entail very important changes in the contingencies and metacontingencies affecting people's lives.

There are many obstacles to the achievement of these new contingencies and metacontingencies. Consider the area of private enterprise. The Soviet leadership had at least three reasons for encouraging the development of private enterprise: (1) to overcome the tremendous shortage of consumer goods, (2) to "tap 'unused labour reserves' such as housewives, students and pensioners (20% of the population in 1988)" (Plokker, 1990, p. 404), (3) to incorporate the desirable parts of the second economy under state control and taxation.

A first obstacle in the path of those who would engage in private enterprise is obtaining permission from the local soviet. Once permission has been obtained, numerous other problems may present themselves. Widespread problems that are very difficult to solve include finding space and obtaining necessary supplies and credit. In an economy marked by severe shortages of all kinds, obtaining supplies is the greatest problem. Some cooperatives contract with state enterprises, and are thus often assured of obtaining supplies; at the same time, however, they are not allowed to sell on the market. Also, cooperatives sometimes are refused help by state enterprise officials, who are legally bound to help them but have no incentive to do so (Plokker, 1990).

A contingency working against private enterprise involves the income earned. Private enterprises must carefully account for their income by keeping detailed cost-accounts (*otchety*). How this income is to be taxed has not yet been settled. "While cooperators consider 'double taxation' (once on the income of the cooperative and once on their personal income) unfair, the public often sees high prices and wages as 'speculation' " (Plokker, 1990, p. 409). The policymakers want to prevent incomes that would be seen as excessively high, but they also recognize that high taxes will diminish free enterprise activities.

The greatest obstacle to the development of private enterprise, however, is the unwillingness of local authorities to cooperate. This resistance seems to be greatest at the lowest level of government (the *raion*). The primary reasons for this unwillingness are said to be a belief that the new policy concerning private enterprise will not last, "fear of the negative effects new activities could have on the local economy, and a strong reluctance to go to any exertion greater than that expressly ordered from above" (Plokker, 1990, p. 409).

There is little of what the Soviets call *material incentive* for local authorities to support private enterprise. This is because only the tax revenue on the cooperative's income goes to the local budget, and this tax is only 3–5%. On the other hand, the progressive tax on the personal income of individual laborers and cooperative members, which may be quite high, goes to the state budget. The local authorities seem to be in an environment in which there is little or no reinforcement for them contingent on helping private enterprise, at least in the absence of any rules specifying that they do so. In addition they have grown up in an environment in which private enterprise activities were presumably punished, at least occasionally, and in which the prevailing rules clearly proscribed such activities.

The most recent problem facing cooperatives has been the appearance of extortionists (many Soviets refer to a Soviet mafia) who threaten to burn down or loot cooperatives unless they are bought off. The frequency of this activity has apparently increased dramatically in the past year (Plokker, 1990). So another negative consequence results from private enterprise in many instances.

Another aversive consequence of engaging in private enterprise is the antagonism it engenders in many Soviet citizens. This antagonism usually centers on the high prices charged by cooperatives and high wages charged by individual laborers. Plokker (1990) cites the view of G. Batygin, editor of the Soviet journal *Sotsiologicheskie Issledovaniya* (*Sociological Research*) that, "people measure the fairness of someone's income simply by its amount: the more it is the more undeserved it must be" (p. 411). At work sites, individual or cooperative workers often encounter hostile reactions by those who work for state enterprises.

Another set of goals and obstacles is entailed in the conversion of Soviet enterprises from military to civilian production (Kincade & Thompson, 1990). Soviet policymakers hope that such conversion will achieve a number of goals, including greatly increasing the availability of consumer goods, sopping up much of the "enormous pool of private savings" (p. 84), and countering strong inflationary pressures. For many workers, money has ceased to function as a positive reinforcer because there are no goods, other than necessities, for which to exchange it (outside of the black market). This situation contributes significantly to the problem of low worker productivity.

Among the obstacles plaguing the conversion effort are the familiar ones of a command economy (the conversion has been centrally directed): "bottlenecks, inadequate transportation networks, low labor productivity and morale, and vertical integration within ministries that leads to inefficient duplication" (Kincade & Thomson, 1990, p. 91). In addition, contingencies developed for producing military goods are inappropriate for producing consumer goods. "Production, fabrication, and assembly techniques suited to making military equipment exclusively . . . are generally not readily adaptable to civilian production, if they can be adapted at all" (Kincade & Thomson, 1990, p. 91). The conversion is further complicated by the requirements of new contingencies that are part of perestroika, such as enterprise accountability and self-financing.

A more general obstacle to bringing about significant changes in economic contingencies and metacontingencies is the lack of consensus among the reformist decision-makers and those who influence them about the sequence and pace of steps to be taken (e.g., Brumberg, 1990; Rumer, 1990). Although virtually all of the reformers agree that the command-administrative system must be replaced, just what should replace it is a matter of much debate, often acrimonious. Two general viewpoints can be discerned. One advocates what is known as "shock-therapy." This is the approach taken in Poland, and involves "immediate abolition of all subsidies, lifting all controls on prices and wages, and closing unprofitable enterprises . . ." (Brumberg, 1990, p. 57, see also Braun & Day, 1990). The other viewpoint argues for a gradual approach to the removal of subsidies and the decontrol of wages and prices. As I write, it is unclear which viewpoint will prevail.

COUNTERCONTROL

Authoritarian societies are always apt subjects for a consideration of counter-control in spite of or perhaps because of the complete lack of countercontrol in such societies. Indeed, the definition of an authoritarian state may be one in which no significant countercontrol is possible. The Soviet Union today is of interest because countercontrol is now developing there.

The development of countercontrol is manifested by the appearance of multiple political parties (although they would not necessarily be called such by Soviets) and multicandidate elections (Tolz, 1990).

The Communist Party of the Soviet Union (CPSU) has relinquished its monop-oly of power, and Gorbachev "is attempting to create a strong power base outside the CPSU" (Tolz, 1990, p. 9). But the law on the newly created post of President that Gorbachev fills provides him with a great deal of centralized power. It remains to be seen to what extent the Supreme Soviet and the Congress of People's Depu-ties will serve as countervailing controls. Other sources of effective countercontrol could include strikes and such manifestations of popular discontent as mass dem-onstrations.

CONCLUSION

There are many contingencies and metacontingencies in the Soviet Union that have not been described here. Almost all of them are changing in significant ways. Among them are those involving ethnic minorities, the mass media, the military, and foreign relations.

To what extent perestroika will move beyond verbal behavior *about* it, to actual farreaching changes *in* rules, contingencies, and metacontingencies remains unan-swered. Any significant changes in rules, contingencies, and metacontingencies will doubtless entail aversive consequences for some segments of Soviet society. Such changes may also result in more reinforcers for all segments of the society, but the uncertainty of their occurrence and the high likelihood that they will be delayed make the task of bringing about the changes difficult.

In addition, the sheer magnitude of the task is arresting. Consider, for example, how difficult it would be for the United States to transform itself from a capitalist society into a socialist one, even if there was an overwhelming consensus in favor of such a change. In the Soviet Union there is no one who has lived in a capitalist society, except as a foreigner. No one has contingency-shaped behaviors that are part and parcel of capitalist contingencies and metacontingencies. If the Soviets change from socialism to something radically different, they will be doing it by learning new rules—rule-governed behavior. In a real sense, they will be doing it "by the book."

Whether the apathy and fatalism (see Chapter 12) of the Soviet masses can be overcome remains to be seen. Suppose, however, that the Soviets do indeed change their society's rules, contingencies, and metacontingencies to those much more like the ones prevailing in capitalist societies, or societies that although not capitalist are nevertheless very unlike present Soviet society. What if they then come to realize that they have still not achieved paradise on earth? What happens when they discover that all societies experience serious problems? Will many Soviet citizens then again become disillusioned and lapse into apathy and fatalism?

REFERENCES

Aslund, A. (1989). *Gorbachev's struggle for economic reform.* Ithaca, NY: Cornell University Press.

Belikova, G., & Shokhin, A. (1989). The black market: People, things, and facts. *The Soviet Review, 30,* 26–39.

Braun, A., & Day, R. B. (1990). Gorbachevian contradictions. *Problems of Communism, 39,* 36–50.

Brumberg, A. (1990). The turning point? *The New York Review of Books, 37,* 52–59.

Hayes, S. C. (Ed.). (1989). *Rule-governed behavior: Cognition, contingencies, and instinctional control.* New York: Plenum.

Hewett, E. A. (1988). *Reforming the Soviet economy.* Washington, DC: The Brookings Institution.

Kincade, W., & Thomson, T. K. (1990). Economic conversion in the USSR: Its role in *perestroyka. Problems of Communism, 39,* 83–92.

Lamal, P. A. (in press). Three metacontingencies in the preperestroika Soviet Union. *Behavior and Social Issues.*

Mann, D. (1990). Nongovernment by decree. *Report on the USSR, 35,* 1–4.

Nove, A. (1990). An economy in transition. In A. Brumberg (Ed.), *Chronicle of a revolution* (pp. 50–71). New York: Pantheon.

Plokker, D. (1990). The development of individual and cooperative labour activity in the Soviet Union. *Soviet Studies, 42,* 403–428.

Rumer, B. (1990). The "Abalkanization" of Soviet economic reform. *Problems of Communism, 39,* 74–82.

Seliunin, V. (1989). A profound reform or the revenge of bureaucracy? *The Soviet Review, 30,* 3–25.

Tolz, V. (1990). The emergence of a multiparty system in the USSR. *Report on the USSR, 2,* 5–11.

Vaksberg, A. (1989). Bone of the mammoth. *The Soviet Review, 30,* 62–75.

Zaslavskaia, T. (1989). The fundamental question of restructuring. *The Soviet Review, 30,* 3–11.

5

Behavioral Analysis of Socialism in Eastern Europe: A Framework for Understanding the Revolutions of 1989

Richard F. Rakos

INTRODUCTION

In 1989 the capitalist industrialized world watched in amazement and satisfaction as each country in Central and Eastern Europe challenged the Soviet-imposed hegemony of communism. Clearly, Gorbachev's (1987; see also Aganbegyan, 1988) perestroika provided the opportunity for such change, as he recognized that the Soviet Union's fortunes were no longer dependent on a socialist buffer zone between it and the West. Indeed, quite the opposite: the Soviet Union needed international cooperation to improve its society (Rakos, in press; Chapter 4). But a more interesting issue is why each Central and East European country jumped at the opportunity to abandon or modify the Soviet-style economic system. After all, despite admitted problems, the socialist system provided for the basic needs of the citizenry. Why did these nations change so quickly?

Two "forces" are usually invoked as explanations. The Soviet withdrawal permitted suppressed nationalism to reassert itself (e.g., Hockenos, 1990) and also unleashed natural desires for political and economic freedom (Waters, 1990). It is the latter impetus, "freedom," that will be the focus of this essay.

Central and Eastern Europe cannot, of course, be considered without recognition that, even under Soviet domination, differences among the countries emerged over the post-World War II period. Yugoslavia, under Tito, began to develop a system of socialist self-management as early as 1950 (McCord, 1989). Hungary introduced the New Economic Mechanism (NEM) in 1968 (Heinrich, 1986), and Poland followed with the similar Reformed Economic System in 1981 (Gomulka, 1986). Each of these modifications attempted to stimulate productivity by increasing worker control over, and involvement in, economic decisions. However, all modifications retained the essential elements of socialism: state control over the means of production and significant central planning (see Chapter 4).

SOCIALISM: AN ECONOMIC PERSPECTIVE

The economic and social consequences of centralized socialism are well documented. Rigid bureaucracies, chronic shortages of consumer goods, stagnant industrial output, inferior technology, minimal innovation, and a generally unsatisfied population that envies capitalistic lifestyles are normative, perhaps inevitable outcomes (Gomulka, 1986; Kornai, 1980, 1986). (Ulman [1988, 1989] contends that Cuba's "rectification" program provides concrete evidence that these outcomes are not inevitable products of true "revolutionary" socialism, but only characterize "bureaucratic" socialism. I briefly will consider Cuba at the end of this essay.) However, these undesired sequelae coexist with others that are positive, such as full employment, subsidized housing and food, and free universal medical care and schooling.

Thus, even with its shortcomings, socialism offers a set of ideals that captures the imagination of many, perhaps because the casualties of capitalism also are obvious. Hungary's socialist ideals, for example, included socialist wage-setting (to everybody according to his work and equal pay for equal work), solidarity (protection of and help for the vulnerable), security (full employment and accessibility to community resources), and societal concern (preeminence of the general interest over those of the individual or small group) (Kornai, 1986). Unfortunately, experience suggests these values are inconsistent with the requirements of economic efficiency, which include incentives to stimulate performance, careful cost-benefit analyses, flexible policies enabling rapid adaptation to changing external conditions, decision-making skills characterized by initiative, innovation and risk-taking, and a mechanism to assign responsibility to individuals for outcomes of decisions (Kornai, 1986).

Kornai (1986) suggests that the economic problems of socialism are centered in its "soft budget constraint"; economic enterprises have soft, perhaps even nonexistent bottom lines, since no industry will be permitted by the state to fail even if inefficiency is a result of mismanagement. Furthermore, the soft budget system is driven by the available resources and their allocation and is therefore "resource constrained." Pure capitalism, by contrast, is characterized by a "hard budget constraint"; bankruptcy will result if profits do not accrue since the state will not intervene. In addition, capitalism is driven by consumer desires and is therefore "demand constrained."

From an economic perspective, soft budgets and resource constraints produce the inefficiencies and dissatisfactions associated with socialism. Official economic behaviors are restricted to those that can best be described as "risk minimizing" (Heinrich, 1986). In Eastern Europe, managers argued for nondemanding production goals, state authorities visciously competed for limited centrally distributed resources, and workers emitted the minimal work behaviors required of them. Furthermore, illegal black markets proliferated (Berend & Ranki, 1985; Heinrich, 1986; Kornai, 1986), and social apathy and skepticism festered (Gorbachev, 1987).

These outcomes can be understood and appreciated from a behavior analytic and an economic perspective; in fact, since individual behavior is, ultimately, the primary concern (cf. Gorbachev, 1987), the behavior analytic perspective may prove even more enlightening.

SOCIALISM: A BEHAVIORAL PERSPECTIVE

The behavioral analysis of cultural phenomena has been facilitated by Glenn's (1986, 1988) distinction between contingencies of reinforcement (CORs) and metacontingencies. CORs, or behavioral contingencies, describe the relationship of individual operant behavior to its consequences in a specified situation. In contrast, the metacontingency is "the unit of analysis encompassing a cultural practice, in all its variations, and the aggregate outcome of all the current variations" (Glenn, 1988, p. 168). A cultural practice is comprised of the interlocking behavioral contingencies (CORs) for a large number of individuals. Whereas contingencies of reinforcement select the behaviors of individuals, metacontingencies select, through cultural outcomes, the interlocking behavioral contingencies that comprise the cultural practice. Metacontingencies, therefore, are mediated by the CORs that control individual behavior. Frequently, especially when a metacontingency is socially planned, the CORs themselves are mediated by verbal behavior in the form of (1) rules bridging the gap between immediate and long-term outcomes (e.g., laws) and (2) social reinforcement. Further, "(b)ecause a cultural outcome is a joint function of the behavior of many people, the outcome may be poorly correlated with the behavior of many of the people engaged in the practice. A cultural practice may produce increasingly ineffective outcomes but continue occurring because the behavior of its individual participants is maintained by stable behavioral contingencies" (Glenn, 1988, p. 170; see Chapter 3 for a further discussion of these concepts). This is precisely what occurred in the Soviet Union and Eastern European states before perestroika (Lamal, in press; Rakos, 1988a, in press).

Central planning established metacontingencies that had the following intended cultural outcomes: (1) state authority, (2) social equality, (3) continually increased industrial production, and (4) a powerful elite class (Lamal, in press; Rakos, 1988a). However, industrial output was compromised by the selection—at least for workers—of competing behavioral contingencies; official work behavior remained under the primary influence of a limited set of verbally mediated reinforcers ("moral incentives"), whereas nonsanctioned labor was controlled by direct material consequences. Economic reforms, such as the NEM in Hungary, established an additional metacontingency designed to foster economic efficiency through the official, though still limited, use of material incentives for workers (Rakos, 1988a). Unfortunately, the interlocking behavioral contingencies selected by the new metacontingency were still not wholly consistent with the goal. A behavioral analysis of the situation suggests that the dominant central planning metacontingencies were the fundamental impediment to economic efficiency, an ideological misjudgment that, in essence, ignored virtually all the behavioral principles involved in contingency management (cf. Rakos, 1988b, 1989).

CONTINGENCY ANALYSIS
OF WORKER BEHAVIOR UNDER SOCIALISM
IN EASTERN EUROPE

A metacontingency, as stated earlier, selects the interlocking contingencies of reinforcement that control the diverse behaviors comprising a social or cultural practice. The metacontingencies arising from socialist central planning, therefore, select CORs for workers, managers, planners, and politicians. These CORs include, but of course are not limited to, activities in the economic sphere. In this section, the CORs controlling work behaviors of ordinary citizens ("workers") living under Soviet-style socialism will be analyzed through discussions of the ingredients comprising a functionally effective COR: the contingency relationship between a response and reinforcer, reinforcer potency, response selection, and stimulus control.

The Relationship of Reinforcement to Work Behavior

Perhaps the most fundamental aspect of socialism is the decoupling of official work behavior and its consequences. In effect, socialism establishes a situation wherein a response and the product of the response are in a noncontingent relationship, thus violating the most basic principle governing the initiation and maintenance of performance. One might presume that this circumstance would occur only under fully developed communism, where the guiding principle is "from each according to his ability, to each according to his needs" (Morrow, 1988). However, in actuality, such noncontingent relationships largely characterize socialism, despite its operative principle of "from each according to his ability, to each according to his work" (Morrow, 1988).

Of course, all behavior is a function of some contingency, and individuals residing in socialist environments are influenced by some consequences. In fact, this contingency is quite straightforward: wages are contingently related to appearing at the work site and inhibiting disruptive responses—but not to working productively. It is this relationship that contributes so significantly to the low productivity and shortages of goods plaguing virtually all socialist systems (Kornai, 1980). When a contingency is established between work and wages, as was done in Hungary, Poland, Yugoslavia, and the People's Republic of China (Gomulka, 1986; Lamal, 1984; Nove, 1983), productivity increases dramatically (Kornai, 1986). This particular contingency involving these countries was enacted while these countries still ensured "full employment." Thus, the common Marxist assertion that capitalistic contingencies motivate productive labor through aversive control—the unremitting threat of unemployment (Ulman, 1988, 1989)—is clearly overstated. But even acknowledging some degree of aversive control here does not weaken significantly the argument: socialism essentially employs a similar strategy in compulsory allocation of, or extremely limited choice among, job responsibilities, unless one makes the supposition that "what workers wish to do . . . correspond(s) to what needs doing" (Nove, 1983, p. 51).

In the absence of the aforementioned contingency, one that Marxists would describe as a system of "material incentives" (Nove, 1983), socialist systems are forced to rely on the idealistic but empirically unsupported assumption that people will work hard because that is what they want to do ("moral incentives"). These moral incentives are in reality social reinforcers and values related to the desirability of socialism. Both social reinforcement and values are verbally mediated conditioned reinforcers. The reliance on such consequences, rather than material goods, as stimuli maintaining work behavior is problematic: for conditioned reinforcers to maintain their potency, they occasionally must be paired with other effective reinforcers. This is particularly true for verbally mediated conditioned reinforcers, since by definition they provide no direct material gain. For example, consistent praise from a work supervisor soon loses its reinforcing quality if it is not paired with material gains such as promotion, expanded responsibilities, and of course, increased salary. Unfortunately, this pairing rarely occurred in Eastern European socialism. On the contrary, social reinforcement and the values of socialism were paired with reinforcers that no longer functioned as reinforcers (i.e., with reinforcers to which the individuals had satiated). In fact, the moral incentives were often paired with aversive stimuli—deprivation of, and long lines and waits for, goods and services—and thereby directly counterconditioned. This arrangement causes the socialist conditioned reinforcers to lose rather than gain power as effective stimuli, resulting in feelings of deprivation, anger, and apathy. Thus, we next turn to a discussion of reinforcer potency.

Reinforcer Potency in Socialist Arrangements

When social and economic conditions are highly noxious and marked by deprivation, the primary reinforcers offered by a socialist environment are powerful. Socialism immediately removes aversive stimulation and reorders priorities to produce positive stimuli; food, shelter, medical care, educational and employment opportunities, social services, and the termination of pain and gross deprivation are likely to become available in a relatively short time. Of course, a strong case could be made that socialism in Eastern Europe—unlike in the Soviet Union—did not develop internally because of abysmal socioeconomic circumstances, which did exist at the end of World War II (Berend & Ranki, 1985) but, rather, was imposed from an external source for political reasons. However, from a behavior analytic perspective, the source of socialism is of limited importance, since the more fundamental phenomenon is that the primary reinforcers provided by socialism do not appear to be sufficient to maintain behavior over long periods of time. Thus the Soviet Union's internally impelled socialism produced problems comparable to those experienced by the Eastern European countries (cf. Aganbegyan, 1988; Gorbachev, 1987; Lamal, in press). Part of the reason that these reinforcers lack long-term potency, often couched in terms of "human nature," is that people "want more out of life." In behavioral terms, this is a problem of satiation: once basic needs are met, the primary reinforcers lose their potency because of repeated acquisition. The maintenance of behavior then requires a wide variety of continually changing secondary (conditioned) reinforcers. These include leisure activities, services, and material goods, as well as the verbally mediated stimuli commonly thought of as values and praise.

Socialism does provide access to a limited array of cultural, artistic, recreational, and spiritual reinforcers (e.g., Heinrich, 1986). But many other conditioned reinforcers are unavailable: spacious living accommodations, diverse food, money for nonessential goods and services ("discretionary spending"), extensive travel, professional education, and often, high-probability behaviors (Premack, 1965)—such as diverse artistic, intellectual, religious, and political expression. Consequently, individuals living under socialism experience satiation to the available reinforcers and come to feel unmotivated and deprived. These feelings will be exacerbated if they have learned to value many potential secondary reinforcers (which they in fact will, as discussed later), yet are provided the opportunity to acquire only a very limited number of them. (And even when a valued secondary reinforcer is obtained through a sanctioned mechanism, it is usually under conditions of unpredictability and tremendous delay, which of course weakens the reinforcer's capacity to strengthen desired behavior.) Although this may be the only way the state has adequate resources to meet the basic needs of the entire populace, many persons nevertheless will experience the arrangement as nonreinforcing or even aversive. This outcome will be associated with emotional responses like frustration, anger, and depression, and is likely to prompt undesirable responses such as aggression, avoidance, and helplessness (see Chapter 12).

Socialism's reliance on moral incentives, social reinforcement, and primary reinforcers might be sufficient in a highly controlled, isolated society. But the postmodern world, through travel, education, and the media, incessantly exposes citizens of socialist states to the incredible array of potentially available secondary reinforcers. Thus, through direct and vicarious conditioning processes, people in developing countries learn that a vast range of goods and services are theoretically available and apparently desirable. This, of course, seriously compounds the problems of restricted reinforcement and satiation, and leads to a black market through which many of the officially unavailable reinforcers can be acquired (Heinrich, 1986; Kornai, 1986; also see Chapter 4). Thus, even in controlled socialist environments, many potent secondary reinforcers exert control over behavior; those environments, like all industrialized ones, are enriched to a large extent.

The endowed milieu of the postmodern industrial state confronts socialism with an additional difficulty: a given rate of reinforcement will support a lower response rate in an enriched environment as compared to a barren one (Herrnstein, 1970). Thus, the ability of socialist values and basic primary reinforcers to control responding is only partially dependent on their strengths as conditioned stimuli; they must also be contingently related (which the primary reinforcers are not) to behavior in a relatively barren or highly controlled environment. However, since industrialized societies offer their citizens an enriched, loosely structured setting, many reinforcers beyond those that are officially sanctioned are either available or potentially available. Herrnstein's hyperbola may provide a behavior analytic clue as to why socialism emerged in nonindustrialized, barren environments (such as Russia and China, contrary to Marx's [1906] prediction), and why it is not working well today in industrialized states. The lack of systematic control intrinsic to industrialized (enriched) environments means that unending secondary reinforcers will be conditioned and functionally introduced into the environment, making what Marx (cf. Cohen, 1978) called "commodity fetishism" inevitable.

The multitude of secondary reinforcers is not the only effect of modernity with which socialism must contend. In addition, regardless of the extent to which any modern state achieves control over behavior, whether through aversive or positive means, that control will be inadequate to restrict the emission of a wide range of behavioral variants and also be too limited to prevent the contingent reinforcement of some of those variants. (Glenn [1988] observes that industrialization—through "revolutions" in the development of energy sources that increased labor efficiency, contraceptive devices that permitted family planning, and job requirements that demanded complex skills—established conditions of "reciprocal behavioral contingencies" between the governors and the governed. One manifestation of this was "some degree of economic countercontrol" by a large middle class. When industrialization prompted the information transfer "revolution," via travel, education, and the media, the ability of the governors to restrain such economic countercontrol was further diminished, this time to the level of functional impotency.) A certain proportion of those behavioral variants will be behaviors not functionally related to or, more important, even inconsistent with, socialist values. This observation leads us to a consideration of response selection.

Response Selection in Socialist Systems

The performance of a response is a function of, among other things, the contingent relationship of the response to meaningful (effective) consequences. The final form of the response develops through the process of shaping, or response differentiation. One of the more intriguing ways of conceptualizing this process was provided by Staddon and Simmelhag (1971), who proposed that all organisms have a large repertoire of behaviors that could be emitted in any particular situation. The principles of behavioral variation determine which response is emitted before the acquisition of reinforcement and include such factors as inherited behavioral tendencies, level of deprivation (motivation), generalization effects from previous experiences in similar situations, and respondently conditioned stimuli. The principles of selection primarily involve reinforcement: when the initial variant does not produce reinforcement, another is emitted, and so on, until one "works." Thus, in Staddon and Simmelhag's view, shaping involves the elimination of ineffective responses until an adaptive one is found. Among other phenomena, this perspective fits well with the observed increase in behavioral variability when an organism is placed on an extinction schedule; the selected response, no longer effective, is abandoned and alternative responses emitted in a new (but futile) attempt to acquire the reinforcement.

Staddon and Simmelhag's analysis enlightens the discussion of socialism in the following way. Socialism limits the range of permissible work behaviors in the interest of the commonweal, relying on rules, social reinforcement, and moral incentives. But this relatively compulsory response selection mechanism is unlikely to be effective in an uncontrolled environment. On the contrary, the principles of variation suggest that the emission of "capitalistic" responses will be highly probable since deprivation exists and the rudimentary variants of such responses are likely to be present through previous experience (e.g., within the family) and observation of compatriots and foreigners. Once emitted, the principles of selection predict that these behaviors will occur repeatedly in those situations where the responses produce potent reinforcement. Their frequency is likely to increase as other variants decrease and further stimulus generalization occurs. Thus, individuals in socialist countries rapidly learn to emit black market and other capitalistic behaviors that acquire unsanctioned but desired reinforcers. As persons learn that capitalistic responses produce reinforcement in increasing numbers of situations, the frequency of "socialist" behaviors will decrease. Further, response generalization will occur: repeated experience will encourage diverse response topographies that all retain the essential functional characteristic.

The sensitivity of humans to the consequences of their behavior suggests that capitalistic initiatives will be high probability responses. Although a case could be made that such responses have attained this status throughout history (cf. Rakos, 1988b), we need only analyze the contemporary environment to see that such responses will achieve that standing today.

The high probability of capitalistic responses is ensured by the modern world with its pervasive and varied means of information transmission. Widespread formal education, television and written media that cross functionally artificial political borders, and increased travel expose citizens of socialist states to countless behavioral variants, many antisocialist and/or capitalist in nature. Technology itself enables humans to emit countless new behavioral variants that produce new reinforcement. As behavior repertoires expand and new reinforcers are introduced, the likelihood of capitalistic responses increases. For example, the convenience of microwave cooking is a new behavioral variant and the microwave oven itself is a conditioned reinforcer made possible by technology. But since behavior is chained in long sequences, the ability to perform the microwave cooking response will be functionally related to the emission of prior behaviors in the chain. In the initial microwave chain, a person must first emit the responses necessary to acquire the microwave; in socialist countries, this will almost certainly be a black-market response.

To summarize, it is likely that individuals in socialist environments will gradually, or perhaps rapidly, learn to emit capitalistic responses, regardless of the point in history in which they live. But the postmodern technological environment increases the probability dramatically.

Of course, there will be some individuals in this situation who do not enter the black market or emit other countercontrolling responses. These are likely to be persons for whom the state-imposed controls are effective; in other words, their response variants are restricted and their exposure to information is limited. These individuals are influenced by the antecedent stimulus control exerted by government, but they are not necessarily responsive to the moral incentives promulgated by the state. In fact many of these individuals emit only the minimum behavior necessary to acquire the sanctioned reinforcers (i.e., show up for work). This response pattern is just as inappropriate from the socialist perspective as capitalistic noncompliance. We might characterize these individuals as exhibiting "learned helplessness" (Seligman, 1975; see also Chapter 12). When aversive consequences cannot be alleviated by any response, the organism ceases behavioral effort and passively endures the noxious stimulation.

Thus, for most people in socialist societies, passive behavior or alternative unsanctioned responses are likely to emerge. Noticeably absent are active countercontrolling responses that might alter the contingencies (see also Chapter 4). In effect, the socialist contingencies teach the individual that the state and state policies (the bureaucracy) are discriminative stimuli associated with nonreinforcement or extinction (S^{Δ}). We now turn to a discussion of the stimuli that guide responding.

Stimulus Control in Socialist Societies

The contingent relationship between a response and a reinforcer introduces a third element, thus forming the three-term contingency. This is the discriminative stimulus (S^d), encompassing the salient features of the environment that are present when the response produces the reinforcer. The discriminative stimulus is thus a learned cue that sets the occasion for the response. It is a predictive stimulus: in its presence, the response is likely to lead to the consequence. As noted earlier, the socialist bureaucratic structure is an S^{Δ}, predicting that a response will not produce the reinforcement and therefore setting the occasion for no response or a response to an alternate S^d.

Behavior control in socialist systems, relying as it does on verbally mediated values and social reinforcement, in effect involves rules and rule-governed behavior (Skinner, 1971). Rules are S^ds that identify the contingent relation between response and reinforcer. To oversimplify, socialism asserts the rule that "appropriate" behavior is good because it is consistent with ideologically defined communal interests and will produce abundant social reinforcement and adequate (but limited) material reinforcement. However, in a socialist world the rules and social consequences still compete with unrestricted material reinforcers and their associated S^ds for control of behavior. Rules are powerful stimuli that can render behavior insensitive to actual contingencies (Catania, 1984; Cerutti, 1989; Hayes, 1989), but only under certain circumstances. Inaccurate rules, general rules, and extended contact with direct contingencies are factors that weaken rule-governed behavior (Hayes, Brownstein, Haas, & Greenway, 1986; Hayes, Brownstein, Zettle, Rosenfarb, & Korn, 1986). These variables generally characterize rules in the socialist system and thus seriously undermine their potency, possibly resulting in the primacy of contingency-shaped behavior.

The relative weakness of socialist rules as controlling stimuli can be further appreciated through a discussion of the matching law, which asserts that organisms on concurrent schedules of reinforcement distribute their responses relative to the rate, delay, magnitude, and potency of reinforcement for each alternative (Catania, 1984). In a classic experiment by Rachlin and Green (1972), pigeons invariably responded to the stimulus associated with an immediate, albeit small, reinforcer, and eschewed the stimulus associated with a delayed but much larger reinforcer. Rachlin and Green also demonstrated that conditions easily could be arranged to induce the pigeons to exhibit self-control by responding to the stimulus associated with the larger delayed reinforcer about two thirds of the time. But the problem for socialism is that its delayed reinforcers are not larger or otherwise more potent than those immediately available for capitalistic responses. Quite to the contrary, the socialist reinforcer is not only delayed but, as discussed earlier, it is also significantly less powerful. Thus, socialist rule-governed behaviors, placed as they are on concurrent schedules with capitalistic contingency-shaped behaviors, are unlikely to be emitted frequently.

The discriminative stimuli associated with the acquisition of material incentives are learned from several sources. One, of course, is direct experience within the socialist environment. However, S^ds may also be learned through observation in travel, education, and the media. Finally, stimulus generalization will expand the influence of S^ds to an increasing number of circumstances.

In addition to discriminative stimuli, other types of stimulus control exert influence that weakens the socialist rule-governed behavior. Establishing stimuli, which arrange conditions that increase the reinforcing value of a stimulus, have increased in visibility as information transfer becomes common. Furthermore, many establishing stimuli are products of technology. The microwave in your kitchen is an S^d for cooking a certain way, one that is reinforced with rapidly (and deliciously?) prepared foods. But microwave technology is an establishing stimulus for wanting rapidly prepared foods; before the development of the microwave, individuals had little or no desire for such rapid preparation. It is through establishing stimuli that the envy of capitalistic lifestyles originates.

Finally, stimulus equivalence classes, the foundations of symbolic behavior, may play a critical role in social and economic behavior. Money is generally conceptualized as a generalized reinforcer, but it also could have another function. Its power could lie less in its direct reinforcement potency and more in its ability to form symmetrical and transitive equivalence classes with numerous goods and services and thus become symbolically equivalent to specific commodities and ammenities. Furthermore, money, via the material and service reinforcers it can acquire and with which it therefore is associated, can also form an equivalence class with the concept of behavioral freedom. In fact, it is possible that, through transitive relations (i.e., money/behavioral freedom, behavioral freedom/

democracy), money and democracy are equivalent concepts, suggesting that the demands for democracy in Eastern Europe in 1989 were in reality demands for money and material reinforcers.

THE CONTINGENCY OF REINFORCEMENT
CONTROLLING WORK BEHAVIOR:
THE HUNGARIAN EXAMPLE

The preceding analysis of the COR encompassing work behavior under socialism can be appreciated further through discussion of a concrete example. Hungary is the focus here because its experimentation with socialism has attracted widespread attention, providing the data for and interest in such an exercise.

The metacontingency underlying central planning in any socialist system is most concerned with producing the long-term outcomes of state authority and social equality. Soviet-style socialism also mandated that industrial production meet continually increasing quotas. Until 1968, Hungary attempted to produce these outcomes by exercising direct control over work behavior and industrial procedures through detailed production, supply, and investment plans, allocation of material resources, and wage and price indicators (Heinrich, 1986). These measures were seen as the core of the process that would select the COR encompassing high-quality work behaviors maintained by abundant primary reinforcers, limited secondary reinforcers, moral incentives (i.e., socialist values), and social reinforcement. As described earlier, this was not the behavioral contingency selected. Instead, a distinctly more capitalistic COR emerged to control the behavior of many individuals (i.e., the black market), whereas a learned helplessness (minimal work) COR was selected for others. Consequently, Hungarians experienced official production levels that were consistently inadequate, resulting in persistent shortages of consumer goods (Kornai, 1986). Therefore, in 1968, Hungary introduced the New Economic Mechanism, a program designed to shift economic behaviors from direct state control to "state guidance" through a series of so-called temporary indirect measures. These included fiscal and budget policy changes, price and wage limits, credit and tariff policy alterations, and preferential direct investments (Heinrich, 1986; Nove, 1983). In essence, the policies were altered to institute a new metacontingency intended to produce the long-term outcome of increased economic efficiency and increased production. State authority and social equality goals remained essentially unchanged. Nevertheless, even this loosening of central control failed to select CORs of workers that resulted in efficient and increased industrial production, despite a new contingency that permitted workers to receive up to 15% of their salary as a bonus related to the profit earned by their enterprise—but with no penalty if the enterprise lost money (Nove, 1983). In Hungary's "first economy," official work behaviors that contributed to the industrial output remained minimal.

The modest impact of the initial attempt to directly link work behaviors with consequences suggests that the potential reinforcer (15% bonus) did not empirically function as a reinforcer. Furthermore, the socialist metacontingency still selected the capitalistic COR, characterized by the emission of high-frequency profit-making responses, or the learned helplessness COR, distinguished by a generally depressed rate of on-task behavior.

State authorities recognized the reality of the situation, prompting the ruling

Hungarian Socialist Workers Party (HSWP) to introduce sweeping new regulations in 1981 at its Twelfth Congress. In essence, these reforms were designed to implant a new metacontingency that would result in the cultural outcome of economic efficiency through improved utilization of untapped labor and initiative "in harmony with the common interest" (as the HSWP phrased it, Heinrich, 1986, p. 147). This had the effect of producing a second economy, characterized by expanded behavioral options and contingent response-consequence relationships. Henceforth, small business and private enterprise would have broad freedoms through the elimination or loosening of restrictions on the quality and quantity of production, capital investment, and employment ceilings (Heinrich, 1986). These changes were modeled after earlier successful ones implemented in the agricultural sector (Berend & Randi, 1985). In essence, through the establishment of hard budget constraints and the opportunity to earn profits, it was hoped that a COR for sanctioned entrepreneurial behavior would be selected. This COR would then contribute to economic efficiency, as measured by goods and services of increased quantity and variety and production methods resulting in increased abilities to develop new products and modify old ones.

Individuals participating in the second economy had two major options. They could work in one of several arrangements that combined public and private entrepreneurship or they could engage in business as a completely private entity.

The public-private combinations were organized in one of two ways (Heinrich, 1986; Kornai, 1986). Small cooperatives consisting of 15–100 persons could be formed by state employees, who then leased fixed capital from the state for a specified cost. Cooperatives had harder budget constraints than state-owned enterprises. They were typically involved in catering businesses and various trades (Kornai, 1986). Professional cooperative groups, specialized units with independent financial status within an existing cooperative, were also organized.

Alternatively, economic work communities (EWCs) could be formed. These groups consisted of 2–30 employees who functioned as private entrepreneurs yet worked under the protection of the state employer, and paid rent for use of the enterprise's fixed assets. In effect, an EWC ran a private business using state facilities (Heinrich, 1986). Principal activities included maintenance, repair, construction, cleaning, painting, other services, and production (e.g., cutting, casting, tool making). By 1984, 5,800 EWCs existed, employing 60,000 individuals. Although half the EWCs were involved in production, their impact on output was minimal (Heinrich, 1986). One major reason for the inefficiency was that, again, the socialist COR was still not selected by the metacontingency; much of the EWC work was accomplished during state working hours. As an official review committee noted in 1984, "the problem of separating work for the factory and for the EWC is still waiting for a solution . . . the manual workers frequently start their better paid EWC job during working hours" (Heinrich, 1986, p. 148). Thus, in effect, a problem observed to result from the first economy metacontingency was still evident in the "second economy" metacontingency: workers continued to engage in private, illegal work during state hours using state equipment.

The second economy also permitted individuals to engage in completely private business, though they were required to apply to the state for approval (Heinrich, 1986). Individuals leased unprofitable, state-owned restaurants, food stores, and small shops. They paid the state a fixed rent but otherwise were completely independent. For example, the private business had to acquire its own tools and raw materials, often through negotiation of supply contracts with state enterprises (Berend & Ranki, 1985; Heinrich, 1986). These businesses could hire up to three workers, employ as many as six family members, and train a maximum of two apprentices. Other private businesses included "after job work" such as taxi services using private cars and maintenance services such as plumbing, carpentry, and mechanical repair (Berend & Ranki, 1985).

Estimates suggested that approximately 170,000 individuals engaged in officially sanctioned private enterprise in the second economy (Heinrich, 1986). Service accounted for 55% of the economic return, with construction contributing 30–35% and commodity production the remaining 10–15%. Sixty percent worked privately fulltime, 29% as a second job, and 11% were pensioners (Heinrich, 1986). Overall, 16% of the labor hours, 33% of the national income, and 40% of personal income were realized in the second economy (Berend & Ranki, 1985). Since a significant progressive income tax only began when annual income exceeded 200,000 forints, which was about four times the average state worker's income, the COR encompassing sanctioned private enterprise was further strengthened.

The data suggest that economic efficiency, the socially planned outcome of the second economy, was partially achieved. The availability of goods and services increased significantly, but there was little growth in productivity, possibly a result of uncontrollable external circumstances (Nove, 1983). However, additional consequences also were evident. For example, though employment remained virtually full (Nove, 1983), other effects threatened the desired social equality (common good); income disparity grew (Nove, 1983), public criticism was directed toward private business people because of the higher prices they charged, and work hours for private entrepreneurs (and often their family members) greatly exceeded those permitted in the state sector (Heinrich, 1986). In addition, the state lost tax revenue because of an underreporting of income on an estimated 62% of returns (Heinrich, 1986). These individual and cultural outcomes are common when capitalistic CORs control work behavior.

The second economy produced both social benefits and concerns. Despite its loosening of behavioral restrictions and expansion of reinforcement opportunities, the metacontingency continued to select profit-making CORs. The potency of the capitalistic COR is most evident in what had been called Hungary's third economy, otherwise known as the black, illegal, or informal economy (Berend & Ranki, 1985; Heinrich, 1986; Kornai, 1986). The black market existed because the capitalistic COR was selected by the metacontingencies established for the first and then the second economies, despite intentions to the contrary. Interestingly, the cultural outcome of the black market apparently was judged to be desirable, since the illegal behaviors were approved, patronized, encouraged, or tacitly tolerated more often than prosecuted by the state (Heinrich, 1986). In fact, regulations were introduced in an attempt to legalize and expand those unplanned contingencies judged to be useful in producing goods and services of high quality. The unofficial but real acceptance of these activities, despite the fact that an application for a permit was not submitted to the state, taxes were not paid, and private capital was illegally used to generate income through nonsanctioned work, suggests that efficiency and mass consumption were powerful and desirable cultural consequences.

The behaviors of the third economy involved service delivery in the intellectual, material, and housing realms (Kornai, 1986). Intellectual services, for which no numerical estimates are available, included those offered by architects, dentists, lawyers, physicians, engineers, translators, typists, and child care workers. Doctors, for example, demanded large sums for their services, yet the percent of patients admitting they paid for medical care despite the availability of free treatment rose from 38% in 1980 to 60% in 1983 (Heinrich, 1986). Material services included general handy work, repair work (e.g., cars, clothing, and telecommunication instruments), painting, construction, and the transport of people and goods. Approximately 400,000 people provided services in housing construction, maintenance, and repair (Kornai, 1986). In fact, almost 50% of first and vacation homes were constructed unofficially, and private capital financed about 65% of the work (Heinrich, 1986). Finally, lodging services were provided by approximately 200,000 individuals, often to tourists but also to others on long-term bases (Heinrich, 1986; Kornai, 1986).

The third economy was characterized by the practice termed *csuszopenz,* or "sliding money" quickly over a counter or desk. Attempts to reduce this "bribe economy" were rendered unsuccessful by the state's inability to offer acceptable alternatives (Heinrich, 1986), or in many cases, any alternatives (Kornai, 1986).

The third economy, directly exemplifying the capitalistic COR, produced an outcome diametrically opposed to the outcome planned by socialist metacontingencies. Instead of each citizen obtaining services of equal quality in his or her turn, the economically powerful obtained reinforcers of higher quality more quickly. Janos Kadar, the First Secretary of the Central Committee of the Hungarian Socialist Workers Party until mid 1988, recognized this in his address to the Party's Thirteenth Congress:

> It is a social necessity and a justified claim that the economic tasks in all production spheres be met primarily during official work hours and only then. I should like to add that there is a work and social aspect to this problem: the working people must be able to create the necessary material basis for life during official working hours (quoted in Heinrich, 1986, p. 151).

Kadar recognized that the first and second economies did not provide this cultural outcome as they were then organized—hence, the toleration of the third economy and capitalistic behavioral contingencies. This unique mix of systems, sometimes referred to as "Kadarism" (Gomulka, 1986), provided for three separate cultural outcomes, each related to a set of economic practices: the first economy produced a basic level of equality and security, the second resulted in somewhat increased production, and the third developed the means and ends of mass consumption and efficient service delivery. Thus, in reality, Hungary in the late 1980s established three distinct metacontingencies that formed a relatively stable society under the political conditions existing in Europe until 1989. When Gorbachev permitted the Hungarians to choose the metacontingencies governing their state, however, they quickly abandoned those that produced the first and second economies and simultaneously sanctioned and expanded the one related to the third economy. The Hungarians made clear and unambivalent judgments of the relative value of various cultural outcomes. It is of interest to note that the adoption of a general capitalist metacontingency has rapidly produced the associated and apparently inevitable cultural outcome of significant unemployment ("Hungary's Economic Reforms," 1989).

Contingencies of Reinforcement in Hungary that Interlocked with the Worker's COR

Metacontingencies select the interlocking behavioral contingencies that comprise a cultural practice. Therefore, to expand the behavioral analysis of socialist central control, this section will briefly examine the contingencies of reinforcement that emerged to control the behavior of Hungarian planners and managers.

The intended cultural outcomes of state authority, social equality, and increased production meant that planners were responsible for issuing directives detailing what and how much should be produced and who (which workers) should do the producing (Nove, 1983). Directive-issuing behavior was maintained by a rich array of social and material reinforcers bestowed by the governing politicians for output that achieved the goal. Since "success indicators" had to be expressed in quantifiable terms, plan goals were expressed in units of measurement: tons, square meters, number of items, and so forth (Nove, 1983). However, goals were rarely achieved, not only because of the poor work productivity discussed earlier, but also because of inevitable fragmentation inherent in running a large industrial state. Thus, efficiency was constrained by the numerous departments involved in production in a complex industrial state and by local interests (Nove, 1983). Most products are in reality a mix of products, necessitating that success indicators be aggregated.

In the Soviet Union of the early 1980s, there were about 12 million "disaggregated" products, but "only" 48,000 plans; " in other words, the *average* 'product' which is the subject of a plan-instruction is an aggregate of 250 sub-products" (Nove, 1983, p. 73). Under such circumstances, goals will be met (and hence reinforcement obtained) only when quantity of outcome is great. Since the quality of, and consumer demand for, a product were irrelevant criteria, the cultural outcome of this mechanism was large tonnage or high numbers of product units of dubious desirability (Nove, 1983). Furthermore, waste was encouraged, since targets expressed in tons encourage the use of the maximum amount of materials and those expressed in currency prompt the use of expensive materials (Nove, 1983). Hence, the COR selected another behavior of the planners. Ministry officials competed viciously for the allocation of centrally distributed resources to enterprises under their aegis (Heinrich, 1986). The outcome of this process formed the basis for shortages: large numbers of undesired or unneeded inferior quality goods were produced. Nevertheless, despite this cultural outcome, the behavior of the planners was maintained by stable behavioral contingencies that produced intermittent reinforcement.

The New Economic Mechanism introduced in 1968 attempted to alter the metacontingency selecting these behavioral contingencies for planners. The material allocation system was discontinued and plan targets became indicative rather than obligatory, except for certain areas such as energy and transport. However, the new rules embodied in the NEM metacontingency were weak and led to the selection of competing behavioral contingencies, resulting in inconsistent application of policy. As Nove (1983) observes, "there were many cases of direct central intervention, including ad hoc subsidies, directions to deliver to specific customers (e.g., to Comecon partners under bilateral agreements), and limits placed on imports and on co-operative enterprise" (p. 123). Thus, when the dramatic changes were introduced in 1981, central control was fundamentally constrained. Planners, to be reinforced, now had to use indirect mechanisms to positively influence production. For example, with prices decentralized, planners informally restrained price rises through consequences to managers, such as promotion and dismissal and the granting of necessary permits and authorizations (Heinrich, 1986; Nove, 1983). Additionally, the banking system assumed more importance for planners. Although the creation of new enterprises, major projects, and social services remained within the direct purview of the center, investments related to production were decentralized. Nevertheless, planners could encourage specific investments by making loans and credits easily available for projects judged to be in the national interest (Heinrich, 1986; Nove, 1983). Thus, after 1981, the behavioral contingencies selected for planners resulted in central guidance rather than central control.

The CORs guiding the behavior of managers can be similarly analyzed. The initiation of the NEM had minimal impact on some of the contingencies of reinforcement governing their behaviors: for example, instead of bargaining over plans (i.e., attempting to secure nondemanding goals [also see Lamal, in press]), they bargained over credits and subsidies (Heinrich, 1986). On the other hand, the economic reform drastically altered other contingencies. For instance, managers assumed increased responsibility for production, earning huge bonuses (up to 80% of their salary) when profits accrued and suffering significant salary reductions (20%) when losses were incurred (Nove, 1983). This led to widespread income disparity and worker dissatisfaction, leading to major modifications of the dispensation of bonuses. After 1981, when central guidance was the policy, the contingencies controlling managers' behaviors were, as noted, less direct. Managers could still earn some bonuses related to profit, but the control exercised by decentralized prices assumed greater importance. Very large profits were viewed with disfavor; promotion and dismissal and approval of required permits and applications were contingently related to internal business decisions. Additionally, managers experienced strong monetary sanctions in the form of supplemental taxes if wage increases exceeded recommended guidelines (Nove, 1983). Further, investment decisions were constrained by the planners' influence over the banks' approval of credits and loans (Nove, 1983). But a soft bottom line remained, and enteprises showing losses were rescued through subsidies or other measures. Thus, managers' business decisions produced consequences, both positive and negative, of modest import. This contributed to the cultural outcome of the first economy under the NEM: somewhat increased production, the maintenance of state authority, and a measure of social equality (e.g., full employment). However, the restraints on positive and negative consequences ensured that production increases would be modest and still too inflexible to meet rapidly changing technological innovations and consumer preferences. Hence, the NEM also introduced the cooperatives and private enterprises that came to comprise the second economy.

CONCLUSION

Metacontingencies are established or emerge within very broad environmental influences or, in Nove's (1983) term, "externalities." Hungary, for example, is a country that lacks abundant supplies of raw materials, particularly the fossil fuels and iron ore essential for industrial output. It is landlocked and dependant on foreign ports for exports and imports (Heinrich, 1986). Other externalities include changes in global economic conditions. Hungary's reliance on agricultural exports was undermined by significant decreases in agricultural prices in the past few decades (Heinrich, 1986). Exposure to Western markets and their manufactured goods increased the competitive pressure on Hungary's own industrial output (Gomulka, 1986). The worldwide inflation that increased dramatically after 1973 produced a large differential between internal and external prices (Nove, 1983). In the late 1970s, worsening trade terms suppressed Hungary's aggregate production and forced the government to increase retail prices faster than wages (Nove, 1983).

These externalities interact with the economic metacontingencies in two ways. First, they may directly undermine the intended cultural outcome, as when bilateral trade agreements, inflation, or trade terms affected Hungary's industrial output. Second, they may increase the likelihood of associated undesired outcomes. Hungary's severe pollution problems are an example of this effect. The reliance on agricultural exports, necessitating widespread use of artificial fertilizers containing nitrates, resulted in severe water contamination. Poor quality domestic fuels and the use of coal instead of expensive imported oil, as well as the large increase in the number of automobiles, has led to poor air quality characterized by high sulphur content that produces acid rain and soil (Heinrich, 1986). "Internalities," it must be noted, have also contributed to pollution. Waste disposal and recycling procedures in Hungary are technologically inadequate for the huge amount of garbage and hazardous waste produced by industry and agriculture, a problem exacerbated by attempts to increase profits. In fact, CORs supporting polluting behaviors were directly selected by the Hungarian economic metacontingencies, as fines were significantly less than purification expenses (Heinrich, 1986).

Of course, externalities, interactions between metacontingencies and externalities, and undesired tangential outcomes of metacontingencies are not unique to socialist systems. Capitalistic countries, for the same or similar reasons, pollute their environment comparably. It is because of the increasing number of externalities in the postmodern world that some degree of social planning is essential; in fact, an argument could be made that national planning without international planning is meaningless since, for example, pollution knows no political boundaries.

But the question raised by the analysis of Soviet-style socialism in Eastern Europe relates to the form and extent of such planning rather than to its necessity, since the laissez-faire capitalism to which Marx reacted no longer exists (Nove, 1983). On a large scale, the authoritarian society of Singapore may be closest today to laissez-faire capitalism; occasionally, small communities such as La Jolla, California, embrace unbridled capitalism within the constraints imposed by the larger society (McCord, 1989). Both capitalist and socialist countries have undertaken vigorous experimentation over the past decades. Denmark and the other Scandinavian nations developed the "social welfare state" but consequently experienced difficulties with production and motivation (McCord, 1989). Yugoslavia experimented with self-management "communism" directly linked to incentives and market forces, producing distinct positive outcomes and numerous negative ones that are difficult to interpret because of "externalities" and nationalistic friction (McCord, 1989; Nove, 1983). Cuba, as noted earlier, implemented its rectification program, relying on voluntary work behavior consequated primarily by moral rather than material incentives (Ulman, 1989).

It is too soon to assess the success of rectification, but several issues are worth raising. First, Cuba is a relatively small, somewhat isolated country of only 10,000,000 inhabitants who, because of periodic waves of emigration of the discontented (Mesa-Lago, 1981), now constitute a fairly homogeneous population. Such a circumstance may provide fertile ground for behavior control through social reinforcement and other moral incentives (Nove, 1983; Rakos, 1989), but has little applicability to most modern nations. Second, the true test of rectification will come when the Soviet Union discontinues its massive subsidies (Brundenius, 1984; MacEwan, 1981; Mesa-Lago, 1981), which likely mask problems of industrial inefficiency (cf. Farber, 1990). And third, the range of potential problems is presently unknown. The current volunteer system requires that workers put in long hours: 6-day work weeks, 14-hour work days, 8-hours of voluntary labor on alternate Sundays, and "emergency" 24-hour shifts are held up as models (Hillson, 1990). The net benefits of this regimen compared to capitalist ones are not obvious. Further, workers who perform poorly and fail to respond to the collective's discipline are not tolerated (Hillson, 1990), but the social consequences of such solidarity are also unclear.

Even observers on the left have great reservations with the "rectification" program. For example, Farber (1990) contends that "(p)olitically, it has entailed a fierce repression of the small human rights movement that had been given a breathing spell during 1987–1989. Economically, it has resulted in a reassertion of Stalinist policies with a Guevarist-Maoist twist: a bureaucratic centralized economy, practically no private economic activity by Cubans, the primacy of so-called moral incentives, and no room for trade union independence or any other form of working-class autonomy from the state" (p. 484).

No system is perfect; indeed, the search for utopia on earth uncovers what we all suspect: the perfect society does not exist (McCord, 1989). But we, of course, must continue to search for the best compromise between the ideal goods and the necessary evils. Pragmatism is likely to be the ideology that guides that search. And in the postmodern world—one that is functionally shrinking because of information transfer—our task will be to balance the humane with the human. Capitalism, in so many ways, is not humane, but as my behavioral analysis implies, it is thoroughly human. Socialism, on the other hand, is clearly humane, but a scientific analysis suggests it is not really human.

There is no resolution to this paradox at present, but the continued scientific analysis of human behavior offers us the greatest opportunity to uncover one. Our task, as Skinner (1971) emphasized, is to design a culture that will survive, and more than that, will survive because it meets the needs of people—a society that is, in other words, both humane and human. To do this, we will have to abandon political ideology and replace it with a commitment to analyze society from the scientific perspective of behavioral analysis. Should we undertake this task, we may find a way to design a society that—despite inevitable inequalities—provides each individual with diverse and satisfying reinforcers well beyond the minimum required for subsistence, an environment wherein numerous desired reinforcers are attainable as a consequence of the emission of productive on-task behavior. Skinner (1971) has argued that "presumeably, there is an optimal state of equilibrium in which everyone is maximally reinforced" (p. 119). Writing about the real world rather than *Walden Two* (Skinner, 1948), he abandoned his utopian vision of an optimal state where everyone is equally reinforced. It is time we follow suit.

REFERENCES

Aganbegyan, A. (1988). *The economic challenge of perestroika.* Bloomington, IN: Indiana University Press.

Berend, I. T., & Ranki, G. (1985). *The Hungarian economy in the twentieth century.* New York: St. Martin's Press.

Brundenius, C. (1984). *Revolutionary Cuba: The challenge of economic growth with equity.* Boulder, CO: Westview Press.

Catania, A. C. (1984). *Learning* (2nd ed.). Englewood Cliffs, NJ: Prentice-Hall.

Cerutti, D. T. (1989). Discrimination theory of rule-governed behavior. *Journal of the Experimental Analysis of Behavior, 51,* 259-276.

Cohen, G. A. (1978). *Karl Marx's theory of history: A defence.* Princeton, NJ: Princeton University Press.

Farber, S. (1990, October 29). Isolation case: No more Soviet aid for Cuba? *The Nation,* pp. 482-485.

Glenn, S. S. (1986). Metacontingencies in *Walden Two. Behavior Analysis and Social Action, 5,* 2-8.

Glenn, S. S. (1988). Contingencies and metacontingencies: Toward a synthesis of behavior analysis and cultural materialism. *The Behavior Analyst, 11,* 161-179.

Gomulka, S. (1986). *Growth, innovation and reform in Eastern Europe.* Madison, WI: University of Wisconsin Press.

Gorbachev, M. (1987). *Perestroika: New thinking for our society and the world.* New York: Harper & Row.

Hayes, S. C. (1989). *Rule-governed behavior: Cognition, contingencies, and instructional control.* New York: Plenum.

Hayes, S. C., Brownstein, A. J., Haas, J. R., & Greenway, D. E. (1989). Instructions, multiple schedules, and extinction: Distinguishing rule-governed from schedule-controlled behavior. *Journal of the Experimental Analysis of Behavior, 46,* 137-147.

Hayes, S. C., Brownstein, A. J., Zettle, R. D., Rosenfarb, I., & Korn, Z. (1986). Rule-governed behavior and sensitivity to changing consequences of responding. *Journal of the Experimental Analysis of Behavior, 45,* 237-256.

Heinrich, H. G. (1986). *Hungary: Politics, economics, and society.* Boulder, CO: Lynne Rienner.

Herrnstein, R. J. (1970). On the law of effect. *Journal of the Experimental Analysis of Behavior, 13,* 243-266.

Hillson, J. (1990, June 8). Cuba: A new way of organizing labor. *The Militant,* p. 11.

Hockenos, P. (1990, April 18-24). Hungary's free election defrosts long-latent nationalist tendencies. *In These Times,* p. 9.

Hungary's economic reforms introduce many to poverty. (1989, March 24). *The Cleveland Plain Dealer,* p. 10-A.

Kornai, J. (1980). *Economics of shortage. Volume B.* Amsterdam: North-Holland Publishing Co.

Kornai, J. (1986). *Contradictions and dilemmas: Studies on the socialist economy and society.* Cambridge, MA: MIT Press.

Lamal, P. A. (1984). Contingency management in the People's Republic of China. *The Behavior Analyst, 7,* 121-130.

Lamal, P. A. (in press). Three metacontingencies in the preperestroika Soviet Union. *Behavior and Social Issues.*

MacEwan, A. (1981). *Revolution and economic development in Cuba.* New York: St. Martin's Press.

Marx, K. (1906). *Capital I.* Chicago: Charles H. Kerr & Co.

McCord, W. (1989). *Voyages to utopia: From monastery to commune, the search for the perfect society in modern times.* New York: W. W. Norton.

Mesa-Lago, C. (1982). The economy: Caution, frugality, and resilient ideology. In J. I. Dominiguez (Ed.), *Cuba: Internal and international affairs* (pp. 113-166). Beverly Hills, CA: Sage.

Morrow, J. (1988). Is socialism flawed? *Behavior Analysis and Social Action, 6,* 23-24.

Nove, A. (1983). *The economics of feasible socialism.* London: George Allen & Unwin.

Premack, D. (1965). Reinforcement theory. In D. Levine (Ed.), *Nebraska Symposium on Motivation.* Lincoln, NE: University of Nebraska Press.

Rachlin, H., & Green, L. (1972). Commitment, choice and self-control. *Journal of the Experimental Analysis of Behavior, 17,* 15-22.

Rakos, R. F. (1988a, May). Metacontingency analysis of Hungarian society. In J. Morrow (Chair), *Contingencies of reinforcement in noncapitalist countries.* Symposium conducted at the annual meeting of the Association for Behavior Analysis, Philadelphia.

Rakos, R. F. (1988b). Capitalism, socialism, and behavioral theory. *Behavior Analysis and Social Action, 6,* 16–22.

Rakos, R. F. (1989). Socialism, behavioral theory, and the egalitarian society. *Behavior Analysis and Social Action, 7,* 23–29.

Rakos, R. F. (in press). Behavior analysis of perestroika. *Behavior and Social Issues.*

Seligman, M. E. P. (1975). *Helplessness.* San Francisco: W. H. Freeman.

Skinner, B. F. (1948). *Walden Two.* New York: MacMillan.

Skinner, B. F. (1971). *Beyond freedom and dignity.* New York: Bantam/Vintage.

Staddon, J. E. R., & Simmelhag, V. L. (1971). The "superstition" experiment: A reexamination of its implications for the principles of adaptive behavior. *Psychological Review, 78,* 3–43.

Ulman, J. (1988). Just say no to commodity fetishism: A reply to Rakos. *Behavior Analysis and Social Action, 6,* 25–31.

Ulman, J. D. (1989). Beyond the carrot and the stick: A behaviorological rejoinder to Rakos. *Behavior Analysis and Social Action, 7,* 30–34.

Waters, R. (1990, June). After the party. *Mother Jones,* pp. 17–21.

6

Organizational Behavioral Analysis in the United States: Public Sector Organizations

William K. Redmon and Leslie A. Wilk

INTRODUCTION

The products of day-to-day performances of individuals sum to define an organization's accomplishments. Without explicit direction from overall objectives to guide collective achievements, performances may be "unlinked" from ultimate purposes and fail to contribute to planned outcomes. Even when objectives are set and individual performances are linked to objectives in effective ways, one must still determine if the objectives describe valuable outcomes for the culture outside the organization. Thus, in general, effective organization management requires that two questions be answered: (1) What should be accomplished by organization members?; and (2) What is the value of accomplishments for survival of the organization? Recently some have suggested that these questions can best be answered by adopting analytical methods that go beyond individual behavior and explicate sources of control for cultural practices. Glenn (1988) suggested that behavior analysts adopt the methods of cultural anthropologists and proposed that behavioral analyses at the cultural level be described in terms of metacontingencies. This approach will be adopted here.

For purposes of this chapter, a metacontingency exists when (1) the performance of more than one individual is the subject of study (i.e., a group), (2) consequences for the collective performance of the group are identified (i.e., events that affect the survival of the group as a whole), (3) a functional relationship between group performance and group consequences is identified, and (4) events that set the occasion for group performances (i.e., antecedents) are identified. Much like an individual operant contingency, a metacontingency requires that changes in consequences influence group performance, and that the presence of antecedents that are correlated with reinforcing consequences (adaptive outcomes for the group) increase the probability of selected patterns of response by the group.

The objective of this chapter is to describe a metacontingency analysis appropriate for organizations in the public sector. As part of this process, the following will be presented: a description of consequences of organization outputs typical of the public sector, examples of intervention at the metacontingency level, extant analytical models that provide a base for further development, and specific ways of proceeding with the development of a working metacontingency model. This chapter will consider only public sector organizations. Private sector businesses differ in important ways and will be addressed in a later chapter.

CHARACTERISTICS OF PUBLIC SECTOR ORGANIZATIONS

Organizations can be categorized in terms of the sources of consequences of their outputs. As implied by the label, public sector organizations serve the public by providing services supported directly or indirectly by government agencies and funded by tax dollars (Mancuso, 1988). Thus, several important sources of consequences are obvious, including the responses of citizens who receive services, reactions by government committees and departments who arrange funding or oversee services, and the actions of the legal system that regulates services and mediates consumer complaints about public entities. In contrast, in the private sector, consumer purchases and market competition directly affect profitability and ultimately are the most critical influences in long-term survival (see Lynn, 1981 for a complete discussion of these issues).

Public sector organizations serve all who qualify for their services. In some cases, this means that service recipients must live within a geographical boundary (e.g., city, state, etc.); in other cases, it means that recipients must meet service criteria (e.g., 65 years of age or older, demonstrate physical disability, etc.). Private sector organizations survive by selling services or products to other businesses (wholesale) or the public (retail); their financial livelihood depends on the direct response of the consumer in the marketplace, and financial profitability is their central objective. In private sector organizations, consumer involvement is seen as a means to an end in that the needs of customers must be considered to survive. In the case of public sector organizations, documentation of consumer involvement is necessary to demonstrate effectiveness, (e.g., number of citizens served); however, involvement with governmental funding sources and regulatory agencies is critical in obtaining needed revenues (Wolf, 1984). For example, public utility rates are set by Public Service Commissions; however, utility companies must present evidence of customer satisfaction before a rate increase is permitted. Similarly, mental health agencies serve clients directly; yet they receive funding from government sources that require that they respond to the requirements of funding agencies (e.g., evaluation reports, budget planning, maintenance of appropriate client records) and provide a minimum level of services.

Private sector organizations also maintain direct control over financial resources generated by profits, whereas public sector operations are not profit-based. Thus, flexibility in use of financial consequences (i.e., change in salary, bonuses) is constrained within public organizations that have little control over this important source of employee motivation.

Exceptions to this division do exist. Private sector organizations may be either profit or nonprofit; and some may provide services like those offered by state and federal agencies (e.g., education, mental health treatment, etc.). However, in such cases, government agencies function as buyers through purchase of services contracts and seldom fund entire organizations year to year as they do with state and federal agencies. Thus, the contingencies that apply to private nonprofit organizations are more like those of the private than public sector.

ORGANIZATIONAL BEHAVIORAL ANALYSIS

Most applications of behavioral analysis in organization settings have been done in the fields of Organizational Behavior Management (OBM) and Performance Management (PM). For purposes of this chapter, we will refer to both areas as Organizational Behavioral Analysis (OBA). OBA is reputed to have begun in the late 1970s when principles used in designing programs in psychiatric treatment were extended to staff management. Since that time, hundreds of applications have been undertaken with considerable success. Over the past 10 years, OBA research studies and applications have been about equally divided across public and private sectors (Balcazar, Shupert, Daniels, Mawhinney, & Hopkins, 1989). However, most of these interventions have been done at the individual-worker level and have focused on day-to-day performances controlled by immediate environmental events. They have not, for the most part, considered the performance patterns of large numbers of individuals across long time periods (O'Hara, Johnson, & Beehr, 1985). A comprehensive behavioral analysis of the organization (private or public) has yet to emerge from our extensive study of individual work performance.

METACONTINGENCY APPLICATIONS IN OBA

Although few applications in OBA have included metacontingency analyses, several have incorporated, directly or indirectly, elements of this approach and have strived to achieve large-scale outcomes that analyze the events that affect the combined contributions of many individuals. Samples will be described here to illustrate how metacontingencies operate in public sector settings and to serve as the basis for discussion of factors important to development of cultural behavioral analysis. Interventions from three areas of the literature will be sampled: staff management in mental health settings, admissions management in universities, and management in municipal government. These examples represent a cross-section of recent programming at the metacontingency level in the public sector and depict common demands placed on public sector organizations by governmental agencies and consumers.

Example Programs

Mental Health Agencies

Mental health agencies have as their central objective the treatment of problems in living presented by citizens in their catchment areas. Serious problems are treated on an inpatient basis, whereas prevention and treatment for less serious problems are provided in community living environments and outpatient clinics. Historically, the mental health treatment system in the United States began with hospital treatment of mental illness for those who could pay for the services and provided little treatment for the poor or working classes (early 19th century to mid 20th century). However, after WW II, several trends began that would change the entire face of this system (Bloom, 1984). First, the use of drugs to treat mental illness led to the release of thousands of patients who were capable of living independently. Second, patients and staff became involved in the design and management of treatment systems. Third, treatment agencies were decentralized so that patients could be closer to the support of families and local communities. This gradual shift from inpatient care to more community-based care led the Joint Commission on Mental Illness and Health in 1961 to recommend systematic changes to improve mental health treatment. Later, the recommendations of the Commission led to new legislation that created a formal community-based mental health treatment system (Community Mental Health Centers Act, 1963). This act required that states and local authorities provide a full range of essential services ranging from prevention to inpatient programs.

In the 1980s local involvement was increased when a new system of funding for mental health services emerged in the form of the community block grants, which were awarded to state and local governments by federal sources (Bloom, 1984). This program required that local authorities determine how funds were spent and that local agencies design and implement mental health service systems. Emphasis on community-based treatment and local control of resources in mental health treatment led to a proliferation of decentralized, community-based services that shifted the control over mental health services away from centralized federal agencies and toward local citizens and governments.

The historical trends just described allow an analysis of the developing mental health system at the metacontingency level. As services have become decentralized and control more localized, public sector mental health services have come under closer scrutiny. Increased pressure has been manifested in several major areas. First, with the ever increasing federal deficit and emphasis on cost control, mental health agencies have been targeted for decreased spending (Williams, 1981). Second, community control has led to increased emphasis on consumer needs, which often are not addressed adequately by centralized service systems (Christian & Hannah, 1983). Third, more consumer demands for services have led to legal challenges that have influenced mental health agencies in the form of common law (precedents built through court cases) and implementation of federal policies via the courts (Martin, 1975). Finally, as cost controls have increased, regulation by government has also intensified. Agencies must meet increasing demands for reporting and verification of their compliance with policies to be eligible to receive federal funds such as Medicaid or Medicare (Fernald, 1986).

Such influences have led to increased emphasis on effective management of mental health programs and especially management of staff and resources to produce effective treatment programs within reasonable budget constraints (for a discussion of productivity in mental health see Duggan, 1983). Over the past 10 years, this gradual movement toward improved treatment practices has led to numerous behavior management programs that have targeted motivation and management of treatment staff in inpatient hospitals and community agencies. Most OBA interventions in mental health have targeted productivity in inpatient settings such as psychiatric hospitals or training centers for people with developmental disabilities. These environments have been the subject of attention for the most part because of historical deficiencies in effective treatment and emphasis on restrictive treatment practices (e.g., seclusion and restraint). In these settings, and others, ineffective programs and unproductive staff translate into unnecessary institutionalization and excessive costs.

In early OBA studies most researchers targeted very specific outcomes relevant to individual facilities or patients. For example, Quilitch (1975) used performance feedback to increase the frequency of submission of suggestions by mental health employees in a state-supported treatment facility. This study targeted staff morale and communication, which were assumed to help solve important problems in service delivery. Several treatment problems were reported to have been solved as a result of staff suggestions. A similar study was done by Kreitner, Reif, and Morris (1977) in a psychiatric hospital where a performance feedback intervention was used to affect three aspects of the treatment system: (1) frequency of group therapy sessions, (2) frequency of individual therapy sessions, and (3) completion of daily duties. Large improvements in staff performance were noted in all three areas after the feedback program was introduced. Later studies followed a similar pattern. Prue, Krapfl, Noah, Cannon, and Maley (1980) provided feedback on performance to aides in a large psychiatric hospital and found that their program increased the extent that staff interacted with patients and produced other unanticipated positive effects (e.g., more staff conversations about treatment issues). Unfortunately, early research rarely extended interventions to multiple environments to affect large numbers of staff and patients or paid more than scant attention to survival goals of the organizations within which data were collected. And most studies involved only isolated tests of individual contingency management with small numbers of staff.

In this context, recent studies have begun to expand the scope of analysis. For example Parsons, Cash, and Reid (1989) carried out a normative evaluation of the "extent and quality" of services delivered in residential service agencies in 22 states. Normative data indicated that institutionalized persons routinely spent two thirds of their time in living units engaged in activities that had no functional value. These authors then designed a comprehensive management system to address this problem and evaluated the outcome in five living units for an extended time period. The results indicated that problems typical of hundreds of treatment units could be solved in ways that left durable and effective programs in place after an initial intervention. Specific target behaviors were defined in terms of client activities that promoted functional skills (i.e., those necessary for independent living). A management system was designed to improve the extent to which staff implemented daily treatment programs. The management system included: clear specification of daily activities to be carried out, assignment of a specific staff role to each employee (described in written form), staff training in implementation of client programs, and supervisory monitoring and feedback to ensure that appropriate staff behaviors were noticed and encouraged. This program was implemented in a facility that included 165 clients in five living units and a complete staff on each unit, including direct care workers and supervisors.

The study by Parsons et al. is a model for large-scale implementation of OBA procedures and provides an example of an analysis at the metacontingency level. First, success is defined in terms that are important to consumers and to regulatory agencies who influence or provide funding. The consequences that were identified were characteristic of the public sector and important to survival of an entire agency or service system (i.e., funding-related). Second, the measures of performance combined individual outputs and defined success at the level of the agency rather than for individual staff members. Third, the program applied a management system made up of elements that could be applied in a variety of similar settings over an extended period of time under realistic conditions. In fact, the program was maintained over an extended period with 110 direct-care staff, 165 residents, and 10 assistant supervisors. Finally, the procedures of the program were described in a way that facilitated its use by others in different agencies (i.e., appropriate agency-level antecedents were developed). Most importantly, Parsons et al. reported evidence of a functional relationship between agency-level performance and outcomes critical for survival. The changes produced by the management program led to improved reviews by the Medicaid office; two reviews following the use of the system reported no "decertification risks" and included a commendation for the new system.

A similar program was implemented by the same research group in schools that served the needs of the severely handicapped (Parsons, Schepis, Reid, McCarn, & Green, 1987). As in the study described earlier, large-scale relevance was established by completing a normative study in 43 classrooms to establish the generality of needs addressed by the intervention. Additionally, an intervention program was designed to influence the functional skills of students through better management of staff performance across several schools and classrooms. Finally, this program was tested over an extended period of time. The results indicated that functional task involvement increased in 21 classrooms across 4 different schools and that the improvements were maintained for at least 2 years. However, unlike the mental health intervention described earlier, no functional relationship between changes in client performance and consequences important to organization survival were described (e.g., public satisfaction, reactions of funding sources or regulatory agencies, etc.).

Universities

U.S. colleges and universities are now facing the greatest decline in high school students in history (Breneman, 1983), and admission management teams are seeking ways to maintain enrollments at survival levels. Changing demographics, shifting student career interests, intensifying competition, and scarcity of college financial aid resources are among the concerns currently plaguing enrollment managers (Kellaris & Kellaris, Jr., 1988; Knight & Johnson, 1981).

Most strategies have emphasized marketing and public relations and have not addressed the performance of administrative, recruiting, or clerical staff members. In this regard, Rogers (1989) has suggested that admissions team building strategies that target philosophy, hiring, training, and performance can solve many pressing admissions problems. Areas such as selection, training, and retention of admissions support staff also have been considered in recent years (Hartnagel, 1986; Snyder, 1989).

These problems have been addressed through programs such as pep talks, changing computer systems, hiring part-time help, information sharing, career development, providing employee recognition and instituting mandatory overtime for all employees during peak processing months. Unfortunately, although typical strategies have emphasized general performance factors, they have failed to assess directly the impact on the number of students recruited from a shrinking market. The relationship between internal interventions and success in the marketplace has been assumed, but not treated explicitly. Regardless of the immediate effects of management programming, state-supported universities require enrollments sufficient to justify funding by state governments and to obtain tuition funds to supplement endowments or appropriations.

Recent OBA studies have adopted an approach that targets staff performances that directly affect recruiting success: "first response" strategies. First response refers to the speed with which universities respond to student applications. Schools that respond quickly are assumed to hold an advantage in that students often accept the first offer that they receive. In this context, Wilk and Redmon (1990) described a staff productivity management program for university admissions personnel that was designed to decrease response time in processing new applications. The management program included a daily goal setting and feedback program that was administered with admissions processors whose speed of response determines turnaround time. In the initial study, the operations supervisor met individually with each of four processors at the beginning of the work day and set goals for type of tasks and quantity of work to be done. Twice during the day, the supervisor checked the performance of each employee to determine if work was within the range specified by the morning goals. If performance was consistent with goals, praise was delivered; corrective feedback was given in cases where performance was not adequate. The results led to large decreases in turnaround time and a 300% increase in productivity within the unit, leading to greater success in achieving "first response" status.

Before, during, and after the program, the speed of response of the admissions unit (i.e., time from receipt of applications to notification of student of admission status) was monitored. Over a period of 2 years, the response time decreased from several weeks to a maximum of a few days. Enrollment also increased substantially during the period of the program. This system was later applied in a larger university with 10 times the staff with similar results (Wilk, 1990). Other universities have contracted for implementation of the same intervention in an effort to increase their competitiveness in the market. Thus, the patterns developed have been shown to be replicable across different settings and individuals.

The program implemented by Wilk and Redmon (1990) represents a metacontingency analysis in several ways. It incorporated a goal that was relevant to the survival of the organization and communicated the cultural requirements to groups of workers on the front lines in an effective and frequent manner. Additionally, the program improved services to constituents of the university, and apparently led to better chances for survival in financial and political terms. Systems like that examined in the Wilk and Redmon study translate the demands of the environment, in this case the public, into requirements for systems and finally, into individual performance standards. In doing so, individual patterns are prescribed because of their value in producing resources for the system. Furthermore, new workers who are employed by the system are trained in the procedures of the system and are assimilated into environments that occasion repeatable response patterns that define the practices of the work culture.

Unlike the mental health program applied by Parsons et al. (1989) described earlier, the Wilk and Redmon program did not determine precisely the functional relationship between the outcomes of the management program and survival (i.e., enrollment increases). Although enrollment increased during the time of the program, it was unclear whether a functional relationship between the management program and the increase existed. Enrollment also increased in other universities that did not use the program during the same time period. Certainly, improvement in first-response status was assumed to be linked to successful recruitment; however, no definitive proof for this connection was presented. This raises a critical problem in metacontingency analyses; functional relationships between large-scale changes over extended periods and survival-related consequences may be difficult to discern. Unlike individual behavior-consequence relations that occur in a relatively brief period under limited circumstances, organization practices are subject to myriad influences.

Municipal Governments

Municipal governments operate extensive service networks and must secure sufficient support and fees from constituents to maintain functioning systems (e.g., sewers, water, streets, etc.). Survival in government requires that leaders and staff members maintain contact with community members and respond to their needs. Nordstrom, Lorenzi, and Hall (1991) reported an intervention within the Codes Division of a midwestern city of 1.5 million. The Codes Division had been plagued by productivity problems and low morale. In fact, these authors reported that the lack of productivity had attracted the attention of the public and threatened to undermine the credibility of the entire department. Thus, change was mandated by public pressure occasioned by publicity regarding misuse of resources, poor productivity, errors, and other problems.

The Codes Division employed 160 people and included 32 managers. The authors designed a training program to improve the management practices of all levels in an effort to improve productivity throughout the division. Managers were trained to apply behavioral principles to employee problems by carrying out projects under the supervision of professional trainers. Training included three components: classroom instruction, behavior change projects, and incentives for effective use of the projects by managers to solve problems.

An acceptable project included several elements: (1) behaviorally defined performance, (2) systematic intervention, and (3) graphed data. Project length ranged from 2 weeks to 11 months. All projects were evaluated in terms of a change ratio (CR) designed by the authors. To calculate the CR, mean performance level before intervention was divided into a mean performance level after intervention. Thus, for example, in a study that produced a mean baseline level of 15% appropriate behavior and 30% after baseline, the CR would be 2.0. The best projects were recognized publicly by the division administration and time off was provided for the winning managers. Exemplary managers also were recognized in the city newsletter.

Nineteen projects were completed (involving from 1–20 employees). Some targeted the performances of department employees; some targeted independent contractors; others focused on the behaviors of management peers. Specific behaviors that were pinpointed included: greeting customers, thanking customers, answering phones promptly, number of inspections completed per day, number of errors in logs, safety, timely deliveries, and others. Typical interventions included: performance feedback from supervisors, daily instructions, graphic feedback, goal setting, correction of incorrect responses, and small tangible incentives. All CRs exceeded 1.0 and 50% were greater than 2.0, indicating that overall the programs were very successful across many different employees, managers, and behaviors.

The city government projects represent a metacontingency intervention in that they focused on multiple small changes designed to influence the overall functioning of a large division. Additionally, the behavior patterns of many different managers and workers were affected by the interventions in ways that would be repeatable in other government offices. Unfortunately, like many other OBA programs, no explicit relationship between project success (changes in practices) and organization improvement (organization consequences) was reported. Only passing mention was made of the effects of the interventions on the public relations problems that led to the program in the first place.

Other OBA Public Sector Examples

In addition to the previously mentioned examples, other recent issues illustrate success and failure of OBA interventions at the metacontingency level in the public sector.

Geller (1990a) lamented the fact that years of behavioral study of environmental protection (e.g., reduction of littering, energy conservation, recycling, car pooling) have led to little lasting effect on cultural practices. In spite of the effectiveness of low-cost behavioral strategies, they have not been adopted on a large scale, and support for them by public institutions is practically nonexistent. Geller maintained that a lack of "government, corporate, and societal support" was responsible and that we should shift our strategies away from isolated research and theorizing to those that promote the influence of our work on the larger culture. Although he did not use the term "metacontingency," Geller's recommended approach is similar to Glenn's (1988) metacontingency analysis.

To describe specific strategies, Geller asked several colleagues who had been active in environmental protection research to identify the reasons for failure and to recommend action for improvements. One theme ran through all of their responses: behavior analysts have failed to influence the public to support and adopt their technology. Some who responded to Geller's request pointed out that we did not publish news of our work in the public media; others indicated that we did not coordinate our efforts as a group, and thus, had little influence on government agencies that might have adopted behavioral programs.

In general it is clear that such efforts were not developed with an eye toward public appeal or its agencies and thus produced few outputs of value at the cultural level. Unlike the examples presented earlier in mental health, government, and universities, which were designed to produce outcomes that affected survival immediately (i.e., funding, reduced complaints from the public, increased enrollment), much of the environmental protection research of the 1970s was done to demonstrate the power of behavioral techniques and not to encourage large-scale adoption of these methods. Cultural behavioral analysis requires that programs lead to a change in important cultural-level consequences and that the relationship between these outcomes and repeated patterns of behavior by cultural members be arranged.

One positive example is that of safety belt promotion. Geller (1990b) described his success in getting large corporations to adopt safety belt promotion campaigns and reported extensive success in saving lives and preventing injuries through this effort. Others have reported similar successes in this area. For example, Rogers, Rogers, Bailey, Runkle, and Moore (1988) arranged for three Florida state agencies to adopt a safety belt promotion strategy that included the use of personal commitments to use safety belts and dashboard sticker prompts on state cars. The results led to a reduction in workers' compensation claims for the agencies involved. In these cases, however, efforts were made to devise effective strategies and to influence important organization-level outcomes (e.g., profits, insurance claims, etc.).

Safety belt promotion programs that have been successful on a large scale have utilized effective individual contingencies (e.g., use of prizes, time off, etc.) and organization-level outcomes that are produced by the collective actions of individuals. Such programs are more likely to lead to adoption by the organizations involved and to develop a cultural practice that continues and supports the change in individual contingency management as an integrated part of long-term functioning.

ISSUES RELATED
TO PUBLIC SECTOR ANALYSES

All of the examples presented thus far addressed metacontingencies to some degree. They all focused on overall outputs of a collection of individual members in an organization. Individual performance was changed as a means of influencing a general organizational outcome, which improved the chances of survival. In these cases and others like them, changes in the performance patterns of one or two individuals would do little to accomplish the goal of the intervention. Only large-scale performance changes could produce success. Furthermore, in all of these cases, the projects were continued over an extended period (i.e., more than one year) and thus cut across changes in personnel, minor policies, environmental conditions, and other individual factors.

In terms of the criteria for metacontingencies, all of the programs cited earlier targeted an organization outcome that was critical for survival. In the Parson's et al. (1987) program, compliance with regulations that affected funding (i.e., Medicaid rules) were targeted. Wilk and Redmon (1990) attempted to improve first-response position in university recruiting because of the assumed relationship between this factor and student matriculation. Nordstrom and colleagues (1991) assisted managers in improving efficiency in a large-scale effort designed to overcome poor publicity and a history of ineffective action in a city government division. Geller (1990b) and Rogers et al. (1988) promoted individual seat belt use, which had economic implications for private and public sector organizations.

Also as pointed out earlier, many OBA applications have either ignored organization-level outcomes or treated them only in passing. Most have focused on individual performance changes and immediate influences of these changes on the functioning of a department or unit. Several issues probably interfere with implementation with programming at the cultural level and reduce the chances that published reports of metacontingency interventions will appear in the literature. We will consider three of these problems here, including (1) scope of influence required, (2) maintenance of intervention components, and (3) separation of contingency elements in time.

Scope

To produce changes that are important to the survival of an organization or culture, many different individuals must be influenced in effective ways. Thus, one must control important motivating events at the top levels of organizations and arrange for these changes to influence groups of individuals through the usual means of control. Unfortunately, as Balcazar et al. (1989) pointed out, most OBA studies have targeted change at the line worker level and only a handful have implemented programs at the executive level. Thus, our technology has been tested and tried at the lower levels where the scope of influence is usually too small to produce changes important to the survival of large groups of people.

Maintenance

Large-scale influences are achieved over long periods with sustained effort. Furthermore, cultural practices are likely to be shifted only when the consequences of adopting new practices make the shift worthwhile. A program that produces improved outcomes at the organization or cultural level is likely to be maintained. One which produces effects at the individual level only, no matter how powerful, is not likely to be supported by governments, public organizations, coalitions, or institutions long enough to have a lasting effect. The examples described earlier illustrate limited OBA success in this regard. However, Balcazar et al. (1989) indicate that most studies in the field do not report data on continuation or maintenance of effects.

Temporal Relation Among Contingency Elements

Unlike immediate contingencies that often operate with simple behaviors and individual actors, metacontingencies involve relationships among events that may be separated by long time periods. Changes in practices may be followed by changes in outcomes, but only after a period of time has passed. Thus, the relationship between management changes (e.g., performance feedback to employees) and their results (e.g., increased consumer satisfaction) may not be discernible by common means.

Malott (1988) addressed this issue and suggested that cultural influences may be controlled by "indirect acting" contingencies rather than "direct acting" ones. Indirect acting contingencies involve consequences that are too delayed or too improbable to influence behavior directly, such as long-delayed organization changes that follow individual behavior patterns. Direct-acting contingencies include those where antecedents and consequences occur in close proximity to behaviors that are changed. According to Malott, behavior analysts could improve their effectiveness at the cultural level by developing a better understanding of indirect acting effects so that we could better bring about change in metacontingencies. Unfortunately, little work has been done in this area.

EXISTING BEHAVIORAL MODELS OF CULTURE

Although no behavioral model appropriate for analysis of cultures has been developed, several candidates have been described by OBA researchers; and some have been used in practice. These attempts can be used to form an historical base for further development of the metacontingency analyses. Three models of this type will be described, including Behavioral System Analysis (Krapfl & Gasparotto, 1982), the Performance Engineering Matrix (Gilbert, 1978), and the Total Performance System (Brethower, 1982).

Behavioral Systems Analysis (BSA)

BSA was derived from a combination of systems analysis and behavioral analysis and incorporates the following critical elements: (1) identification of organiza-

tionally significant outcomes, (2) emphasis on complex contingencies of reinforcement and punishment, and (3) use of the complex contingencies to study the effects
of behavior of the individual on organization outcomes. BSA borrows concepts
from traditional systems analysis and behavioral analysis and combines them into a
model that can be used to analyze entire social systems. A behavioral system
includes inputs, processes, outputs, and feedback loops. Inputs consist of resources needed by the system to operate (e.g., raw materials, money, etc.). Processes include the actions taken to transform the inputs into outputs (e.g., the
delivery of therapy to a client). Outputs are the finished products that are consumed by those who receive services or buy products from an organization and
must be of sufficient value to obtain resources to energize the inputs and maintain
the system. Feedback includes information or resources that result from the output
which, in turn, influence processing and/or inputs. Feedback permits the system to
make adjustments to improve the viability of outputs and increase the chances of
survival. Figure 6-1 presents a diagram of a simple performance system.

Performance Engineering Matrix (PEM)

The PEM depicts an organization in terms of six levels of generality including
philosophical, cultural, policy, strategic, tactical, and logistics (see Table 6-1).

Philosophy describes "ideals" that transcend specific cultures and goals and are
statements about what "should be." At the cultural level, goals are described and
give meaning to performance. At the policy level, models for implementing cultural goals are established and include mission statements. At the strategic level,
objectives for individual jobs or roles are described. Tactics describe day-to-day
duties of individuals. Finally, logistics refer to resources needed to carry out tasks.

Although Gilbert (1978) described all six levels, he ultimately reduced the
working model down to three: policy, strategic, and tactical. These three comprise
the abbreviated version of the PEM. The most apparent use of the PEM is to
describe outcomes at each of the levels so that they are linked together and provide
a purpose at more general levels for specific tasks and activities at more specific
levels. Gilbert recommends that models, methods, and measures be specified at

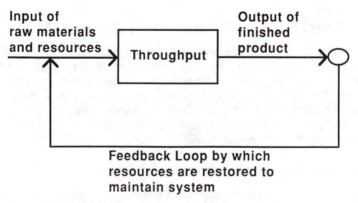

Figure 6-1   Diagram of an organization as a system.

Table 6-1 Description of levels included in the performance engineering matrix based on Gilbert (1978)

Level of vantage	Description
Philosophical	Ideals that state philosophy of life
Cultural	Goals of culture within which organization resides
Policy	Statement of purpose of organization in terms of mission
Strategy	Roles of members of organization required by jobs
Tactics	Duties and responsibilities of members
Logistics	Resources required to carry out tasks

each level so that outcomes can be implemented and evaluated. Methods include programs, procedures, and operations that are used to produce accomplishments that meet important objectives. For example, a program might specify that employees should be recognized for producing high quality manufactured tools in a metal-working plant (i.e., establish a quality culture). In this case, the program that provides recognition based on quality is an incentive method, whereas the data used to set criteria for quality awards and to track quality of outputs serve as a measure. Both relate to a model that identifies high quality as a critical accomplishment for the organization.

Total Performance System (TPS)

Brethower (1982) maintains that organization functions can best be described in terms of a system that depicts organization processes and outputs and the reaction of the environment to the outputs. He termed this model a Total Performance System (TPS). A TPS includes six major elements, many of which are borrowed from traditional systems analysis: input, processing system, output, receiving system, receiving system feedback, and processing system feedback (Brethower, 1982). These elements are depicted in Figure 6-2.

Input, processing, and output are similar to that of BSA described earlier. However, the TPS adds to BSA specialized feedback loops important to long-term survival. The receiving system consists of those who "receive" and use outputs. Receiving system feedback involves contact with consumers to learn about their reactions to the outputs. For example, a university might interview employers of its graduates or the parents of students to determine their levels of satisfaction with the skills of graduates. In this case, the parents and employers would be part of the receiving system and their satisfaction with the skills of their children or employees would be termed "receiving system feedback." Processing system feedback is internal to the system and represents a check on the output before it is delivered to the receiving system. Processing system feedback permits the organization to make midstream corrections in its outputs to increase the chances that they will be accepted by the receiving system. Processing system feedback is much like an internal quality control loop, where the standards are matched to those of the receiving system. In the example of the university, internal standards for graduation, course grades, and other immediate outcomes might be set to match those demanded by employers of graduates. These internal checks on outcomes increase the chances of eventual success in the environment outside the organization and allow correction of ineffective actions early in the process.

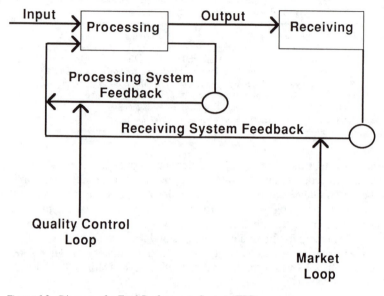

Figure 6-2   Diagram of a Total Performance System (TPS).

In all three of the systems described, individual performances are monitored and measured. However, the importance of individual behavior is defined by relevance to the overall objective of the system. For example, in the PEM, tactical-level performances must be related to job outputs, and job outputs must be related to the mission of an organization before one can know how to change performance in beneficial ways. Furthermore, if policy-level measures are monitored and found to be lacking, one can "troubleshoot' the system by working down to jobs to identify contributors to the problem and then to tactics to identify specific performances that may be lacking.

The three models presented in this chapter incorporate elements of a cultural analysis on which future refinements can be based. They all relate well to the concept of metacontingency as described earlier in this chapter and by Glenn (1988). In all cases, explicit reference is made to the mission or organization-level objectives and to the relationship between these outcomes and individual work. Furthermore, all emphasize context and the relationship between a functioning performance system and the environment in which it must operate. This is handled most explicitly by the TPS, where the role of the consumer or receiving system is formally treated as part of the system and the connection between the processing system and the receiving system is depicted clearly.

Unfortunately, references to the TPS or PEM in the OBA literature are practically nonexistent. Only one such study has appeared in the *Journal of Organizational Behavior Management* (Brethower & Wittkopp, 1987). Most descriptions of the steps to be followed in OBA interventions (Brown, 1982; Daniels & Rosen, 1974) begin with pinpointing a target behavior and proceed to measurement, intervention, and evaluation, totally omitting consideration of the relationship between pinpointed performance and important organization outcomes. In some cases rules for pinpointing remind one to choose only behaviors that are important, but guidelines for making this choice are not given. More explicit methods of targeting behaviors that are relevant to the organization's survival are urgently needed to create "relevant" OBA interventions.

The basic OBA model could be strengthened by adding elements of the TPS or PEM to traditional procedures so that pinpoints are linked to goals important to survival at a cultural level. Both the TPS and PEM provide specific guidelines for creating such linkages and, if combined with detailed measurement and intervention techniques, could lead to a more complete cultural intervention model. Furthermore, this framework could make the relationship between individual performances and organization outcomes more explicit for workers and managers who are responsible for creating and maintaining relevant performance.

CONCLUSION

Overall, the content of this chapter provides reason for optimism. First, initial efforts in applying metacontingencies have met with some success and thus provide an impetus for future efforts. Large-scale, relevant changes in organizations have been produced with little dilution of behavioral principles. Second, existing models provide a good base for immediate extension of our current work to a full-scale behavioral cultural analysis. Third, it appears that these strategies are workable even in the public sector, where organization and culture outcomes tend to be ill-defined. Finally, an extensive base of individual behavior change methods has already been produced and can be potentiated through a model that links this powerful technology to important cultural outcomes so that intervention effects have meaning beyond immediate circumstances.

SUMMARY

The focus of this chapter has been on Organizational Behavioral Analysis (OBA) in the public sector with particular emphasis on analysis by metacontingencies. The defining features of a metacontingency were described and include the following: (1) the performance of more than one individual is the subject of study (i.e., a group); (2) consequences for the collective performance of the group are identified (i.e., events that affect the survival of the group as a whole); (3) a functional relationship between group performance and group consequences is identified; and (4) events that set the occasion for group performances (i.e., antecedents) are identified.

Major sources of control in public sector organizations were presented including the responses of citizens who receive services, reactions by government committees and departments who arrange funding or oversee services, and the actions of the legal system that regulates services and mediates consumer complaints about public entities. Examples of OBA programs in the public sector were presented to illustrate a technology of behavior management that considers both individual and organizational benefits. Examples were selected from the fields of mental health, education, municipal government, and public safety promotion.

Finally, obstacles to the development of effective metacontingency interventions and suggested analytical models were considered. The most promising of existing models are the Performance Engineering Matrix suggested by Gilbert (1978) and the Total Performance System suggested by Brethower (1982). In both cases, the coordinate roles of individual and organization are considered, creating a backdrop for future work that is compatible with a metacontingency framework.

REFERENCES

Balcazar, F. E., Shupert, M. K., Daniels, A. C., Mawhinney, T. C., & Hopkins, B. L. (1989). An objective review and analysis of ten years of publications in the *Journal of Organizational Behavior Management*. *Journal of Organizational Behavior Management, 10*(1), 7-37.

Bloom, B. L. (1984). *Community mental health: A general introduction.* Monterey, CA: Brooks-Cole.

Breneman, D. W. (1983, March). The coming enrollment crisis. *Change*, pp. 14-19.

Brethower, D. (1982). Total performance systems. In R. O'Brien, A. Dickinson, & M. Rosow (Eds.), *Industrial behavior modification* (pp. 350-369). New York: Pergamon.

Brethower, D. B., & Wittkopp, C. (1987). Performance engineering: SPC and the total performance system. *Journal of Organizational Behavior Management, 9*(1), 83-103.

Brown, P. (1982). *Managing behavior on the job.* New York: Wiley.

Christian, W. P., & Hannah, G. T. (1983). *Effective management in human services.* Englewood Cliffs, NJ: Prentice-Hall.

Daniels, A., & Rosen, T. (1984). *Performance management: Improving quality and productivity through positive reinforcement.* Tucker, GA: Performance Management Publications.

Duggan, M. (1983). *Productivity in mental health: Measuring, monitoring, motivating.* Boulder, CO: Western Interstate Commission for Higher Education.

Fernald, C. D. (1986). Changing medicaid and intermediate care facilities for the mentally retarded (ICF/MR): Evaluation of alternatives. *Mental Retardation, 24*, 36-42.

Geller, E. S. (1990a). Behavior analysis and environmental protection: Where have all the flowers gone? *Journal of Applied Behavior Analysis, 23*, 269-273.

Geller, E. S. (1990b). Performance management and occupational safety: Start with a safety belt program. *Journal of Organizational Behavior Management, 11*(1), 149-174.

Gilbert, T. (1978). *Human competence: Engineering worthy performance.* New York: McGraw-Hill.

Glenn, S. S. (1988). Contingencies and metacontingencies: Toward a synthesis of behavior analysis and cultural materialism. *The Behavior Analyst, 11*, 161-179.

Hartnagel, D. (1986). Supporting the support staff. *College and University, 61*(4), 275-281.

Kellaris, J. J., & Kellaris, W. K., Jr. (1988). An exploration of the factors influencing students' college choice decision at a small private college. *College and University, 63*(2), 187-197.

Knight, B., & Johnson, D. (1981). Marketing higher education. *Educational Record, 3*, 28-31.

Krapfl, J., & Gasparotto, G. (1982). Behavioral systems analysis. In L. W. Frederiksen (Ed.), *Handbook of organizational behavior management.* (pp. 21-38). New York: Wiley.

Kreitner, R., Reif, W. E., & Morris, M. (1977). Measuring the impact of feedback on the performance of mental health technicians. *Journal of Organizational Behavior Management, 1*, 105-109.

Lynn, L. E., Jr. (1981). *Managing the public's business: The job of the government executive.* New York: Basic Books.

Malott, R. W. (1988). Rule-governed behavior and behavioral anthropology. *The Behavior Analyst, 11*, 181-203.

Mancuso, J. R. (1988). *Mancuso's small business resource guide.* New York: Prentice-Hall.

Martin, R. (1975). *Legal challenges to behavior modification: Trends in schools, corrections and mental health.* Champaign, IL: Research Press.

Nordstrom, R. R., Lorenzi, P., & Hall, R. V. (1991). Managers in city government: Behavior training programs. *Journal of Organizational Behavior Management, 11*(2), 189-211.

O'Hara, K., Johnson, C. M., & Beehr, T. A. (1985). Organizational behavior management in the private sector: A review of empirical research and recommendations for further investigation. *Academy of Management Review, 10*(4), 848-864.

Parsons, M. B., Cash, V. B., & Reid, D. H. (1989). Improving residential treatment services: Implementation and norm-referenced evaluation of a comprehensive management system. *Journal of Applied Behavior Analysis, 22*, 143-156.

Parsons, M. B., Schepis, M. M., Reid, D. H., McCarn, J. E., & Green, C. W. (1987). Expanding the impact of behavioral staff management: A large-scale, long-term application in schools serving severely handicapped students. *Journal of Applied Behavior Analysis, 20*, 139-150.

Prue, D. M., Krapfl, J. E., Noah, J. C., Cannon, S., & Maley, R. F. (1980). Managing the treatment activities of state hospital staff. *Journal of Organizational Behavior Management, 2*, 165-183.

Quilitch, H. R. (1975). A comparison of three staff-management procedures. *Journal of Applied Behavior Analysis, 8,* 59–66.

Rogers, M. E. (1989). Building a winning admissions team. *College and University, 65*(1), 5–13.

Rogers, R. W., Rogers, J. S., Bailey, J. S., Runkle, W., & Moore, B. (1988). Promoting safety belt use among state employees: The effects of prompting and a stimulus-control intervention. *Journal of Applied Behavior Analysis, 21,* 263–269.

Snyder, D. (1989). Hiring support staff *can* be a win/win affair. *College and University, 64*(3), 300–305.

U.S. Congress, P.L. 89-105. *Mental Retardation Facilities and Community Mental Health Centers Construction Act of 1963.* Washington, DC: U.S. Government Printing Office, 1963.

Wilk, L. A. (1990). *The effects of performance feedback and goal setting on the productivity and satisfaction of clerical workers.* Unpublished doctoral dissertation, Western Michigan University, Kalamazoo, Michigan.

Wilk, L. A., & Redmon, W. K. (1990). A daily-adjusted goal-setting and feedback procedure for improving productivity in a University admissions department. *Journal of Organizational Behavior Management, 11*(1), 55–75.

Williams, J. L. (1981). Health care costs: Why should we worry? *New England Journal of Human Services, 1,* 31–37.

Wolf, T. (1984). *The nonprofit organization: An operating manual.* New York: Prentice-Hall.

7

Organizational Behavioral Analysis in the United States: A View from the Private Sector

William K. Redmon and Judy L. Agnew

INTRODUCTION

Glenn (1988) proposed that behavior analysts apply the principles of cultural anthropology, especially those of cultural materialism (Harris, 1979), in analyzing the behavior patterns of organized groups. She suggested that a model of behavioral analysis at the cultural level (metacontingencies) be developed to supplement existing approaches at the individual level (behavior contingencies). Numerous studies related to this strategy have been carried out in Organizational Behavioral Analysis (OBA) over the past 10 years in public and private sector organizations (Balcazar, Shupert, Daniels, Mawhinney, & Hopkins, 1989). And OBA is the area within the field of behavioral analysis that serves as the most likely base for development of a workable metacontingency model. This chapter will review OBA strategies used in the private sector and consider the application of a metacontingency analysis appropriate for private sector operations. Four main topics will be addressed, including the defining features of private sector organizations, a description of OBA applications in the private sector, examples of applications involving metacontingencies, and recommendations for development of a metacontingency model.

For purposes of this chapter, a metacontingency is assumed to exist when (1) the performance of more than one individual is the subject of study (i.e., a group), (2) consequences for the collective performance of the group are identified (i.e., events that affect the survival of the group as a whole), (3) a functional relationship between group performance and group consequences is identified, and (4) events that set the occasion for group performances (i.e., antecedents) are identified. Much like an individual operant contingency, a metacontingency requires that changes in consequences influence group performance, and that the presence of antecedents that are correlated with reinforcing consequences (adaptive outcomes for the group) increase the probability of selected patterns of response by the group.

PUBLIC AND PRIVATE SECTOR ORGANIZATIONS

Private sector organizations depend on profits from the consumer marketplace for their survival. Their efficiency in managing expenses and offering products or

125

services that will satisfy consumers is directly related to success. Unlike public sector organizations, the private sector is not protected from market fluctuations by government funding or political support systems. As Lynn (1981) noted, "Whatever the similarities of task, activity, or even social setting, private management is oriented toward economic performance as determined in markets, whereas public management is oriented toward the public interest as determined in political forums" (p. 114).

These differences have important implications for management strategies and especially for organization change. Public sector organizations must satisfy the public (e.g., provision of fire and police services) or client groups (e.g., mental health services), whereas private sector organizations must satisfy their customers to the extent that they will spend money to purchase products or services. In the former case, benefits accrue to the public, whereas in the latter case, the business owner reaps the benefits of success directly (Blau & Scott, 1963).

Like public organizations, private sector businesses can be defined functionally in terms of typical consequences of organization practices. Private businesses survive only if they are profitable; thus, financial outcomes comprise the most critical category of consequences. Because private organizations are concerned with financial survival, their ultimate goals are easily defined. However, to say that all private organizations exist to make money is to oversimplify the relationship between markets and businesses. Certainly, private organizations, as well as public ones, must attend to the welfare of the supporting public in the process of producing profits, and must be sensitive to the needs of customers whether they be purchasers or taxpayers who support government programs. For example, many companies in the United States attribute their success to excellence in customer service (e.g., timely delivery of products, replacement of defective products, careful consideration of customer preferences, etc.) and focus their efforts on maintaining service quality. Thus, although profits certainly must be earned to survive, these companies believe that they can best continue to be profitable by providing good service. In this context, they build training programs, incentive systems, and marketing plans around service objectives and uphold service quality as their primary mission.

Emphasis on profits leads to many practices that distinguish private from public organizations. Lee (1987) summarized several important features in this regard. First, private organizations try to minimize costs so that profit margin is maximized. Second, unlike government agencies that operate as monopolies, private organizations must survive in competitive markets; thus, they must be sensitive to changes in competition and adjust their practices accordingly. Third, demands for profitability provide managers in the private sector with more flexibility in controlling finances and personnel than those of the public sector. For example, they may terminate employees or close entire operations to control financial health, a practice applied only under the most extreme circumstances in government agencies where civil service rules dictate personnel actions.

Finally, when private businesses earn profits, they often retain these funds for use in additional development or as incentives to maintain the conditions that led to the profits initially. When employees perform in a way that increases profits, the company may reward them with performance-contingent pay. In the public sector, this relationship between performance and profits is weak or nonexistent. Public employees who perform well may not influence funding; in fact, funding may be reduced or eliminated for reasons unrelated to effectiveness (e.g., when the tax base is insufficient to fund mental health services).

ORGANIZATIONAL BEHAVIORAL ANALYSIS (OBA) IN THE PRIVATE SECTOR: AN OVERVIEW

OBA includes research and applications that have been carried out in the areas of Organizational Behavior Management (Frederiksen, 1982) and Performance Management (Daniels & Rosen, 1984). According to Kreitner (1982), the field

> . . . involves the process of making specific job-related behaviors occur more or less often, depending on whether they enhance or hinder organizational goal attainment through systematic manipulation of (1) antecedent conditions that serve as cues and (2) immediately pleasing or displeasing consequences. (p. 4)

In general, OBA includes several important elements including ongoing measurement of overt behavior, intensive study of individuals in within-subject designs and use of operant analyses to identify the causes of behavior and develop change strategies (Frederiksen, 1982). OBA is reputed to have begun in the mid 1970s when behavior management technology was extended from psychiatric treatment systems to organization management. Since that time OBA studies have been about equally divided across public and private sectors (Balcazar et al., 1989).

Private sector interventions have been described in two major literature reviews over the past 10 years. The first was done by Andrasik (1979), the second by Merwin, Thomason, and Sanford (1989). In the review by Merwin et al., a clear picture of the field is presented. Thirty-five studies were reviewed; only two directly addressed the performance of managers, whereas a majority targeted the performance of direct service or manufacturing workers (e.g., hotel employees, textile operators, fast food workers, etc.). Others targeted the performance of salespersons who worked for real estate companies, retail stores, or manufacturing firms. In spite of the fact that this review addressed private sector interventions, only about half of the studies described reported data on the financial impact of their interventions. Most of the dependent measures referred to individual worker performances such as safe practices (e.g., use of earplugs), absenteeism (e.g., number of days absent from work), stealing (e.g., number of missing products), or sales (e.g., number of contacts and follow-ups). One study that targeted manager performance measured total sales/cash shortage, whereas another focused on self-management by a small business owner.

Merwin et al. (1989) also compared the characteristics of studies considered in their review with those reviewed by Andrasik 10 years earlier. This comparison revealed an increase in the proportion of studies reporting reliability data on dependent measures, a large increase in use of follow-up measures to assess durability of interventions, and an increase in the percentage of studies reporting cost benefit data.

EXAMPLES OF METACONTINGENCY ANALYSES IN THE PRIVATE SECTOR

In spite of many improvements in OBA research over the past few years, the reviews cited earlier indicate that most studies have emphasized heavily individual contingencies and intraorganizational factors. Relatively little attention has been given to consequences important to survival of organizations in the marketplace, and few studies have linked individual outputs with culturally meaningful influences. In spite of the lack of attention given to metacontingencies, several OBA strategies appear to hold great promise in this area. The purpose of this section is to consider examples of these interventions to illustrate how they might be used as a starting point for future development of a model of organizational cultural analysis.

Before describing examples, some clarification of the defining features of a metacontingency is needed. The terms "individual contingencies" or simply "contingencies" refer to events that operate at the individual level. For example, an individual contingency includes an immediate antecedent stimulus (e.g., a supervisor assigns a task) and an immediate consequence (e.g., supervisor praise) surrounding an individual response (e.g., completion of one task). The term "metacontingency" refers to relationships between environment and behavior that operate at a more global level and includes the combined performance of many individuals within an organization (e.g., the production of a supply of products), antecedent stimuli that influence group performances (e.g., a sales opportunity in the market), and consequences relevant to an entire factory or company (e.g., earned profits for an entire product line). In this context, the terms "organizational responses" and "organizational practices" will be used to refer to the responses made by a group of individuals that are influenced by consequences important to the survival of the group (i.e., adaptive response to demands of the marketplace).

Because a metacontingency deals with the behavior of groups of people over time, the responses and outcomes are cumulative. Individual instances of behavior that are inappropriate may be reinforced and maintained in the short run, even if they are detrimental to long-term success. However, over the long term, successful organizations are those that respond in ways that satisfy the demands of the marketplace and provide products or services that meet the needs of consumers. These organizations must monitor conditions external to the organization and implement internal management programs that promote individual performances that sum to create effective general outputs.

Presented here are three common OBA applications that demonstrate how metacontingencies might be applied in organizations.

Example Interventions: Compensation Systems

For an organization to survive, individual contingencies must support behavior that will ultimately lead to the achievement of organizational goals. In theory, compensation systems are good examples of practices that align individual and organization success in that employees can be paid for production of goods and services that ultimately lead to increased profits. For example, a salesclerk is paid to sell goods to customers and the selling of goods to customers results in profits for the organization. On an individual level, selling behavior represents a response that is maintained by an hourly wage and/or commission. On a metacontingency level, the compensation system for all employees, including the salesclerk, represents a "practice" on the part of the organization that is maintained by consequences provided by the marketplace. Furthermore, the compensation system affects many individuals who currently sell products and strengthens a similar pattern for new employees who are shaped by the culture in which the compensation system is embedded.

Unfortunately many compensation systems do not align individual performances and organization benefits. Most traditional systems pay employees based on what they should do, rather than what they actually do and deliver payment based on hours worked rather than work accomplished. Traditional procedures for determining compensation involve several steps (Henderson, 1985). First, a job analysis is done for each position in the organization to identify job elements. Second, job evaluation is done whereby tasks are rated in terms of their importance to organization functions. As a result of this process, several factors, called "compensable factors," are identified and used as criteria for determining pay levels. Some examples of compensable factors include effort, skill, responsibility, and working conditions (Muchinsky, 1990). By itself, this method of determining compensation provides virtually no link between employee performance and pay. Under such conditions, a person who holds a position that includes important compensable factors will be paid a large wage regardless of how well the tasks are completed or whether they are completed at all.

To supplement content-based compensation systems, many organizations attempt to factor in productivity through routine performance appraisals. Although base salary is determined by compensable factors, merit raises, bonuses, or other supplementary pay is awarded based on performance ratings. Unfortunately, many performance evaluation methods are subjective and applied infrequently, thus creating only a weak link between performance and pay. This link may be weakened further by inclusion of factors such as seniority, which have little to do with productivity (Henderson, 1985; Landy, 1989).

Although traditional compensation systems are used in most organizations, attempts have been made recently to create a stronger relationship between pay and performance by adding monetary incentives to base pay (Abernathy, 1990; Perry, 1988; Skrzycki, 1987). The motive behind this movement is not necessarily an interest in providing fairer compensation to employees, but rather an interest in increasing overall productivity to more efficiently achieve organizational goals. One way to become more competitive is to increase productivity (Mawhinney, 1986). Faster production leads to a reduction in the labor costs associated with producing each unit of product or service, which allows a company to offer products or services at lower prices. Finally, lower prices lead to increased sales and increased sales eventually lead to increased company profits.

A number of different monetary incentive programs have been applied, all aimed at increasing productivity and decreasing labor costs. However, not all of them have been successful. For example, one of the most popular incentive techniques is profit sharing whereby employees are paid a portion of company profits, usually on a quarterly or annual basis (Metzger, 1964; Henderson, 1985). Profit sharing works on the assumption that if employees have a stake in the success of the organization they will work harder to produce greater profits for the company and themselves. From a behavioral perspective, profit sharing has one major flaw—the individual contingencies that support daily performance are weak because of long delays between behavior and consequences. Furthermore, good performance may go unreinforced because of a poor relationship between company profits and individual effectiveness. Even if an employee works hard the possibility exists that, despite her good efforts, the company will not do well and no bonus will be received. Finally, even assuming that hard work will guarantee a bonus, the progression toward the bonus is slow and cumulative. Employees must work hard day after day until the cumulative effect of increased company profit eventually results in the bonus.

A second kind of incentive system, referred to as "individual monetary incentives," represents a better example of an organizational practice that arranges the conditions needed to support individual behaviors that underlie the achievement of organizational goals (Abernathy, 1990). Unlike other incentive systems, pay-for-performance programs pay employees based on performance levels. Typically, employees receive a base salary and incentives are paid in addition to base salary contingent on objective measures of productivity (Frisch & Dickinson, 1990).

Individual incentive programs differ from profit sharing in that the contingencies working at the individual level are direct-acting as opposed to indirect-acting (for a discussion of these types of contingencies, see Malott, 1988). Individual incentive pay is usually delivered with each paycheck as opposed to once per quarter or year, thus representing a considerable reduction in the delay of delivery. Furthermore, individual incentives are "probable," that is, workers are guaranteed incentive money contingent on productive behavior: if they work hard they will receive incentives; if they do not work hard, they will not. Finally, although incentives may be considered "small," each and every unit produced above a standard results in money earned. Thus pay is less dependent on "cumulative" production across extended time periods than profit sharing.

An excellent example of the effectiveness of individual monetary incentives was reported by Union National Bank of Little Rock, Arkansas. In 1987, 70% of the bank's 485 employees were on individualized incentive programs. This system represents a true organization-wide practice in that it is applied to almost all levels of employees from entry-level clerks to senior vice presidents. In general, the incentive system has resulted in 200–300% productivity improvements, which has translated into significant movement toward organizational objectives (Dierks & McNally, 1987).

The first incentive program was introduced in the proof department. Proof operators were paid based on their daily output (i.e., number of checks completed). During baseline, average performance was 1,065 checks per hour. After the introduction of incentives, performance increased to 3,500 checks per hour. When these results were published, the proof operators were earning incentives equal to 50–70% of their base salary. In addition, turnover decreased from 110% to zero, absenteeism declined from 4.24% to 2.23%, and, perhaps most significantly, the number of employees required dropped from eleven full time and three part time, to three full time and six part time. The overall savings resulting from checks being processed faster was $100,000 a year.

A second incentive system described by Dierks and McNally involved bank tellers. Performance improvements for this group included an increase in the number of new accounts sold, an increase in number of transactions processed, and improvements in daily cash outages. Since this job involved more than one task, point values were assigned for performance level on each task. Points were totaled daily, and tellers were paid incentives based on the number of points earned. Before the introduction of incentives, tellers earned an average of 32 points. After introduction of incentives, average points earned rose to 71 points. More specifically, the yearly cash outage decreased from $15,961 to $13,772, and the average hourly transaction rate increased from 17.9 to 29.5. So, while the tellers earned more money by being more productive, the bank enjoyed an increase in customer volume of 67% and was able to reduce the number of tellers required.

The proof operator and teller incentive programs are only two of the incentive systems in place at Union National Bank. Programs have been designed for all staff levels. The organizational goals achieved by these compensation systems include cost savings, the ability to attract and retain effective employees, and a reduction in the number of employees required to carry out bank business. Thus, the organizational practice of paying employees based on performance has been selected as an effective practice at the metacontingency level.

Performance-based pay systems can be linked directly to organization profit levels so that adaptive flexibility is built into incentive programs. For example, Union National Bank provided pay to individuals based on the value of their performance to the bank by calculating the value of each outcome and paying an employee a percentage of that value when the outcome was achieved. In this way, money paid out was never more than the income generated by the performance for which the pay was provided. This method protects the organization and maintains a sensitive relationship between financial incentives and income. This arrangement is not possible in most public sector organizations because income is not directly related to productivity. When funding is provided by government grants or appropriations by the legislature, budgets are set in relation to political objectives and not productivity. Thus, a public sector organization that sets up a pay for performance system may find itself with insufficient funds to pay promised incentives (for an exception, see *Performance Management Magazine,* 1990).

Other advantages of flexible compensation systems make them useful in an adaptive sense. Pay for performance programs allow an organization to adjust quickly to change in market consequences. By linking wages to productivity, organizations have more control over labor costs, and thus more "wage flexibility" (Perry, 1988; Skrzycki, 1987). In times of economic downturns, organizations can reduce production along with wages and labor costs. Although this may be undesirable from the individual employee's standpoint, the alternative may well be unemployment (Weitzman, 1984). If an organization cannot cut expenses, workers may be laid off, or the company may shut down completely. In a traditional compensation system, little wage flexibility is available in that employees are paid based on factors unrelated to productivity and organization health. (e.g., compensatory factors, seniority, etc.). Thus, reducing production will have virtually no impact on labor costs. Because pay-for-performance systems tie individual contingencies to organizational contingencies, individual consequences can co-vary with organizational consequences.

A related form of flexibility afforded by pay-for-performance programs is the ability to modify the nature of the work completed. If a change in the world economy dictates a change in organization practices, a company can quickly adjust compensation so that employees who were being paid to engage in one set of behaviors, can be paid to engage in different behaviors (e.g., those associated with a new production technique or product). Recently, experts have emphasized the necessity of this kind of flexibility in adapting to a volatile global economy (e.g., Peters, 1987).

Unions and Pay for Performance

Discussion of pay for performance inevitably raises the issue of unions. Any analysis of organizational metacontingencies in the private sector must include unions. As O'Brien (1990) notes, unions are ". . . in the best position to get groups of workers to respond as units" (p. 203). Thus, unions can influence behavior patterns, either to be more in line with the existing metacontingencies or to work against the overriding contingencies. Interestingly, the OBA field has not addressed the influence of unions. O'Brien (1990) reviewed publications in the OBA literature and found virtually no reference to unions. He reported that the *Journal of Organizational Behavior Management* has published no articles in which the word "union" appears in the title. Furthermore, major review articles and books in the field do not discuss the role of unions in performance management or compensation programming. Traditionally OBA consultants have been viewed as working for management, for the good of management, and therefore may be seen as the enemy of unions (O'Brien, 1990). Similarly, OBA consultants usually view unions as a disruptive force in their intervention attempts. Unions bring with them a set of complicated rules and may impede an organization's ability to change rapidly in response to changes in the metacontingencies.

In perhaps no other kind of OBA intervention is union resistance likely to be stronger than pay-for-performance interventions. The stereotypical response to such programs is that they are simply a vehicle for getting more work out of employees for less money. As O'Brien points out, however, unions should not resist pay-for-performance systems such as those proposed by OBA that are based on objective work measurement. Paying employees based on objective performance rather than subjective indicators should help to ensure fair representation for workers. As O'Brien (1990) noted, "Once objective data systems are in place, management can no longer reward or punish on whim. With our sophisticated measurement techniques, why shouldn't unions employ OBM consultants to design merit pay systems of their own?" (p. 203). Although the potential for abuse of incentive systems does exist, similar possibilities hold true for any effective technology. One method for avoiding such abuse is for unions and management to work together to create and maintain incentive programs that will profit both individual employees and the organization as a whole. Such cooperative behavior as an organizational practice is adaptive according to the current analysis in that it ensures the alignment of individual and metacontingencies.

Example Interventions: Supervisory Feedback Systems

Although organization-wide monetary incentive systems are effective in aligning individual contingencies and organization outcomes, they are by no means the most common method in use. Within the field of OBA, the most popular intervention has been supervisory feedback systems. Over half of the studies published in the *Journal of Organizational Behavior Management* in the last 10 years have used some type of performance-based feedback (Balcazar, Hopkins, & Suarez, 1986; Balcazar et al., 1989).

Traditionally, the supervisor has been viewed as the major vehicle for the development and maintenance of employee behavior. Most strategies that prescribe methods for altering employee motivation, place major responsibility, either explicitly or implicitly, on the supervisor. OBA interventions are no exception; most behavioral management systems involve control over antecedents and consequences by a supervisor. Such involvement is reasonable given that part of any supervisor's job is to direct employee performance. Additionally it is important to note that feedback delivered by a supervisor is likely to be more powerful than that delivered by a coworker or by a consultant, because the supervisor has control over many of the reinforcers associated with individual performance (e.g., pay raises, promotion, work assignment, access to time off, etc.).

Because supervisors are responsible for ensuring that subordinate behavior contributes to organization objectives, it is important that they be responsive to changes in metacontingencies. Traditional supervisory systems are often ineffective in this respect primarily because they are punitive. Good performance is typically ignored, whereas poor performance is punished, often with little corrective guidance (Bourdon, 1982; Dierks & McNally, 1987). It is assumed that employees know what is expected of them, and thus, require no explicit feedback. Only behaviors that are clearly incorrect or undesirable are noticed. Behaviorally based feedback systems, on the other hand, focus on the reinforcement of appropriate employee behaviors rather than the punishment of inappropriate patterns. This approach requires that appropriate performance be specified clearly and supported by motivational conditions, and, in practice, has led to dramatic increases in productivity (Balcazar, Hopkins, & Suarez, 1986).

It would be incorrect to assume that the simple institution of a behavioral feedback system guarantees individual behavior that is in line with metacontingencies. To establish a clear link between individual performance and organization goals, supervisors must target behaviors that are directly related to organization success in the marketplace. Unfortunately, target behaviors may be chosen solely because they serve the needs of the division or department for which the supervisor is responsible, whether or not those needs are in line with overall organizational goals (Brethower, 1982).

Perhaps one of the best examples of a behavioral feedback intervention, which explicitly and successfully linked individual performance with organization success, was described by Zemke and Gunkler (1982). They applied an "organizational-results-referenced performance management system," based on what they termed "the business proposition." The business proposition requires that management arrange clear relationships between employee performance and organization objectives, and that organization objectives be clearly related to profits. The authors noted that although senior management is usually in touch with the business proposition, other levels of the organization may not be. Thus, the goal of results-referenced interventions is to "make organizational results and their values more immediately evident and usable" (p. 567). In the terminology used in the present chapter, the goal is to strengthen metacontingencies by making the relationship between individual performance and organization success clear.

Zemke and Gunkler (1982) applied their results-referenced intervention in a theme park. The intervention began with consultations with senior management to determine the overall mission of the park. Consultants determined that the success of the park depended on repeat business; thus customer satisfaction was identified as the top priority. A precise definition of customer satisfaction was stated, and a survey was created to assess guest perceptions of the park's performance. The survey was conducted daily and the results became the measure of achievement of organizational goals. After a baseline period, survey results were posted for all staff to see. The simple posting of guest perceptions had little effect on business success as measured by subsequent changes in guest satisfaction. The second manipulation involved implementing a token economy that was linked to guest satisfaction levels. Tokens were delivered by supervisors and managers to employees who engaged in behaviors that were determined to produce increased satisfaction on the part of guests. The details of the token economy are worth nothing because they demonstrate how the economy was linked to overall objectives. Each token was assigned a face value; however, the redemption value of the tokens depended on daily guest satisfaction levels. When guest satisfaction was high, the tokens were worth more than on days when satisfaction was low. To ensure delivery of the tokens, managers and line supervisors were required to award a minimum number of tokens per day and were taught to use the tokens to reinforce desired behaviors. Temporary subsystems were implemented where and when necessary (e.g., a lottery system at the end of the season to prevent absenteeism and turnover), and multiple backup reinforcement systems were developed (e.g., special awards). The results indicated that the token economy resulted in increased guest satisfaction, and that the removal of the economy led to a decrease in satisfaction.

An additional results-referenced subsystem was instituted in those areas of the park that brought in additional money above and beyond the general gate admission fee (e.g., games areas, gift shops, refreshment areas). The amount of money earned per day was calculated and posted, and employees were awarded tokens contingent on the previous day's income. This system resulted in a significant increase in sales and a 360% return on investment. In summary, the organizational-results-referenced performance management approach as outlined by Zemke and Gunkler (1982) represents an excellent example of how individual contingencies can be linked to organization outcomes. As these authors pointed out, the advantage to such an approach is that it creates a "checks-and-balances system that keeps errant subsystem intervention strategies from going too far astray" (p. 582).

As with compensation systems, feedback systems that produce immediate influences on individual employee behavior can be used to respond quickly to changes in market consequences. If a change in the market dictates a change in organizational practices, organizations that can produce the necessary changes quickly will be more likely to survive. Without direct and sensitive control over individual contingencies that support employee behavior, adaptive responding at the organizational level is not possible.

Example Interventions: Training and Technological Advances

According to Hinrichs (1976), training involves the process of changing the behaviors of individuals in a way that improves their contribution to the effectiveness of the organization. Through training programs, organization members learn to carry out relevant tasks at levels of proficiency that ultimately improve profits and increase the chances of survival. Additionally, employees may be taught rules that maximize their understanding of and response to an organization mission. General rules of this type may lead to increases in individual performances that are consistent with general organization goals, even in the absence of explicit instructions. Many different formats are used to deliver training, ranging from the most informal, such as on-the-job training, to formal instruction in off-site classrooms (Howell & Dipboye, 1986). Typically, skills to be trained are identified in a needs analysis, which is used to justify training in terms of organization priorities (Landy, 1989), and cost-benefit analyses are completed to assess the effects of training strategies on profits (Ross, 1982).

Recent studies have emphasized the importance of training and education in creating organizations that are adaptive and successful in a rapidly changing marketplace. In this regard, a study by the Massachusetts Institute of Technology Commission on Industrial Productivity found that companies in countries that utilize on-the-job training (e.g., Japan and Germany) are more successful because they develop broader relevant repertoires more rapidly than those in countries that use more formal approaches (e.g., United States and Britain) (Dertouzos, Lester, & Solow, 1989). This report also described a tendency on the part of U.S. companies to replace workers whose skills have become obsolete rather than retrain them, a practice that further supports formal training methods and stands in direct opposition to more flexible, continuous on-the-job retraining methods. In general, flexible training programs provide a means of adjusting to changes in the marketplace that affect profits and promise greater success in a global economy such as that of the auto industry where competitive advantage depends heavily on worker proficiency.

Worker training strategies are perhaps best illustrated in the area of quality control technology where U.S. companies are attempting to build new programs. In the past 10 years, significant improvements in the quality of Japanese products has resulted in the loss of business for many American companies (Mainstone & Levi, 1987). In response to this situation, many U.S. companies have implemented innovative quality control programs as a way of improving their market position. This practice has led to, among other things, widespread support of W. Edwards Deming's Statistical Process Control (SPC-D) approach to quality improvement that was tested primarily in Japan (Deming, 1982). Deming's approach includes both a management philosophy and a set of statistical techniques used to evaluate and improve specific product quality. The goal of SPC-D is the prevention of quality problems rather than the detection of problems after the fact. Thus, statistical techniques are applied during the production process rather than after the product is complete. To monitor quality throughout the entire production process, each employee involved in production must be trained in SPC-D techniques.

The basic premise underlying SPC-D is that all processes produce variation in output and that variation has two possible sources that Deming labels "normal" and "abnormal." "Normal" variation is considered to be a function of factors inherent in the system and thus is seen as "chance" variation that can never be completely eliminated and is not likely to cause quality problems (Deming, 1975). "Abnormal" variation is considered to be a function of unusual or nonrandom factors that are not inherent to the system and are likely to result in quality problems. The primary function of SPC-D is to identify and correct abnormal sources of variation. Several steps are included: (1) Output variation is measured via the use of specially designed control charts; (2) at regular intervals throughout the day, each employee draws a sample of several products from the process at her stage of production; (3) critical indicators of quality are assessed for each element in the series sampled; and (4) sample means and ranges are calculated and plotted on the control charts. If the sample means are normally distributed around the grand mean, then the process is considered to be "in control" (meaning the variation is normal) and does not need attention. If the sample means deviate significantly from the grand mean, then the system is said to be "out of control" (meaning the variation is abnormal) and a problem exists. Through continual assessment of product quality during the manufacturing process, SPC-D allows the early detection of potential problems—ideally early enough to avoid the production of substandard products. By training all employees in these techniques, high-quality finished products are more likely. Because SPC-D techniques are similar regardless of stage of production or type of product, implementation is arranged through organization-wide training programs for line workers and management. As such, SPC-D training represents a good example of linkages between individual performance and effective organizational response to markets that demand better products (e.g., the automobile market).

It should be noted that SPC-D exemplifies not only an organization-wide training program, but also includes the implementation of other cultural contingencies designed to work in concert with the statistical techniques. Most notably, this approach requires that management give all employees the power to control operations so that production of substandard products can be prevented (Deming, 1982). If an employee must wait for supervisory approval to shut down an operation, low-quality products may be produced for the duration of the delay. Thus, a lack of employee autonomy will hinder the prevention of poor-quality production through early detection. As with other practices that affect the behavior of a group of individuals, the empowering of employees is an organizational practice that is assumed to lead to the production of high-quality products and thus represents an adaptive adjustment to market demands.

In summary, training programs designed to develop a quality culture through implementation of SPC-D provide another example of control through metacontingencies. Market demands for improved quality are translated into strategies that include (1) widespread training of new technical skills, and (2) changes in rules that relate individual practices to organization success. As a result of this type of program, individuals are provided with the means to work directly to decrease threats to organization survival.

ISSUES RELATED TO PRIVATE
SECTOR METACONTINGENCIES

All of the examples presented in this chapter represent methods of relating individual performance patterns to organization-level consequences. In all cases, groups of employees were affected by the methods described. In all cases, some evidence was presented to indicate that the responses of organizations that arranged metacontingencies were more adaptive than those that did not. Certainly, companies in countries that have adopted flexible pay systems, responsive training programs, and effective supervisory methods have fared well relative to those that have not (Dertouzos et al., 1989).

Of course the influence of these strategies depends to a great degree on how well individual and organization levels are linked by effective management. Certainly, effective metacontingencies must include clear messages regarding survival-related performances required on the part of the work force (antecedents) and delivery of powerful individual reinforcers contingent on behaviors related to organization success (consequences). For example in the case of pay-for-performance, behaviors that increased profits were reinforced by increased individual payments. And in the results-referenced supervisory feedback system, supervisor-controlled reinforcers were made contingent on performances that related directly to organization goals.

EXISTING MODELS OF CULTURAL ANALYSIS IN OBA

As indicated in the chapter on public sector interventions, several models relevant to metacontingency analyses have been described by OBA practitioners. These include Behavioral Systems Analysis (BSA) (Krapfl & Gasparotto, 1982), the Performance Engineering Matrix (PEM) (Gilbert, 1978), and the Total Performance System (TPS) (Brethower, 1982). The same models are relevant in the private sector. The details of these models will not be repeated here; readers may refer to the public sector chapter for more information. However, an analysis of private sector contingencies in terms of the TPS will be presented for purposes of illustration.

The TPS includes the following elements: (1) input of raw materials and resources, (2) a processing system where raw materials are transformed, (3) outputs that are the finished products, (4) a receiving system that consumes outputs, and (5) two feedback loops. The feedback loops include information from internal checks on the outputs before they are sent to the receiving system and information from the receiving system that indicates whether outputs satisfy the demands of consumers. The receiving system represents the marketplace, and receiving system feedback occurs in the form of financial return and customer satisfaction, as well as more general responses concerning the value of products or services to the larger culture (e.g., complaints regarding pollution or safety of products).

In the private sector, where profits rule, financial return is the most critical form of feedback; certainly, no business will survive for other purposes unless expenses can be paid. However, the characteristics of outputs that lead to profit must also be identified so that internal control systems can be arranged to ensure that outputs will indeed be acceptable to the receiving system. Quality control is the best example of internal control systems whereby quality of products or services is monitored during the production process to avoid producing outputs that will not return profits. Marketing studies and consumer satisfaction surveys are typical sources of data used to identify specific output features that best influence the consumer.

The TPS can be used to represent a metacontingency. Organization-level outcomes are described by criteria for receiving system satisfaction (e.g., market demands). Internal individual requirements are depicted by internal feedback (e.g., quality control). The degree to which the criteria applied by these two sources match, determines the extent to which individual contingencies and organizational success are linked. If the internal feedback loop is set to monitor criteria that match exactly those of the market, then internal processes are likely to contribute directly to profitability. If these two sets of criteria differ appreciably, internal actions may deviate often from success-related practices. The extent to which internal management applies the standards of the receiving system determines the degree to which an organization focuses individual effort on ultimate cultural success.

CONCLUSION

This chapter presented an analysis of metacontingencies typical of private sector organizations and illustrated existing applications in the OBA field. The examples provided demonstrated how the efforts of a large number of individual workers could be utilized to improve profits or profit-related functions (e.g., quality control). Additionally, current analytical models that provide an approximation of a metacontingency approach were reviewed and directions for future development were suggested.

The examples presented in this chapter were neither identified as metacontingency analyses by their authors nor were their results analyzed in terms of behavioral systems or any other cultural framework. Few OBA reports mention this level of analysis and, as such, fail to contribute to the development of a large-scale operant model. Gilbert (1978) criticized the field for its emphasis on behavior without respect to purpose or ultimate goals. He suggested that we focus on accomplishments that are worthy in terms of organization missions. His advice appears to have been ignored.

Hopefully this chapter, and other writings like it, will stimulate productivity in OBA by reminding researchers and practitioners that a powerful behavior change technology must be applied in the service of more general purposes to be useful to the culture.

REFERENCES

Abernathy, W. B. (1990). *Designing and managing an organization-wide incentive pay system.* Memphis, TN: W. B. Abernathy & Associates.

Andrasik, F. (1979). Organizational behavior modification in business settings: A methodological and content review. *Journal of Organizational Behavior Management, 2,* 85–102.

Balcazar, F., Hopkins, B. L., & Suarez, Y. (1986). A critical, objective review of performance feedback. *Journal of Organizational Behavior Management, 7,* 65–89.

Balcazar, F. E., Shupert, M. K., Daniels, A. C., Mawhinney, T. C., & Hopkins, B. L. (1989). An objective review and analysis of ten years of publications in the *Journal of Organizational Behavior Management. Journal of Organizational Behavior Management, 10*(1), 7–37.

Blau, P. M., & Scott, W. R. (1963). *Formal organizations, a comparative approach.* London: Routledge & Kegan Paul.

Brethower, D. M. (1982). Total performance systems. In R. O'Brien, A. M. Dickinson, & M. Rosow (Eds.), *Industrial behavior modification* (pp. 350–369). New York: Pergamon.

Bourdon, R. (1982). Measuring and tracking management performance for accountability. *Journal of Organizational Behavior Management, 4,* 101–112.

Daniels, A. C., & Rosen, T. A. (1984). *Performance management: Improving quality and productivity through positive reinforcement* (2nd ed.). Tucker, GA: Performance Management Publications.

Deming, W. E. (1975). On some statistical aids toward economic production. *Interfaces, 5,* 1–15.

Deming, W. E. (1982). *Quality, productivity, and competitive position.* Cambridge, MA: Center for Advanced Engineering Study, Massachusetts Institute of Technology.

Dertouzos, M. L., Lester, R. K., & Solow, R. M. (1989). *Made in America: Regaining the productive edge.* New York: Harper-Collins.

Dierks, W., & McNally, K. (1987, March). Incentives you can bank on. *Personnel Administrator,* pp. 61–65.

Frederiksen, L. W. (Ed.). (1982). *Handbook of organizational behavior management.* New York: Wiley.

Frisch, C. J., & Dickinson, A. M. (1990). Work productivity as a function of the percentage of monetary incentives to base pay. *Journal of Organizational Behavior Management, 11*(1), 13–33.

Gilbert, T. (1978). *Human competence: Engineering worthy performance.* New York: McGraw-Hill.

Glenn, S. S. (1988). Contingencies and metacontingencies: Toward a synthesis of behavior analysis and cultural materialism. *The Behavior Analyst, 11,* 161–179.

Harris, M. (1979). *Cultural materialism.* New York: Random House.

Henderson, R. I. (1985). *Compensation management: Rewarding performance* (4th ed.). Reston, VA: Reston Publishing.

Hinrichs, J. R. (1976). Personnel training. In M. Dunnette (Ed.), *Handbook of industrial and organizational psychology* (pp. 221–253). Skokie, IL: Rand-McNally.

Howell, W. C., & Dipboye, R. L. (1986). *Essentials of industrial and organizational psychology* (3rd ed.). Chicago: Dorsey Press.

Krapfl, J., & Gasparotto, G. (1982). Behavioral systems analysis. In L. W. Frederiksen (Ed.), *Handbook of organizational behavior management* (pp. 21–38). New York: Wiley.

Kreitner, R. (1982). The feedforward and feedback control of job performance through organizational behavior management. *Journal of Organizational Behavior Management, 3*(3), 3–20.

Landy, F. J. (1989). *Psychology of work behavior* (4th ed.). Pacific Grove, CA: Brooks-Cole.

Lee, R. D., Jr. (1987). *Public personnel systems* (2nd ed.). Rockville, MD: Aspen.

Lynn, L. E., Jr. (1981). *Managing the public's business.* New York: Basic Books.

Mainstone, L. E., & Levi, A. S. (1987). Fundamentals of statistical process control. *Journal of Organizational Behavior Management, 9*(1), 5–22.

Malott, R. W. (1988). Rule-governed behavior and behavioral anthropology. *The Behavior Analyst, 11,* 181–203.

Mawhinney, T. C. (1986). OBM, SPC, and Theory D: A brief introduction. *Journal of Organizational Behavior Management, 8,* 89–105.

Merwin, G. A., Jr., Thomason, J. A., & Sanford, E. E. (1989). A methodology and content review of organizational behavior management in the private sector: 1978–1986. *Journal of Organizational Behavior Management, 10*(1), 39–57.

Metzger, B. (1964). *Profit sharing in perspective.* Evanston, IL: Profit Sharing Research Foundation.

Muchinsky, P. M. (1990). *Psychology applied to work.* Pacific Grove, CA: Brooks-Cole.

O'Brien, R. M. (1990). Working the other side of the street: Can organizational behavior management help unions to change management? In W. K. Redmon & A. M. Dickinson (Eds.), *Promoting excellence through performance management* (pp. 193–205). New York: Haworth.

Performance Management Magazine. (1990, Winter-Spring). An evolving system at Spectrum Center. Tucker, GA: Performance Management Publications.

Peters, T. (1987). *Thriving on chaos.* New York: Harper & Row.

Perry, N. J. (1988, December 19). Here come richer, riskier pay plans. *Fortune,* pp. 51–58.

Ross, P. C. (1982). Training: Behavior change and the improvement of business performance. In L. W. Frederiksen (Ed.), *Handbook of organizational behavior management* (pp. 181–218). New York: Wiley.

Skryzcki, C. (1987, May 24). Linking wages with performance. *The Washington Post,* pp. H1, H3.

Weitzman, M. (1984). *The share economy: Conquering stagflation.* Cambridge, MA: Harvard University.

Zemke, R. E., & Gunkler, J. W. (1982). Organization-wide intervention. In L. W. Frederiksen (Ed.), *Handbook of organizational behavior management* (pp. 565–583). New York: Wiley.

8

Behavioral Analysis in Higher Education

Joel Greenspoon

INTRODUCTION

A behavioral analysis of higher education is fraught with numerous dangers. The differences in the contingencies and metacontingencies among universities and colleges can be enormous. There are differences in the administration of a private liberal arts college and a private liberal arts university. There are administrative differences between the sectarian and nonsectarian colleges. And there are tremendous differences between the private and public colleges and universities. Under these conditions, any behavioral analysis of higher education will be limited and may be applicable to a relatively small sample. At the same time, there may be some facets of a behavioral analysis that are applicable to a fairly broad range of academic institutions. Within this disclaimer, this chapter will now address a behavioral analysis of higher education in the United States.

SOME BASIC CONSTRUCTS
OF BEHAVIORAL ANALYSIS

Behavioral analysis is a unique approach to the analysis of behavior. Certain constructs have become basic to such analyses. Since these constructs provide the basis for the analysis, it is important that they are clearly and rigorously defined. Though there are some differences among behavior analysts about these definitions, these differences tend to be rather trivial.

The contingency is the basic construct in behavior analysis. It consists of the antecedent, the behavior, and the consequence. The antecedent is the environmental event(s) that is directly related to the emission of a behavior. Some of these antecedent events may function as discriminative stimuli. A discriminative stimulus is a stimulus in the presence of which there is an increased probability that a specific behavior will be emitted. The discriminative properties of a stimulus are acquired and may differ from individual to individual. Other antecedent events may be classified as establishing operations (Michael, 1982). The establishing operation (EO) is an operation or series of operations that increase the effectiveness of some object or event as reinforcement and evokes the behavior that has in the past been followed by that event or object. Behavior is what the person says or does. The consequence is the event(s) that occurs following a behavior. A consequence that increases the frequency of the behavior it follows is called a positive reinforcer. A consequence that suppresses the frequency of the behavior it follows is called a punisher. A consequence whose avoidance or escape results in an increase in the frequency of the behavior that leads to the avoidance or escape is called a negative reinforcer. As we proceed in the analysis, we shall provide specific examples of each of the components of the contingency.

The metacontingency (Glenn, 1988) is also used in an analysis. According to Glenn (1988) "the metacontingency is the unit of analysis encompassing a cultural practice, in all its variations, and the aggregate outcome of all the current practices" (p. 168). There are group practices that have outcomes that relate to the functioning of administrators and faculty. Alumni associations, legislatures, church officials, student bodies, and faculty are groups that engage in practices that have outcomes.

The alumni association of a university or college may engage in activities that impact extensively on both the faculty and administration. There may be variations in the practices of alumni association, but there are also some commonalities in these practices. Though the alumni association of a private college or university has practices that may differ from some of the practices of the alumni association of a public institution, there are some similarities. The alumni association of a private college that becomes involved in raising money for the college generates outcomes that have an impact on many different facets of the college. The alumni association of the public college may embark on a campaign to influence the state legislature on matters that relate to the functioning of the college or university. The alumni association comprises what Harris (1979) calls a permaclone. The individuals comprising the association change over time, but there is a continuity to the practices of the association until the practices fail to produce the desired outcome. Any change in the practice of the association will usually be very gradual, even though the behavior of individual members may change much more dramatically. Additional examples of metacontingencies will be described later.

FACULTY CONTINGENCIES

This section examines some of the contingencies that generally prevail for faculty members. It is necessary to remember that not all of these contingencies apply in every higher education institution. However, to understand today's contingencies, we have to examine some of the changes that have occurred in higher education over the years, especially the last 50 years, that are associated with changes in the metacontingencies.

Early History

The primary objective of higher education in the American colonies was to educate the young people, initially only men. The earliest colleges in the colonies were all founded by religious groups. The education of ministers was a primary function of the college, although none of these colleges, except for William and Mary, had charters that expressly designated them as only seminaries for the training of ministers. As more and more colleges were founded, their charters became increasingly secular. The secularization of the colleges was associated with certain changes in the metacontingencies. The metacontingencies of these early colleges reflected the religious group that founded the college. For example, most of the colonial colleges clearly specified that the president must be of a particular religious faith and had religious tests for the faculty. The founders of Brown University specifically ruled out religious tests for the faculty. Despite the religious emphasis of the colonial colleges, none of them required students to adhere to a particular religious faith, although attendance at chapel was usually compulsory.

Environmental changes directly affect the contingencies that may operate in the academic community. The changes in the environment of the Massachusetts Bay Colony were affected by changes occurring in England. When William Cromwell was in power in England, the Puritans were able to control virtually every facet of life in the colony, including Harvard College. The Congregational Church through the Overseers exercised considerable control over Harvard. Though very popular with the Overseers, Henry Dunston, technically the first president of Harvard, resigned because of the controversy over his views on infant baptism. As was the case for many presidents since him, Dunston's efforts to obtain more funds from the General Court resulted in a financial investigation that seemed to cast doubt on his competency (Hofstadter, 1955a, 1955b).

The death of Cromwell and the restoration of the monarchy in England resulted in changes that affected the colony. Support for the Puritans in the Massachusetts Bay Colony was not as strong as when Cromwell was in control. In addition, the colony was prospering, creating increasingly important merchant and artisan classes. These classes were more concerned with a college curriculum that prepared students for vocations other than the ministry. By the early 18th century clergymen graduates became a minority among all graduates, and by the end of the 18th century four fifths of all graduates were going into nonministerial occupations.

These environmental changes with the accompanying changes in the metacontingencies had a profound effect on the faculty. Initially at Harvard the only person who could be considered a professional educator was the president. The president taught courses, but much of the education was in the hands of tutors. Tutors were generally students who were studying for the ministry. They taught until they completed their own education and received an appointment as the minister of some church. College teaching was not considered to be a profession. As a consequence, the president and other administrators (e.g., finance officer when the college became larger) provided the continuity to the college. Harvard was established for 85 years before the first professor was appointed.

The absence of a permanent faculty led to a development that differentiated the colonial colleges from their European counterparts. And it is a difference that prevails down to present time. The governing body of European universities tended to be the faculty. In the colonies, the governing body was a board that, with the possible exception of the president, consisted of clergymen and state officials—individuals who were not directly involved in the education of the students. Since these individuals had responsibilities other than the day-to-day operations of the college, they usually granted control over such operations to the president. As a result, the president of the college emerged with a lot of control over the contingencies for the faculty and students. This control was to be exercised within the guidelines established by the governing body. Since the president usually was a member of the board, he was in a position to influence the guidelines.

Even after colleges began to appoint permanent faculty members, the president frequently continued to exercise extensive control over the faculty. Hofstadter (1955a) reported that President Porter of Yale forbade William Graham Sumner from using Herbert Spencer's (1874) *Study of Sociology* as a text. Academic freedom was virtually unknown even into the latter half of the 19th century. James

Hart (1878) wrote a treatise about German universities in which he advocated the adoption of the German concept of *Lehrfreiheit,* which he defined as the right of the professor to be free to teach what he chooses, as he chooses.

Modern Times

Today there is a greater sharing of the control of the contingencies of the faculty. The extent of this sharing varies from institution to institution. In the final analysis, the governing body legally has control over the personnel decisions affecting the faculty in that it must approve all personnel decisions. However, for all practical purposes the personnel decisions rest with the president since the governing board usually approves all of the president's personnel recommendations. The president, on the other hand, may approve all personnel recommendations that are submitted through, in some cases, a laborious, time-consuming process of faculty and administrative committees.

The specification of most of the contingencies for faculty members in the larger colleges and universities usually originates within the department, the basic unit of administration of the faculty. The chief administrative officer is the chair, although there may still be some departments that have heads. In theory a head may act on matters without the advice and consent of the faculty within the department. A chair is the chair of the committee of the whole, the entire faculty within the department. The departmental faculty vote on all matters relating to the operation of the department, including personnel matters. The chair, in turn, has the responsibility of administering the policies developed by the department within the policies that have been developed for the college or the university. The governance policies developed by the department may be subject to approval by higher administrative units. Departmental policies cannot conflict with the policies of higher administrative units. The department, for example, cannot develop personnel policies that conflict with the college or university's personnel policies. In practice there are heads who behave as chairs and chairs who behave as heads.

Specific Contingencies

The particular contingencies established for faculty members vary considerably from institution to institution. There are several general areas that are considered in many institutions, although their relative importance may vary depending on the size and nature of the institution.

These general areas include teaching, research or scholarly activity, departmental/university service, and, in some cases, community service. Teaching is frequently stated as the number one area in many institutions, but it often takes a back seat to the research/scholarly activity. Teaching refers to the behaviors emitted by the faculty members designed to facilitate and maximize behavior acquisition by the students. Though it should be apparent that the effective instructor emits behavior in the classroom, laboratory, and/or studio that differ from the behaviors emitted by the ineffective instructor, it is relatively rare for an instructor to be evaluated on such behaviors. All too often the instructor is evaluated on such vaguely defined factors as personality, interpersonal relationships, and the like. When students are involved in the evaluation process, they are rarely asked to describe the behaviors of the instructor. Though we usually assess or evaluate a machine on its performance, we rarely evaluate an instructor in terms of the performance of his/her product—the students.

There are methods for assessing how much the student has learned that eliminates much of the subjectivity that now prevails. One method utilizes a pre- and posttest over the material of the course. The two tests are the same; the only difference is that the pretest is administered on the first class day and the posttest on the last class day. The difference is a measure of how much the student has learned.

Many faculty object to this method. It is possible for a faculty member to teach the test, thereby ensuring that the students will show large gains. This is a valid concern, but it can be dealt with effectively by having other faculty members create the test based on the objectives developed by the instructor. If the instructor develops a set of objectives describing the behavior of the students at the end of the course, it should be possible for other faculty to develop a test that represents these objectives. This method could also be used if a pretest could not be used.

Many faculty members oppose the development of measures of teacher effectiveness based on student performance. There is no question that such measures put pressure on the faculty member to perform. Being an excellent story teller or a good actor may not be effective in getting students to learn. At the same time being a good story teller or an undemanding faculty member may result in frequently doing well on the subjective student evaluations that are now so commonplace.

There are some instructional techniques that put the emphasis on the behavior of the student, not the instructor. In other words, these techniques require the student to emit a large amount of behavior, thereby enabling the instructor to shape the behaviors that are pertinent to the subject matter of the course. Skinner's (1968) programmed instructor (PI) and Keller's (1968) and Keller and Sherman's (1974) personalized self-instruction (PSI) are two techniques that emphasize student behavior. Neither technique has gained very wide acceptance, although both techniques are based on behavior analytic principles. Both techniques require a tremendous amount of work by the instructor before an effective program can be developed. Poor quality programs were detrimental to the development of PI. PI was designed to free the instructor from the teaching of rote material and to allow him or her more time to spend on more complex and complicated material. There were some who objected to the seeming mechanical and mechanistic way that PI presumably functioned.

PSI, like PI, required a tremendous amount of time and effort of the instructor, especially if there were no adequate teaching assistants. PSI requires the student to attain a level of mastery before moving on to the next unit. PSI, therefore, does not fit very well into the traditional time-based system that prevails in higher education. Registrars in particular object to the difficulties that are created because PSI does not operate within the traditional time frame. Deans object because they cannot understand why there are so many high grades, especially since every student who completes the course may get an "A". Other administrators, especially the finance officer, object because PSI courses are labor intensive, presumably increasing the cost of educating the students. I am not aware of any study that has been conducted to determine the relative cost of a PSI and a traditional course.

Though both PI and PSI were initially enthusiastically received by many in higher education, neither one has maintained this initial enthusiasm. It is apparent that both PI and PSI use the student, the product of our educational system, as the measure of the effectiveness of the instructor. Consequently, the evaluation of teacher effectiveness continues to be the subject of much debate but relatively few acceptable solutions.

Metacontingencies and Teaching

The process of teaching frequently represents an area of conflict of metacontingencies, especially in the public institutions. Providing high-quality education to those who enter the institution is a proclaimed objective of every higher education institution. However, this outcome is jeopardized by the basis on which funds are provided to the institution by the state legislature. Though funding practices vary from state to state, there is usually a high positive correlation between the credit hours generated and head count and the amount of money provided by the legislature. Though more student credit hours mean more money, the ratio of the two usually requires the institution to have very large classes, especially in the first 2 years of undergraduate school. In many states there are minimum numbers of students that must be enrolled if the class is to be taught. Having a class of 150–500 students frequently requires the faculty member to adopt practices that are not compatible with the objective of providing a high-quality education. The objective of the legislature is to provide funds such that it remains within the budgetary restrictions that prevail. When there are budget crunches, an increasingly common phenomenon in many states these days, the budgets for higher education are frequently adversely affected. These two outcomes—a balanced state budget and high-quality education—are frequently incompatible.

The private sector also has its budgetary problems. Many private colleges and universities, some very prominent ones, have been confronted with deficits. Despite the financial problems that may beset them, the private institutions attempt to maintain a reasonable student/faculty ratio that is compatible with the attainment of quality education. Some private institutions have found it necessary to increase teaching loads of the faculty as they wrestle with their financial problems. Though teaching loads may increase, the class size usually remains relatively small.

The issue of teaching loads is another possible source of conflict between the metacontingencies of the institution and society. Many states have mandated that the standard teaching load is 12 hours, usually four 3-hour courses. However, other faculty activities are considered in the computation of teaching load so that most faculty members rarely teach more than three courses and frequently only two. Private institutions have comparable, sometimes even lower, teaching loads.

To individuals who are not familiar with the demands made on faculty members, the 9-hour teaching load sounds likes a sinecure. State legislatures frequently sound alarm over the seemingly light loads of the faculty. When considering the teaching loads of public school teachers and community college faculty members, legislatures frequently discuss increasing the teaching demands on the faculty. Institutional administrators are frequently asked to justify a faculty member's spending only 9 hours a week in the classroom. The fact that a faculty member can come and go as he/she pleases is seemingly incomprehensible to the worker who is tied to his machine or desk for 40 hours a week. That the faculty member spends many hours in preparing a 3-hour course, frequently has committee assignments, and is engaged in research/scholarly activities is not something that is readily apparent to the average individual. Even college graduates who would seemingly be more aware of the time demands on a faculty member are frequently among those who complain about the seemingly soft job of a faculty member.

Metacontingencies and Tenure

Another issue involving the faculty that frequently leads to a conflict of meta-contingencies between the faculty and society involves the concept of tenure. Most higher education institutions award tenure to faculty members after a period of time. Tenure means that the individual faculty member is protected against capricious discharge and is designed to enable the faculty member to pursue the "truth" without fear of being discharged for saying and doing things that may not conform to the community's concept of "truth." Contrary to popular belief tenure is not a guarantee of a position. The lay person and society in general do not understand the concept of tenure and the role that it plays in meeting the objectives of the institution. The search for the "truth" does not always lead to conclusions that conform to the prevailing views in a community. When this occurs, there is frequently a demand the offending faculty member be fired. Firing under these conditions would be considered contrary to the conditions of tenure. It is interesting to note that there have been court decisions that have provided employees in the public marketplace with some of the protection provided by tenure. At the same time, legislatures have from time to time debated the merits of tenure at state institutions and have considered alternatives that would reduce or eliminate some of the protection now accorded by tenure.

One example of an alternative is term tenure. Term tenure means that the faculty member is accorded the protection of tenure during a specified period of time. At the end of that period of time the faculty member is evaluated and recommended for another term or terminated. The objective of term tenure is presumably the termination of faculty members whose performance does not warrant retention. Term tenure may be another issue in which there is a clash of metacontingencies. This time the clash is between the faculty and the administration. The outcome of term tenure from an administrative standpoint is the maintenance of high-quality performance by the faculty. The contention is that there are some faculty members who "retire" once they have attained tenure. Meanwhile, they occupy a faculty position but presumably are not functioning at a level that warrants retention. Since they have tenure, they are very difficult to terminate. This issue has gained additional pertinence in recent years because enrollment at many institutions has stagnated or even declined. These tenured faculty have to be retained and that means that untenured faculty of high quality may have to be terminated.

The faculty, however, tend to emphasize a different outcome from term tenure. They see it as a vehicle by which unpopular faculty members or faculty members whose behavior may have irritated the administration or some segments of the population can be terminated without the difficulties associated with terminating a tenured faculty member. It is somewhat reminiscent of the situation some years ago when the president of a prominent university was advocating the termination of tenure on the grounds that it would "get the faculty members off their asses." The faculty response was "that it would get them off their asses and on their knees."

An interesting development with respect to tenure is taking place at the University of California-Berkeley. What makes it so interesting is that the initiative for this modification of tenure came from the faculty. Tenured faculty members would be reviewed periodically to determine if they were worthy of their positions. Conceivably a tenured faculty member deemed unworthy could be terminated. The argument being used in this situation is similar to the argument used by the administration in support of term tenure. The counter arguments are comparable to the arguments raised against term tenure.

The courts have been involved in the tenure issue, especially with respect to the denial of tenure. The position of the courts seems to be that they do not want to interfere in the operation of an institution. If the institution establishes and functions according to due process procedures, the courts will not interfere or reverse decisions made at the institution.

Unions and Higher Education

The tenure issue, as well as other issues of importance to the faculty, has given rise to the appearance of unions on the college campus. Many faculty members consider unions and collective bargaining to be antithetical to the collegial climate. Gray and Davis (1980) contend that the alienation of higher education and labor unions arises from different social and economic roles. They contend that faculty members consider the unions to be outsiders who constitute a serious threat to the established order, which the faculty consider to be their domain. At the same time unions and collective bargaining have become an important part of the scene in many higher education institutions.

There are three major unions involved in organizing and representing the faculty. They are the American Federation of Teachers (AFT), of the AFL-CIO, the National Education Association (NEA), and the American Association of University Professors (AAUP). Neither the NEA nor AAUP originated as a union, but the AFT did. Both the NEA and AAUP became unions reluctantly. Consequently, each of these unions may function differently, some more or less in accord with the principles of behavioral analysis.

One important factor affecting union activities is that legislation mandating the issues to be negotiated vary from state to state. When President Kennedy issued an executive order in 1962 allowing government employees to organize and engage in collective bargaining, he opened the door to efforts to unionize state and local employees. However, each state had to enact enabling legislation that mandated the issues to be negotiated. Many states, about half according to Kaplin (1985), enacted such legislation, but there was great variability in the mandated issues. California, for example, grants employees the right to "meet and confer" with administration representatives, but does not specify any issues that must be negotiated. On the other hand, New York, New Jersey, Pennsylvania, and Michigan have very strong collective bargaining laws that included educational institutions. It is not too surprising that efforts to organize faculties have been most successful in those states.

Another important factor is the National Labor Relations Board (NLRB). The NLRB's jurisdiction over private institutions was asserted in a case involving Cornell University (1970). The court later upheld the NLRB's jurisdiction over private institutions in *NLRB* v. *Wentworth Institute* (1975). A critical factor in these cases was the institution's involvement in interstate commerce. If a private institution is large enough to have a significant effect on interstate commerce, it comes under the jurisdiction of the NLRB. At the same time, public institutions are exempt from NLRB jurisdiction, but are subject to state control.

Another important factor is the involvement of the faculty in the governance of the institution. The U.S. Supreme Court ruled in *NLRB* v. *Yeshiva University* (1980) that the faculty of Yeshiva University were sufficiently involved in the governance of the University to be considered managerial and, consequently, the University did not have to negotiate with the union certified as the representative of the faculty. In *Loretta Heights College* v. *NLRB* (1984) the U.S. Circuit Court ruled that the faculty were not sufficiently involved in the governance of the College to be considered managerial and the College would have to negotiate with the union certified as the representative of the faculty.

Another critical factor is the faculty itself. Ladd and Lipset (1973) reported on a survey they conducted among faculty at a number of different colleges and universities. The faculty at prestigious institutions were more liberal and conceivably more supportive of unionization than the faculty at the less prestigious institutions. However, the results showed that younger faculty at the less prestigious institutions were more favorable toward unionization than the faculty at the more prestigious institutions. Generally, faculty who had published and had research grants were less supportive of unionization than faculty who were primarily engaged in teaching, despite the fact that the latter were at institutions where the faculty were less involved in the decision-making process.

Although the way in which a union may function varies from union to union and institution to institution, there appears to be a significant conflict between the union and behavior analytic principles. Kemerer and Baldridge (1975) probably identified this conflict when they stated that "collective bargaining is a system of governance and decision making difficult to reconcile with the collegial image of academic governance" (p. 3). Ladd and Lipset (1973) stated that there is a clash between the meritocratic culture of the research-oriented academic and the egalitarian culture of the union. The union functions with respect to the group outcome, a metacontingency. The union negotiates for the group so that the consequences are essentially assessed in terms of the group. The meritocratic culture and behavioral analysis place greater emphasis on the individual's behavior as a basis for consequences. It is interesting to note with respect to the meritocratic culture that Boyd (1973) contends a factor involved in the increasing interest in unionization is a growing dissatisfaction with the merit basis of pay. He stated, ". . . a number of faculty members believe that the whole idea of merit pay, based as it is on financial reward and punishment, smacks too much of the marketplace and rests on values inappropriate to an academic community" (p. 15).

A basic premise of behavioral analysis is that to increase or maintain the frequency of a desired behavior requires reinforcement of that behavior. Merit pay, if indeed based on the behavior of the individual faculty member, is one of the reinforcers that is used to affect that end. In institutions where the faculty exercises considerable control over the criteria of performance and the attendant merit increase in pay, there is less interest in unions according to Ladd and Lipset (1973) than in those institutions where the administrators exercise total control over salary increases.

As Ladd and Lipset (1973) and Kemerer and Baldridge (1975) point out, the union tends to place greater emphasis on seniority than merit as the basis for reinforcement, at least the reinforcement provided by the institution. Not all faculty reinforcement comes from the institution. A seniority basis for reinforcement can lead to what is frequently called noncontingent reinforcement. Noncontingent reinforcement is defined as providing reinforcement independent of any specified behavior. Many younger faculty complain about "deadwood." Deadwood are faculty who may have contributed at one time but no longer contribute to the department or unit. In a behavior analytic-based system these faculty would receive no institutional reinforcement if they no longer emitted reinforceable behaviors. In a seniority-based system they would continue to receive reinforcement.

A behavior analytic system makes all reinforcement contingent on specifiable and specified behaviors. The unionized system is certainly a much simpler system to administer since the basis of reinforcement is not behavior-based. A behavior analytic system requires a detailed analysis of desired behaviors since desired behaviors serve as the basis of reinforcement.

The issue of who specifies the desired behaviors becomes a critical issue in a behavior analytic system. If the faculty specify the desired behaviors, the system may be markedly different than if the administration, the trustees, or the legislature specified the desired behaviors. One factor cited by Kemerer and Baldridge (1975) in the growing interest in collective bargaining is the increasing control of institutions, especially public institutions, by boards that are further and further removed from the individual campus. In many states each institution has a board of trustees; the system to which the institution belongs may have a board; and then there may be a super board that oversees all of the higher educational institutions in the state.

In addition to the issue of who determines the desired behaviors is the issue of who decides that a faculty member has emitted the desired behaviors. In a behavior analytic approach the specification of the desired behaviors should be so rigorous that there is little or no question that the behaviors have occurred. The union approach that de-emphasizes specific behaviors would not be confronted with this problem. Once the faculty member has fulfilled the probationary period, all other decisions are based on seniority.

The egalitarian emphasis of the unions may not be completely in conflict with a behavior analytic approach. Though behavior analysis does not support an undiscriminated distribution of reinforcement, it does emphasize procedures designed to develop and maintain behaviors that maximize the probability of reinforcement. For example, if research and publications were an important basis for reinforcement, a behavior analytic approach would emphasize the development of procedures designed to have every faculty member engage in research and generate publications. If every faculty member is emitting the desired behaviors, then the distribution of reinforcements is simplified and approaches an egalitarian basis emphasized by the union.

An important issue that affects the union's efforts to organize a faculty revolves around the concept of shared governance. The 1966 Statement on Governance of Colleges and Universities embodies the principle "that decision making requires both the fulltime efforts of professionalized bureaucrats or bureaucratized professionals and the part time but intensive governance of the faculty, with lesser roles for the trustees and students" (Mason, 1974, p. 2). This statement on governance was adopted by the AAUP and endorsed by the American Council on Education and the Association of Governing Boards of Universities and Colleges.

The sharing of governance, if indeed it is shared, would probably embody many of the principles of behavioral analysis and satisfy some of the objections of the unions, at least one union—the AAUP. Though the sharing of governance has seemingly occurred in the prestigious private and public institutions, it has not occurred too frequently in the less prestigious institutions. It appears that as the financial resources available to higher education lessen, at both the public and private levels there has been an increased tendency for boards of trustees and the institutional administration to assume more power and authority and deviate further and further from the concept of shared governance. This development, if true, could lessen the already weak role of behavior analytic principles. It could, perhaps, lead to an increasing tendency on the part of faculty to organize in unions to exert more influence on the decision-making process.

Unions have a history of assuming an adversarial position, although there seems to be a lessening of that stance and a moving toward the concept of shared governance in industry. The union in higher education is in a much more formidable position to assume an adversarial position than the individual faculty member. However, the single most powerful weapon in this adversarial relationship is the strike, a weapon that is banned for state employees in many states. The strike is a powerful weapon, but it is a form of aversive control. Behavior analysts tend to eschew aversive control, although many recognize situations where it may be necessary. Behavior analysts tend to prefer the use of positive control to attain behavioral objectives.

Scholarly Activity as a Contingency

Many institutions place great emphasis on the research/scholarly activity of the faculty. The research area has attained increasing emphasis at many institutions since the federal and state governments began to spend large amounts of money in support of research. The dollars of grant and contract money and the number of publications have become important measures of the worth of the faculty member and enter into a variety of personnel decisions. Both of these contingencies may be unfair to faculty members of various disciplines. The amount of grant money is not evenly available across all disciplines. Research in some areas may require months and months before a publishable article is possible. Research in other areas may be completed in a few days or weeks. The quality criterion for the acceptance of an article for publication varies considerably from journal to journal in virtually every discipline. The persistent researcher will be able to find some journal that will publish it. Estes (1956), in reviewing the field of learning for the *Annual Review of Psychology*, made the observation that "many, perhaps the majority, of the studies will soon be forgotten by all but their authors" (p. 1). With the publishing contingency in operation, some faculty members will publish anything that can be accepted. One faculty member who was submitting an article that he acknowledged was not very good or very well done commented, "Deans don't read them; they just count them." However, other faculty members submit only articles that they believe will have an impact on the field.

Evaluating research and scholarly output is very difficult. Numbers alone may be the simplest and easiest way, but simply counting has some serious drawbacks, since high-quality publications carry the same weight as lesser quality publications. There is probably no single criterion by which publications can be evaluated. It is true that most evaluators place a greater weight on articles published in refereed journals than nonrefereed journals. Publication in refereed journals is no assurance of quality since friendly editors may be more inclined to accept articles from close personal friends.

The evaluation of publishing a book also varies considerably. In some disciplines, especially the humanities, publishing a book may be meeting a more demanding contingency than publishing an article. Publishing a book in the physical and biological sciences may not be evaluated as highly because most books utilize extensively the work of others. This assessment may vary as a function of the nature of the book. A book in which the author develops a new theory may be assessed much more highly than a book that reviews the literature in a given area.

Assessing the value of papers presented at regional, national, and international meetings is also very difficult. Invited presentations are usually assessed more highly than papers that are submitted and then presented. Papers presented at national and international meetings are usually more highly regarded than papers presented at regional or state meetings. It is generally accepted that papers presented at meetings do not meet as rigorous criteria for acceptance as articles submitted to journals.

A related contingency involves offices held in professional organizations, journal editorships, refereeing articles submitted to journals, grant panel memberships, election to prestigious societies, (e.g., National Academy of Science), and awards and honors bestowed by various organizations (e.g., Nobel Prize). The weighting of these contingencies varies from department to department within an institution and from institution to institution. Most of these contingencies are closely related to the publishing contingency. Election to the National Academy of Science or being awarded the Nobel Prize requires publication of research and/or theoretical articles. Editing a journal, refereeing articles, and sitting on grant panels are usually assigned to individuals who have demonstrated knowledge and skills in the discipline, and this demonstration is usually through publishing.

The Service Contingency

The contingency involving service to the department and institution frequently is in the form of committee assignments. Many committees are elected by the members of the department or some other administrative unit. Evaluation committees often consider the number of committees indicative of the contribution of the faculty member to the department or institution. Counting committee assignments may be no more indicative of service to the institution than counting the number of publications is to the research contingency. The performance of the faculty member in committee deliberations may be more important. Some faculty members may be elected or appointed to many committees, but contribute little or nothing to the activities of the committees. The activities of the committee itself must be considered. Some committees deal with trivial issues and may rarely meet. Other committees may deal with issues critical to the faculty, the department, or the institution. These issues are not often considered in evaluating a faculty member with respect to service to the institution.

The issue of faculty committees in and of itself is one that can lead to conflict between the contingencies established by the administration and those considered important by the faculty. How much importance is attached to a committee recommendation, especially if the recommendation is contrary to the contingencies of the administration? It is not uncommon for the administration to create a faculty committee to deal with a "hot potato." If the recommendations of the committee are congruent with the contingencies of the administration, the administration will accept them and then ascribe responsibility to the committee. On the other hand, if a committee's recommendations are not congruent with the contingencies of the administration, the administration may change or reject them. Committees can be used by the administration to turn faculty against faculty, a situation that can lead to almost total control by the administration.

Service to the Community Contingency

The importance of service to the community in assessing a faculty member depends on the relationship between the community and the institution. The "town-gown" relationship has a long history in both the United States and Europe. One important consideration in this relationship is that there are frequent clashes involving conflicting metacontingencies. The objectives of most higher education institutions involve educating those who attend and the search for "truth." Too often the community looks on the institution as a source of jobs for the townspeople plus customers for the various products sold by local merchants. Right at the outset the outcomes of the institution are markedly different for the two groups, and conceivably could be incompatible. The situation may be further complicated by the fact that the institution does not pay any property taxes as a public or tax-exempt institution. Some townspeople may believe they have to pay higher property taxes because the institution does not.

Academicians tend to consider a higher education institution to be a vehicle for change. The controllers of contingencies in the community are frequently opposed to change. Again, there is a conflict of metacontingencies that may lead to serious conflict between the institution and the community. The institution is frequently conceptualized as a community of scholars. Since the search for "truth" is an integral activity of scholars, many scholars may espouse views and advocate changes that run contrary to the prevailing views of the community. During the period of time when southern institutions were in the throes of desegregation, there were many clashes involving faculty who favored desegregation and many townspeople who opposed it. One of the most acrimonious situations in recent years occurred during the early 1950s, the era sometimes called the era of McCarthyism. There was great concern among many that the faculties of higher education institutions were communists and "pinks" and that they were in the process of subverting the youth of the country. The espousal of outcomes by faculty members that ran contrary to the outcomes of higher education voiced by political and civic leaders resulted in branding such faculty members as communists. Faculty members in many institutions were asked to sign oaths professing their renunciation of communism and loyalty to the United States. Many faculty members considered such oaths to be a violation of their constitutional rights and an infringement on their efforts to search for the "truth." Eventually the environment changed, loyalty oaths were discarded, but many institutions and faculty members suffered as a consequence of it.

To minimize the possible conflict of community and institutional metacontingencies, many administrators place a high value on the involvement of the faculty in the community. This involvement can take a variety of forms. Some faculty members consult with various businesses and organizations. Others may make speeches and presentations to civic, church, and social groups. Some may become involved in the political activities of the community, even running for political office.

There are some faculty members who consider the community service criterion to be unfair, since their disciplines may not be amenable to involvement in the community. Community service is not necessarily based on one's discipline. Other faculty members contend that community involvement requires time and effort that are better spent on their activities at the institution. And there are some who contend the institution does not "belong" to the community in which it is located and there is no particular need to become involved in the community's affairs.

These contentions have some validity. The administration, on the other hand, attempting to minimize conflicts that may adversely affect the institution, may also have a legitimate position. The contention revolves around whether community involvement should be one of the contingencies governing the behavior of the faculty. If faculty members are able to meet the other contingencies and have time to become involved in community affairs, then they should do so. On the other hand, if the faculty member elects to meet the other contingencies and not participate in community affairs, he or she should be able to exercise that option without any aversive consequences.

We have looked at some of the contingencies that prevail with respect to faculty. The establishment of contingencies is one thing; providing the conditions that are conducive to the meeting of the contingencies is another. For example, it is relatively easy to establish the contingency involving research, but the conduct of research requires certain conditions. Some areas of research require a considerable amount of money for equipment and supplies, a large amount of space, and time. It behooves an administration to analyze the situation to determine if the contingencies and metacontingencies of the institution are reasonable and realistic in terms of the conditions that can be provided for meeting these contingencies. To establish a contingency with respect to excellence in teaching and then require faculty members to teach a large number of courses with large enrollments may be unrealistic.

CONSEQUENCES

What are the consequences for faculty members, who established the consequences, and who controls the distribution of these consequences? These questions are the ones that seem to be the basis for many of the conflicts between faculty and administration. Consequences are provided for behavior and for a consequence to function as a positive reinforcer, the frequency of the behavior followed by that consequence must increase or be maintained. Some consequences may be provided immediately after the emission of the behavior, but many other consequences may be delayed, some for rather long periods of time. Some consequences provided faculty members arise within the institution, but there are consequences that arise from outside the institution.

Positive Consequences

There are some rather obvious positive consequences such as salary increases, retention, promotion, and tenure. These consequences usually have their origin within the department or smallest administrative unit. In very small units the initial recommendation may arise with the administrative head of the unit. In a department of three or four faculty members, the chair may make personnel recommendations without input from the faculty. Larger departments or units usually have a faculty committee that makes recommendations of these consequences to the unit chair. Salary recommendations are usually in terms such as high, average, low, or none. The chair of the unit then makes recommendations to the dean. The chair's recommendations may be influenced by the committee's recommendations depending on how the chair assesses the committee members. In strong, well-developed units the chair's recommendations may be identical to or reflect slight modifications of the committee's recommendations.

The dean, after receiving the chair's recommendations, makes recommendations to the academic vice president or dean of faculty. The dean may consult with others or have a committee that reviews the recommendations that come from the various units. The vice president, perhaps after consultation with others, makes recommendations to the president. The president, in conjunction with the chief financial officer and his or her staff, prepares the budget that is submitted to the governing body. The president usually, but not always, accepts the personnel recommendations of the academic vice president. When the governing body approves the budget, then the personnel recommendations are finalized.

In state institutions it is possible that the legislature may control salary increases by specifying any salary increase as a fixed percentage for all faculty members. If that occurs, then the legislature has in effect eliminated salary increases as a positive reinforcer, since a faculty member's salary adjustment is not contingent on any behaviors that are specific to the academic community. The "across the board" salary increase is met with a mixed reaction by the faculty. The faculty members who have emitted the behaviors that are usually prized in the academic community are opposed to such salary adjustments. The faculty members who have emitted few, if any, behaviors highly prized in the academic community are more favorably disposed to the "across the board" increase. If salary increases, tenure, retention, and promotion are to function as positive reinforcers, they must be directly related to the behaviors of faculty members that enable the institution to meet its goals and objectives.

In some states the legislature may specify a percentage of the salary increase to be across the board and another percentage that is to be merit. This approach is usually more acceptable than across the board, although there is a watering down of the potential reinforcing properties of the salary increase.

Some state institutions are able to avoid the difficulties created by "across the board" salary increases by utilizing funds that are independent of state appropriations. These funds may be derived from endowments or other gifts to the institution or funds generated by the institution locally.

There are other potential reinforcers for the behaviors of faculty members. Publications, especially publications that are well received by others in that area of research, may be powerful reinforcers for behaviors associated with research. Papers presented at meetings that are well received by the audience may be effective reinforcers for research behaviors. Favorable reference by others in their articles and papers is an effective reinforcer for research behaviors for many faculty members. Many reinforcers of research behavior may be verbal. Colleagues may tell the faculty member that his or her research is excellent. Prizes and awards are frequently provided faculty members for outstanding research. Many institutions have awards for outstanding research by faculty members. Perhaps these kinds of reinforcement may be lumped under a category called recognition.

There is another important source of reinforcement for research activities. This reinforcement involves receiving research grants and contracts. Research grants and contracts not only increase the research capability of a faculty member, but also receiving such grants and contracts often entails other beneficial effects, such as increased salary, promotion, and tenure.

The behaviors involved in teaching may be provided a variety of reinforcers. Students may comment favorably about a particular course. They may tell their friends to take a particular faculty member's course or courses. Course enrollment, especially electives, may serve as a form of reinforcement. There may be some question about the behavior for which students provide reinforcement. The faculty member's behavior that may be reinforced by the students is joke telling, easy grading, and/or giving few or no outside class assignments.

In many institutions students are provided the opportunity to evaluate their instructors. These student evaluations may be used in the assessment of the faculty members for personnel recommendations and/or decisions. The student evaluation of faculty members rarely involves describing the behavior of the faculty member. There are many faculty members and administrators who believe the student evaluations are more of a popularity contest than an identification of significant behaviors of the faculty members.

There are other reinforcements that are frequently provided for effective reaching. Many institutions have some form of "outstanding teacher" award. The process of identifying the "outstanding teacher" varies from institution to institution. In some institutions the students have complete control over the naming of the outstanding teacher. In other institutions it may be a joint student-faculty function. It is extremely rare for the criteria for outstanding teacher to be specified in behavioral terms. The outstanding teacher award is usually presented at a public convocation and carries a monetary component.

Many scholarly and professional organizations provide an award for outstanding teaching and outstanding research behaviors. The American Psychological Association provides such awards on an annual basis.

Negative Reinforcers and Punishers

There are some negative reinforcers and punishers that may be provided by a variety of sources for various behaviors. Negative reinforcement involves the avoidance of or escape from some aversive consequence and an increase or maintenance of the behavior that led to the avoidance or escape. On the other hand, punishment is the providing of an aversive consequence for some behavior that leads to a suppression of the frequency of the behavior.

Faculty members have to be careful to avoid charges of discriminatory practices, especially with respect to grading. There are cases in which students have sued faculty members because they failed to receive the grade in a course they believed they deserved. Instructors have been charged with discriminating against students by excessive demands in their courses or maintaining standards that are essentially unattainable or not comparable to standards maintained by other instructors in the institution. Many institutions provide mechanisms through which students can file charges against faculty members for a variety of behaviors in addition to discriminatory grading practices and excessive demands. One of the more serious charges in recent years is sexual harassment of female students by male faculty members. Female students have charged male faculty members with demanding sexual favors in return for a good grade in the course.

These kinds of charges can destroy the career of a faculty member, even if the charges are not substantiated. If the charges are supported by evidence, a faculty member may be discharged even if he has tenure. John B. Watson was driven out of the academic community as a function of his alleged extramarital activities. In many cases it seems as though the burden of proof rests with the faculty member. The faculty member must prove that he is not guilty of the charges, a position that is contrary to the contention that a person is innocent until proven guilty. Faculty members have resigned rather than go through the quasilegal proceedings that may be involved in refuting the charges.

There have been reports of female faculty members who have been subjected to sexual harassment from male colleagues, chairs, or higher administrative officers. There have been reports of female faculty members who have been subjected to discriminatory practices with respect to retention, promotion, and tenure considerations. Some of these charges have made their way into the courts. The entire process is very aversive to the female faculty member even if she wins the case.

For many faculty members, the most aversive facet of the academic environment is the politics that are occasionally more important than performance. Many departments have cliques or groups that tend to be supportive of the members of the clique and work against anyone who is not a member. Efforts are expended to gain control over important departmental or institutional committees, especially committees that are involved in personnel matters. Favorable personnel actions may depend more on who you know rather than what the faculty member has done.

The situation may become more serious as many institutions are not growing larger and the competition for retention, promotion, and tenure becomes more intense. Many institutions have placed a cap on the percentage of faculty who will be tenured. An untenured faculty member must not only meet the criteria related to scholarly activity and teaching, but avoid alienating anyone who may be in a position to influence personnel decisions. This situation is greatly ameliorated when there are faculty shortages. Predictions of faculty shortages, especially in the sciences and mathematics, are currently being made. Faculty shortages unquestionably increase the faculty member's bargaining position.

There are other situations that arise within a department that require actions and may be influenced by political considerations. The determination of which faculty members teach which courses is very important to most faculty members. In a large department there will be more than one faculty member who may be qualified to teach a particular course. Faculty members whose behavior may have annoyed an influential colleague may find that he or she is punished by being denied the opportunity to teach some highly desired course. The specification of courses that will be required of all majors in the department is another important consideration. Some faculty members prefer to teach required courses and other faculty members prefer not to teach them. Again, assignment to courses may be used to punish a faculty member for behavior that irked an influential colleague. At the same time it should be noted that the assignment of faculty to courses may be used to reinforce certain behaviors of faculty members.

There are other conditions that may be used as reinforcers or punishers of the behavior of faculty members. Preferred teaching times and/or classrooms may be used to reinforce various behaviors of a faculty member, but unpreferred teaching times and/or classrooms may be used to punish various behaviors of a faculty member. Office assignments can be used in a similar fashion.

Travel monies and money for research equipment and supplies can be allocated as reinforcement or punishment for desired or undesired behavior. In some departments travel money is equally allocated among all faculty members regardless of whether or not the faculty member is presenting a paper at the meetings. Though this method of allocation seems eminently fair, it fails to utilize travel money as a reinforcer for research or scholarly activity. And, of course, denying travel money to a faculty member can be used as a punisher for some behaviors. The same situation can exist for research equipment and supplies. There are faculty members who continue to receive research support in the form of equipment and supply monies despite the fact that they have failed to produce a publication or a paper presentation at some scholarly meeting. And there are faculty members who receive no support because they have run afoul of the political power structure within the department.

Most of these problems or difficulties could be prevented if the criteria for these sources of reinforcement or punishment were stated in behavioral terms. If the contingencies were clearly stated in a rigorously defined language, then there would be fewer questions about whether a faculty member met the contingency. For example, if the basis for obtaining travel money were clearly stated in behavioral terms, there would be fewer disputes about its distribution, especially if travel money was used as a reinforcer for research-oriented behaviors and behaviors involved in making a presentation at a professional meeting. Unfortunately, some of the contingencies may not be stated explicitly so that the faculty member does not know what behavior is being demanded of him or her.

Changing Contingencies

Sometimes contingencies change because the objectives of the institution change. Faculty members may be hired under one set of contingencies, but as the objectives of the institution change, the contingencies change. The faculty member may have accepted the position primarily because of the existing contingencies. The change in contingencies may make it much more difficult for the faculty member to meet the new contingencies. An illustration of changed contingencies is the institution that changes from a teaching-oriented institution to a research-oriented institution. Over the years a number of institutions changed from teachers' colleges to universities. When the institution was a teachers' college, there may have been no research contingency for promotion, tenure, or pay raises. As a university the institution may establish a research contingency. Faculty members who may have met the contingencies of a teacher-oriented institution may no longer be able to meet the contingencies of a research-oriented institution.

The statement of the contingencies to the prospective faculty member may be considered a form of establishing operation. That is, the description of the contingencies that prevail provide the motivation for the faculty member when he or she accepted the position. When the contingencies change the faculty member may become very disgruntled when passed over for promotion and after receiving only nominal salary adjustments.

We have discussed some of the contingencies and consequences for the faculty members, but we do not contend that we have described all of the contingencies or consequences. There will be contingencies and consequences that will be unique to each institution. A faculty member at the University of Colorado is alleged to have stated that being in the beautiful location of Boulder, Colorado, was worth half his salary. Not all of the contingencies and consequences apply to every institution. I have tried to describe some of the more common faculty contingencies and consequences.

ADMINISTRATOR CONTINGENCIES

What are the contingencies and consequences for administrators? The contingencies and consequences for administrators will vary as much from institution to institution as they do for faculty members. Since administrators do not have tenure as administrators, their continuance in an administrative position is frequently at the discretion of higher level administrators. For example, the dean may remain a dean as long as the vice president for academic affairs considers his or her performance to be satisfactory. A change in the higher levels of administration is frequently accompanied by changes at the lower levels of administration.

What are the contingencies and consequences that attract people to administrative positions? There is as much variability here as in any thing else in the academic environment. Some faculty members may find that the reinforcers for faculty behavior are no longer effective in maintaining their behavior. They may report that teaching and research are not fun any more. To do the kinds of things they would like to do requires them to be in a position to exercise more control than is available to them as faculty members or even as departmental chairs. They may have ideas for new or changed programs that can be implemented only if they are in a position of authority and responsibility. Being able to create a successful program is a powerful form of reinforcement for many academicians. Moreover, the exercise of control is a very effective source of reinforcement for many individuals. Administrative positions generally provide more opportunities to exercise control than faculty positions.

The "Professional Administrator"

The "professional administrator" is one who enters the administrative environment after a very brief exposure as a faculty member. Why individuals make early entry into administration is not too clear and probably varies from individual to individual. Some may enter administration because they have found that the prevailing reinforcements for faculty members are ineffective for them. Some may have found that the demands made on them as faculty members were very aversive. Others may be lured by the higher rate of compensation and the added perquisites afforded administrators. And there may be some who find the increased interactions with important political, civic, and social leaders to be very reinforcing.

The difficulty confronting professional administrators is that they do not have a good understanding of the contingencies that control the behavior of the faculty members. Faculty members actually exercise some control over administrators, albeit not as much as the faculty members believe they should. Faculty members who have risen through the faculty ranks before becoming administrators are aware of this situation and can accept it. The professional administrator, on the other hand, may not accept any faculty control and be controlled only by the contingencies provided by the higher administrative personnel, including the governing body. This kind of situation almost invariably leads to an adversarial relationship between the faculty and administration, a situation that is not conducive to the attainment of the institutional objectives. Moreover, the adversarial relationship is conducive to an increase in lawsuits and there has been a significant increase in lawsuits over the past 30 years. The increase in lawsuits alleging discrimination in some personnel realm was facilitated by congressional action. Congress in 1972 amended the Civil Rights Act of 1964 and the Equal Pay Act. According to LaNoue and Lee (1987), there was only one discrimination suit in the 1960s despite the social activism of the period. They reported the number of court decisions involving discrimination lawsuits against academic institutions rose to 20 from 1970–74, 87 from 1975–79, and 118 from 1980–84. The increase in the number of lawsuits may also have been facilitated by growing unionism on campus, which was described earlier.

Competing Contingencies

Most administrative personnel find that they are frequently subject to competing contingencies. The higher administration generates contingencies, but the units lower in the organizational structure also create contingencies. For example, a dean may find that the vice president for academic affairs has created a limit on the amount of money available for the purchase of equipment. This amount was provided by the chief financial officer who has to exercise control over the budget. The dean, in making equipment money available to the departments, may find that the departments are requesting more money than is available. Departmental chairs may contend that if they do not get the requested monies they will have to cut out some programs, reduce the number of laboratories, drop courses, or reduce the number of sections of popular courses. These steps could lead students to complain because they cannot enroll in certain courses or must change programs because a program as been deleted.

The dean, confronted with this situation, may demand more money from the academic vice president. However, the academic vice president controls contingencies and consequences for the dean. The control exercised by the academic vice president may affect the behavior of the dean and his or her demands. The only control the dean exercises in the interactions with the academic vice president are the soundness of the basis of the request for the additional funds and the threat of resignation. The dean who is reluctant to resign the deanship may be reluctant to be forceful in making demands on the academic vice president. Moreover, neither the soundness of the request nor the threat of resigning may be effective in extracting more money from the academic vice president.

Most administrators find that they frequently encounter the metacontingencies of the community because the community leaders conceptualize the administrators in the same way that they conceptualize executives in a company. They tend to assume that the administrators have, or should have, total control of the situation at the institution at all times. When a faculty member behaves in a manner contrary to the metacontingencies of the community, the community leaders tend to contact an administrator. Faculty members' behavior conflicting with the community metacontingencies is one of the major aversive events for many administrators. An example of this kind of conflict is a faculty member speaking to a minority group and suggesting legal actions that may be taken with respect to segregation in the public schools in a community that has strongly resisted integrating the public schools. The dominant cultural group considers the outcome of school integration to be a reduction in the quality of education as well as other undesired outcomes. This group especially resents a faculty member who speaks on behalf of school integration who is or should be a member of the dominant cultural group. They also resent that their tax dollars are being spent to support a faculty member who speaks out against the metacontingencies of the dominant cultural or social group. Community leaders may demand that the faculty member be disciplined, perhaps fired. However, to discipline or fire a faculty member in this situation could be considered an abridgement of freedom of speech and could lead to a lawsuit.

Administrators by and large are greatly concerned about lawsuits. Though the courts may be reluctant to interfere in the operation of an institution, they have done so on a number of occasions in the past 25 years. Many administrators have backed down in a position or action in the face of a threatened lawsuit. Some faculty members have capitalized on the administration's reluctance to go into court to gain promotion, tenure, salary increases, and other reinforcements, even if the faculty member has not emitted the behavior that warrants the demanded reinforcers. When the administration is confronted with a demand to take a course of action that could lead to a lawsuit, it looks for ways and means to placate the demands of community leaders and faculty without providing a basis for a lawsuit.

The administrators of the private institution can find themselves in a similar situation. The faculty member who leads a protest against a company that contributed thousands of dollars to the institution may find that the administrators take a rather dim view of such action. At the same time the administrators can do little or nothing about the situation as long as the faculty member does not violate any community, state, or federal laws.

The President

The president of the institution is the highest ranking administrator and has primary responsibility for the day-to-day operation of the institution. In large institutions today, the president is no longer capable of overseeing every aspect of the day-to-day operations. Consequently, there has been a tremendous increase in the number of administrators in most institutions, but especially in the larger institutions. There is a variety of administrators carrying various titles who are actually more involved in the daily operations than the president. The president of a public higher educational institution is more concerned with public relations and maintaining a good relationship with important political, civic, and social leaders than the educational practices of the institution. For many years, the presidents of public institutions were not involved with generating gifts and grants to the institution as the legislature provided the requisite funding. In recent years the public sector has found it necessary to invest more time and effort in raising money from private sources as legislatures have been forced to curtail monies for higher education. The president has usually taken the lead in this endeavor. One result of this development is that the president has come into more and more contact with the metacontingencies that prevail in the corporate world and with the wealthier members of the community. These metacontingencies are frequently quite different from the metacontingencies of the political and higher educational sectors.

One result of this increased interaction with the metacontingencies of the corporate world is a growing concern about the operation of an educational institution in a manner similar to that of a corporation. The concept of the bottom line that is commonplace in the corporate world is now being heard more and more in the academic environment. There are some who believe that the educational entity must adopt more and more of the practices and procedures of the corporate environment. Conversely, there are those who contend that it is not possible to operate an educational institution in the same way as a corporation.

Increasing interactions with the metacontingencies of the corporate world has also resulted in a significant change in the requirements of a president of a public institution of higher education. Demonstrated scholarship on the part of a candidate for president is not as important as behaviors necessary to interact with the leaders of business and industry. Demonstrated scholarship would be nice, but other considerations have become more important. Having strong connections with top-ranking officials of the federal government, especially of granting agencies, is a strong asset for an aspiring president. The rise of the professional administrator means that fewer candidates for administrative positions have acquired the credentials of the traditional academician, since the professional administrator will have spent relatively little time as a faculty member. The aspiring president must have acquired behaviors that are closer to the behaviors of the aspiring president of a corporation as the budgets of many institutions are in the hundreds of millions of dollars. There are institutional presidents today who have no academic background and have come from the corporate world.

The private sector of higher education has always relied on private sources for the funds to operate the institutions. Obtaining adequate financial support has been a continuing problem for the private institution. Some of the best known and most respected private institutions have occasionally found themselves with operating deficits. The president has always been in the forefront in soliciting funds for the institution. During the past 10–15 years, the costs of education have risen sharply and the private sector has scurried to find the funds necessary to keep functioning. In the 1950s a rule of thumb that was frequently applied in the private institution was that student aid should be provided for not more than 25% of the students. Another frequently applied rule of thumb was that tuition should account for less than 50% of the budget. The tremendous increase in tuition in recent years has necessitated raising the percentage of students receiving financial aid to over 50% in many private institutions today. The reduction in a variety of federal government programs aiding students has placed more of the financial burden on the institution itself.

The presidents of private institutions have to be especially productive to raise the funds necessary to meet the ever-increasing costs of operating an institution. Many consider that the crowning achievement of President Bok of Harvard was increasing the endowment to 5 billion dollars during his 20-year tenure. Even with this large endowment, Harvard is planning a campaign to raise an additional 2.5 billion dollars. But Harvard is not alone in its efforts to raise money. Many private institutions are planning or conducting campaigns to raise money.

Given the importance of raising money in both the private and public sector, the president of an institution must have the behaviors that are effective in raising money. One of the major reinforcements for a president is probably getting a large gift from a corporate or private donor. Other sources of reinforcement for presidents include attracting nationally and internationally noted individuals to speak at convocations and graduation exercises. Having noted individuals (e.g., Nobel and Pulitzer Prize winners) join the faculty is a significant reinforcement for presidents and other administrators such as academic vice presidents and deans. The national and international recognition attained by an institution in a source of reinforcement for the administrators and, perhaps, the faculty.

I have tried to provide an overview of some of the metacontingencies, contingencies, and consequences that prevail in higher educational institutions in the United States. As mentioned before, I do not claim to have exhausted the list for any of these three concepts. We must remember that the components of metacontingencies and contingencies are acquired. Since the United States is a pluralistic society, it is not possible to specify that a given metacontingency is present in every part of that society or in every subculture. Higher educational institutions are located all over the country in a variety of communities and regions. The prevailing metacontingencies in any of these locales may differ from those in another locale. The same situation exists with respect to contingencies. There is usually a definite relationship between the contingencies and metacontingencies. The institution in a given locale will reflect to a greater or lesser degree the metacontingencies that prevail in the community. The degree of conflict between the community and the institution is inversely related to the extent to which the institution has accepted the metacontingencies of the community.

The components of the contingency and metacontingency are acquired. The control exercised by the environment over the behavior of a faculty member of an administrator is primarily acquired. Much of the acquisition has occurred before the faculty member or administrator became associated with the institution. And the control exercised by the contingency has been acquired individually. Because the contingency is individually acquired, the extent of the control exercised by the contingency will vary between individuals. "Control" here simply means the probability of occurrence of a behavior in a given environment. If a given environmental situation exercises little control over a behavior of a faculty member, it simply means there is a low probability that that behavior will be stopped by that faculty member in that situation. The same environment may exercise a high degree of control of the same behavior of another faculty member.

Most consequences have acquired their consequential properties. As a result, what may be an effective consequence for one faculty member or administrator may be totally ineffective for another. To assume that a given consequence will be effective for every person is fraught with great danger. Many administrators make this assumption about the effectiveness of a given consequence for all faculty members and then are surprised when it does not have the expected effect. Consequences have to be tailored to the individual faculty member to maximize their effectiveness. Promotion in rank may be a powerful reinforcer for one faculty member's behavior, but tenure may be more powerful for another's. A personal computer may be a more powerful reinforcer for a faculty member's behavior than a salary increase. Since the individual's history is intimately associated with the consequential properties that various objects and events have acquired, it may behoove administrators to become more aware of the individual's history. To do so may enable consequences to be provided that will maximize the contribution of every faculty member and administrator to the attainment of the objectives of the institution.

REFERENCES

Boyd, W. B. (1973). Collective bargaining in academe: Cause and consequences. In C. R. Hughes, R. L. Underbrink, & C. C. Gordon (Eds.), *Collective negotiations in higher education: A reader* (pp. 11–28). Carlinville, IL: Blackburn College Press.

Cornell University, 183 NLRB 329 (1970).

Estes, E. K. (1956). Learning. In P. R. Farnsworth & Q. McNemar (Eds.), *Annual review of psychology* (pp. 1–38). Palo Alto, CA: Annual Reviews.

Glenn, S. S. (1988). Contingencies and metacontingencies: Toward a synthesis of behavior analysis and cultural materialism. *The Behavior Analyst, 11,* 161–180.

Gray, L., & Davis, W. (1980). Labor and higher education: Impetus to new alliances. In H. Stack & C. M. Hutten (Eds.), *Building new alliances: Labor unions and higher education* (pp. 1–11). San Francisco: Jossey-Bass.

Harris, M. (1979). *Cultural materialism.* New York: Random House.

Hart, J. M. (1878). *German universities: A narrative of personal experience.* New York: D. Appleton & Co.

Hofstadter, R. (1955a). *The development of academic freedom in the United States.* New York: Columbia University Press.

Hofstadter, R. (1955b). *Academic freedom in the age of the college.* New York: Columbia University Press.

Kaplin, W. A. (1985). *The law of higher education* (2nd ed.). San Francisco: Jossey-Bass.

Keller, F. S. (1968). "Good-bye, Teacher." *Journal of Applied Behavior Analysis, 1,* 79–89.

Keller, F. S., & Sherman, J. G. (1974). *The Keller plan handbook.* Menlo Park, CA: W. A. Benjamin.

Kemerer, F. R., & Baldridge, J. V. (1975). *Unions on campus.* San Francisco: Jossey-Bass.

Ladd, E. C., & Lipset, S. M. (1973). *Professors, unions, and American higher education.* Washington, DC: American Enterprise Institute for Public Policy Research.

LaNoue, G. R., & Lee, B. A. (1987). *Academics in court.* Ann Arbor, MI: University of Michigan Press.

Loretta Heights College v. NLRB, 742 F.2d 1245 (10th Circ. 1984).

Mason, H. I. (1974). Faculty unionism and university governance. In J. H. Schuster (Ed.), *Encountering the unionized community* (pp. 1–26). San Francisco: Jossey-Bass.

Michael, J. (1982). Distinguishing between discriminative stimuli and motivational functions of stimuli. *Journal of the Experimental Analysis of Behavior, 37,* 149–155.

NLRB v. Wentworth Institute, 515 F.2d 550 (1st Cir. 1975).

NLRB v. Yeshiva University, 100 S.Ct. 856 (1980).

Skinner, B. F. (1968). *The technology of teaching.* New York: Appleton-Century-Crofts.

Spencer, H. (1874). *The study of sociology.* New York: D. Appleton & Co.

9

Behavioral Analysis of Clinical Practice in the United States

K. Anthony Edwards

INTRODUCTION

It has now been 111 years since Wilhelm Wundt opened the doors of the first experimental psychology laboratory at Leipzig, Germany (Boring, 1957). Introspection, or the private events known primarily as thinking and feeling, were extensively studied, giving the world the first established laboratory for examining the human "mind." As metaphysical as this might now appear, as Boring noted, Wundt actually "began the antimetaphysical tradition that still persists" (p. 332). Seventeen years later (in 1896), Lightner Witmer, one of several first-generation experimentalists in the United States from Wundt's school, opened the first psychological clinic and coined the term "clinical psychologist" (Boring, 1957; Levine & Levine, 1970; Strickland, 1988; Sundberg, Tyler, & Taplin, 1973). The first client was an elementary school child who had trouble spelling, an educational problem. Clearly, or perhaps ironically, both private events and spelling are problems of verbal behavior that today's behavior analysts witness.

Since those early beginnings, a rich history has followed circuitous routes through a more or less long and thorny road toward an applied behavioral analysis. Other routes have also been followed, and it is through these that the dominant "traditional" field of clinical practice has emerged, one that closely imitates medical practice (Blau, 1983). Some applied behavior analysts insist it is time to dress in the clothing of clinical psychologists (e.g., Dougher, 1988). Others who are learning-theory oriented argue for the return of learning-theory based clinical practice (Levis, 1990; Stampfl, 1987; Wolpe, 1987). However, most applied behavioral clinicians may not fully understand or appreciate where it is they want to go and where they may arrive. "Rather than emerging as an independent profession," Blau (1983) stated, ". . . the larger number of practicing psychologists are under the direction or limitation of other professionals in settings that restrict rather than enhance the delivery of psychological services to the consumer" (p. 57).

Clinical psychologists are broadly trained as scientist-practitioners and offer a range of skills including assessment, intervention, and consultation. They conduct a mixture of psychotherapeutic interventions based on training and experience; administer intelligence, aptitude, and personality tests; and examine neuropsychological functioning and marital adjustment. Clinicians serve as expert witnesses in a wide range of court cases; they design, direct, and monitor programs relating to substance abuse, self-destructive behavior, and the criminal justice system; they work in an assortment of different medical settings using psychological methods and tools required in health service.

Clinical psychologists do not often work independently. They usually perform their services in psychology departments, university clinics, hospitals, prisons, community mental health centers, agencies, courts, and treatment centers. Psychologists in these institutions rarely impact on policy, and there is little freedom for clinicians to decide how to best use their skills. Clinical psychologists are usually "an interim professional, receiving consultations or service requests and filling these within the constraints and expectations of a host institution" (Blau, 1983, p. 58).

For the most part, the behaviors of clinical psychologists in these settings tend to be shaped and maintained by the agencies and the histories of those agencies. Individuals who attempt to create their own job description, as murky as the original might be, tend to last a short time, or so it appears (see also Malott, 1986).

Several studies have examined what clinical psychologists are and what they do (Alberts & Edelstein, 1990; Conway, 1988; Garfield & Kurtz, 1976; Guevremont & Spiegler, 1990). In one recent study (Conway, 1988), most clinical psychologists were clinical practitioners (59%), some academicians (20%), and the remainder were researchers (5%), consultants (5%), supervisors (2%), administrators (8%), and other (1%). They were employed in private practice (23%), at a university psychology department (22%), and "other" (12%). The remainder were about evenly divided among mental hospitals (8%), general hospitals (6%), outpatient clinics (5%), community mental health centers (5%), medical schools (7%), and universities/other (7%). It was noted that 55% of the clinical psychologists declared their theoretical orientation as "eclectism"; 11%, psychoanalytic; 10%, learning theory; and the remaining 21% declared their orientation as neo-Freudian, interpersonal, cognitive, existential, humanistic, biological/neuropsychological, or other.

Garfield and Kurtz (1976) reported the characteristics of clinical psychologists of the 1970s. Little of the total percentage of clinician's time was devoted to "behavior modification." However, little time was devoted to any particular technique; one wonders what activities are actually occurring in the 25.07% of the time designated as "individual psychotherapy." Nearly 10% considered their theoretical orientation "learning theory," 7.14% stated "other," and 54.97% considered themselves "eclectic." Again, one wonders how much eclectic time was spent doing what. Note too that only eclectic and psychoanalytic emphases were proportionately greater than learning theory.

Guevremont and Spiegler (1990) more recently examined the clinical practices of behavior therapists. All members of the Association for Advancement of Behavior Therapy listed in the 1988 directory who indicated they were engaged in clinical practice ($n = 2,277$) were contacted, but less than half of the questionnaires were returned ($n = 988$). The most frequently used therapy techniques were indicated as, in descending order, reinforcement, cognitive restructuring, behavioral rehearsal, relaxation training, and problem-solving. The most frequently used assessment procedures, in descending order, were interviews, self-report inventories, self-recording, and behavior rating scales. Least frequently used assessment procedures were projective techniques, neurological tests, and psychophysiological measures.

Alberts and Edelstein (1990) recently reported that 308 graduate training programs report offering at least one course in behavior therapy or specified training in the scientist-practitioner model. The behavioral emphasis of their program was rated 3.0 or higher on a 5-point scale by 219 respondents, where 1 = "none" and 5 = "very great amount." Further analysis showed that clinical psychology programs, at the master's level, offered the largest number of behavior therapy courses, whereas school psychology offered the fewest. Doctoral level programs in educational psychology offered the largest number (M = 5.88), whereas counseling psychology offered the least (M = 2.75). School (M = 5.33) and clinical (M = 5.03) followed closely behind educational psychology programs. A further analysis of the weight of theoretical/conceptual analysis was conducted for 49 programs. The results are perhaps encouraging. Behaviorism is hardly meeting its demise; furthermore, radical behaviorism seems to be alive and thriving. Whether it will have an effect on the field of clinical psychology is yet to be determined.

Clinical psychology has been defined as an applied science utilizing the principles of psychology to understand and help alleviate human problems (Bellack & Hersen, 1980). Psychology is considered a cross between science and the humanities. It is a profession historically connected to psychoanalysis, testing, and therapy. Clinical psychologists are usually trained as both scientists and practitioners.

A thorough review of Hersen, Kazdin, and Bellack's (1983), Walker's (1981), and Wolman's (1965) handbooks is recommended for a well-rounded overview of clinical psychology as well as a comparison and contrast of where the field has been for the past generation and where it is going. Other books describe the private practice from a "setting up business" perspective (Pressman, 1979; Pressman & Siegler, 1983), a general perspective (Bellack & Hersen, 1980; Hokanson, 1983; Sundberg et al., 1973), and a relatively full range of techniques and materials required for a behavior therapy private practice (Kaplan, 1986). No texts are yet available describing a behavior analytic clinical practice, but one is needed.

CONTINGENCIES OF CLINICAL PRACTICE

Blau (1983) argues that the clinical psychologist should: (1) essentially receive regularly scheduled training to skillful, full-time practitioner role models throughout graduate school; (2) be exposed to and be supervised under a wide range of widely accepted assessment procedures and techniques—"therapeutic intervention, crisis consultation, and consultation involving consumer-generated help-requests" (p. 60); (3) be credentialed by an incremental increase in professional practice licensure and mandatory continuing education and reevaluation of clinical skills; and (4) provide services under the independent practice model, if clinical psychology is to justify itself and remove other professions as supervisors.

Graduate training, Azrin (1977) argues, has not produced effective treatments based on understanding behavior. Focusing on learning principles, clinical outcome, and scientific evaluation of treatments produces more effective clinicians. He emphasizes an applied research strategy focusing on problems and outcomes rather than on method. Clinical practice disallows the use of long baselines for no treatment because patients are in need of help and they are usually paying for services. The rule in Azrin's work was to use the shortest baseline possible to establish a trend. "A prerequisite in this strategy was scientific rigor regarding objective specification of the procedures, quantitative and objective specification of the behavioral outcome, controlled experimental evaluation, a conceptual foundation for the procedures, and the primacy of data over speculation" (Azrin, 1977, p. 148).

A large number of psychologists entered into private practice in the 1950s (Blau, 1983). Gradually, independent practice became more widely accepted by the American Psychological Association, practitioners became eligible for third-party payment, hospital privileges were surreptitiously granted to some, the general public came to accept psychologists, and in many cases turned away from psychiatry. Psychologists have also gradually become part of the community delivering services without supervision by medical professionals.

However, in spite of a solid base, "clinical psychology has taken the medical and psychiatric profession as a partial model" (Blau, 1983, p. 58). Granted, "The medical profession, with its tradition of helpfulness, concern, and responsibility, is a respectable model" (Blau, 1983, p. 58). But is this the model psychologists want? Members of the medical profession support a disease model (Blau, 1983; Ullmann & Krasner, 1965). As a result of the lack of a model, teaching, and appropriate rules, those who are designing and implementing clinical education and training have been inadequate in preparing clinicians for practice dealing with the "real world" in the community. Therefore, clinical psychology has fallen short in providing services to those who need it. "Because psychologists are rarely trained for independent, applied professional roles, they are less likely to be in a position to deliver their services and make their value known" (Blau, 1983, p. 58).

Ferster (1972) describes how the behavior of therapists is differentially reinforced by changes occurring in their patients' behaviors. According to Ferster, the clinician's training and experience, the training and experience of clients, and the theory under which the therapist is operating structures and directs therapy, whereas the focus on the individual's behavior changes the theory and affects the experience on which treatment is based. "The theory suggests what to look for, but when it ceases to be useful, the experiential therapist shifts to his observations of the patient's behavior and his own experience" (Ferster, 1972, pp. 1–2).

Much in the same way the "child is the father of the man," according to Freud, "the client is the therapist of the clinical psychologist." The client's behaviors set the occasion for the therapist's behaviors. To refuse to "set aside the tool bag" when a new problem appears, continuing to "use a hammer to insert a screw," is short-sighted at best. To avoid the client setting the rules for the therapist, clinicians need to rely on outcome research. Is there enough of it? Definitely not. Do clinicians rely on it? Probably not enough. Do they change strategies because of outcome research? Not likely. Epling and Pierce (1986) have argued convincingly that basic research is little utilized by clinicians and that basic and applied researchers have much to offer each other.

METACONTINGENCIES OF CLINICAL PRACTICE

Clinicians tend to behave and report their behavior as most of us do. We tend to consider our behavior on the "cause and effect" or contingency level. A client appears at the office, states a presenting problem, and therapy or testing begins. Additionally, however, the clinician's license hangs on the wall, displayed so that the potential client can see it. The secretary/bookkeeper notes the patient's arrival and departure in a book for billing to an insurance company that will base the amount of money paid to the clinician on whether he or she is listed in the National Register of Health Service Providers of Psychology. The insurance company will also determine whether it will pay for the diagnosis given. Additionally, some other forms are filled out and guarantees of confidentiality are given. A copyrighted test purchased from a publishing company is given, and the fee for the test is indicated on the billing form. During treatment, an audiotape or videotape might be played, some homework assignments might be given, and a book might be loaned to the patient.

All of these activities or events are part of the culture and are accepted, recommended, or criticized by other members of the clinical psychology culture. Clinicians' behaviors are affected by the actions of others in the culture and they behave likewise toward others. They serve on ethics committees, budget committees, or planning committees with other members of the culture, and they decide among themselves the ethical practices, money allocations, or programs that will be effected on other members of the culture. Some of these practices will become relatively permanent and some will disappear, depending on which have benefited, punished, or had no effect on other members of the culture.

The unlicensed "psychologist" is condemned for using this label. The psychologist who engages in sexual activity with a client is taken to court for breaking the law. Other members of the culture voice approval or disapproval for the activity or for the law. Organizations such as the American Psychological Association's Divisions 12 and 42, Division 1 of the Wisconsin Psychological Association, and the Brown County Psychological Society endorse certain clinical cultural practices such as hospital privileges, licensure through the National Register, third-party payments to clinicians, and clinicians' rights to prescribe medication. All of these have been, are being, or probably will be enacted through legislation. They have, and will, considerably change the course of clinical practice.

In an important contribution (e.g., Glenn, 1987, 1989) to the struggle to bridge the gap between behavioral analysis and cultural materialism, Glenn (1988) defined some key concepts of Harris' version of anthropology (also see Harris, 1979; Lloyd, 1985; Vargas, 1985). Cultural materialism (a branch of a science of culture) and behavioral analysis (an approach to a science of behavior) share characteristics that are important. In behavioral analysis the unit of analysis is the contingency of reinforcement. However, "The metacontingency is the unit of analysis encompassing a cultural practice, in all its variations, and the aggregate outcome" (Glenn, 1988, p. 168). Relationships between operant behaviors and environmental events are related to natural consequences of ontogenic behavior. Behaviors tend to maintain until for some reason, a need for change comes about. When behaviors are affected by an environment comprised of others, a cultural practice emerges. Behaviors of new members are shaped and maintained by those in the culture who are affected.

As Glenn (1988) states, "The outcomes of cultural practices must, of course, be specified empirically" (p. 168). As in the earlier mention of a clinician having sex with a client, the number of clinicians engaged in sexual activities is the outcome of cultural practices as defined by ethics committees and other leaders in the cultural community. The number of clinicians who misdiagnose is an outcome of clinical cultural practices as a function of insurance company demands for specific diagnostic categories considered payable or not payable. The number of clinics whose members have their licenses hanging on the wall is an outcome of clinical cultural practices as defined by examiners rules.

> The functional relationship between cultural practices and their outcomes feeds back into cultures through the selection process. If variations in the practice fail to keep pace with changes in the metacontingencies, the practice is no longer selected. Practices that "fit" their environment produce outcomes that maintain permaclones (i.e., the continuous practices of a group comprised of individuals gradually replaced over time). This is selection of the third kind. (Glenn, 1988, pp. 168–169)

The practice of clinical psychology is no exception to Glenn's selection rule.

THE FUTURE OF CLINICAL PRACTICE

Krasner (1990) presents an exceptionally optimistic perspective of clinical behavior modification/therapy. First, he claims that the terms are basically synonymous in the literature. Second, he states that the field has grown and expanded to a remarkable degree. Consider, for example, the "research, applications, publications, organizations, journals, conferences, training programs, and individuals identified with it (and against it). . . ." (p. 3). Many would disagree with this optimism. For example, Skinner (1990) notes the impact of cognitivism and believes it has diverted useful energies in the wrong direction. Activities have been both directed away from cultural concerns and on individuals with little hope for any future productivity. The journals, publications, and other activities have been wastefully focused. The important global issues are described in Russell (1950, 1957), Wheeler (1973), Zifferblatt and Hendricks (1974), Malagodi (1986), Harzem (1987), Catania and Harnad (1988), in Skinner's many publications (for a complete listing, see Catania & Harnad, 1988), and in Harris' prolific writings (e.g., Harris, 1964a, 1964b, 1974, 1975, 1977, 1979, 1981, 1985, 1987, 1988, 1989).

Some complain that students are not learning the roots of applied behavioral analysis. What is especially needed is for professors of behavior analytic clinical practices to look at what they are doing with their students. Malott (1986) comes close. Professors of psychology tend to train their potential experimental scientists to believe they must do experimental research and publish in scholarly journals; anything less is inadequate. Although it is implied they should not be teachers, administrators, or practitioners, most get these jobs and then attempt to maneuver them into research positions.

> They evaluate their jobs in terms of how many research opportunities there are. And they hang their heads in shame when they are not able to publish as much as their colleagues in the big-time universities . . . [W]e are condemning the majority of our graduates to live as unhappy misfits in jobs they will eventually find themselves in . . . [T]o suggest another model is to blaspheme. (Malott, 1986, pp. 5–6)

Krasner (1990) quotes Wolpe (1986) as stating, " 'despite its well-documented record of success in the treatment of the neuroses, behavior therapy is little taught in departments of psychiatry because of an inaccurate image based on misinformation' (p. 192)". Fully 25% of the 72 chapter authors of the book in which Krasner is writing are cited as affiliated with departments of psychiatry. I would certainly hope that at least some of them are teaching some courses in behavior therapy and, indeed, that some of them are dispelling at least some of the misinformation about behavior therapy. Twenty years ago one would have had to look very hard to find 25% of the authors of any behavior modification/therapy textbook affiliated with departments of psychiatry. Is this further evidence of a marriage of clinical psychology and psychiatry?

One defining property of the problems of clinical practice is the definitions provided in the DSM-III-R (American Psychiatric Association, 1987), the psychiatrist's and clinical psychologist's bible. As definitions are becoming empirical, and somewhat more closely approximating behavioral definitions, they should become more acceptable to behavior analysts. If behavior analysts get involved in defining, then the definitions will be still more acceptable (especially to behavior analysts).

What will especially influence clinical practice are the environments in which clinical practice is conducted. As long as clinical practice is conducted in the office, institutions, or away from the settings in which the problem behaviors occur, there is not likely to be much significant change in behavior patterns. Economic factors such as amount of payment for services provided over time certainly affects clinical practice; patients who receive Medicaid are less well-served than patients who are funded by an insurance policy paying 100% of the costs. As with all health services, threats such as lawsuits and claims of fraud or abuse (valid or invalid) affect clinical practice. Support and other feedback from professional colleagues at meetings in particular, but locally as well, affect clinical practices. Colleagues sharing the same general physical environment, philosophical position, and clinical style affect clinical practice. Finally, but not completely, books, films, lectures and other information available at meetings inform the clinician on the current research and techniques developed.

CLINICAL CASE STUDY

A clinical setting familiar to the author is described here to provide an example of how applied behavior analysts can benefit society on the cultural level.

Prison inmates are a large part of the national population, and this group is steadily increasing. In 1979, there were over a quarter of a million inmates in state prisons (Travisono, 1984). In 1987, over a half million adults were incarcerated, almost double in 9 years (Travisono, 1988). Almost 2 million adults are on probation (Travisono, 1988). Between July 1, 1986 and June 30, 1987, almost a quarter of a million individuals were admitted to prison, over 232,000 were released, about 5,000 escaped, and 835 died. Nearly all will return to their previous environments and behaviors and more than half will return to prison.

Furthermore, a large percentage of inmates are considered "mentally ill." Of the quarter of a million plus (278,141) inmates in prison on the first day of 1978 (Weiss & Henney, 1980), 10,895 were transferred to mental health facilities that year (Steadman, Monahan, Hartstone, Davis, & Robbins, 1982). Edwards (1988a) suggested that most transfers occurred from segregated units (protective custody, death row, segregation). It appears that 15–20% (Clanon, 1981; Roth, 1980) or more (James, Gregory, Jones, & Rundel, 1980) of inmates warrant psychological or psychiatric attention and more than 5% may require hospitalization (Roth, 1980).

There are very few psychologists working with these clients, and there are far fewer applied behavior analysts. Edwards (1988b) estimates that there is about one psychologist per 800 inmates. Most of these psychologists work in maximum security prisons. And most prison inmates have or are eligible for a DSM-III-R diagnosis (American Psychiatric Association, 1987). Few studies of this population are reported by applied behavior analysts.

Possibly, because of this, the medical (i.e., clinical) model is becoming stronger in prisons, and psychologists are becoming a part of the medical branches of departments of corrections. Clinical psychologists conduct intake interviews, do crisis intervention, provide psychotherapy, and conduct group therapy. This appears to be nonthreatening and relatively nonproductive in terms of dealing with cultural metacontingencies.

Bartollas (1985) notes that "formal treatment modalities based on social learning principles are on the decline in juvenile and adult corrections. The Federal Prison System no longer conducts such programs, and the federal government will no longer fund behavior modification programs" (p. 133). How did this happen? This may have been a consequence of erroneous information and an uninformed public. As a result of communication problems, one of the few possible opportunities to correct maladaptive destructive adult and juvenile behavior was erased. As Bartollas (1985) continues, "Yet, reinforcing inmates for positive behavior is one of the most universally accepted principle in corrections. In correctional institutions throughout the nation, residents receive additional privileges as they accept institutional rules and procedures and as they show more positive attitudes" (p. 133).

As an alternative to behavioral analysis, cognitive therapy seemed safe to use in prisons. Because it was similar to the vernacular (Skinner, 1990), it was easy to understand and thus was successful for awhile. Cognitive psychology seemed to have helped in corrections. The dust had to settle before anyone could recover from the Martinson (1974) edict that, with regard to psychological services in corrections, "nothing works" (see also Wilson & Herrnstein, 1985). But Skinner is correct on one count (and many others)—the "vernacular refined for the study of mental life is scarcely more helpful than the lay version, especially when theory began to replace introspection" (p. 1210). Indeed, it would have been more useful to have had behavioral analysis. "It would have helped in two ways, by clarifying the contingencies of reinforcement to which the vernacular alludes, and by making it possible to design better environments—personal environments that would solve existing problems and larger environments or cultures in which there would be fewer problems" (Skinner, 1990, p. 1210). However, it was not so simple to see this in the correctional setting that prohibited "behavior modification," and theorizing is not allowed in settings where crises occur at a higher than average rate such as a maximum security prison; without models, teaching, and rules favoring behavioral analysis, progress is at a standstill.

Whether we like prisons or not, they are here to stay for a long time. They, like nursing homes, appear to be a "necessary evil" (Edwards, 1980; Edwards & Sheldon-Wildgen, 1980; Risley & Edwards, 1976). Applied behavior analysts are needed to provide models for prison psychologists. Behavior analysts can serve as clinical directors (teachers, models, and rule makers) monitoring research, planning packages, supervising graduate and undergraduate students, training staff, and performing "clinical" functions. What has been done in the past is far too limited, has been met with suspicion, and was internally fought until rendered ineffective. What behavior analysts can now do for prisons is unlimited: The research is still there to be done; clients are still available in massive numbers with multiple problems; staff need training more than ever before; and packages still need to be developed. As Stolz (1981) stated: "Is anybody out there, does anybody care?" (p. 491).

There is little need to repeat what has been said quite well by Baer, Wolf, and Risley (1968, 1987) concerning the current dimensions of applied behavioral analysis in general and by Morris (1980) on the dimensions of applied behavioral analysis in criminal justice. Behavioral analysis must be behavioral, applied, and analytic. In prisons, this can provide what Skinner (1990) argued for: better treatment.

Regarding this matter, Remington (1981) has stated: ". . . when behavior modification techniques are introduced within a prison setting, many advantages are gained" (p. 122). Positive reinforcement more effectively replaces aversive methods. Inmates favorably perceive this. Educational and vocational achievements are better managed using contingencies. He further argues, however, that "unless inmates are given a substantial role to play in the design of the contingencies under which they work, and unless these contingencies can be shown to reduce recidivism, then even a scheme as effective as that described by Ayllon and his colleagues can amount to no more than a humane and effective method for the management of institutional behavior" (p. 122). Although there seems to be little wrong with "a humane and effective method for the management of institutional behavior," inmates will find little to recommend change if it fails to provide them with a better life, more immediate access to release, and the like. Actually, inmates are usually little affected by reduced recidivism because its consequences are too far distant.

Emery and Marholin (1977) discuss behavioral technology at two levels. The first is that which goes no further than the study itself. Yes, it works, but so what? No one uses the data, no one incorporates the procedures. Stolz (1981) further argues that no one reads the reports and perhaps no one even cares whether or not it works. King (1981) says that for these programs to generalize, we have to accept this: "Revolutionaries at middle age must accept their quiet domestic life or refuel their passion by taking on larger battles" (p. 510). He goes on to state that it is a marketing problem. "A marketing orientation begins with the consumer's needs and wants and designs its products and services and their dissemination around the habits, customs, and preferences of its consumers" (p. 508). Who is the consumer in a prison? The prisoner, prison administration, or society?

Psychologists in prisons are operating adrift. They have no "father of correctional psychology." They have no model, theory, or anything else. They tend to work at surviving within the system in more ways than most psychologists or applied behavior analysts. Not only are the administrators of the system often hostile to change (and to the entire concept of psychology), but so is the client who is in need of treatment. Can corrections benefit from the technologies of applied behavioral analysis?

CONCLUSION

Sundberg et al. (1973) conclude their discussion of the future of clinical psychology by stating:

In contrast with the outlook ten years ago [now about 30 years ago], the charting of a few alternative directions for clinical psychology no longer seems feasible. Instead we look toward a pluralistic profession with many specialized kinds of work being carried out in many setting-client-activity situations. Professional organizations and training programs will evolve to facilitate such pluralistic development. (p. 537)

In their overview of experimental research methodology in clinical psychology, Kratochwill and Mace (1983) presented some general characteristics and limitations of experimental methods and argued that clinical psychology "should adopt a scientific/empirical focus in theory, research, and practice" (p. 218). Risley (1972) argues emphatically that therapy cannot advance very far without measurement and an alliance between therapy and experiment; applied behavioral analysis requires the incorporation of measurement into therapy. This, he states:

will serve to improve the service rendered to a client, showing unequivocally when therapy is not being therapeutic (i.e., is not correlated with significant improvements in the client's behavior). Measurement alone would eliminate many of our current therapeutic routines by demonstrating that no marked improvement occurs when these routines are followed. (Risley, 1972, p. 47)

The impact of applied behavioral analysis is likely to be felt in the clinical area in terms of verbal behavior (Dougher, 1988; Michael, 1984; Skinner, 1957; Winokur, 1976), behavioral assessment (Haynes, 1983), and the quantitative laws of conditioning (Herrnstein, 1977). The forthcoming bridge between behaviorism and cultural materialism will significantly change (as it already has) the course of the applied behavior analysis culture and will decidedly have an impact on clinical behavior analysis.

Harzem (1987) stated, ". . . contemporary society needs, for survival, the kind of knowledge that a science of psychology can provide, so as to bring under control political-economic-military events that have become, through technology, so powerful and so dangerous" (p. 176). He closes by stating that those who have been stimulated by Skinner's social concerns must begin to unify their social awareness and their serious work, pursue scientific questions relating to the human issues of today. Although no one can know what will result by way of structure and general function, the fundamentals of a science of human behavior now exists and needs to be built. "The virtues of being a psychologist lie in the building of this new science of psychology. They lie, too, in the reformation of this much maligned yet desperately needed of academic disciplines . . . the matter is deadly serious" (Harzem, 1987, p. 180).

Zifferblatt and Hendricks (1974) argued for an applied behavioral analysis of population control almost a generation ago. "The problem of designing environments to insure proper use of technology," they state, "is far too crucial to the world to remain unexamined by the tools of science" (p. 750). Applied behavior analysts are capable of dealing with behavioral problems, and social problems in the final analysis are problems involving human behavior. These problems are challenging our survival, the survival of our children, and the survival of our children's children. The problem that faces the science that knows how to deal with issues involves making behavioral changes that will aid survival.

Azrin (1977) emphasizes that applied research emphasizes outcome, clinical significance, situational complexity, population heterogeneity, a systems approach, subject preferences, practicality and cost benefits, and side effects. The guiding principle is outcome. Understanding is not enough for applied psychologists. There is an implicit contract and understanding that students taking courses and nonstudents who pay the taxes that support research for academic psychology believe that the research will lead to benefits for them. Basic research will become applicable to solve human problems. Azrin (1977) has justified these mandates in terms of his work with overcorrection, habits, and the job club, among many others.

One critical feature of clinical psychology that cannot be ignored is that it is the individual client who is the primary concern. Too quickly, one tends to lose sight of this. As Hayes (1983) notes:

> Clinical interventions are largely oriented toward the needs of individual clients . . . It implies that understanding the individual is the major goal of clinical knowledge. Logically, it also implies that case analyses should be an important method in clinical psychology. (Hayes, 1983, p. 181; See also Azrin, 1977)

In designing a cultural approach to clinical behavior analysis, these considerations must be made. Is behaviorism the philosophy that will provide us the science to save us from science and technology? Those who seem to understand the philosophy appear to believe so. If we wish to construct a proper culture of clinical psychology, behaviorism coupled with cultural materialism is the baseline.

SUMMARY

> Nature, even human nature, will cease more and more to be an absolute datum; more and more it will become what scientific manipulation has made it. Science can, if it chooses, enable our grandchildren to live the good life, by giving them knowledge, self-control, and characters productive of harmony rather than strife. (Russell, 1957, p. 87)

Skinner (1990) carefully considered three kinds of variation and selection. These account for the behavior of the organism at any given point in time and space as their product. The first is the biological, discussed in relation to respondent behavior preparing "a species only for a future that resembles the selecting past" (Skinner, 1990, p. 1206). The second kind of selection has to do with "operant conditioning, through which variations in the behavior of the individual are selected by features of the environment that are not stable enough to play any part in evolution" (Skinner, 1990, p. 1206). The third kind of selection is the selection of cultural practices that largely depended on verbal behavior. "Modeling, telling, and teaching are the functions of the social environments called cultures. Different cultures emerge from different contingencies of variation and selection and differ in the extent to which they help their members solve their problems" (Skinner, 1990, p. 1207). As "contingencies" are different for respondent and operant behaviors, they are different for operant and cultural behaviors.

It has been over a century since Wilhelm Wundt opened the first experimental psychology laboratory. It has been almost a century since one of his students, Lightner Witmer, opened the first psychological clinic and coined the term "clinical psychologist." Psychology in general and clinical psychology in particular have undergone a great many definitional refinements since then, for better or for worse. Skinner, for one, has for decades and in numerous publications argued that cultural practices such as those involved in the practice of clinical psychology require critical examination.

Three questions essential to a behavioral analysis of clinical practice include: (1) What is clinical practice; what do clinical psychologists do and how is the concept defined? (2) What are the contingencies involved in clinical practice; why do clinicians do what they do from a behavior analytic perspective? and (3) What are the metacontingencies of clinical practice; what holds it together as its super-structure? These questions have been briefly addressed in this chapter, but they demand more detailed discussion.

Clinical practice can be designed as can all cultural practices. What changes have historically occurred in the contingencies and metacontingencies of clinical practice that are responsible for shaping and maintaining its current patterns? What is going on right now that will change the direction of clinical practice in the future? Who are the designers and who is watching them? And, what changes are probably "on the verge of occurring," or are imminent? It should be apparent that clinical psychology is becoming closer to clinical psychiatry in model, in teaching, and in practice. If this happens, clinical psychology may ultimately be little different than the cultural products to which Torrey (1986) refers; his book, *Witchdoctors and Psychiatrists: The Common Roots of Psychotherapy and Its Future,* should be read by all aspiring clinical practitioners of any philosophical bent.

Behavior analysts are in an intellectual and technological position to influence positive change in clinical practice. Positive change applies not only to the well-being of the practitioner (as guild-builders tend to emphasize), but also to the consumer. It is likely that applied behavior analysts are not yet in a political position to instrument much change. Yet, to make changes, behavior analysts must become involved in policy change. It would be most welcome for behavior analysts to more freely apply contingency management strategies with other behavior analysts, such that they might feel better about being engaged in behavioral analysis. Unfortunately, we are not all clones of B. F. Skinner, equipped with his genius and afforded his contingencies and metacontingencies. It would indeed help if some shaping, prompting, and positive reinforcement for approximations toward Skinner's behaviors were applied to our own practitioners.

> *A critical problem may be that the outcomes of current practices are so far removed from the behavioral contingencies supporting individuals' behavior that unproductive variations of cultural practices continue being replicated. The solution to this problem may involve bringing behavioral contingencies within reach of cultural outcomes. (Glenn, 1988, p. 178)*

This applies to clinical practice and other cultural behaviors.

REFERENCES

Alberts, G. M., & Edelstein, B. A. (1990). Training in behavior therapy. In A. S. Bellack, M. Hersen, & A. E. Kazdin (Eds.), *International handbook of behavior modification and therapy* (pp. 213–226), (2nd ed.). New York: Plenum Press.

American Psychiatric Association. (1987). *Diagnostic and statistical manual of mental disorders* (3rd ed.), (Revised). Washington, DC: Author.

Azrin, N. H. (1977). A strategy for applied research: Learning based but outcome oriented. *American Psychologist, 32,* 140–149.

Baer, D. M., Wolf, M. M., & Risley, T. R. (1968). Some current dimensions of applied behavior analysis. *Journal of Applied Behavior Analysis, 1,* 91–97.

Baer, D. M., Wolf, M. M., & Risley, T. R. (1987). Some still-current dimensions of applied behavior analysis. *Journal of Applied Behavior Analysis, 20,* 313–327.

Bartollas, C. (1985). *Correctional treatment: Theory and practice.* Englewood Cliffs, NJ: Prentice-Hall.

Bellack, A. S., & Hersen, M. (1980). *Introduction to clinical psychology.* New York: Oxford University Press.

Blau, T. H. (1983). Roles and professional practice. In M. Hersen, A. E. Kazdin, & A. S. Bellack (Eds.), *The clinical psychology handbook* (pp. 57–62). New York: Pergamon Press.

Boring, E. G. (1957). *A history of experimental psychology* (2nd ed.). New York: Appleton-Century-Crofts.

Catania, A. C., & Harnad, S. (Eds.). (1988). *The selection of behavior: The operant behaviorism of B. F. Skinner: Comments and consequences.* New York: Cambridge University Press.

Clanon, T. L. (1981). Psychiatry in the California correctional system: Past and present. *Federal Probation, 47,* 33–37.

Conway, J. B. (1988). Differences among clinical psychologists: Scientists, practitioners, and scientist-practitioners. *Professional Psychology: Research and Practice, 19,* 642–655.

Dougher, M. J. (1988). Clinical behavior analysis: Why we need a special interest group. *Behavior Analysis, 23*(1), 33–34.

Edwards, K. A. (1980). Restoring functional behavior of "senile" elderly. In J. M. Ferguson & C. B. Taylor (Eds.), *The comprehensive handbook of behavioral medicine: Volume 3: Extended applications and issues* (pp. 45–63). Jamaica, NY: SP Medical and Scientific Books.

Edwards, K. A. (1988a). Some characteristics of inmates transferred from prison to a state mental hospital. *Behavioral Sciences and the Law, 6,* 131–137.

Edwards, K. A. (1988b). *What behavior analysts can do in prisons: A need for middle management.* Paper presented at the meeting of the Association for Behavior Analysis, Philadelphia, May.

Edwards, K. A., & Sheldon-Wildgen, J. (1980). Providing nursing home residents' rights. In G. T. Hannah, W. P. Christian, & H. B. Clark (Eds.), *Preservation of client rights: A handbook for practitioners providing therapeutic, educational, and rehabilitative services* (pp. 319–344). New York: Free Press.

Emery, R. E., & Marholin, D. (1977). An applied behavior analysis of delinquency: The irrelevancy of relevant behavior. *American Psychologist, 32,* 860–873.

Epling, W. F., & Pierce, W. D. (1986). The basic importance of applied behavior analysis. *The Behavior Analyst, 9,* 89–99.

Ferster, C. B. (1972). An experimental analysis of clinical phenomena. *The Psychological Record, 22,* 1–16.

Garfield, S. L., & Kurtz, R. (1976). Clinical psychologists in the 1970s. *American Psychologist, 31,* 1–9.

Glenn, S. S. (1987). Rules as environmental events. *The Analysis of Verbal Behavior, 5,* 29–32.

Glenn, S. S. (1988). Contingencies and metacontingencies: Toward a synthesis of behavior analysis and cultural materialism. *The Behavior Analyst, 11,* 161–179.

Glenn, S. S. (1989). Verbal behavior and cultural practices. *Behavior Analysis and Social Action, 7,* 10–15.

Guevremont, D. C., & Spiegler, M. D. (1990). *What do behavior therapists really do? A survey of the clinical practice of AABT members.* Paper presented at the meetings of the Association for the Advancement of Behavior Therapy, San Francisco, November.

Harris, M. (1964a). *The nature of cultural things.* New York: Random House.

Harris, M. (1964b). *Patterns of race in the Americas.* New York: Walker.

Harris, M. (1968). *The rise of anthropological theory: A history of theories of culture.* New York: Crowell.

Harris, M. (1974). *Cows, pigs, wars & witches: The riddles of culture.* New York: Random House.

Harris, M. (1975). *Culture, people, nature: An introduction to general anthropology.* New York: Crowell.

Harris, M. (1977). *Cannibals and kings: The origins of cultures.* New York: Random House.

Harris, M. (1979). *Cultural materialism: The struggle for a science of culture.* New York: Random House.

Harris, M. (1981). *America now: The anthropology of a changing culture.* New York: Simon and Schuster.

Harris, M. (1985). *Good to eat: Riddles of food and culture.* New York: Simon and Schuster.

Harris, M. (1987). *Death, sex, and fertility: Population regulation in preindustrial and developing societies.* New York: Columbia University Press.

Harris, M. (1988). Group and individual effects in selection. In A. C. Catania & S. Harnad (Eds.),

The selection of behavior: The operant behaviorism of B. F. Skinner: Comments and consequences (pp. 46–48). New York: Cambridge University Press.

Harris, M. (1989). *Our kind: Who we are, where we came from, where we are going.* New York: Harper and Row.

Harzem, P. (1987). On the virtues of being a psychologist. *The Behavior Analyst, 10,* 175–181.

Hayes, S. C. (1983). The role of the individual case in the production and consumption of clinical knowledge. In M. Hersen, A. E. Kazdin, & A. S. Bellack (Eds.), *The clinical psychology handbook* (pp. 181–195). New York: Pergamon Press.

Haynes, S. N. (1983). Behavioral assessment. In M. Hersen, A. E. Kazdin, & A. S. Bellack (Eds.), *The clinical psychology handbook* (pp. 397–425). New York: Pergamon Press.

Herrnstein, R. J. (1977). The evolution of behaviorism. *American Psychologist, 32,* 593–603.

Hersen, M., Kazdin, A. E., & Bellack, A. S. (Eds.). (1983). *The clinical psychology handbook.* New York: Pergamon Press.

Hokanson, J. E. (1983). *Introduction to the therapeutic process.* Reading, MA: Addison-Wesley Publishing Company.

James, J. F., Gregory, D., Jones, R. K., & Rundell, O. H. (1980). Psychiatric morbity in prisons. *Hospital and Community Psychiatry, 31,* 674–677.

Kaplan, S. J. (1986). *The private practice of behavior therapy: A guide for behavioral practitioners.* New York: Plenum Press.

King, L. (1981). Comment on "Adoption of innovations from applied behavioral research: 'Does anybody care?'" *Journal of Applied Behavior Analysis, 14,* 507–511.

Krasner, L. (1990). History of behavior modification. In A. S. Bellack, M. Hersen, & A. E. Kazdin (Eds.), *International handbook of behavior modification and therapy* (pp. 3–25). (2nd ed.). New York: Plenum Press.

Kratochwill, T. R., & Mace, F. C. (1983). Experimental research in clinical psychology. In M. Hersen, A. E. Kazdin, & A. S. Bellack (Eds.), *The clinical psychology handbook* (pp. 197–221). New York: Pergamon Press.

Levine, M., & Levine, A. (1970). *A social history of helping services: Clinic, court, school, and community.* New York: Appleton-Century-Crofts.

Levis, D. J. (1990). The experimental and theoretical foundations of behavior modification. In A. S. Bellack, M. Hersen, & A. E. Kazdin (Eds.), *International handbook of behavior modification and therapy* (pp. 27–51). (2nd ed.). New York: Plenum Press.

Lloyd, K. E. (1985). Behavioral anthropology: A review of Marvin Harris' *Cultural materialism. Journal of the Experimental Analysis of Behavior, 43,* 279–287.

Malagodi, E. F. (1986). On radicalizing behaviorism: A call for cultural analysis. *The Behavior Analyst, 9,* 1–17.

Malott, R. W. (1986). Experimentation in behavioral psychology: The flight to the laboratory. In A. Poling & R. W. Fuqua (Eds.), *Research methods in applied behavior analysis: Issues and advances* (pp. 1–6). New York: Plenum Press.

Martinson, R. (1974). What works?—Questions and answers about prison reform. *Public Interest, 38,* 22–54.

Michael, J. (1984). Verbal behavior. *Journal of the Experimental Analysis of Behavior, 42,* 363–376.

Morris, E. K. (1980). Applied behavior analysis for criminal justice practice: Some current dimensions. *Criminal Justice and Behavior, 7,* 131–145.

Pressman, R. M. (1979). *Private practice: A handbook for the independent mental health practitioner.* New York: Gardner Press.

Pressman, R. M., & Siegler, R. (1983). *The independent practitioner: Practice management for the allied health professional.* Homewood, IL: The Dorsey Press.

Remington, R. E. (1981). The token economy in prison settings: How much has it achieved? *Criminal Justice and Behavior, 8,* 119–123.

Risley, T. R. (1972). Behavior modification: An experimental-therapeutic endeavor. In R. D. Rubin, H. Fensterheim, J. D. Henderson, & L. P. Ullmann (Eds.), *Advances in behavior therapy* (pp. 37–52). New York: Academic Press.

Risley, T. R., & Edwards, K. A. (1979). *Behavioral technology for nursing home care: Toward a system of nursing home organization and management.* Lawrence, KS: Center for Applied Behavior Analysis.

Roth, L. (1980). Correctional psychiatry. In W. Curran, A. McGorry, & C. Petty (Eds.), *Modern legal medicine, psychiatry, and forensic science.* Philadelphia: Davis.

Russell, B. (1957). What I believe. In P. Edwards (Ed.), *Why I am not a Christian: And other essays on religion and related subjects* (pp. 48-87). New York: Simon and Schuster.

Russell, B. (1950). The science to save us from science. *New York Times Magazine*, March 19, 1950. (Also published in San Jose State College Associates in Psychology (Eds.), *In quest of value: Readings in philosophy and personal values* (pp. 23-29). San Francisco: Chandler Publishing.)

Skinner, B. F. (1957). *Verbal behavior.* New York: Appleton-Century-Crofts.

Skinner, B. F. (1990). Can psychology be a science of mind? *American Psychologist, 46,* 1206-1210.

Stampfl, T. G. (1987). Theoretical implications of the neurotic paradox as a problem in behavior theory: An experimental resolution. *The Behavior Analyst, 10,* 161-173.

Steadman, H. J., Monahan, J., Hartstone, E., Davis, S. K., & Robbins, P. (1982). Mentally disordered offenders: A national survey of patients and facilities. *Law and Human Behavior, 6,* 31-38.

Stolz, S. B. (1981). Adoption of innovations from applied behavioral research: "Does anybody care?" *Journal of Applied Behavior Analysis, 14,* 491-505.

Strickland, B. R. (1988). Clinical psychology comes of age. *American Psychologist, 43,* 104-107.

Sundberg, N. D., Tyler, L. E., & Taplin, J. R. (1973). *Clinical psychology: Expanding horizons* (2nd ed.). Englewood Cliffs, NJ: Prentice-Hall.

Torrey, E. F. (1986). *Witchdoctors and psychiatrists: The common roots of psychotherapy and its future.* Northvale, NJ: Jason Aronson.

Travisono, D. N. (Ed.). (1984). *Juvenile and adult correctional departments, institutions, agencies, and paroling authorities: United States and Canada.* College Park, MD: American Correctional Association.

Travisono, D. N. (Ed.). (1988). *Juvenile and adult correctional departments, institutions, agencies, and paroling authorities: United States and Canada.* College Park, MD: American Correctional Association.

Ullmann, L. P., & Krasner, L. (Eds.). (1965). *Case studies in behavior modification.* New York: Holt, Rinehart and Winston.

Vargas, E. A. (1985). Cultural contingencies: A review of Marvin Harris's *Cannibals and kings. Journal of the Experimental Analysis of Behavior, 43,* 419-428.

Walker, C. E. (Ed.). (1981). *Clinical practice of psychology: A guide for mental health professionals.* New York: Pergamon Press.

Weiss, J. C., & Henney, J. S. (1980). Crime and criminals in the United States. In E. Bittner & S. Messinger (Eds.), *Criminology review yearbook* (pp. 697-727). Beverly Hills, CA: Sage.

Wheeler, H. (Ed.). (1973). *Beyond the punitive society: Operant conditioning: Social and political aspects.* San Francisco: W. H. Freeman and Co.

Wilson, J. Q., & Herrnstein, R. J. (1985). *Crime and human nature: The definitive study of the causes of crime.* New York: Simon & Schuster.

Winokur, S. (1976). *A primer of verbal behavior: An operant view.* Englewood Cliffs, NJ: Prentice-Hall.

Wolman, B. B. (Ed.). (1965). *Handbook of clinical psychology.* New York: McGraw-Hill.

Wolpe, J. (1986). Misrepresentation and underemployment of behavior therapy. *Comprehensive Psychiatry, 27,* 192-200.

Wolpe, J. (1987). The promotion of scientific psychotherapy: A long voyage. In J. K. Zeig (Ed.), *The evolution of psychotherapy* (pp. 133-142). New York: Brunner/Mazel.

Zifferblatt, S. M., & Hendricks, C. G. (1974). Applied behavioral analysis of societal problems: Population change, a case in point. *American Psychologist, 29,* 750-761.

10

Analysis of Preventive Medical Services in the United States

Melbourne F. Hovell, Robert Kaplan, and Frank Hovell

INTRODUCTION

Preventive medicine is a recognized medical specialty that promotes clinical services designed to prevent disease, injury, and premature death. Preventive medicine is a subset and a product of the broader field of public health. Clinical procedures, including instructional and counseling services as provided by a physician, are emphasized in preventive medicine. This field also employs the physician in the role of political activist, influencing health policy for disease prevention (Johns, Hovell, Ganitas, Peddecord, & Agras, 1987).

Curative medicine differs from preventive medicine and public health in the degree and type of emphasis on prevention. For instance, given a flood with many people injured, the medically oriented triage professional treats the patient with a severed femoral artery; the preventive medicine specialist sterilizes drinking water and gives typhoid vaccine. Both interventions are needed, but the ultimate needs of the population may be served better by preventing illness and injury in large proportions of the population and not by providing inherently limited medical care for acute illness or injury.

The broader field of public health includes many disciplines: medicine, environmental health science, psychology, nursing, and others. Interventions performed by public health specialists range from clinical services to environmental engineering (Last, 1986). Ultimately the goal of preventing avoidable morbidity and premature mortality requires the efforts of all public health disciplines and specialists. Although many specialists and interventions are necessary to prevent disease, this chapter focuses on preventive services best provided by practicing physicians.

PUBLIC HEALTH AND CLINICAL PERSPECTIVES

Two competing perspectives guide prevention interventions. The first is the clinical perspective. In this view, a clinician is concerned primarily with the welfare of each patient. Preventive medicine follows the public health perspective. This perspective focuses on the welfare of the community (Hovell, Elder, Blanchard, & Sallis, 1986). Preventive interventions are designed to benefit a defined population rather than specific individuals. For instance, air pollution control procedures presumably reduce risk of toxic effects of automobile exhaust and other pollutants for whole communities.

Competition for Limited Resources

Sometimes these perspectives are at odds. Health services, preventive and curative, consume finite resources. Investing in one expends resources that might have been invested in the other. From the clinical perspective, there is virtually no limit to treatment for a given patient, regardless of cost. Investing $50,000 in heart surgery for a 60-year-old male follows the clinical perspective. However, expensive surgery uses resources that could have been invested in heart disease prevention. Following the public health perspective, investing $50,000 in smoking prevention might reach many hundreds of youth and could prevent many from smoking or acquiring heart disease as adults. The emphasis on prevention could result in many more individuals living long and high-quality lives. However, since resources are finite, this result will be at the expense of some acutely ill individuals.

Magnitude of Effect—Definition of Success

Interventions differ in their degree of effectiveness or magnitude of effect. Some prevention services may be powerful, whereas others are only minimally so. The pediatrician who administers the Sabin polio vaccine to well children virtually assures zero risk of polio, and the effect is essentially lifelong. Conversely, asking smokers to quit may appear ineffective. However, from a public health perspective, seemingly ineffective prevention efforts may have important benefits for the population. Russell and colleagues demonstrated that physicians who advised smoking patients to quit were able to increase the quit rate from 3–5%, a 67% increase relative to controls not asked (Li, Coates, Ewart, & Kim, 1987; Russell, Wilson, Taylor, & Baker, 1987). Projected to the whole population, simple advice could result in over 2 million quits in the United States. Thus, some interventions, when applied to large numbers of people, benefit an important minority of the population. Low-cost interventions provided to the whole community need only benefit a small proportion of the population to be worthwhile (Hovell & Black, 1989). Physicians see more than 70% of adults, at least once per year; thus, they could greatly affect the population's welfare even when few individuals benefit from particular preventive services (National Center for Health Statistics, 1983).

Compliance with Prevention Standards

The U.S. Preventive Services Task Force published a *Guide to Clinical Preventive Services* and the American Medical Association has made specific recommendations about preventive services (American Medical Association, 1983; *Guide to Clinical Preventive Services,* 1989). These services include immunizations, well patient screenings, and medical treatments for biological risk factors such as elevated blood pressure, blood sugar, or cholesterol. With increasing recognition that lifestyles play important roles in disease etiology, physicians are encouraged to prescribe changes in diet, increased exercise, decreased cigarette use, and limited alcohol use. Although practitioners are more apt to prescribe preventive services most consistent with traditional medical treatment (e.g., antihypertension medication) than to attempt behavior modification, none is provided reliably by practicing physicians (Becker & Janz, 1990). The majority (80%) of physicians report preventive services for most patients (Maibach, Scutchfield, & Hovell, 1984; McAlister et al., 1985). However, these reports are likely to be overestimates of preventive interventions, resulting from varying definitions of prevention and inaccurate reporting of actual performance. The type of preventive service also makes a difference. Practitioners in the San Diego State University (SDSU) health service center recorded virtually no referrals for preventive services during baseline or after interventions specifically promoting such referrals (Johns, Hovell, Drastal, Lamke, & Patrick, in press). Until more objectively measured, self-reported compliance rates are questionable.

These observations raise two questions about preventive medicine: (1) Which services should physicians provide and which should be provided by others? (2) What conditions determine a practitioner's likelihood of performing preventive services reliably?

DISEASE ETIOLOGY AND THEORY

Over the last 25 years the top 10 causes of premature mortality were degenerative diseases such as cardiovascular diseases, cancer, diabetes, and special types of trauma (e.g., automobile and nonautomobile related injury, homicide, and suicide). Although infectious diseases have not disappeared and new epidemics have appeared in the last 20 years (e.g., AIDS, Toxic Shock, Legionnaires disease), the degenerative diseases account for the vast majority of the morbidity and mortality in developed countries. The etiology of these diseases is complex and multifactorial, involving lifestyles, basic genetics, and sometimes infectious agents. Both genetics and viral infections have been implicated in the etiology of diabetes; eating and exercise patterns may contribute to the occurrence of some types of diabetes and almost certainly contribute to diabetes control. Shifts in morbidity and mortality patterns toward diseases and injuries resulting from risky lifestyle have dictated that prevention efforts include reduction of high-risk behaviors. In some instances controlling infectious diseases requires changes in behavior. There is no more dramatic example than AIDS. No cure exists. Treatment yields little or no extension in life expectancy, and the only effective means of control is preventing risk behavior and exposure to the HIV.

These morbidity and mortality patterns call for both physician and nonphysician public health interventions. We must increase seat belt use, decrease driving while intoxicated, and decrease the amount of carcinogens in our air, water, and food supply. Continued chlorination and expanded fluoridation of public water supplies will sustain and extend the prevention of numerous infectious diseases. These interventions will be implemented by persons other than physicians: teachers, police, environmental engineers and others. Physicians should be political advocates for these interventions.

The Health Belief Model

Preventive medicine currently relies on counseling procedures, also known as cognitive services, for changing risk behavior. Implicitly, these procedures follow variants of the health belief model or related theory of behavior. This model asserts that people make rational decisions based on knowledge and "cost-benefit" judgments (Ajzen & Fishbein, 1980; Rosenstock, 1974). From this model, educational procedures provide information, and counseling procedures persuade people to revalue costs (including fears) or benefits. This, then, leads one to make rational decisions and, presumably, changes in lifestyle. The health belief model emphasizes changing knowledge and attitudes as prerequisites for behavior change. In so doing, it likely distracts attention from more powerful behavior change determinants.

The Operant Model

The Operant Model makes no assumptions about cognitive mediators of behavior. It focuses on discrete environmental variables, most notably contingencies of reinforcement, schedules of reinforcement, and stimulus control (Skinner, 1953, 1974). This model has yet to be incorporated fully into preventive medicine. If preventive medicine specialists were trained to understand operant conditioning and to use behavior modification techniques, a more sophisticated preventive service model would emerge (Millenson & Leslie, 1979).

In the operant model, reinforcement is the effect of certain consequences of behavior. Consequences that result in increased frequency or rate of behavior are reinforcing. Such consequences include food or social events (e.g., a smile). The concept of reinforcement includes the concept of contingency: the reliable association of a particular event as a consequence of a particular behavior. Behavior reliably followed by a reinforcing consequence increases in frequency. Concepts of punishment and extinction are similarly defined functionally. Consequences that decrease the rate of behavior they follow are said to be punishing. Behavior that is neither reinforced nor punished will return to the baseline rate. This is extinction. When a nurse ignores a patient's overuse of the hospital call button, he/she ceases to provide social attention. Normally this decreases the rate of trivial calls— extinction.

Some consequences can acquire reinforcing properties; these are learned. Some reinforcers can become generalized by association with a wide variety of other reinforcers. The most notable is money. Money can be exchanged for all other types of reinforcers (e.g., food, housing, and recreation). The reinforcing properties of money are relatively independent of deprivation states for any particular other reinforcer, such as food. Complex schedules of reinforcement and punishment combine to determine specific patterns of behavior. These contingencies probably determine physicians' practice patterns.

Physicians and Behavior Modification

The practice of preventive medicine should include interventions to prevent heart disease, cancer, and even trauma. These services should include behavior modification techniques.

Physicians will require a greater understanding of learning theory to employ behavior modification techniques correctly and completely. Recognizing that some form of "reward" (contingencies of reinforcement) is critical to increasing "protective behavior" will lead to contingency management interventions; conversely, the health belief model leads to education about health benefits. Evidence to date suggests that the former is more effective. The etiology of numerous diseases includes lifestyle behavior patterns: eating, exercise, drug use and abuse, and safety behavior. To control these diseases, physicians must understand fully their etiologies, including the determinants of behavior. Although medical schools are increasing the behavioral science curriculum, they have yet to include sufficient training in learning theory and behavior modification procedures for routine use in preventive medicine.

PREVENTION SERVICE MODELS

Physician-provided preventive services might include varied activities—multiple practitioners with few inherent limits on depth of services possible (Johns et al., 1987). One model involves the physician screening patients, and then providing immunizations and medical treatments. Elevated blood pressure may be treated with medication. In a more aggressive model, the physician counsels patients to alter their diet, exercise, and general lifestyle to reduce elevated blood pressure.

A still more aggressive model employs medical and allied health specialists. The physician may refer patients to dieticians for detailed nutrition counseling, to nurse specialists for diabetic (or other) special instruction, to exercise physiologists for detailed exercise evaluation and instruction. This model assumes that the allied health professionals' expertise complements the physician's prevention efforts. This could be extended by return visits for follow-up services and by providing some instruction in small group formats.

Prevention and Contingency Management

We have employed contingency management to increase the rate of physical activity in children with cystic fibrosis (CF) (Kilbourn, Hovell, Menna, & Harwood, in preparation). In this study, behavioral specialists, in cooperation with medical specialists, taught parents of CF children to use a contingent privilege system to reinforce increased physical activity. Although the secondary prevention value of exercise remains to be demonstrated for CF patients, this illustrates a combined behavioral/medical specialist model of preventive medicine. Future applications could be implemented by physicians, if trained to design and manage behavior modification programs (Katz & Zlutnick, 1975).

Referrals and Preventive Medicine

Finally, all professional specialists should refer clients to other specialists. Internists refer for surgery when such treatment is needed. Physicians rarely refer for behavioral/psychosocial services. One type of prevention model yet to be established reliably would have physicians refer patients to behavioral specialists to attain greater changes in lifestyles related to disease prevention, injury control, and promotion of well-being. This model might be a critical intervening step until physicians acquire formal training in behavior modification. It always may be the preferred model for prevention issues well outside the expertise of most physicians. Social problems related to homicide, suicide, family violence, and even injury control often exceed the professional skills and interests of physicians. In these instances, physicians should be held accountable only for referral.

These models of preventive medicine are not all-inclusive, and they cannot be adopted with the certainty that they are effective. However, they represent most forms of preventive service. The more aggressive models may be predicted to be effective based on numerous behavioral risk factor modification trials that employed similar procedures (Elder, Hovell, Lasater, Wells, & Carleton, 1985).

To benefit completely from preventive medicine, physicians need to be rewarded for practicing preventive services. A conceptual analysis of existing contingencies of reinforcement and stimulus control influences may provide guidance in engineering reliable preventive services.

BEHAVIORAL ANALYSIS OF PREVENTIVE SERVICES

We will use principles of operant conditioning to speculate about the likely control of preventive services practiced by physicians. Among the principles considered, we have emphasized contingencies of reinforcement. Formal education is discussed in terms of learning history.

Medical School: Establishing Skills as Reinforcers

Probably one of the most important determinants of preventive services is the general learning history of the practitioner in concert with formal professional training. Physicians self-select into medical training. They apply to and enter medical school because of a history that has made physician behavior (or its consequences) reinforcing. Most medical students "want to help" ill people recover. The process of helping is reinforcing. Students are shaped to master basic biology and are reinforced by solving biological questions or surgical manipulations. Such shaping continues in medical school such that medical services become powerfully reinforcing behavior. The surgeon who correctly sutures the arteries in a heart transplant is no doubt powerfully reinforced by his/her observation of a competent surgical procedure, perhaps even if the patient dies.

Thus, self-selection into medicine implies that helping people has become powerfully reinforcing. This learning history, especially after honing by medical school, may decrease the likelihood of preventive services. We view the reinforcement derived from performing curative care as contingencies maintaining alternate, if not incompatible behavior. Even if physicians see prevention as important, they enjoy practicing curative medicine.

The practitioner may not have the counseling skills or be able to discriminate between effective and noneffective counseling. Few or no schools now teach all medical students techniques of behavior modification following operant conditioning theory. In short, many preventive services have not been taught or learned well. Plus they are not themselves reinforcing behaviors. The failure of medical schools to establish prevention service skills in the context of establishing sophisticated curative skills further mitigates against the practitioner adopting routine prevention services (Bartlett, 1984; Dismuke & Miller, 1983).

The intense attention to biological technology in medical education is appropriate, in that many acute illness conditions require both sophisticated machinery and technical knowledge of pathophysiology. However, it may be insufficient in light of changing disease patterns. Unfortunately, medical school staff are themselves expert in biological sciences and less so in behavioral sciences. They may be inadequately prepared to recognize the need for additional types of training, and they are not well prepared to determine the detailed curriculum, even if they see the need.

For example, the increased emphasis on counseling skills in medical schools is appropriate, but is based on a shallow understanding of behavioral principles and behavior change techniques. This is especially true in light of increased competence in the population. Fifty years ago, the typical patient probably was a farmer or white collar worker with a limited formal education. Such patients were not equipped to follow complex instructions from their physician. Today, the average patient has some college education, often pertaining to disease prevention or treatment. The patient is both more educable and more demanding of education. The physician must have considerable counseling skills even to provide new information or correct misinformation, let alone institute behavior modification procedures.

On-Going Contingencies of Reinforcement for Medical Services

Medical services result in a number of different types of probable reinforcing consequences. Among the more obvious are feedback regarding cure (or prevention) of disease, social gratitude from patients and families, and fees for services. These consequences are generally considered positive reinforcers. In concert with these contingencies, consequences that may be negative reinforcers are likely. Among these are failure to cure (or prevent) disease, social criticism from patients, families and the general public, professional organization sanctions, legal liability, and increased malpractice insurance rates (resulting from successful claims). These consequences operate concurrently in complex schedules, and these schedules change over time. It can be presumed, axiomatically, that the individual's practice behavior depends on his or her current schedule of reinforcement for preventive versus curative services, in the context of his or her learning history.

Health promotion specialists have repeatedly questioned why preventive medicine is not widely practiced. One of the major reasons is that it may not be profitable. Table 10-1 below shows rates for reimbursement for a variety of preventive services relative to rates of reimbursement for other services. Economically, there is no rationale for physicians to engage in preventive practices. Al-

Table 10-1 Costs for various medical services

Service	Time required (min)	Charge[a]
Brief nutrition counseling	15	16.50
Nutrition counseling	45	44.00
Extended clinic visit (Fam Med)	45	68.50
Influenza vaccination	5	28.00
Electrocardiogram	10	60.50
Flex sigmoidoscopy	10	129.00
Vasectomy	45	331.25
Cataract surgery	45	2,200.00

[a]Based on estimates of prevailing rates for San Diego, CA, 1990.

though most physicians are well meaning, they are too busy treating acute problems (for which they receive financial reinforcement) to attend to prevention needs.

Cost Containment—Contingency Management Interventions

One reason for emphasizing preventive services is that medical care costs have grown out of control (Somers, 1984). The United States spends about 11% of its GNP on health care, whereas equally advanced societies spend about 8%. Later we will consider the role of prevention in reducing these costs. However, first we must consider general efforts to control health care spending. Several different efforts to control escalating health care costs represent natural experiments from which we can see the effects of financial contingencies on physician practice patterns. Since 1980 there have been waves of cost containment strategies represented by various acronyms. Most are known as managed care plans. More than 60 million Americans are now enrolled in some sort of program that attempts to control costs. These include Health Maintenance Organizations (HMO) and Preferred Provider Organizations (PPO). In HMOs an employer typically pays a fixed fee to an HMO, which in turn provides all necessary health care for the employee. These plans may or may not require a copayment from the employee. In PPOs, the employers pay a specific plan that includes independent health care providers. In exchange for caring for employees of the plan, the independent provider agrees to take a fee fixed by the plan.

Another attempt to control costs involves reimbursements of hospitals by Diagnosis Related Group (DRG). Hospitals are reimbursed for the median length of stay by diagnosis rather than the actual length of stay by the patient. This has created incentives to move patients out of hospitals more promptly and ultimately to reduce costs for other aspects of care. Indeed some cost savings have been realized under these systems. Yet, these systems have become extremely complex. DRGs, for example, now allow for a remarkable number of local adjustments, secondary diagnosis adjustments, teaching related adjustments, and other practices. Even with these strategies, health care costs have continued to rise.

Perhaps the most recent strategy is to control physicians' fees. A new strategy known as Resource-Based Relative Value Scaling (RBRVS) attempts to define the value of a physician's service based on several components, including training required, time required, work required, and other factors. Under this system, some highly reimbursed procedures may be reimbursed at a lower rate. Conversely, some aspects of primary care, including patient counseling, may be reimbursed at a higher rate (Hsiao, Braun, Dunn, & Becker, 1988; Hsiao et al., 1988). Congress and the Health Care Financing Administration are very serious about this approach. They have created a Physicians' Payment Review Organization to refine the approach with the eventual hope of implementing it in the near future. Some observers have speculated that RBRVS will increase the use of preventive services because they will allow physicians to gain greater payment for cognitive services.

One potential problem with RBRVS is an incentive to increase volume. If a physician receives $100.00 to do an electrocardiogram and his customary allowable charge is reduced to $50.00, evidence suggests that he will double his volume (Wennberg, 1990). Operant studies suggest that, when the environment is closed (there are no alternative responses that lead to reinforcement), response rate increases to maintain levels of reinforcement. According to this argument, the system will increase the volume of tests but not necessarily decrease total expenditures. It will be difficult to increase volume for preventive services because they are time consuming to administer. Thus, even though there may be more reinforcement for cognitive services under RBRVS, the rate of response cannot be increased to make prevention profitable.

How Reimbursement Can Affect Use of Services

Most models of health care assume that the amount of service used reflects the medical need for those services. For example, we would assume that the number of hysterectomies performed in a community represent the number of women who required that procedure. However, systematic studies revealed that use of services varies remarkably among communities where the need should be the same. For example, women in some communities are nine times as likely to have a hysterectomy as women with the same characteristics in a bordering community. Men with the same symptoms are 13 times as likely to have a prostate operation in some communities as in others with similar demographic characteristics (Roos, 1984; Wenneberg, Freeman, & Culp, 1987; Wennberg, 1990). Wenneker, Weissman, and Epstein (1990) reported that patients in Massachusetts were much more likely to have cardiac procedures if they had private insurance than if they were covered by Medicaid or had no insurance. These findings prevailed even with adjustments for seriousness of illness. The data suggest that providers are influenced by the income they received for performing services, not simply the medical need.

Many examples help clarify why costs for nonpreventive services have escalated. In most cases this is because the systems have allowed for the billing of multiple procedures. The charges for these procedures are not necessarily linked to their difficulty or their underlying costs. For example, Bunker, Fowles, and Schaffarzink (1982) noted that the customary charge of arthroscopy is about $500. During an examination of the knee, a small piece of redundant membrane may be seen. The redundant membrane is of no clinical importance, but it can be removed making the procedure a synovectomy, which can be billed at $1,300. When this was allowed, the number of synovectomies greatly increased. Many patients with serious osteoarthritis of their knees require operations for replacement of both knees. Since it is often desirable to minimize exposure to anesthetics, physicians began operating on both knees simultaneously. Insurance companies, recognizing the time saving in the double operation introduced policies that allowed only a 50% increase in payment for the second knee above what was allowed for the first. Surgeons reacted by scheduling separate operations for each knee. This resulted in increased (back to the original) fees, hospital, anaesthesia, and laboratory costs, not to mention the additional risks and inconvenience to the patient. The reimbursement policy resulted in higher costs, and more complex and dangerous medical procedures.

Numerous examples suggest that contingencies affect the rate of use of medical services. For example, the State of New Hampshire was concerned that patients covered by Medicaid were getting too many unnecessary prescriptions. In response to this problem they implemented a policy restricting the number of prescriptions that could be reimbursed to three per month. Time series analysis conducted before and after the implementation of this policy and in comparison to a control state (New Jersey) demonstrated a dramatic reduction in pharmaceutical use as a result of the policy. Whether this adversely affected patients is unknown. However, it probably influenced physician prescribing behavior (Soumerai, Avoran, Ross-Degnan, & Gortmaker, 1987). Another series of interesting experiments demonstrated that feedback to physicians can influence their practice behavior. Martin, Wolfe, Thiboudeau, Dzau, and Brunwald (1980) assigned resident physicians to one of three groups in an attempt to reduce medical test ordering. One group received a financial incentive if they ordered fewer tests, the second group reviewed the medical charts with an experienced senior staff person, whereas the third group served as control. Both review and financial incentives resulted in reduced test ordering. Physicians often are unaware of financial consequences of their own practice behaviors. In one study, physicians were assigned at random to two groups. One group received feedback about how much patients would be charged for services. The comparison received no feedback. There was a slight reduction in the number of tests ordered when physicians received feedback. However, when feedback ended, test ordering in the two groups became equivalent (Tierney, Miller, & McDonald, 1990). These studies demonstrate that physician behavior is controlled by monetary and feedback contingencies.

Evidence suggests that various types of feedback regarding primary care services can increase quantity and possibly quality of services (Hershey, Porter, Breslau, & Cohen, 1986; Mitchell & Fowkes, 1985). Similarly, Project INSURE has shown that training and financially compensating primary care physicians for preventive services can increase the frequency of these services relative to curative care (Logsdon, Rosen, & Demak, 1982; Logsdon & Rosen, 1984). These studies confirm the reinforcing properties of feedback and payment, and they suggest that arranging schedules of reinforcement can increase specifically preventive services.

However promising these studies may be, prevailing schedules are not likely to maintain prevention services and, as an aside, may not differentially sustain effective services. Among all reinforcers noted earlier, money appears the most powerful. Payment by patients, private insurance companies, and government entitlement programs are complex contingency management systems. Programs such as Medicare, Medicaid, MediCal (in California), and Blue Cross-type private health insurance define the services to be compensated and compensation rates. Individual practitioners are unable to negotiate individual rates. Invariably, rates set by government and large private insurance programs are lower than the charges normally extended to the individual patient when not covered by insurance or government programs. From the practitioner's experience, private insurance and government sources of compensation are inadequate, given overhead expenses and relative to the potential income lost had services been provided to a privately paying individual. In effect, physician's service behavior operates under multiple concurrent schedules analogous to laboratory choice experiments, where most practitioners will provide services to patients who generate higher fees. This can be seen in lower quantity (de facto rationing), lower quality, and sometimes the absence of services for the poor, the elderly, and populations in unattractive or rural settings (Hurley, 1990; Newhouse, 1990; Reinhardt, 1990; Rooks, 1990; Stoll, 1990).

Third-Party Payment for Cognitive Services

Perhaps for understandable reasons, third-party payers are not willing to compensate practitioners for cognitive services. Compensation tends to be for discrete diagnostic testing and equally discrete medical prescriptions. Limited amounts of nutrition counseling and physical therapy instruction are compensated, but often at rates that preclude the physician from delivering such services directly. The latter may be viewed as an asset to the public by encouraging referral to allied health specialists. However, it probably reduces the frequency of nutrition counseling and related cognitive prescriptions.

Third-party payers are understandably reluctant to pay physicians to talk to patients. The ability to define the beginning and end of an instance of service and the difficulty in defining effective or appropriate techniques of risk reduction lead to fears of paying practitioners unlimited amounts of money for questionable outcomes. Although physicians are reimbursed for some curative care procedures with uncertain efficacy, it is unlikely that reimbursement policies for prevention services are going to change until services of affordable characteristics and with known effectiveness for modifying risks of disease and ultimately disease rates are identified. As preventive medicine adds more effective interventions for lifestyle change, such as contingency management techniques, third party payers may be more willing to compensate practitioners for preventive services. Indeed, this touches on a special problem of compensation for services versus outcomes.

Reinforcing Performance Versus Effectiveness

Although the "art of medicine" reflects the knowledge barrier that limits cure (or prevention) from being guaranteed, the failure to compensate differentially for successful treatment undoubtedly influences quality of care. Traditionally, physicians are paid for their time, not for preventing or curing disease.

Certain preventive services lend themselves to objective verification (or a near approximation) and, as such, may be reliably compensated. Immunizations are classic examples. In this case, the performance of service is verifiable and its efficacy is known. However, recommending smoking cessation is not now reliably compensated. It seems that such a service, while only influencing perhaps 3–10% of smoking patients to quit, would be worth a small compensation (e.g., $1.00 per smoking patient). Verification could be based on copies of written "cessation prescriptions" given to the patient. Where the service can be verified and where there is reasonable evidence of population benefit, modest compensation contingencies will need to be developed to insure provision of preventive services. Where the effectiveness of preventive service is best measured on a population basis, such as a 3–10% greater rate of smoking cessation after advice to quit, the compensation could be based on group rates (all smokers attending a given clinic or seen by a given physician) determined periodically, rather than the successful cessation of a given individual. Unfortunately, even if the service can be verified, efficacy of many potential preventive interventions is not yet known or accepted by third-party payers. Furthermore, attribution of responsibility for prevention is especially difficult. The outcome to be assessed is the absence of disease in a defined time period. If one remains healthy, who is to say it was a result of actions performed by a physician (or any other professional). The difficulty in attributing wellness to a specific service makes both individual patients and third-party payers reluctant to reimburse physicians for preventive services.

Response Costs

Reimbursement for services by insurance and government entitlement programs are not without costs. Most require extensive billing records to be completed by the physician and patient. Most set limits on the services to be compensated, review claims, and decline to pay for some services provided. Payment for services based on specific fees for diagnostic related groups is an example of limiting hospital fees for service. Members of PPOs may be caught between the rationing limits of the insurance company, which may not pay for certain services, and their professional decision that the service is critical. Failure to provide the service may lead to patient complaints and may have malpractice ramifications. In this situation, the practitioner usually provides the service, bills the insurance company, and later learns the service is not covered. Often government entitlement programs prohibit the practitioner from charging the patient for the uninsured proportion of the bill. In these instances, the practitioner may suffer financial loss for providing "best advice" care.

In addition to the loss of revenue based on charges denied, the cost of billing and rebilling entitlement programs can be expensive. Some practitioners devote one or more employees to complete insurance and entitlement records. It is common for billings to be submitted, denied after long delays (or only partially paid), and for repeat billings to be necessary. In some instances, the cost of billing exceeds the amount of income to be received for a given patient. These response cost consequences lead some physicians to withhold treatment for certain patients or for certain types of care.

Prenatal medical care, a form of well-patient management that is known to prevent low birth weight babies and other complications of pregnancy, has resulted in serious risk to the practitioner (*A Children's Defense Budget Fiscal Year 1989,* 1988; *Blessed Events and the Bottom Line,* 1987; Institute of Medicine, 1988; Ingram, Makuc, & Kleinman, 1986). These risks, in turn, have resulted in few practitioners providing prenatal care to high-risk pregnant women. High-risk (i.e., uninsured) women who report to clinics or private offices for prenatal care and who are provided service must depend on government systems of compensation to the provider. Compensation for these services fails to equal that provided by working-insured women. High-risk women often experience medical complications for which more expensive medical care is needed and again compensation is at a much reduced rate. Because the poor are at high risk, the proportion who experience complications requiring surgery and possibly resulting in death of the fetus is higher than for middle-class patients. As may be true for all women, medical complications and loss of a baby may evoke malpractice law suits. The risk is so great that many practitioners cannot afford the malpractice insurance costs if they provide prenatal services to high-risk women (Rosenbaum & Hughes, 1988). In effect, government policies (contingency management procedures) and the insurance and legal consequences have so evolved that they systematically punish practitioners for delivering preventive services to the subpopulation most in need.

Because many curative services command higher fees, even eliminating response costs for preventive services may be insufficient to insure increased preventive services. For reliable provision of preventive services, government and insurance compensation programs must not cost the practitioner more than could be earned by delivering the preventive service. The process of billing, documentation, and accountability must be simple, straightforward, and require little staff time. Compensation should be as rapid (without delay) as possible. As political sentiment shifts in favor of compensating preventive services, compensation systems must allow for response cost.

Generally, preventive services do not result in malpractice litigation, perhaps because most services represent very low risks. However, careful study of the malpractice insurance and legal liabilities involved in medicine is needed to create systems of accountability that will provide appropriate sanctions for medical errors and at the same time not punish practitioners for delivering preventive services—especially for the subgroups most in need. This is a complex and critical area of investigation where the threat of malpractice suits and the high costs for certain services may generalize to other preventive services for which risks are low, especially if the preventive services are not compensated.

A special form of response-cost could occur for preventive medicine as it has in dentistry. If preventive services are established as routine for all patients and if powerful interventions are developed, provision of preventive services will decrease the rate of acute illness and related fees for curative care. Physicians' incomes will decrease, especially if fees for prevention do not compensate fully for the decreased patient visits. In dentistry, the use of fluoride in the drinking water and the reliable teaching of daily tooth brushing have reduced dental disease such that practitioners no longer earn as much income as expected. This is not likely in preventive medicine because powerful interventions are not now available. However, the government and insurance architects of health policy must consider the potential revenue loss to sustain preventive services in the context of increasing effectiveness.

Consumer Reactions and the Magic Bullet

Although major government and insurance company policies for compensating physicians for preventive service are critical for the routine provision of such service, the reaction from patients as consumers may be an important limiting factor. Patients attend clinic and physician offices primarily in response to pain or dysfunction. They come to the doctor to obtain "cures." Patients are subject to principles of reinforcement; they come with lifestyles that are powerfully reinforcing, even if contributing to disease. For the physician to advise (or prescribe) change in diet, exercise, alcohol use, drug use, cigarette cessation, and so forth is to ask patients to discontinue highly reinforcing (or reinforced) behavior. Usually these prescriptions are provided in absence of alternative sources of reinforcement. Most patients will not change, or will not change for long, based on the physician's advice. Even if the advice is beneficial on a population basis (e.g., 3–10% quit smoking), most will not experience cure without considerable delay as diet and other behavior changes take effect. The loss of reinforcement normally derived from usual lifestyle behavior and the failure to "cure" the problem for which the patient reported to the physician are likely to result in repeated requests for treatment and a quick cure. If not forthcoming, the physician can expect criticism, in some cases anger, and in some cases patients may initiate suit for "malpractice." Others will turn to a new physician, thereby removing all future income from the original practitioner. This can be seen in many arthritis patients who "shop" for physicians who can effectively control chronic pain (Kasteler, Kane, Olsen, & Thetford, 1976).

Even if the provision of preventive services never reduces curative care income, there is a problem with patient attendance to physician offices for preventive purposes. Preventive medicine now takes advantage of patients coming to the office for acute care; relatively few come for preventive services specifically. As the need for and as the availability of preventive services for risk behavior patterns increase, there will need to be increased attention to recruiting people to the office to receive services in absence of pain or dysfunction. Obtaining reliable attendance to appointments for curative care and relief from pain or dysfunction is difficult (Frankel & Hovell, 1978). Relatively powerful contingencies of reinforcement and "advertising" (prompting) procedures will be needed to bring patients into contact with providers of preventive medicine care.

The consuming public has learned to expect immediate cures. The magic bullet is the implicit model of care for patients and practitioners. Administering a single drug without disturbing side-effects and without loss of reinforcement derived from risk-taking behavior is the type of treatment expected. Lean schedules of medical "breakthroughs," and common use of certain medications sustain these expectations. The use of aspirin for headache teaches that relatively immediate relief is possible by taking a pill. Thus, the patients' expectations are for immediate cure without loss of existing reinforcers.

The public's demand on physicians' use of medication can be expected to increase. This will be a result of the advertising practices of pharmaceutical companies. Increasingly, medications attained only through prescription are being advertised on television and in the print media. These advertisements are directed at the public, promise therapeutic effectiveness, and encourage would-be patients to ask their physicians for a particular medication by commercial name. Although these advertisements may promote more active involvement on the part of patients in their own care, they are likely to increase the demands and social contingencies affecting physician behavior. These influences are likely to work against provision of preventive services in favor of popular presumed cures (Perri & Dickson, 1987).

Stimulus Control

Although all antecedents that have discriminative stimulus functions derive these functions as a consequence of reinforcement contingencies, they can be important influences of physicians' practice of preventive services without directly manipulating reinforcement contingencies. In our investigations we have shown that a simple and inexpensive prompting procedure can increase physicians' preventive counseling services (Johns et al., in press). A list of behavioral risk factors (e.g., smoking) was attached to the front of medical charts in the Student Health Service Center. With this was a notice asking each physician to review each risk condition and prescribe appropriate risk-reduction actions. The rate of review and risk reduction prescriptions, as measured by chart records, was significantly increased. However, there was no increase in referral to specialists and this rate was essentially zero. Similarly, reminder procedures, using computer technology, have been successful in promoting increased screening (e.g., mammogram) procedures (Turner, Day, & Borenstein, 1989).

These results suggest that preventive services for which compensation is already available (e.g., screening examinations) and services that are easy to provide (e.g., recommend decreased dietary fat), even if not specifically compensated, can be increased in rate by prompting procedures. Additional research is needed to determine how long increased rates of preventive services can be sustained in the presence of sustained prompts. Interestingly, even in a health center where a physician's salary is not related to fee for service, referral to other specialists was not provided. Future investigations should explore the variables responsible for referral actions.

Public Health Perspective and the Type of Feedback

As described earlier, the public health perspective is concerned with the health of the population. This implies examination of group data, where a population is the unit of analysis, to assess the effectiveness of an intervention. For example, the clinical perspective for smoking cessation focuses on individual patient outcomes and precludes differential feedback about population effects of antismoking campaigns. The clinician expects large magnitude effects (i.e., cures) in a specific patient and for all patients. In this context, asking 100 smokers to quit and incidentally observing that about 90 fail to quit is not likely to be reinforcing. This is a failure to discriminate a public health benefit to the population, where an important minority of the 100 patients may benefit from the physician's advice. Physicians need to be trained to assess the population benefits of a preventive service. In the smoking cessation analogy, the practitioner needs to know the population baseline quit rate in absence of his or her request to stop. This rate is about 3%. Comparing a 5% quit rate to a 3% baseline represents a very large relative change and is likely to be discriminated as a reinforcing outcome. Although simply observing change associated with treatment procedures is not satisfactory research methodology for concluding causal relationships, it might provide an important applied feedback mechanism for shaping preventive services.

Physicians are not trained to discriminate population benefits, to recognize the type of data needed to discriminate possible benefits, or to collect the type of data needed to attain the necessary feedback regarding preventive services. Formal training in the public health perspective and associated data collection and interpretation procedures may be critical prerequisites to the establishment of routine preventive services. In absence of such training and feedback, physicians' behavior is likely to drift, operating as a function of accidental dramatic "cures" that appear reliable, whereas the physicians are unable to "see" the more reliable population effects of their services.

Population-based data may be the best basis for third-party payers to reimburse physicians for outcome success. Many preventive procedures are not likely to yield clear benefits to any specific patient; rather, the service may benefit an unpredictable subset. Insurance companies could not reimburse physicians only for successful outcomes and expect them to receive sufficient income to maintain the service. Insurance companies could provide remuneration for preventive services based on two criteria: routine payment for providing the service, and intermittent fees for attaining or exceeding a population criterion success rate. For example, the practitioner could receive $1.00 for each smoking cessation prescription written. With appropriate data available regarding the proportion of patients who quit per quarter year, the physician would receive $100.00 for achieving a quit rate of at least 5%. Of course the exact degree of change needed to be a clear health benefit and the amount of money to be paid should be determined by cost/benefit analyses and type of patients receiving the service. Establishing such contingencies could sustain the preventive services and the population data collection needed to qualify for payments. This would sustain the data feedback system noted earlier, thereby increasing the incidental reinforcement to be attained simply from discriminating important changes possibly resulting from the practitioner's service.

IS HEALTH PROMOTION PROFITABLE?

One important justification for health promotion programs is that they reduce health care costs. Yet several authors have challenged the cost effectiveness of prevention or health promotion programs. In an intriguing book, Russell (1986) posed the question, "Is Prevention Better than Cure?" In this she notes that most analyses fail to account adequately for all costs of preventive services. More recently Warner, Wickizes, Wolfe, Schildroth, and Samuelson (1988) examined the conventional wisdom that work place health promotion programs yield financial dividends for companies. The literature shows that most studies published before 1986 suggest that health promotion programs increased profitability. However, these studies often relied on anecdotal evidence from analyses with serious design limitations. Thus, Warner et al., (1988) recommended healthy skepticism for readers of the literature.

The most recent considerations of cost/benefit and cost effectiveness for preventive medicine have correctly called for more accurate assessments. With more accurate analyses, promised financial savings are likely to disappear for many preventive medicine procedures, especially those focused on lifestyle behavior. This is a complex issue that pivots around the cost of delivering service, the relative effectiveness of intervention, and the reduction in costs related to the morbidity/mortality to be prevented.

The first issue, effectiveness, is critical. Most behavioral services focus on counseling/educational techniques. Cognitive services are perhaps the least effective interventions for changing lifestyles, keeping them changed, and doing so for the majority of patients who receive these services. Counseling for weight control may be an example. Most patients discontinue treatment, most do not adhere to advised diet prescriptions, most lose little weight; those who lose tend to regain it. Such services cannot be cost effective or cost beneficial; they are not yet effective.

Conversely, very inexpensive and easy to deliver services, such as advice to quit smoking, may prove both cost effective and cost beneficial. These minimal interventions may work with very few patients but in relation to the cost of delivering the service provide a financial savings. We know of no cost benefit analyses of minimal interventions, so final conclusions about cost savings must await additional investigation.

Contingency management is most apt to change lifestyles, but this has yet to be included in the routine practice of preventive medicine. Even if included, it will cost much more than traditional cognitive procedures and as such may not prove to save costs.

To further confound the issues, Fries (1990) has pointed out that there appears to be a ceiling effect for longevity and that competing forms of morbidity increase in probability with age. Thus, changing risk factors for one cause of premature death may not yield much increased longevity, as a result of competing sources of morbidity/mortality. In these instances, the possible health benefits and cost savings may be lost. These issues argue for simultaneous multiple risk-factor modification. However, only a few risk factors are known and even if many more were known there may be a biological limit to life extension. Knowledge barriers will limit both effectiveness and potential cost savings.

As the effectiveness of preventive medicine interventions increase, no doubt some will prove cost effective and cost beneficial; others will not. Some of those that do not yield cost savings, nevertheless, may be effective in preventing morbidity and mortality. These interventions may require government sanctions (punishments) for failure to provide and government reimbursement to sustain effective but costly prevention services.

CONCLUSION

There is growing political and philosophical support for preventive medicine. Increasingly, this includes efforts to change lifestyle risk behavior patterns of the patient population. Evidence suggests that the majority of physicians support the use of preventive services, but they may actually perform preventive services less reliably, especially those that require change in patient behavior. The relative failure to provide these services is very likely a consequence of formal learning history, where curative medicine procedures have become powerfully reinforcing and on-going contingencies of reinforcement sustain curative care rather than preventive services. Nevertheless, initial investigations have demonstrated that physicians are responsive to stimulus control and reinforcement procedures; when prompted or paid for preventive services, these services increase in frequency. More research is needed to identify the best forms for stimulus control and to identify the most cost-effective schedules of reinforcement for establishing and sustaining preventive services.

With additional health services research and with architectural advice from behavioral specialists expert in operant conditioning, entitlement programs and private insurance companies could design contingency management policies (remuneration rules) that would sustain reasonable rates of preventive service. These policies would need to take into account the effectiveness of the preventive service to be reinforced, the response costs involved in attaining remuneration, and competing sources of reinforcement for curative care services. These changes could decrease the costs incurred by insurance companies as a result of preventable morbidity. If savings occur, they may serve as reinforcement for sustaining remuneration for preventive services. If savings are insufficient to be reinforcing, government policy actions (reinforcement or punishment) may be needed to require such reinforcement procedures. The remuneration for preventive services is a likely prerequisite for both performance in practice and for change in formal medical education. As schools of medicine begin to train new physicians in formal assessment and intervention techniques to affect prevention of disease and as the public health perspective is formally included in the curriculum, the process of providing preventive medicine may become as reinforcing as some curative care procedures may be now. The speed and extent of establishing preventive medicine practices as routine could be enhanced by formal adoption of principles of learning and the public health perspective as the basis for preventive medicine. The operant model of behavior as a conceptional foundation for both physician practice and patients' behavior change promises to make an important contribution to the achievement of the nation's health objectives (U.S. Department of Health and Human Services, 1990).

REFERENCES

A children's defense budget fiscal year 1989: An analysis of our nation's investment in children. (1988). Washington, DC: Children's Defense Fund.

Ajzen, I., & Fishbein, M. (1980). *Understanding attitudes and predicting social behavior.* Englewood Cliffs, NJ: Prentice-Hall.

American Medical Association. (1983). Medical evaluations of healthy persons. (Council on Scientific Affairs). *Journal of the American Medical Association, 429,* 1626–1633.

Bartlett, E. (1984). Teaching health education in medical education: Selected perspectives. *Preventive Medicine, 13,* 100–114.

Becker, M., & Janz, N. (1990). Practicing health promotion: The doctor's dilemma. *Annals of Internal Medicine, 113,* 419–422.

Blessed events and the bottom line: Financing maternity care in the United States. (1987). New York: Alan Guttmacher Institute.

Bunker, J., Fowles, J., & Schaffarzink, R. (1982). Evaluation of medical-technological strategies: Effects of coverage in reimbursement. *New England Journal of Medicine, 306,* 620–624.

Dismuke, S., & Miller, S. (1983). Why not share the secrets of good health? The physician's role in health promotion. *Journal of the American Medical Association, 249,* 3181–3183.

Elder, J. P., Hovell, M. F., Lasater, J., Wells, B., & Carleton, R. (1985). Applications of behavior modification to community health education: The case of heart disease prevention. *Health Education Quarterly, 12,* 151–168.

Frankel, B., & Hovell, M. (1978). Health service appointment keeping: A behavioral view and critical review. *Behavior Modification, 2,* 435–464.

Fries, J. F. (1990). An introduction to the compression of morbidity. In P. R. Lee & C. L. Estes (Eds.), *The nation's health* (pp. 35–41). Boston: Jones and Bartlett Publishers.

Guide to clinical preventive services: An assessment of the effectiveness of 169 interventions. (1989). (Report to the U.S. Preventive Services Task Force). Baltimore: Williams and Wilkins.

Hershey, C., Porter, D., Breslau, D., & Cohen, D. (1986). Influence of simple computerized feedback of prescription changes in an ambulatory clinic. *Medical Care, 24,* 472–481.

Hovell, M., & Black, D. R. (1989). Minimal intervention and arthritis treatment: Implications for patient and physician compliance. *Arthritis Care and Research, 18,* 20–34.

Hovell, M., Elder, J., Blanchard, J., & Sallis, J. (1986). Behavior analysis and public health perspectives: Combining paradigms to effect prevention. *Education and Treatment of Children, 9,* 287–306.

Hsiao, W., Braun, P., Dunn, D., & Becker, E. (1988). Resource-based relative values: An overview. *Journal of the American Medical Association, 260,* 2347–2353.

Hsiao, W., Braun, P., Dunn, D., Becker, E., DeNicola, M., & Ketcham, T. (1988). Results and policy implications of the resource-based relative value study. *New England Journal of Medicine, 319,* 881–888.

Hurley, J. (1990). Simulated effects of income-based policies on the distribution of physicians. *Medical Care, 28,* 221–238.

Ingram, D., Makuc, D., & Kleinman, J. (1986). National and state trends in use of parental care. *American Journal of Public Health, 76,* 415–423.

Institute of Medicine. (1988). *Prenatal care: Reaching mothers, reaching infants.* Washington, DC: National Academy Press.

Johns, M., Hovell, M., Drastal, C., Lamke, C., & Patrick, K. (in press). Promoting prevention services in primary care: A controlled trial. *American Journal of Preventive Medicine.*

Johns, M., Hovell, M., Ganitas, T., Peddecord, M., & Agras, S. (1987). Primary care and health promotion: A model for preventive medicine. *American Journal of Preventive Medicine, 3,* 346–357.

Kasteler, J., Kane, R. L., Olsen, D. M., & Thetford, C. (1976). Issues underlying prevalence of "doctor-shopping" behavior. *Journal of Health and Social Behavior, 17,* 328–339.

Katz, R., & Zlutnick, S. (Eds.). (1975). *Behavior therapy and health care.* New York: Pergamon Press.

Kilbourn, K., Hovell, M., Menna, D., & Harwood, I. (in preparation). Promoting physical activity in cystic fibrosis children: Analysis of a privilege system.

Last, J. (Ed.). (1986). *Maxcy-Rosenu public health and preventive medicine.* New York: Appleton-Century-Crofts.

Li, V., Coates, T., Ewart, C., & Kim, Y. (1987). The effectiveness of smoking cessation advice given during routine medical care: Physicians can make a difference. *American Journal of Preventive Medicine, 3,* 81–86.

Logsdon, D., & Rosen, M. (1984). The cost of preventive health services in primary medical care and implications for health insurance coverage. *Journal of Ambulatory Care Management, 7,* 46–55.

Logsdon, D., Rosen, M., & Demak, N. (1982). The INSURE program on lifestyle preventive health services. *Public Health Reports, 97,* 308–317.

Maibach, E., Scutchfield, F., & Hovell, M. (1984). A survey of primary care physicians preventive services: Implications for smoking cessation counseling. *Patient Education and Counseling, 6,* 113–115.

Martin, A. R., Wolfe, M. A., Thiboudeau, O. A., Dzau, V., & Brunwald, E. (1980). A trial of two strategies to modify the test-ordering behavior of medical residents. *New England Journal of Medicine, 303,* 1330–1336.

McAlister, A., Mullen, P., Nixon, S., Dickson, C., Gottlieb, N., McCuan, R., & Green, L. (1985). Health promotion among primary care physicians in Texas. *Texas Medicine, 81,* 55–58.

Millenson, J., & Leslie, J. (1979). *Principles of behavior analysis.* New York: Macmillan.

Mitchell, M., & Fowkes, F. (1985). Audit review: Does feedback on performance change clinical behavior? *Journal of the Royal College of Physicians, 19,* 251–254.

National Center for Health Statistics. (1983). *Physician visits: Volume and interval since last visit,* (vital and health statistics; series 10, no. 144). Hyattsville, MD: U.S. Government Printing Office.

Newhouse, J. (1990). Geographic access to physician services. *Annual Review of Public Health, 11,* 207–230.

Perri, M., & Dickson, W. (1987). Direct to consumer prescription drug advertising: Consumer and physician reactions. *Journal of Pharmaceutical Marketing and Management, 2,* 3–25.

Reinhardt, V. (1990). Rationing the health-care surplus: An American tragedy. In P. Lee & C. Estes (Eds.), *The Nation's Health* (pp. 104–111). Boston: Jones and Bartlett Publishers.

Rooks, J. (1990). Let's admit we ration health care–then set priorities. *American Journal of Nursing, 90,* 38–43.

Roos, N. P. (1984). Hysterectomy: Variations in rates across small areas and across physicians' practices. *American Journal of Public Health, 74,* 327–355.

Rosenbaum, S., & Hughes, D. (1988). The medical malpractice crisis and poor women. In Institute of Medicine, *Prenatal care: Reaching mothers, reaching infants* (pp. 229–243). Washington, DC: National Academy Press.

Rosenstock, I. M. (1974). Historical origins of the health belief model. *Health Education Monographs, 2,* 328–335.

Russell, L. (1986). *Is prevention better than cure?* Washington, DC: The Brookings Institute.

Russell, M., Wilson, C., Taylor, C., & Baker, C. (1979). Effect of general practitioners' advice against smoking. *British Medical Journal, 2,* 231–235.

Skinner, B. F. (1953). *Science and human behavior.* New York: Macmillan.

Skinner, B. F. (1974). *About behaviorism.* New York: Knopf.

Somers, A. (1984). Why not try preventing illness as a way of controlling Medicare costs? *New England Journal of Medicine, 311,* 853–856.

Soumerai, S. B., Avorn, J., Ross-Degnan, D., & Gortmaker, S. (1987). Payment restrictions for prescription drugs under medicaid: Effects of therapy, cost and equity. *New England Journal of Medicine, 317,* 550–556.

Stoll, B. (1990). Choosing between cancer patients. *Journal of Medical Ethics, 16,* 71–74.

Tierney, W. M., Miller, M. E., & McDonald, C. J. (1990). The effect on test ordering of informing physicians of the charges for out-patient diagnostic tests. *New England Journal of Medicine, 322,* 1499–1504.

Turner, B., Day, S., & Borenstein, B. (1989). A controlled trial to improve delivery of preventive care: Physician and patient reminders? *Journal of General Internal Medicine, 4,* 403–409.

U.S. Department of Health and Human Services: Public Health Services. (1990). *Healthy people 2000: National health promotion and disease prevention objectives.* Washington, DC: Government Printing Office.

Warner, K. E., Wickizer, T. M., Wolfe, R. A., Schildroth, J. E., & Samuelson, M. H. (1988). Economic implications of workplace health promotion programs: Review of the literature. *Journal of Occupational Medicine, 30,* 102–112.

Wennberg, J. E. (1990). Small area analysis in the medical care outcome problem. In L. Sechrest, E. Perrin, & J. Bunker (Eds.), *Strengthening causal interpretations of non-experimental data.* Washington, DC: Agency for Health Care Policy and Research.

Wennberg, J. E., Freeman, J. L., & Culp, W. S. (1987). Are health services rationed in New Haven or over utilized in Boston? *Lancet, 23,* 1185–1189.

Wenneker, J. E., Weissman, J. S., & Epstein, A. M. (1990). The association of payer with utilization of cardiac procedures in Massachusetts. *Journal of the American Medical Association, 264,* 1255–1266.

11

Contingencies and Metacontingencies in Correctional Settings

Janet Ellis

INTRODUCTION

The nation's prison population jumped by a record 46,004 inmates in the first 6 months of 1989 for a total of 673,565 men and women behind bars. These figures have broken a federal record; they represent the highest annual increase in the 64 years that the Bureau of Justice Statistics has counted prisoners (Metts, 1989). These data come as no surprise. As Nietzel and Himelein (1987) declared, "One of the greatest ironies of current corrections is that the lock-'em-up-longer philosophy regarded as reactionary only 20 years ago is now considered to be the cutting edge in penology" (p. 130).

The long-term outcomes of this philosophy may drastically change our lives, both economically and socially. Why hasn't going to prison served to deter criminal behavior? What's been done in prison to try to change the probability of future criminal behavior? "Much more can be done through applied behavior analysis when the problem is understood" (Skinner, 1978, p. 43). This chapter focuses on trying to understand the problem by examining: (1) applications of behavioral technology in prisons; (2) contingencies and metacontingencies extant in such institutions and in our culture that may account for the alarming rise in crime rates, as exemplified in increased numbers of incarcerations.

Throughout this book, authors have used a technical vocabulary in discussing their topics. They have defined certain concepts (e.g., behavior, technology, contingencies, metacontingencies) as these terms applied to their subject matter. This procedure is necessary because each chapter focuses on a different facet of the cultural kaleidoscope. In this chapter, contingencies and metacontingencies will be explained in terms of Glenn's analysis (1985, 1986, 1988), wherein she discriminates between technological and ceremonial behavior and introduces the concept of metacontingencies as these apply in a behavior analytic framework.

Briefly, this chapter explains why correctional settings and the behavior of those working in such settings may be considered ceremonial and why behavioral interventions in prison are considered technological. Behavioral programming for delinquent and adult offenders is also described; likewise, the role of correctional staff (security and treatment-oriented personnel) is examined in light of the apparent failure to change criminal behavior. The chapter closes with a description of the metacontingencies accounting for current cultural views on prisons, prisoners, and society's role in rehabilitation, then concludes with a suggested redefinition of the role of applied behavior analysts in the field of corrections.

DEFINING TERMINOLOGY

Certain terminology, specific to behavior analysis, is used in discussing the issues involved in implementing behavioral programs in correctional settings and in examining the role that societal policies have played in determining consequences for criminal behavior. The following technical vocabulary will be defined: control, behavioral technology, contingency of reinforcement, operant behavior, metacontingency, ceremonial and technological behavior.

"Control" is a word that generally connotes domination by a powerful person or by rule with punishing consequences for failure to follow. When behavior analysts refer to "control," they are using it to explain the effect of applying an independent variable (an intervention) to the dependent variable (behavior). If the contingencies created by the independent variable (e.g., the contingencies in a behavioral self-management contract) change the dependent variable (e.g., eating behavior of the contractee) then the contractual contingencies controlled eating behavior—caused eating behavior to change. In this chapter "controlling" behavior will be used interchangeably with "causing" behavior to occur. Next, we shall define behavioral technology, which will be the generic term for independent variables under consideration in this chapter.

Technology is generally a technical method of achieving a practical purpose. The technical method we are specifying is behavioral technology, or the implementation of scientifically discovered and empirically verified procedures to change behavior-environment relations (i.e., to control or cause the emergence of new behavior). The behavior of interest is criminal behavior—activity that violates laws prohibiting this behavior and for which there is an authorized punishment (Wilson & Herrnstein, 1985), and the focal environment is the correctional institution. We shall analyze interactions between criminal behavior and the prison environment using the contingency of reinforcement (COR). A COR consists of the behavior of a given person in a given environment (e.g., repeated instances of an inmate from his cell threatening to harm a guard) and the changes in that environment that are always or sporadically contingent on that behavior (the guard then approaching the cell and warning the inmate to be quiet or else).

Using the COR as our basic unit of analysis, we're going to look at criminal operant behavior. Operant behavior is activity that produces consequences that, in turn, cause an increase or a decrease in frequency of that behavior. For example, yelling threats, banging on the bars, and demanding to talk to a doctor produces a guard at the cell for an inmate. All these behaviors are in the same operant group or class because they all function to produce the same consequence: a guard at the cell. In another example, a delinquent can obtain money by stealing it from a family member, by robbing a drive-in grocery store, by selling a stolen car. So, all these behaviors are in the same operant class because they involve "easy" or "cheap" behavior (i.e., behavior involving little sustained effort) and produce a common consequence—money in the delinquent's pocket.

Metacontingency is defined here as "the unit of analysis describing the functional relations between a class of operants and a long-term consequence common to all the operants" (Glenn, 1986, p. 2). For instance, the number of inmates living in prison in any state is the outcome of the state's criminal justice practices.

For example, in 1989 the number of inmates in Texas prisons (and in county jails) was the outcome of a federal court ruling that Texas state prisons must stop admitting inmates when the system is within 95% of court-ordered capacity.

Glenn (1985, 1986) distinguished between ceremonially and technologically maintained behavior. Technological behavior is behavior maintained by nonarbitrary changes in the environment—by its usefulness, value, or importance to the behaving person and others. Calculators, steam shovels, written symbols, token economies, behavioral contracts, and programmed instruction are products of technological behavior. Technological control ensures change, because technological behavior is maintained only if it proves useful to the culture. Engineers who design rockets do not retain those designs if the rocket does not function to specification. In contrast, ceremonial behavior is behavior maintained by social reinforcers "deriving their [reinforcing] power from the status, position, or authority of the reinforcing agent independent of any relation to changes in the environment directly or indirectly benefitting the behaving person" (Glenn, 1986, p. 3). Because of this arbitrary feature, ceremonial behavior typically involves aversive control. Examples of ceremonial control include: capricious parental demands on children; grading "original papers" in terms of the content of student opinion; apartheid rules governing behavior of black South Africans that function to keep white South Africans in control of the major economic and political resources; church edicts that limit diets to certain foods and that mandate wearing only certain types of clothing. In summary, as Glenn points out, ceremonial control maintains itself because of its advantage to those with the control. And she defines some of the dimensions of ceremonial behavior as tending to be "static, resistant to change, and when widespread establishes institutional patterns that bind the culture to the past" (1985, p. 18). State institutions—including prison systems—are characterized by metacontingencies that enable ceremonial behavior and account for administrative and staff behavior in the prison.

POLITICAL METACONTINGENCIES CREATING AND MAINTAINING CEREMONIAL BEHAVIOR IN PRISON SYSTEMS

In most states the governor is the titular head of the state's correctional system and can initiate budgetary planning for prisons and can veto legislative funding arrangements. The governor appoints the state director of corrections or has input into this decision. These appointees are usually political and may change when the governor leaves office. According to Hawkins and Alpert (1989), 78% of state prison directors have 2 or fewer years of experience in that position; 5–10% have been working in that job 2–4 years. Directors are often appointed from within the ranks of the prison wardens. If the appointment is internal (within the same state), the new director may favor the prison unit where he or she was most recently the warden. Another frequent occurrence is that unpopular, ineffective, or even incompetent personnel may be promoted to a director position to remove them from a volatile position elsewhere in the system (Hawkins & Alpert, 1989).

ECONOMIC METACONTINGENCIES
MAINTAINING CEREMONIAL BEHAVIOR
IN PRISON SYSTEMS

In addition to the role of these political metacontingencies in accounting for the top prison leadership, there are certain economic contingencies that bear on who is hired to actually work in the trenches—dealing with the inmates on a daily basis in the prison itself: the prison guards. Guards are likely to be white high school graduates from rural areas. Prisons are usually located in these areas for two reasons; urban areas do not need prisons as an employment source and their citizenry actively oppose such institutions. Prisons may be a detraction to large industries considering a move to the area. To the contrary, many rural towns, with no major employer, may offer tax incentives and donate land for the prison site. Citizens in such towns are likely to be employed by the prison and to remain at their jobs (despite, in many cases, aversive work conditions) because of the lack of available economic choices (Hawkins & Alpert, 1989).

A quasimilitary structure best describes the organizational chain of command in a prison. Officers wear uniforms; a major, captains, lieutenants, sergeants and line officers form the battalion headed by the unit's warden. As in a military structure, the lower echelon officers not only do not question the rationale for the rules they follow, but also many of these officers have never seen, in written form, the rules they are paid to enforce. These rules are handed down verbally by their superior officers, many of whom have also never read the rules. Wetzel and Hoschouer (cited in Holburn, 1987) described such institutions as "bureaucratic procedures organized and controlled by ineffective rules and regulations described (often contradictorily) in voluminous policy manuals and management directives" (p. 283).

CEREMONIAL BEHAVIOR IN PRISON SYSTEMS

Glenn (1985) defined status as the "power to control the behavior of others through social reinforcement (independently of the usefulness of the behavior to the one behaving)" (p. 19). In the prison system wardens and security officers have status in that they exert rigid control over the behavior of both prison staff and inmates; this control over the behavior of others and the consequences deriving from such control has become institutionalized, since persons with such power are inclined to maintain the status quo. Likewise, Glenn points out that those without much status (i.e., prison guards) are also likely to find a threat to the status quo aversive possibly because many of their own reinforcers have been mediated by those having status. In short, ceremonial control involves processes that provide institutional resistance to (technological) progress; and, thus, when systems are ceremonially controlled they are not susceptible to implementing contingencies that could possibly result in constructive changes.

TECHNOLOGICAL BEHAVIOR
IN PRISON SYSTEMS

Given these circumstances, when society (through its courts) intrudes into prison systems and orders reform in treatment of inmates and changes in hiring and training of staff, technological behavior is mandated in correctional institutions. At this point, behavior analysts, as purveyors of technology, may enter the picture. Generally, the goal of behavioral interventions is to help people acquire appropriate behavior rather than to decrease rates of inappropriate behavior. The outcome of successfully implemented technology is human behavior that is effective in the current and in future (natural) environments, because this behavior is maintained by its reinforcing consequences. An effective technological intervention in a prison setting not only teaches new repertoires to the inmates, but also enhances the effectiveness of the prison security staff behavior—both at work and at home. For example, training guards to praise appropriate inmate behavior when they observe it benefits the inmate-behaver, the guard, and the prison system. It may increase the frequency of that inmate's changed behavior; the guard has learned a skill that can be practiced at home and at work; if the rate of suitable behavior increases, the rate of violent, assaultive behavior may decrease across time, thereby benefitting the prison. The next part of this chapter describes such behavioral interventions in closed institutional settings (i.e., prisons, as opposed to community residential settings or day program facilities), which house juvenile and adult offenders.

BEHAVIORAL INTERVENTIONS
FOR JUVENILE DELINQUENTS
IN CORRECTIONAL INSTITUTIONS

Although few might argue the importance of the environment in evoking, shaping, reinforcing, and punishing behavior (Colman, 1975), apparently society has concluded that prison environments are appropriate settings for modifying delinquent behavior. Prisons are becoming commonplace residences for increasing numbers of young persons. One in nine persons is referred to juvenile courts by their 18th birthday (O'Donnell, 1977), and over 500,000 children and adolescents are housed in juvenile and adult correctional facilities in the United States (Farrow, 1984). Also, approximately 80% of these youthful offenders are illiterate (Davidson, 1988). One official lamented that his state was able to turn "fresh, bright-eyed first graders into hardened criminals in 10 years" (Hoppe, 1990, May 16, p. 8A).

An assumption underlying behavioral interventions (regardless of the behavior being trained/modified) is that students fail to learn when environmental conditions are not appropriate for learning to occur (Lindsley, 1965); or, conversely, all students are capable of learning some behavior when there is an appropriate motivational system and instructional program. Prisons, by virtue of their mandate from the culture to deter/punish criminal behavior, generally focus on "deceleration objectives" (Glenn & Hutchison, 1990)—that is, eliminating inappropriate behavior, rather than on reinforcing appropriate behavior that occurs or on training acquisition behavior. Prisons, then, might appear unlikely environments in which to acquire much generalizable appropriate behavior.

What have behavior analysts done to modify the behavior of the incarcerated juvenile delinquent? Briefly, they have designed and implemented token economies/point systems. Using these as basic motivational systems, they have taught, through programmed instruction, academic behavior (e.g., reading, math, social studies, etc.). Additionally, they have included social skills training. As Burchard and Lane (1982) summarized, "It is now estimated that in almost every state, there is some variation of a token-economy system within an institutional setting" (p. 615).

Cohen and Filipczak (1971), in their seminal study involving a point system in a prison setting, created *A New Learning Environment.* This project will be described in some detail because it was a prototype for interventions that followed over the next 10 years. This comprehensive program (called the CASE II Model), instituted at the Washington, DC, National Training School for Boys, was designed as a 24-hour/day educational project involving programmed learning opportunities. The boys earned points for working at their academic courses and for passing tests at 90% mastery criterion. Students entered the program at their individually assessed educational level, and all modularized units were self-paced. The points they earned for engaging in appropriate behavior could be use to purchase a variety of back-up goods and services (from dessert to private study cubicles to opportunities to have their clothes dry cleaned and eventually to have escorted and later unescorted trips away from the prison).

This program met generally accepted behavioral criteria for interventions in any setting: (1) the operants trained would also be reinforced in the boy's natural environment; (2) the behavior trained could be consistently, objectively observed, measured, and monitored; (3) appropriate behavior was consequated as soon as possible after its occurrence; (4) programmed consequences maintained desirable behavior over extended periods of time; (5) consequences bridged the delay between targeted behavior and back-up consequences. And, most importantly, Cohen and Filipczak controlled the relevant contingencies critical for a successful intervention in any setting: (1) they hired and trained the staff; (2) they had adequate funds (i.e., to offer staff bonuses for programs designed and implemented by the correctional staff and for extensive back-up consequences for the point system); (3) the program was housed in a completely remodelled, redesigned four-story building separate from the main prison. In short, these researchers had both the responsibility and the authority necessary to implement their project.

Dean and Reppucci (1974) at the Connecticut School for Boys and Hobbs and Holt (1976) at the Alabama Boys Industrial School established 24-hour-a-day, token-economy-based rehabilitation programs to train academic and social skills. Nay (1974) also instituted a comprehensive training program with three differences: (1) the population was female delinquents; (2) targeted skills included vocational behavior; (3) Nay also included training certain staff behavior—giving direct, clear instructions to the delinquents and socially reinforcing appropriate inmate behavior. Interestingly, staff behavior changes in the appropriate direction were greater than those of the inmates. (*Note:* This chapter will not discuss the appropriateness of criteria for measuring successful outcomes, since these are often set by the institution and may be interpreted differently from criteria established by the behavioral research design.)

These types of extensive and inclusive motivational systems for juveniles in prison appear to have flourished from the mid-1960s through mid-1970s and then appear to have phased down into scattered projects focusing primarily on literacy skills of single subjects (e.g., Bippes, McLaughlin, & Williams, 1986; Burchard & Harrington, 1985–86). This definite move away from programs in correctional institutions apparently stems from the current alternatives to incarcerating delinquents—group homes (e.g., Achievement Place), transition programming from prison to half-way houses back into the home, and community-based alternatives. Yet behavior analysts faced obstacles working in correctional settings that may also have accounted for the decrease in behavioral interventions. These will be discussed later in this chapter.

BEHAVIORAL INTERVENTIONS
FOR ADULT OFFENDERS
IN CORRECTIONAL INSTITUTIONS

Prisonization theory states that prisoners adapt to their environment in ways that later make it difficult for them to survive lawfully in the free world (Zamble & Porporino, 1990). Prisons not only constrain much behavior, but also they provide little in the way of contingencies that would instigate, reinforce, and maintain progressive behavioral changes. This assertion is based on personal observations of daily events in prison systems. First, events that could be delivered contingent on appropriate behavior (e.g., attention from staff) are often mandated by law to be delivered noncontingently (e.g., attention from staff when offender makes demands or threats). Secondly, positive inmate behavior (e.g., cooperating with prison rules) enters into two contingencies simultaneously. Prison staff provide a very low-density schedule of reinforcement and peers provide a high density punishment schedule (e.g., threatening and often physically attacking the inmate) for cooperating with the system and, consequently, receiving even more attention from staff. Third, the largest number of reinforcers are available both from peers and from staff for negative behavior (i.e., any responses producing signs of damage to the prison system or personnel). Fourth, as Allyon and Azrin (1968) suggested, a way of increasing the reinforcing effectiveness of an event for people is to watch others engage in some behavior that is immediately followed by strong reinforcers. So, unwanted behavior that is consistently and strongly reinforced by peers and staff is effectively modeled for new inmates and thereby perpetuated.

Generally, the prison environment is arranged such that personnel attend to preventing or consequating unwanted behavior ("deceleration" behavior) rather than on arranging the environment to produce short- or long-term behavior changes that may earn the offender reinforcers in the free world. For example, Vito (1985) suggests that a shift of prison management philosophy is needed to remedy the image of work as punishment.

Given these prison contingencies, the same question arises: What have behavior analysts done to modify the behavior of the incarcerated adult offender? Curiously, this question has the same technological answer as that provided for juvenile offenders: token economies/point systems. Apparently, behavior analysts have depended on these well-known and possibly overused approaches for the same reasons the author bases her interventions on these systems, because they are: (1) relatively easy to set up in a short amount of time, (2) easy to demonstrate to prison staff, and (3) an effective vehicle by which to involve staff in the day-to-day running of the program. Also, more complex procedures involving stimulus control, schedules of reinforcement, or varying aspects of the reinforcer (e.g., amount, type, etc.) are difficult to implement (i.e., to ensure that these variables do indeed enable prediction and control of the behavior under study) even in a laboratory setting. Such procedures are almost impossible to carry out in most institutional settings (i.e., state schools, state hospitals, prisons) with their ever-present, uncontrolled sources of bootleg (unauthorized) reinforcement.

Parallel to Cohen and Filipczak's CASE II Model program for delinquents, behavioral undertakings with incarcerated adults had their seminal project—the Experimental Manpower Laboratory for Corrections (EMLC) located at Draper Correctional Center in Elmore, Alabama. Milan and McKee (1976) operated a 24-hour, 7-day/week cellblock token economy that approximated the features of the CASE II design: they took over one cellblock and structured both educational and vocational activities for 56 inmates. Like Cohen and Filipczak, Milan and McKee had total responsibility and authority for running their project. They suspended usual prison consequences for rule violations and had funds to furnish attractive back-up consequences for points accumulated. Milan and McKee used this maximum security prison cellblock to investigate the effect of various independent variables on developing appropriate inmate repertoires. They studied the effect of three motivational conditions: (1) guard efforts to motivate inmates to participate, (2) noncontingent awarding of points, and (3) contingent awarding of points for program participation. Then Milan, Throckmorton, McKee, and Wood (1979) examined the effect of unannounced attendance checks on rule-following behavior versus earning one half hour of time off the cellblock dependent on rate of following prison rules. They also investigated the relationships between magnitude of reinforcement and performance of targeted behaviors. Milan, Wood, and McKee (1979) studied use of response chaining to maximize inmate involvement in educational activities when tokens alone failed to obtain optimal participation. These landmark research projects provided the basis for others (e.g., Allyon, Milan, Roberts, & McKee, 1979; Bassett, Blanchard, & Koshland, 1975; Kandel, Allyon, & Roberts, 1976). But, sadly, this trend met the fate that befell behavioral interventions for incarcerated delinquents. Apparently, these types of programs are nonexistent today, despite indications that "more juvenile and adult offenders are in detention facilities, training schools, and prisons each year than there are mentally ill and developmentally delayed persons in institutions" (Milan, 1987, p. 219). "The paucity of research [even non-research-oriented programs] conducted in the last decade suggests that behaviorists, for whatever reasons, have retreated from closed institutions for juvenile delinquents and adult felons" (Milan, 1987, p. 219).

One possible reason for this retreat may have to do with problems encountered by behavior analysts in gaining the cooperation of the on-site prison personnel (guards, social workers, and administrators) in putting the program contingencies into effect.

ROLE OF INSTITUTIONAL STAFF
IN IMPLEMENTING
BEHAVIORAL TECHNOLOGY

The political and economic metacontingencies described earlier ultimately account for the practices of the correctional staff, which involve the behavior of administrators, guards, and social workers. But, these practices present competing contingencies for direct contact staff (guards, social workers, program designers) trying to carry out habilitative/rehabilitative programs in correctional institutions. This discussion describes these competing contingencies generally and then notes specific examples of their effect on the behavior of institutional staff.

Glenn (1985) notes that since rules emerging from ceremonial practices tend to maintain the status quo, if technology threatens to disrupt the status quo then rules that suppress technology will be devised. It follows, then, that wardens are unlikely to seek intervention programs that would expand the power of their treatment staff or guards. Likewise, the upper-echelon officers and the on-line guards, all of whom spend a great deal of time and effort maintaining the status quo (as per warden's instructions), also do not welcome or want changes.

Competing Contingencies Resulting in Lack of Motivation to Change Behavior

Wardens often appear to respond to treatment personnel as the enemy because such persons exist because of philosophical changes in cultural views or because treatment personnel are legally mandated to be in the prison (Hawkins & Alpert, 1989). This viewpoint has trickled down to the guards. For instance, in various prison settings guards frequently complained to this author and her colleagues that they saw themselves losing power while inmates, as they are accorded due process rights, are gaining in power and influence. And guards see treatment personnel as the harbinger of inmate power. It is not surprising then that a very small percentage of correctional budgets are spent on offender programs according to Gendreau and Ross (1984). Security's goal for any program plan implemented for inmates is institutional control; whereas, treatment personnel see their goal as rehabilitation of the offender. In our experience, guards could detail explicitly and exactly what they did not want the inmates to do or be able to do, but treatment personnel had no predetermined criteria for labeling an intervention as successful and no particular behavioral outcome they wanted to produce.

Another factor that accounts for security's unified viewpoint is embodied in their job training. Crouch and Alpert (1982) say, "The formal training of guards stresses that inmates are untrustworthy, conniving and even dangerous, and thus deserve constant suspicion" (p. 171). Perhaps, the effect of such training can be noted in the changes in guards' verbal and nonverbal behavior that are correlated with time they have been working in the prison—the longer the time period the more aggressive and punishing their interactions with inmates appear to be (Ellis, personal observation; Bassett & Blanchard, 1977; Crouch & Alpert, 1982).

Competing Contingencies Involved in "Changing Behavior"

The behavior analyst and security officers talk about this topic in quite different ways although they both use the phrase "changing behavior." Guards typically are describing immediate changes in inmate behavior—decreases in yelling, decreases in noncompliant behavior, decreases in violent and assaultive behavior. When behavior analysts describe changing behavior, we are describing immediate and long-term changes in guard and social worker behavior as well as in inmate behavior. We are interested in changing controlling variables to produce appropriate new behavior rather than in decreasing inappropriate behavior. Giving an outsider control over contingencies that account for behavior of guards and treatment personnel is, clearly, inimical to prison administrators' interests.

In addition to these competing contingencies, there remains the issue of relevant criteria for behavior change. Allyon and Azrin (1968) focused on teaching behaviors that would continue to be reinforced after training. As mentioned earlier, there is a low rate of inmate appropriate behavior; in addition to the inconsistent (often nonexistent) consequences that follow appropriate behaving, there is the problem of no appropriate discriminative stimuli for free world behavior in the prison environment. Inmates do not make choices or exercise options while in prison. In the free world it is the failure to make good choices and/or to know what options to exercise and under what conditions that can lead to further imprisonment. There are no differential consequences for inmate behavior in the prison. Behavioral guidelines in a prison setting usually take the form of, "Don't do _____," thereby predisposing personnel to observe unwanted behavior. Because alternative (i.e., appropriate) behavior may take any other form, its occurrence is rarely noted as desirable by prison staff and even more rarely reinforced.

Effect of Competing Contingencies on Correctional Staff Behavior

Laws (1974) described problems he encountered in operating a token economy in a maximum security psychiatric hospital. Supervising the contingencies requires "a high level of motivation on the part of the staff" (p. 36); Laws could neither reinforce appropriate nor punish inappropriate staff behavior but had to rely on staff assurances of cooperation. Their behavior ranged from "enthusiastic participation" to "blatant sabotage." The program failed to meet its targeted goals.

Fox (1984) attributes the built-in conflicts between custodial and treatment personnel to their mutually exclusive goals. "Custodial staff and administration want a quiet prison and many do not object to 'locking them up and throwing the key away' " (p. 105). Social workers want inmates out of prison as wage-earning, law-abiding citizens. Like Fox, my own observations indicated that guards see treatment-oriented staff as "bleeding hearts on the side of the inmates." Cullen, Lutze, Link, and Wolfe (1989) interviewed correctional officers to measure their support for custody and rehabilitation of criminal offenders. The respondents favored incapacitation and retribution over rehabilitation as a motive for incarceration, and custody as the appropriate goal of the prison.

Musante (1975) summed up the difficult situation facing underpaid, overworked prison guards and social workers. The guards, in particular, are asked to implement a program in which they may be required to provide reinforcers for appropriate inmate behavior. Usually, guards regard these incentives as "bribes" for behavior that "should come naturally" to the inmate because it is the "right thing to do."

Economic and political metacontingencies combine to produce prisons manned by personnel with little or no educational preparation for correctional work, no merit system to provide a motivational component for learning new behavior, and insufficient training to maintain a behavior modification program in an institutional setting. These poorly trained personnel, who behave in an environment that can be considered barren at best and aversive at worst, are as victimized by prison policies as are the inmates. What has accounted for these prison contingencies that have failed to reduce recidivism or produce effective behavior change programs?

Metacontingencies have shaped public policy toward incarceration much as prison contingencies have shaped the offender's behavior. Both the prison system and the offenders usually get noticed when they engage in behavior that results in aversive outcomes for the public. For example, correlated increases in rates of substance abuse and violent criminal behavior have led to longer prison sentences that have led to overcrowding in prisons. This situation often results in: (1) shorter sentences for those already in prison, (2) need for more custodial staff, (3) increased probability that a repeat offender will be released who then will commit another crime. Likewise, overcrowding and the concomitant deterioration of living conditions in prisons have resulted in prison riots. Usually such events result in more restrictive rules—more punishment-oriented contingencies—that may affect society as adversely as they affect the inmates (e.g., more prisons result in higher taxes). Before we can discuss the contingencies that may change what happens in our correctional system, we must account for the current contingencies that appear to exert control over correctional policy today. We cannot account for current contingencies without examining the metacontingencies giving rise to the public's stance on incarceration and rehabilitation.

METACONTINGENCIES ACCOUNTING FOR CURRENT VIEWS ON PRISONS, PRISONERS, AND SOCIETY'S ROLE IN REHABILITATION

Skinner (1953) defined a social system as "a controlling agency together with the individuals who are controlled by it" (p. 335). At this point we are interested in two controlling agencies, government (as exemplied in politics/public policies/ laws) and economics (as exemplified in the process of division of wealth), which account for much of the behavior of groups in our social system—or culture. These two controlling agencies have had a major impact on today's correctional system.

Current Political and Economic Metacontingencies Affecting Prisons and Prison Policies

According to Struckhoff (1983–1984), we have a "new electorate," consisting of social minorities (e.g., the elderly, gays, women, the physically handicapped) and racial minorities. These groups are using their vote to promote their goals. They are calling for accountability in politics and laws (e.g., financial accountability for political candidates; equal job opportunities). These metacontingencies have resulted in the legal decisions that have forced the prison system out of its prior self-imposed isolation and into the public limelight.

Economic metacontingencies (e.g., an ever-expanding nucleus of a permanent underclass) are resulting in rising crime rates and changes in laws that have strongly impacted the prison system. "While previously corrections functioned as a relatively small warehousing operation within society, it is now a multibillion dollar enterprise . . . affecting all levels of government and accounting for substantial amounts of consumer dollars in the form of taxes" (Struckhoff, p. 111).

Current Competing Contingencies

As the competition for tax dollars increases among various state institutions (hospitals, schools, and prisons), as funds become less available, as laws governing policies for these institutions become more restrictive (thereby costing more tax dollars to run), there may be chaos in prison systems in the future. Most large state institutions make changes slowly at best and are finding it difficult to develop the flexibility they need to keep pace with ever accelerating changes in public policies (contingencies). As an example of the chaotic policies being developed in corrections today, we can look at the public's view of punishment versus rehabilitation for criminal behavior. Cullen, Golden, and Cullen (1983) gathered data that suggested that juvenile rehabilitation continues to receive public support; however, the public also supports the notion that young criminals are responsible for their actions and are currently being treated too leniently. Interestingly, these researchers reported that although judges and lawyers and prison inmates support child-saving policies (such as shorter sentences and longer probation periods) legislators, prison guards, and the general public support more punitive sanctions for delinquents. And Akers (1965) reminds us that increasing penalties for crimes has the negative effect of making punishment less likely. Increasing punitive sanctions has been accompanied by increases in legal measures by which punishment is avoided. This is evident in the history of traffic infractions. Today as the fines for speeding grow more stringent there are now more ways to avoid detection: radar machines, lawyers specializing in traffic ticket cases, increases in speed limits.

Given this confusing array of contingencies, this author rephrases an earlier question: What can behavior analysts do to modify not only the behavior of the offender, but also of the prison system? The following material describes special populations of incarcerated offenders for whom no current effective programming exists. The author suggests focusing our technology in areas where the prison system administration appears to recognize it needs assistance.

ROLE FOR BEHAVIOR ANALYSTS
IN CORRECTIONAL SETTINGS

Bartol (1980) observed that the longer one is in prison the less likely it becomes that there will be any development or improvement of social and vocational behaviors necessary for legal survival in the free world. Although this comes as no surprise, current legal policies almost ensure that some delinquents will spend at least some critical part of their lives in prison. According to statistics (*Denton Record-Chronicle,* 1987), in 1985 108,000 youngsters between the ages of 10 and 17 years were arrested in Texas. (This number increased in 1986.) Of these, 2,300 were committed to some form of correctional setting and 40% of those 2,300 were incarcerated. Herman (1987) offered data indicating that between 1984–87 27.5% of the children released from correctional institutions for adolescents in Texas eventually were sent back to their original facility or to the adult prison system.

If the current solution is longer sentences for more delinquents and adult offenders, behavior analysts are going to have to modify behavior technology to deal with these larger numbers. Zamble and Porporino (1990) offer what they call the "ultimate challenge of corrections: To create 'total environments' " (p. 70). Franks (1984) distinguished between first-order change (rearranging specific parts of a system) and second-order change (modifying the functioning of the system itself) and notes that applied behavior analysis needs to focus on second-order change when dealing with crime-related problems. Barak-Glantz (1981) sums up this challenge: "It is counter-productive to create the hell of hopelessness in prison. We will maximize the benefits of corrections by creating a community that is lawful, safe, industrious, and hopeful" (p. 57). And who better than behavior analysts to create these positive learning and working environments?

Such an environment would require total environmental control—separate facilities or a separate wing within a prison, the opportunity to select staff and provide motivational events for staff cooperation, staff training in behavioral technology (as accomplished by Smith, Milan, Wood, & McKee, 1976), a resident behavior analyst to remain on site after the program is implemented, sufficient funding that can be flexibly used, and a powerful, well-placed, cooperative prison administrator. These contingencies might be arranged through federal funding channels.

Milan (1987) outlines an approach that encompasses the opportunity to create total environments when he suggests that "the cautious support of a small number of model programs under controlled conditions and supervised by qualified professionals seems the most appropriate course of action for behaviorists to adopt" (p. 170).

And what populations in the correctional setting might benefit most from this total environmental approach? There are some special offenders who have multifaceted problems in addition to their inappropriate criminal behavioral repertoires.

Special Populations of Incarcerated Offenders

The growing numbers of elderly inmates is creating a problem for prisons because they do not have suitable programs (educational, vocational, recreational, rehabilitation), and the elderly inmate is highly likely to be physically assaulted and otherwise victimized in prison (Vito & Wilson, 1985). Another group, the mentally retarded offenders, estimated to number 12,640 nationwide (Denkowski & Denkowski, 1985), constitute a population of inmates for whom nothing different has been done for the last 20 years (Denkowski & Denkowski, 1985). Although prison systems are being legally mandated to develop special programs for this population (Pugh, 1986), much remains to be accomplished. Behavior analysts are uniquely qualified to work with this group, as Glenn and Hutchison (1990) make the point that "there has probably been no area whose growth and development has been so closely tied to behavioral applications as has been the field of mental retardation" (p. 3).

A third special population of offenders who have been bypassed in terms of programming and whose pervasive behavioral deficits indicate they need effective programming are the segregated inmates (juvenile and adult). These offenders have been placed in isolation for various reasons ranging from their assaultive behavior to their own protection from other inmates. They generally have been "filed in warehouse fashion until such time as they are deemed returnable to the general population or transferable to another institution" (Rhoades, 1970, p. 21). These inmates are in single cells and remain inside their "houses" 24 hours/day, except for a daily shower and a 1-hour recreation period. (This is the population for whom the author has designed programs for the past several years.) These inmates have become a focal point for attention by the federal courts; therefore, prison systems may soon be casting about for technologists to plan effective interventions with these offenders.

As long as the federal court is sending special master(s) into a prison system to monitor compliance with the court orders, the upper-level administrators seem likely to cooperate (albeit in a limited fashion) with the interventionist. If the subsequent program is successful (i.e., helps staff maintain order and inmates participate without being coerced), the possibility exists that the program will be continued (although in a modified version) after the special master leaves.

Private Prisons

There is now an alternative to state/federal prisons—the private prison. These facilities are designed to give short-term offenders (minimum security risks) educational and vocational skills. As these inmates are almost ready to leave prison, they may be more motivated to cooperate. Private prisons may prove to be the correctional settings ready for our services. Since these are operated as any other business, the focus is on efficient and effective outcomes at the lowest cost. Data-based, student-paced literacy programs (e.g., direct instruction) and a structured approach to job searching while training the necessary behavior (e.g., Job Club) could prove valuable to a correctional institution whose bottom line is whether or not the services they are offering are profitable for the company and meet the customer's (the state's) needs. Ironically, privatization "may skim off the better quality inmates, leaving state facilities with a residue of hard-core incorrigibles" (Hawkins & Alpert, 1989, p. 229). If this proves to be the case, it is yet another reason why prisons may be interested in our technology.

For instance, in Texas the private prisons apparently are having serious problems: "4 private prison units, touted as national models, are performing so poorly that their operating contracts may be cancelled . . ." (Hoppe, 1990, p. 1A). A behavioral consultant interested in a business sector that will be relatively unaffected by world crises might consider private prison work.

For some applied behavioral scientists, on-site work in a correctional setting may prove to be too time consuming and too difficult to manage along with other responsibilities (e.g., academia, consulting jobs). For these and the less venturesome, there is the equally exciting realm of applied research.

Applied Research Options

A final suggested opportunity lies in the area of analog laboratory experimentation (e.g., Frisch & Dickinson, 1990). Variables that cannot be directly manipulated in a prison setting can be simulated in the laboratory, using the data obtained as the basis for future interventions. Also, well-controlled experimental designs will allow us to evaluate stringently the success of our results. For example, one simulation might indicate whether or not the prison's practice of trying to control behavior by invoking long-term, low-probable consequences could, in fact, be made effective (i.e., goodtime credits—for every 30 days of cooperative behavior 30–40 days are removed from the sentence). Such a research-based solution might help affect a change in prison policy (Ellis, 1990).

But the fact remains that the place to study contingencies that account for the failure of our criminal justice system with regard to modifying criminal behavior is in a prison setting (Ellis, 1989). It is important that any behavior analyst interested in full-time work in such a setting negotiate carefully and in writing what support will be provided before going to work. Consulting with prison systems, rather than trying to make changes from within, may be the safest and most promising route to take.

SUMMARY AND CONCLUSIONS

This chapter has examined the metacontingencies that have created the usually aversive environmental contingencies commonly existing in prisons. By viewing prison administrative behavior as ceremonial and behavioral interventions as technological, the resistance commonly encountered by behavior analysts entering/working in prisons can be more clearly understood. Although there have been no behavioral technologists reporting their work in prisons for the past 16 years, there is certainly a need for such interventions in today's prisons. Also, there are special subpopulations of inmates whose problems are proving too encompassing to be managed by prison personnel with no behavioral training. For whatever reasons, behavior analysts have not opted to work in correctional settings; yet those who reported their efforts years ago were successful in modifying in-prison behavior. Prison literature indicates a move toward transitional community-based programs for offenders; however, if these inmates leave prison with inappropriate (even dangerous) repertoires, what will become of our society as we know it today?

To paraphrase Glenn and Hutchison (1990), "Our failure, as a society, to use technology to develop the repertoires of institutionalized [persons] may be seen as a dysfunctional cultural practice" (p. 23). As professionals interested in and committed to making our world a safer environment and to creating a more productive, peaceful setting in which to live and work, behavior analysts have a responsibility to the culture to find ways to implement a technology that is both humane and effective in the service of humankind.

REFERENCES

Akers, R. L. (1965). Toward a comparative definition of law. *Journal of Criminal Law, Criminology and Police Science, 56,* 293–300.

Allyon, T., & Azrin, N. (1968). *The token economy.* New York: Appleton-Century-Crofts.

Allyon, T., Milan, M. A., Roberts, M. D., & McKee, J. (1979). *Correctional rehabilitation and management: A psychological approach.* New York: Wiley.

Barak-Glantz, I. L. (1981). Toward a conceptual schema of prison management styles. *Prison Journal, 61*(1), 42–60.

Bartol, C. R. (1980). *Criminal behavior: A psychosocial approach.* Englewood Cliffs: Prentice-Hall.

Bassett, J. E., & Blanchard, E. B. (1977). The effect of the absence of close supervision on the use of response cost in a prison token economy. *Journal of Applied Behavior Analysis, 10*(3), 375–379.

Bassett, J. E., Blanchard, E. B., & Koshland, E. (1975). Applied behavior analysis in a penal setting: Targeting "free world" behaviors. *Behavior Therapy, 6,* 639–648.

Bippes, R., McLaughlin, T. F., & Williams, R. L. (1986). A classroom token system in a detention center: Effects for academic and social behavior. *Techniques, 2*(2), 126–132.

Burchard, J. D., & Harrington, W. A. (1985–86). Deinstitutionalization: Programmed transition from the institution to the community. *Child and Family Behavior Therapy, 7*(4), 17–32.

Burchard, J. D., & Lane, T. W. (1982). Crime and delinquency. In A. S. Bellak, M. Hersen, & A. E. Kazdin (Eds.), *International handbook of behavior modification and therapy* (pp. 613–652). New York: Plenum Press.

Cohen, H. L., & Filipczak, J. (1971/1989). *A new learning environment.* Boston: Author's Cooperative, Inc.

Colman, A. D. (1975). Environmental design: Realities and delusions. In T. Thompson & W. S. Dockens, III (Eds.), *Applications of behavior modification* (pp. 409–423). New York: Academic Press.

Crouch, B. M., & Alpert, G. P. (1982). Sex and occupational socialization among prison guards. *Criminal Justice and Behavior, 9*(2), 159–176.

Cullen, F. T., Golden, K. M., & Cullen, J. (1983). Is child saving dead? Attitudes toward juvenile rehabilitation in Illinois. *Journal of Criminal Justice, 11*(1), 1–13.

Cullen, F. T., Lutze, F. E., Link, B. G., & Wolfe, N. T. (1989). The correctional orientation of prison guards: Do officers support rehabilitation? *Federal Probation, 53*(1), 33–42.

Davidson, H. S. (1988). Meaningful literacy education in prison? Problems and possibilities. *Journal of Correctional Education, 39*(2), 76–81.

Dean, C. W., & Reppucci, N. D. (1974). Juvenile correctional institutions. In D. Glaser (Ed.), *Handbook of criminology* (pp. 865–894). Chicago: Rand McNally.

Denkowski, G. C., & Denkowski, K. M. (1985). The mentally retarded offender in the state prison system: Identification, prevalence, adjustment, and rehabilitation. *Criminal Justice and Behavior, 12*(1), 55–70.

Denton Record Chronicle (Thursday, October 1, 1987). 3A.

Ellis, J. (1990, May). *32 months of applied behavior analysis in a correctional setting: Oxymorons and other competing contingencies.* Paper presented at the meeting of the Association for Behavior Analysis-International, Nashville, TN.

Ellis, J. (1989). Iron bars DOTH a prison make: Description of a correctional setting. *Behavior Analysis & Social Action, 7*(1&2), 4–9.

Farrow, J. (1984). Medical responsibility to children. *Clinical Pediatrics, 23*(12), 699–700.

Franks, C. M. (1984). Behavior therapy: An overview. In G. T. Wilson, C. M. Franks, K. D. Brownell, & P. C. Kendall (Eds.), *Annual review of behavior therapy: Theory and practice* (pp. 1–38). New York: Guilford Press.

Frisch, C. J., & Dickinson, A. M. (1990). Work productivity as a function of the percentage of monetary incentives to base pay. In W. K. Redmon & A. M. Dickinson (Eds.), *Promoting excellence through performance management.* Binghamton, NY: Haworth Press.

Fox, V. (1984). The politics of prison management. *The Prison Journal, 64*, 97–112.

Gendreau, P., & Ross, R. R. (1983-84). Correctional treatment: Some recommendations for effective intervention. *Juvenile & Family Court Journal, 34*(4), 31–39.

Glenn, S. S. (1985). Some reciprocal roles between behavior analysis and institutional economics in post-Darwinian science. *The Behavioral Analyst, 8*(1), 15–27.

Glenn, S. S. (1986). Metacontingencies in *Walden Two. Behavior Analysis & Social Action, 5*(1&2), 2–8.

Glenn, S. S. (1988). Contingencies and metacontingencies: Toward a synthesis of behavior analysis and cultural materialism. *The Behavior Analyst, 11*(2), 161–179.

Glenn, S. S., & Hutchison, E. (1990). *Behavioral services in MR institutions: A second look.* Manuscript submitted for publication.

Hawkins, R., & Alpert, G. P. (1989). *American prison systems: Punishment and justice.* Englewood Cliffs: Prentice-Hall.

Herman, K. (1987, October 1). Violent youths held in comfort. *Denton Record-Chronicle*, 1C & 3C.

Holburn, C. S. (1987). Exposing a hoax and rebuilding a culture: A review of Wetzel and Hoschouer's *Residential teaching communities. The Behavior Analyst, 10*(2), 283–285.

Hobbs, T. R., & Holt, M. M. (1976). The effects of token reinforcement on the behavior of delinquents in cottage settings. *Journal of Applied Behavior Analysis, 9*(2), 189–198.

Hoppe, C. (1990, May 16). Private prisons failing to meet goals, audit says. *Dallas Morning News*, pp. 8A, 20A.

Hoppe, C. (1990, August 8). Terrell quits as state criminal justice chief. *Dallas Morning News*, p. 1A.

Kandel, H. K., Allyon, T., & Roberts, M. D. (1976). Rapid educational rehabilitation for prison inmates. *Behaviour Research and Therapy, 14*, 323–331.

Laws, D. R. (1974). The failure of a token economy. *Federal Probation, 38*(1), 33–38.

Lindsley, O. R. (1965). Direct measurement and prosthesis of retarded behavior. *Journal of Education, 147*, 62–80.

Metts, L. (1989, September 11). U. S. prison population posts record six-month increase. *Dallas Morning News*, p. 3A.

Milan, M. A. (1987). Token economy programs in closed institutions. In E. K. Morris & C. J. Braukmann (Eds.), *Behavioral approaches to crime and delinquency* (pp. 195–222). New York: Plenum Press.

Milan, M. A., & McKee, J. M. (1976). The cellblock token economy: Token reinforcement procedures in a maximum security correctional institution for adult male felons. *Journal of Applied Behavior Analysis, 9*(3), 253–275.

Milan, M. A., Throckmorton, W. R., McKee, J. M., & Wood, L. F. (1979). Contingency management in a cellblock token economy: Reducing rule violations and maximizing the effects of token reinforcement. *Criminal Justice and Behavior, 6*, 307–325.

Milan, M. A., Wood, L. F., & McKee, J. M. (1979). Motivating academic achievement in a cellblock token economy: An elaboration of the Premack principle. *Offender Rehabilitation, 3,* 349–361.

Musante, G. J. (1975). Behavior modification in prisons and correctional facilities. In W. D. Gentry (Ed.), *Applied behavior modification* (pp. 109–129). St. Louis: The C. V. Mosby Company.

Nay, W. R. (1974). Comprehensive behavioral treatment in a training school for delinquents. In K. A. Calhoun, H. E. Adams, & K. M. Mitchell (Eds.), *Innovative treatment methods in psychopathology* (pp. 203–243). New York: Wiley.

Nietzel, M. T., & Himelein, M. J. (1987). Probation and parole. In E. K. Morris & C. J. Braukmann (Eds.), *Behavioral approaches to crime and delinquency* (pp. 109–133). New York: Plenum Press.

O'Donnell, C. R. (1977). Behavior modification in community settings. In M. Hersen, R. M. Eisler, & P. M. Miller (Eds.), *Progress in behavior modification, vol. 4* (pp. 69–117). New York: Academic Press.

Pugh, M. (1986). The mentally retarded offenders program of the Texas Department of Corrections. *Prison Journal, 61,* 39–51.

Rhoades, W. J. (1970). A rehabilitation program for maximum security segregation units. *Journal of Correctional Education, 22,* 21–24.

Skinner, B. F. (1953). *Science and human behavior.* New York: Free Press.

Skinner, B. F. (1978). *Reflections on behaviorism and society.* Englewood Cliffs: Prentice-Hall.

Smith, R. R., Milan, M. A., Wood, L. F., & McKee, J. M. (1976). Correctional officer as a behavior technician. *Criminal Justice and Behavior, 3,* 345–360.

Struckhoff, D. R. (1983–84) Corrections: On the brink of. . . . *Journal of Offender Counseling, Services and Rehabilitation, 8*(1/2), 107–115.

Vito, G. F. (1985). Putting prisoners to work: Policies and problems. *Journal of Offender Counseling, Services and Rehabilitation, 9*(3), 21–34.

Vito, G. F., & Wilson, D. G. (1985). Forgotten people: Elderly inmates. *Federal Probation, 49*(1), 18–24.

Wilson, J. Q., & Herrnstein, R. J. (1985). *Crime and human nature.* New York: Simon & Schuster.

Zamble, E., & Porporino, F. (1990). Coping, imprisonment, and rehabilitation: Some data and their implications. *Criminal Justice and Behavior, 17*(1), 53–70.

12

Apathy and Irresponsibility in Social Systems

John H. Kunkel

INTRODUCTION

This chapter describes three aspects of modern societies and outlines the contributions that behavioral analysis can make toward a better understanding of these phenomena. Low rates of important activities (apathy and fatalism) and counterproductive behavior (irresponsibility) are common features of urban-industrial society. The incidence of these actions—and others—varies within and among subcultures, over decades, and even during a person's life span. The following sections outline the answers to four common questions: Why are some people apathetic? Why are some people irresponsible? Why are some people neither? Why is there such variability in social behavior?

When behavior analysts enter the larger world that has been the domain of anthropologists and sociologists, political scientists and economists, they face a difficult choice: to begin anew, disregarding much or all of existing knowledge in these disciplines, or to use whatever "old knowledge" seems appropriate. Behavior analysts are likely to find the first alternative rather attractive: their work would not be contaminated by existing errors and limitations, and they would not have to devote much time to reading about the discoveries in other disciplines. The second alternative has its dangers, such as the inadvertent transfer of errors and limitations from another discipline, but these are probably outweighed by its major advantage: access to important data, useful concepts, and significant propositions about dynamic social systems.

The behavior analyst who is ready to use existing knowledge in the relevant social sciences must be willing to consider research and look at data, concepts, and propositions that at first glance may appear strange, as if from another world. However, this is still the world of human beings who behave and interact, a world of individuals whose daily lives reflect the operation of psychological principles. This chapter analyzes several aspects of rule-governed behavior in large social systems, based on research in social psychology. The discussion demonstrates that the behavior analytic perspective makes it possible to combine data and propositions from sources as disparate as sociology and social psychology. Indeed, it will become apparent that behavioral analysis is the major bridge between those two disciplines.

THREE SOCIAL PHENOMENA

During the 19th century and into the 20th, ethnographers often used "apathy" and "fatalism" to explain various aspects of daily life in other, usually non-

European, preindustrial cultures. More recently, these terms have been used by sociologists also to describe individuals and subcultures in urban-industrial societies. Apathy and fatalism, and to a lesser degree irresponsibility, have often been viewed as components of problems such as poverty, illiteracy, and unemployment (e.g., Banfield, 1970). In addition, these terms are frequently used to describe presumed internal factors and processes that lead either to low levels of behavior or to actions that, in the eyes of an observer, are counter-productive. Hence, they are believed to contribute to a lesser quality of life for many individuals and families.

On a smaller scale, social psychologists have recently begun to analyze apathy and fatalism as components of learned helplessness. In numerous laboratory experiments and field studies researchers have discovered major psychological and social determinants of low rates of behavior, and on this basis have been able to suggest ameliorative and preventive programs (e.g., Peterson, Villanova, & Raps, 1985).

Apathy and Fatalism

The term "apathy" is commonly used when a wide range of activities occur at a very low rate, in various situations, and for a considerable length of time, often to the individual's detriment. When only a few actions occur at a low rate, or only for short periods, or in only a few specific situations, we are likely to call a person lazy or tired, rather than apathetic. Many people consider "fatalism" to be the major root of apathy. The term is commonly used to describe an individual's presumed internal condition and a specific perception of the world and the human being's position within it.

The empirical referents of fatalism are either low rates of behavior or an individual's verbal statements about the widespread dissociation between present behavior and later events. In particular, we call people "fatalistic" when they tell us that aversive events are likely to happen and cannot be avoided, usually because an action's consequences are perceived to be either random or the results of factors over which one has no control (e.g., luck, "city hall"). In addition, fatalism often includes the belief that much (or most) of the world is chaotic, unpredictable, and uncontrollable, and that one experiences more aversive events than one considers fair or would expect by chance.

The problematic nature and negative implications of apathy and fatalism are much more visible in case studies than in statistical analyses. Oscar Lewis' (1959, 1964, 1966) haunting descriptions of family life in Mexico and New York have not been surpassed. As an anthropologist, he was able to weave daily activities, psychological processes, and the social context into a seamless explanatory fabric. In the culture of poverty that he described in excruciating detail, there are few if any links between a person's behavior and later events, and individuals exert little if any control over the world in which they are enmeshed. Indeed, these classic studies show that Lewis was a good behavior analyst before the field matured, and that he analyzed rule-governed behavior before that term was born.

Irresponsibility

This term is a label that observers use to summarize activities that in their judgment are likely to have more negative and/or fewer positive consequences for the actor and other people than would different behaviors that might have been performed instead. These activities reflect either an individual's (perhaps limited) behavioral repertoire or a specific perception of outcomes and their probabilities. Observers implicitly assume that they have a better understanding of the world and a clearer view of outcomes than does the actor.

To the behavior analyst, irresponsibility refers to the selection of an activity (or level of performance) that is linked to highly probable negative consequences for the actor or other people, which could have been minimized or avoided if a different action (or level of performance) had been chosen. The behaving individual, of course, may well have a different perception of the consequences (and their probabilities) linked to various activities and performance levels within the behavioral repertoire.

The range of behaviors that could be labeled as irresponsible is wide indeed and might include most actions of daily life—depending on circumstances. Some actions are almost always in this category, as when a person drinks heavily before driving home at night; here, either or both actions (and certainly their combination) would be viewed as irresponsible. The label of other behaviors depends more directly on the observer's knowledge of a situation. We might call unprotected sexual intercourse irresponsible behavior when we know that a couple does not wish to have more children or if we believe that they already have too many; but we would not use the label if they were trying for their first baby—unless we knew of a high probability of transmitting a genetic defect.

The Variability of Behavior

In complex, dynamic, urban industrial societies with large heterogeneous populations we expect that members of various subcultures behave in a great variety of ways. Yet we find considerable variability of behavior even within groups of individuals with ostensibly similar characteristics, such as middle class white males of European ancestry and urban background. Most social scientists take behavioral diversity for granted and ascribe it to differential socialization and divergent norms among and even within subcultures. Yet one should wonder about additional processes that might be at work.

The following sections outline some of the contributions that behavior analysis in conjunction with social psychology can make toward a better understanding of these interesting phenomena.

THE BEHAVIORAL ANALYSIS
OF LOW-RATE ACTIVITIES

As behavior analysts, we focus attention on the observable activities of a society's or community's members. We also pay attention to the social context, its structure and operation, as determinants of these activities. In these two respects our interest coincides with that of anthropologists, economists, and sociologists. But as behavior analysts we are not concerned with various inferred internal conditions of individuals, which are presumed to underly various activities. Instead, we postulate a small set of behavioral principles that have a solid empirical foundation in hundreds of careful studies performed during the last 50 years. In these two respects we do differ greatly from most social scientists.

The following two examples show the operation of learning principles within social systems of varying sizes. We see here the crucial role that past consequences of behavior play in determining future actions. From such analyses we can determine which modifications must be introduced into groups and communities if the behavior of members is to be changed. The second example is especially significant in that it shows how a large community can be fundamentally altered by the introduction of a few new contingencies.

The Problem of Social Loafing

For several decades now it has been known that groups have a variety of effects on their members: sometimes people work harder when they are with others, more often individuals accomplish much less in groups than when they are alone. The latter findings are so pervasive and consistent, in fact, that "social loafing" has become a legitimate topic of inquiry.

In the original studies, performed in the mid 1880s, but not published until 1913, the French agricultural engineer Max Ringelmann asked volunteer male students to pull a rope alone or with from one to seven companions (Kravitz & Martin, 1986). In the latter setting, individuals pulled only half as hard as when alone. During the last 20 years, a number of experiments have been designed to explore various facets of social loafing. The behaviors studied in modern laboratories have ranged from physical efforts (e.g., shouting, pumping air) to intellectual tasks (e.g., vigilance, solving puzzles). Decrements in performance are usually curvilinear, with a leveling off in groups larger than four. Social loafing is greatest when the group members' pooled activities are relatively simple, inherently uninteresting, and routine. Decrements of behavior occur in both sexes, and it does not matter whether the study has a between- or within-subject design.

For more than a century, researchers have wondered about the nature and roots of this fascinating phenomenon. For example, according to the classic modern experiment (Latané, Williams, & Harkins, 1979), the decline in behavior can be substantial—50% in four-person groups and 60% in six-person groups. Careful analysis of the data revealed that about half of the reduction in performance was a result of inadvertent mutual interference and difficulties in coordination, whereas 50% was a result of individuals deliberately exerting less effort. Since then, most experiments have incorporated designs that eliminate the confounding variables of interference and coordination. Yet the results still show a consistent and significant loss of individuals' performance in groups (e.g., Harkins & Szymanski, 1989). Hence, an important question arises: Why do people in groups loaf so often and so much?

A comprehensive answer has emerged rather slowly, in part because early studies focused on internal processes of groups and individuals. Ringelmann explained his results in terms of coordination problems inherent in any group effort, and that view prevailed for the next 60 years (e.g., Steiner, 1972). Unspecified "faulty social processes," which operate in addition to problems of physical coordination, were also considered as possible explanations (e.g., Ingham, Levinger, Graves, & Peckham, 1974).

In a series of often ingenious experiments performed during the last 15 years, social psychologists gradually discovered the pieces of this interesting puzzle. The crucial step was the realization that in most group settings, members' performances are combined to yield a group's production. Hence, any one person's efforts are quite anonymous: group members typically receive neither benefit nor blame for their actions. This lack of feedback allowed subjects to "reduce their efforts when they felt less personally responsible" (Ingham et al., 1974, p. 382). The degree to which an individual's behavior is "hidden" depends, of course, on the nature of the task and the size of the group—up to a point (e.g., Kerr, 1983). Following this line of argument, a series of experiments during the 1980s gradually revealed that loafing is reduced and can be eliminated when certain conditions prevail within a group. These add up to the establishment of significant contingencies for a group member's action. The most important conditions are:

1. Individual members' efforts can be identified by others and/or themselves (e.g., Kerr & Bruun, 1981; Williams, Harkins, & Latane, 1981);
2. Individual members' efforts can be measured and evaluated by others and/or themselves (e.g., Harkins & Jackson, 1985). It has recently been discovered that the evaluation of group products also reduces loafing (Harkins & Szymanski, 1989);
3. This evaluation may be based on objective criteria or may involve a comparison with the behaviors (or standards) of one's own group, various other social units (e.g., the experimenter), or the individual member (e.g., Harkins & Szymanski, 1989; Szymanski & Harkins, 1987);
4. When the task is difficult and/or significant for the individual, or when group members perform different tasks, social loafing is reduced even when there is no potential for evaluation (e.g., Brickner, Harkins, & Ostrom, 1986; Harkins & Petty, 1982; Jackson & Williams, 1985);
5. Additional factors have been suggested, among them the experimental task's creative component, the behavior's complexity, the partners' efforts, and the degree of group cohesion (e.g., Johnson & Harkins, 1985). But it is not yet clear how these variables and possibly others influence social loafing.

The present state of knowledge is summarized by the basic postulate that "the potential for evaluation is central to the loafing effect" (Harkins, 1987, p. 11). Corollaries add details, but future work is not likely to modify the basic nature of the explanation.

These studies have uncovered the principles that underlie individuals' behaviors in groups with various structures. For example, most groups that perform additive tasks operate in such a way that there are no direct contingencies for members' activities—be they loafing or working hard. Other group structures and operations lead to different relations of members and their actions (e.g., whether individuals' contributions are simply added to a group's product or counted before being added, and whether or not such counting is accompanied by a comparison with other people's contributions). In most experiments, groups are ad hoc collections of strangers, unless the variable of "cohesion" is introduced by analyzing the work of, for instance, members of Alpha Gamma Sigma.

We can see the processes of social loafing on a large scale in the economic disaster of Russia's agriculture. Soviet collective farms are organized in ways that encourage social loafing; hence, they are notoriously inefficient. The few farmers who are allowed to use small private plots (after a day's work on the Collective) cultivate only about 1.3% of the nation's arable land. Yet they produce more than

20% of all food (Feshbach, 1982). In Israel, on the other hand, collective farms are organized somewhat differently and are quite efficient. The crucial difference is that Kibbutzim are inhabited by volunteers who subscribe to a unifying ideology that emphasizes work and the common good.

A Peasant Community in Peru

On a larger scale, apathy and fatalism play crucial roles in economic development—or the lack thereof—in both agricultural and modern societies. Here again statistical studies cannot give us as comprehensive a picture as do careful, long-term descriptions of particular groups. Descriptions of peasant communities in the Third World and of disadvantaged subcultures in urban-industrial societies provide much useful information about the nature of apathy and fatalism—their roots and implications. The most impressive example of a community whose inhabitants' activities changed radically in less than a decade is the Vicos hacienda in Peru. Apathy and fatalism had prevailed in that isolated Andean village for centuries before 1952, when the anthropologist Alan Holmberg leased the hacienda (Dobyns, Doughty, & Lasswell, 1971).

The major causal factor of apathy and irresponsibility was the absence of significant linkages between the peasants' activities and the events that befell them. The hacienda's owner (or his resident manager) ruled the village with an iron hand. Each family had to provide 3 days a week of unpaid labor on the hacienda's fields, and unpaid maid service at the manor also was frequently required. For decades, the hacienda's potato crop had been dismal, only partly because of poor seeds. In accordance with tradition, each family had the use of some poor land for growing subsistence food (also mainly potatoes), but in return a variable percentage of the crop had to be given to the patrón. If a family's harvest was poor, they barely had enough to eat; if the harvest was good, a larger percentage had to be delivered to the patrón, leaving little for the family. Thus, working on the hacienda's lands was not rewarded in any way, and working hard on one's own field held few rewards. Villagers who guarded the hacienda's herds were not paid, and neither were the men who were stationed at mountain passes to collect tolls. No wonder labor in the fields was desultory, many animals were lost, and few tolls were collected!

As the new patrón, Holmberg was able to make fundamental changes in the hacienda's operations. Most important, he abolished unpaid labor and instituted a system of wages for laborers, shepherds, and toll collectors. He provided better seed potatoes and encouraged new, more effective agricultural methods. The repayment of loans and rents for private fields was carefully specified—hence villagers who produced a good harvest kept most of the proceeds. During the first year only a few villagers accepted Holmberg's offer, mainly because his prediction of a favorable outcome was not widely believed. But when harvests improved greatly and Holmberg did not raise rents, more families joined the next year. Within 4 years almost all Vicosiños used the new methods. The potato harvest of the hacienda also increased greatly, which made funds available for such community projects as a new school.

Holmberg instituted similar changes in the educational and political systems of Vicos. When good teachers were hired and the previous system of student exploitation was terminated, attendance and performance increased greatly. Holmberg gradually transferred control of these institutions to the villagers, who learned to run the school well and soon were expert politicians. Within a decade, the community was well enough organized and had enough surplus funds from the sale of abundant harvests to purchase the hacienda for the village. Apathy and irresponsibility had disappeared in less than half a generation!

The common element in all the relatively simple procedures that Holmberg employed was the establishment of new linkages between the villagers' activities and various consequences (Kunkel, 1986). After the patrón's capricious treatment of the peasants ended (e.g., unpaid labor, variable rents), the villagers were able to predict and control important aspects of their social context. In less than a decade, changes in behavior, new activities, and higher rates of effective action had transformed the once "sleepy village" into a thriving community.

The Vicos project is an excellent illustration of applied behavioral analysis on a large scale (population: 1,700). It also demonstrates that apathy, fatalism, and irresponsibility are categories of behavior that can be modified quite easily, rather than internal conditions or personality factors, which presumably are quite difficult to change. However, Holmberg was able to change the hacienda's structure and operation—and thereby some crucial behavior-consequence linkages of the Vicosiños' daily lives—because he had complete control over the hacienda. If he had had only partial control, or if he had employed different psychological principles, or if he had not been a decent human being interested in the villagers' welfare, the project would have been much less successful. Unfortunately, the turmoils of today's Peru, especially the violence and great unrest in the high Andean valleys, have made the ultimate success of Vicos questionable. Holmberg might well agree with Simon Bolivar that he has plowed in the sea.

BEHAVIORAL PRINCIPLES
AND SOCIAL STRUCTURE

Activity sets that are usually labeled apathy and irresponsibility arise from certain combinations of psychological processes and social structures to which some members of small groups, communities, and the larger society are exposed. By analyzing these combinations and their constituent elements, we can determine what might be done to reduce the consequent problems.

The psychological processes involved are the basic behavioral principles summarized in this well-known paradigm:

$$S^D \longrightarrow B \longrightarrow S^{r/a}$$

Most activities (singly or in chains) are the central elements of such behavior triads. However, in daily life many activities have more than one discriminative stimulus and also have various consequences. The basic paradigm is expanded as shown in Figure 12-1. The several consequences may be positive (S^r) or negative (S^a), vary in nature and magnitude, and occur over a wide time span.

Some consequences of activities reflect the physical world, as when we accidentally drop a hammer and bruise our toes. Other consequences consist of the actions of human beings in our context, as when people answer our questions. A friendly reply to a polite inquiry even by a stranger reflects the norms of our society—but not necessarily of other cultures (e.g., Turnbull, 1972). Social interaction consists, essentially, of the connected behavior triads of two or more per-

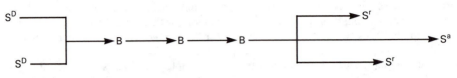

Figure 12-1 The behavior triad.

sons. These connections have the form of equivalences: one person's behavior is equivalent to another person's discriminative stimulus, or positive or negative consequence. Thus, behavior triads are combined to form lattices, as shown in Figure 12-2.

In this simple dyadic interaction, Joe's behavior (B_1) is equivalent to an S^D for Josephine, whose behavior (B_2) is equivalent to a positive consequence (S^r) for Joe and also an S^D for Joe's subsequent actions (B_3). Activities of several people connected by numerous equivalences are termed a social structure. For example, in a hospital regulations specify both the horizontal linkages between behavior and its antecedents and consequences, as well as the vertical connections; thus, it is deemed "proper" for doctors to give orders to nurses rather than vice versa.

The lattice in Figure 12-2 allows us to visualize another important aspect of social interaction: feedback. If Joe's behavior (B_1) is rewarded (by B_2), he learns that B_1 was the "right" behavior; B_1 was performed adequately; and there are links between B_1 and Josephine, and between Josephine's S^D and her action (B_2). We note that Joe's control over later events depends on his behavior and the degree of competence with which it is performed, as well as on the connections among individuals (in the form of equivalences)—in short, the components of a social structure.

Conversely, if Joe's action has no consequences, he learns that B_1 was the "wrong" behavior, or B_1 was not performed well enough, or there are no links between B_1 and Josephine, or between Josephine's S^D and her action (B_2). Joe's lack of control over later events, then, depends not only on his actions and competence, but also on the connections among the individuals who are part of the social structure.

Daily life contains a myriad of interactions varying in complexity and scope. Some interactions are simple and direct, such as a conversation, whereas others are complex and indirect, as when we deal with a bureaucracy. Although most interactions involve other individuals, it is often expedient to consider groups or larger units rather than individuals. For example, a student interacts with a great

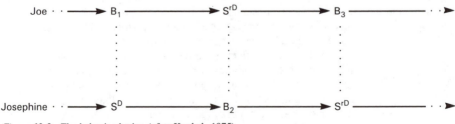

Figure 12-2 The behavior lattice (after Kunkel, 1975).

variety of individuals, but it makes sense to combine some of these persons into "the faculty," "the library," or even "the university."

Peasant communities and primitive tribes have relatively simple social structures. Practically all social interactions are direct, involve relatively few participants, and occur within short time frames. Furthermore, norms are usually widely shared leading to a high predictability of other people's reactions. Hence, one would expect that most individuals have a relatively high sense of control over their social context: if one behaves "correctly" one can expect to gain positive outcomes and avoid negative events from the social context.

Urban-industrial societies consist of numerous social structures, ranging from simple organizations to complex bureaucracies. Many interactions of daily life are indirect, often involve several individuals, and may occur over a lengthy time span. Furthermore, less widely shared norms reduce the degree to which other people's reactions can be predicted—unless we know the individuals well.

For behavior analysts, the crucial variable that differentiates urban-industrial societies from their predecessors is the high proportion of indirect interactions in daily life. Interactions are direct if the chain (of activities and people) between an individual's action and its consequences is short—as is the case in Figure 12-2. In this elementary social structure both participants can predict the consequences of their behaviors, and they know what to do to elicit their partner's desired response. Thus both are likely to have a high sense of control over the social context.

A large proportion of interactions that make up daily life in urban-industrial societies are indirect, involving lengthy chains of (often unknown) people and their actions. The lattice in Figure 12-2 would be greatly expanded to include more people and behaviors: Joe's action (B_1) is an S^D for Josephine's behavior (B_2), which is an S^D for K's action (B_K), which is an S^D for L's action (B_L) and so forth, until finally Z's behavior (B_Z) is equivalent to an outcome for Joe's behavior (B_1). The longer the chain the more errors are possible, even if all participants adhere to the norms of their positions, and the larger the time frame. It may not be easy to determine which behavior was eventually reinforced or ignored. For example, if I wish to have an income tax error corrected, a large number of anonymous people and their actions are likely to become involved—so many, in fact, that I may prefer to "forget the whole thing" unless the error is large and in my favor. When the chain between behavior and its consequences is long, largely unknown, and time consuming, the outcome of any one action is likely to be less predictable and less controllable—or at least people will have the perception that it is. Apathy, fatalism, and alienation are major aspects of individuals' lives in social systems where such indirect linkages form significant components of daily events.

NORMS AND RULE-GOVERNED BEHAVIOR

As behavior analysts have long realized, there is more to complex human action—especially within modern, dynamic societies—than mere contingencies. When anthropologists and sociologists study social systems, the smallest elements are individuals and their activities. However, most analyses of social systems also consider norms among the fundamental units. Norms relate a person's behavior to its context and consequences. The classic definition of norm is "any standard or rule that states what human beings should or should not think, say, or do under given circumstances" (Blake & Davis, 1964, p. 456). Norms guide people's activities by linking the behaviors that a culture defines as "appropriate" in a specific situation to various consequences. Any person's behavior within a social system is the "result of assessing the consequences of [conformity and] nonconformity rather than a result of the 'internalization' of the norm" (Blake & Davis, 1964, p. 466). For example, in Vicos Holmberg successfully replaced old norms that encouraged apathy with new norms that rewarded effort. By gradually fading out of the picture, he ensured that the new norms were accepted by the community instead of being defined as externally imposed.

Clearly, the essence of norm as conceptualized by sociologists and anthropologists corresponds to the basic behavior triad mentioned earlier: $S^D \rightarrow B \rightarrow S^{r/a}$. Furthermore, the principles that govern human activities are considered to be psychologists' learning principles, even when these remain implicit. Behavior analysts should feel rather comfortable in such company.

In recent years, behavior analysts have begun to focus considerable attention on rule-governed behavior as distinct from contingency-governed actions (Hayes, 1989). When rules are defined as "verbal descriptions of behavioral contingencies" (Malott, 1988, p. 184), rule-governed behavior is "regarded as behavior under the control of verbal contingency-specifying stimuli" (Zettle, 1990, p. 44). Such specification can originate in the context—as Holmberg told villagers how to repay debts from their harvest—or is inferred by the individual—as group members do when there are no public guidelines. Many sociologists share this view of how rules and norms affect behavior: "social norms are rules for conduct. The norms are the standards by reference to which behavior is judged and approved or disapproved" (Williams, 1968, p. 204). The major difference between behavior analysts and sociologists is that the former devote great care to the elucidation of rules and their operation (e.g., Malott, 1989).

In his summary of present knowledge regarding rules, Reese (1989) points out that there are at least three rather different kinds of rules that govern human behavior:

1. *Natural rules* reflect the physical universe in which we live (e.g., physicists' "laws"). Illustration: the faster a car is moving, the greater the distance needed to stop.
2. *Normative rules* reflect social and cultural prescriptions of what people should do (e.g., sociologists' "norms"). Illustration: persons who drive should use seat belts.
3. *Normal rules* reflect what people usually do (e.g., in daily life). Illustration: most people who drive today do not use seat belts.

These three kinds of rules are effective analytical tools for the study of most aspects of social systems. Indeed, anthropologists and sociologists have devoted much of their labor during the last century to the elucidation of normative and normal rules—their origin, operation, and change. Yet few researchers have paid much attention to the vexing question of why so many people frequently disregard many normative rules in many different ways. A common answer is that people do not conform to a societal norm because they may be guided by their subculture's competing and perhaps conflicting norms. Instead of wondering about additional determinants of behavior, social scientists have simply accepted the fact that only a variable percentage of people conform to a variable degree to a culture's great variety of norms.

Such an approach is reasonable when the proportion of adherents to a norm is high, if only because explaining the few exceptions would be rather costly in terms of additional hypotheses. But the wisdom of this easy course is questionable when the proportion of exceptions and the degree of variability are high. For example, only about one quarter of Americans (Geller et al., 1987) and about half of Canadians (Malenfant & Van Houton, 1988) use seat belts. Unfortunately, those who study social systems typically lack the analytical tools that are needed to search for—let alone discover—solutions.

Let us consider the problem of low adherence to norms by looking at two simple activities familiar to practically all adults. We would expect that people wash their hands after they use the bathroom, and buckle up when they drive. After all, hygiene and personal safety rank high in most people's lives. Yet far fewer than half of all drivers use seat belts, even in states where this is required by law (e.g., Geller et al., 1987), and barely half of all individuals who use the facilities wash their hands afterward. One revealing study indicated that 90% of users washed their hands when another person was present, but only 15% washed when they were alone (Pedersen, Keithly, & Brady, 1986). Thus we face an intriguing question: Why do some very simple behaviors, which everyone knows, occur at such a low rate—when the benefits are so clear?

Behavior analysts are more likely to find answers than social scientists, if only because their perspective typically focuses on individuals and their relations with the environment. Yet even this perspective has limitations, which reflect the field's rather narrow research concerns and its reluctance to consider research in other fields. To understand social systems, behavior analysts need to consider the relevant work of investigators in other disciplines.

During the last 40 years, social psychologists have paid considerable attention to factors that shed light on the variability of normative behavior. These researchers have developed a number of well-founded propositions and mini-theories that help explain people's often low and variable adherence to social norms. The starting point is the realization mentioned earlier, that it is not the norm itself but the expected outcome of actions that determines an individual's behavior. The mere presence of another person in a washroom, for example, is likely to result in implicit disapproval if one leaves without washing.

Hence, it makes sense to speak of a fourth set of rules:

4. *Personal rules* are verbal contingency-specifying stimuli that reflect an individual's perceptions of the larger world. These perceptions may be derived from one's own and others' experiences or can be based on information from various sources. Some personal rules are autonomous, whereas others are related and may form orientations toward the complex world in which any person is enmeshed. I use the term "personal rule" instead of self-rule, because the latter's meaning is too narrow; Zettle (1990, p. 44) defines self-rules as "contingency-specifying stimuli produced by one's own verbal behavior."

The following sections describe a small segment of the immense social psychological literature that is relevant for the behavior analyst's study of complex social systems. Current research in the area of personal rules describes the processes that so often lead many people to break many of their society's norms. In the course of this brief survey we will also make an intriguing discovery: although most of the relevant studies are couched in cognitive language, much of the actual research is clearly behavioral. Independent and dependent variables, as well as experimental designs and measurements, typically focus on the observable activities of individuals in various types of social structures.

PERSONAL RULES AND ATTRIBUTION

A major thrust of modern social psychology has been the study of attribution—the causes to which people ascribe (1) their own and other people's activities, and (2) various events that befall them (e.g., Kelley, 1973). I will emphasize the second area, and in particular the experimental and field research about linkages between an individual's activities and their consequences. This contextual orientation leads attribution researchers along paths that are similar to those followed by behavior analysts. Indeed, the paths are likely to converge as it becomes increasingly evident that the significant propositions about attribution are congruent with behavioral principles and major aspects of rule-governed behavior.

General Attribution

We begin with a simple example: on a Saturday morning Joe is eagerly driving to the lake and receives a speeding ticket in a village not far from the beach. "That lousy speed trap," he complains to his friends "from now on I'll take a different route." "Oh, come on," Josephine laughs, "you should have obeyed the sign. Didn't you see it just after the 'Kiwanis' board?" It would not be difficult to guess who of the two has received more tickets—and is likely to receive more in the future.

Whether or not Joe "learns his lesson" (i.e., to slow down after speed limit signs) depends on the factors to which he attributes the ticket. If his attribution process includes himself (e.g., "I should have obeyed that sign"), some modification of behavior is likely to occur. In terms of Figure 12-2, Joe establishes a link between B_1 (his driving) and B_2 (the officer issuing a ticket). But if only external factors enter into his attribution (e.g., "I'm the victim of an unfair speed trap"), no speed-reducing behavior is likely to be learned. In terms of Figure 12-2, Joe establishes no link between B_1 (his driving) and B_2—the ticket comes from nowhere, so to speak. Thus the general proposition is: Whether or not events that occur subsequent to activities are conducive to learning new behaviors (or performing old actions in appropriate situations) depends on the sources to which the subsequent events are attributed.

In this example, the individual has a choice of attributions because the situation is ambiguous or at least open to several interpretations. We can understand Joe's view and sympathize: "What a trap! Only one little sign!" But we can also understand Josephine and add, "One sign is enough." When circumstances are clearcut, most people make the "correct" attribution, which is obviously or logically required by events. Even then, however, there may be differences among people's perceptions, and the observer's definition of what is "obvious" and "logical" may not coincide with an individual's opinion. A student who does not study and then does poorly on an examination may yet attribute the resulting low grade to the "hard test" or "unfair instructor" rather than to laziness.

Research on the linkage between present attributions and future actions has some fascinating implications for the work of behavior analysts. Although social psychologists are not wont to say so—largely because they are not familiar with the topic—attribution research elucidates some of the processes involved in rule-governed behavior. The attributions that people make regarding events that befall them establish connections between particular actions in specific circumstances and various consequences (positive, negative, or none at all). These connections, in turn, are the basis for rules that later govern behavior. The implications for the learning, maintenance, modification, and extinction of behavior are significant: correct attributions facilitate the learning and maintenance of appropriate and effective actions, whereas faulty attributions make the learning and maintenance of appropriate and effective actions very difficult and sometimes impossible.

Thus far, behavior analysts have shown little interest in a person's causal attribution and its implications for later events, partly because most of their studies have focused on single subjects or a few, and simple actions within short time frames. "Individual differences" of results are an expected aspect of such work; indeed, variations in subjects' attributions are likely to show up mainly in differential rates of learning and thus may escape behavior analysts' attention altogether. But in the study of large social systems, with their great variety of activities that are important in the lives of people, attribution becomes a significant variable.

The heterogeneity of populations and the great variability of behaviors in dynamic urban-industrial societies should alert the behavior analyst to the complexity of determinants of even the simple activities of daily life. One set of factors is the variability of perceived linkages between behavior and its consequences, summarized as attributions. Over the years, social psychologists have discovered that most people attribute the events that befall them, especially in ambiguous situations to "causes" whose characteristics range along one or more of three major dimensions (e.g., Heider, 1958; Weiner, 1986): (1) global—specific; (2) stable—unstable; and (3) personal—external.

The global-specific dimension reflects the common-sense meaning of these terms. Thus a global attribution of success might focus on "my IQ," whereas a specific attribution of a poor exam score might include "inadequate study for this test."

The stable-unstable dimension again reflects the common-sense meaning of the poles. Thus one might attribute failure in Chemistry 101 to stable factors such as the notion "I don't have a math brain," whereas a disastrous date might be attributed to the unstable factor "I had a terrible headache."

The personal-external dimension with its implications of a controllable context is the most significant aspect of attribution and therefore will be discussed separately. In the literature the label internal-external is commonly used, but I substitute the word "personal" to avoid confusion with the usual meaning of "internal," which in this case is inappropriate.

There is no implication that one or the other pole of each dimension is better or worse; clearly, such evaluations depend on the nature of the factor involved. If an attribution includes "my high intelligence," for example, that global, stable, and personal factor would be positive, whereas "my low intelligence" would be negative, with correspondingly different implications for future behavior.

Most people are rather consistent in their attributions of the events that befall them, and especially the various successes and failures that are part of daily life; hence, it makes sense to speak of a person's attributional style. The variety of such styles is quite large: one person might attribute most or all events to factors with similar characteristics (e.g., global, or unstable), whereas another person may attribute failures to one set of characteristics and successes to quite different elements. The following examples indicate the variations, power, and implications of attribution.

Example 1: Academic Performance

A person's attributional style affects not only the interpretation of specific past events but also has implications for the future. One illustration of dozens that could be cited is a study of students' performance and mood. In a longitudinal field study, Metalsky (1982) and his colleagues discovered that students whose attributional style regarding negative events emphasized personal and global factors (such as "my low intelligence") showed more of a depressive mood reaction after doing poorly on an examination than did students whose style emphasized external and specific factors (such as "an unfair test"). Other studies (summarized by Peterson & Seligman, 1984) provide consistent evidence that a wide range of "negative life events," when combined with a personal-global attributional style for them, are likely to lead to feelings of helplessness.

Example 2: Helplessness and Depression

For more than 20 years, social psychologists have been fascinated by "learned helplessness," a phenomenon akin to apathy and fatalism. The constituent propositions of the revised theory (Abramson, Seligman, & Teasdale, 1978) have given rise to a large number of studies. In general, this work indicates that a person's attributional style regarding negative events affects the probability of later helplessness and its extreme form, depression. In a recent study, Peterson and Barrett (1987) found that students' attributional style influences the ways in which they relate to university life and how they study and learn. Students who attribute negative events to personal, stable, and global factors do less well academically yet seek less help from academic advisors, have less specific goals, and are more likely "to blame aspects of their character for academic disappointments and failures" (Peterson & Barrett, 1987, p. 605) than do students with the opposite attributional style. The implications for dropping out of university or not even applying for college are evident, as are the effects on upward—and downward—mobility.

It has been pointed out repeatedly (e.g., Sweeney, Anderson, & Bailey, 1986) that the road to helplessness and depression consists of downward spirals—of rule-governed behaviors that are self-validating and lead to apathy. When we attribute failure to personal and global factors we subscribe to rules such as: (1) I am not good at many things, and/or (2) most of my actions are not rewarded. Hence, we are likely to try less hard in the future, and that lower effort may well lead to more failure. The rules are now supported by new evidence, and when the next opportunity for action arises, we are less likely to do anything. This almost guarantees failure (and again the rules are supported).

At the same time, research by social psychologists suggests various ways of breaking out of the spiral toward apathy. Chief among these is the employment of "defensive attributions," which are widespread among normal, that is, non-depressed, individuals. The most common defensive attribution has two components: (1) failures and negative events are ascribed to external and/or specific factors such as "a hard test," whereas (2) successes and positive events are ascribed to personal and/or global factors such as "my high IQ" (e.g., Zuckerman, 1979). As behavior analysts would say, such defensive attributions forge a strong B → S^r linkage and weaken the B → S^a connection.

Research on attribution style and helplessness suggests that the rules that govern a person's behavior are acquired from others or inferred from one's experiences. They are selected from a range of alternatives, and they can be changed. The formulation of rules is gradual and involves a series of steps in which a rule is tentatively inferred and tested against events in the real world, modified if necessary, and tested again, until the person is satisfied (e.g., Hilton & Slugoski, 1986).

Locus of Control

The most important dimension of attribution is the personal-external continuum. During the last quarter century, social psychologists have devoted considerable attention to individuals' beliefs regarding the origin of events that befall them and, in particular, the possibility of controlling these events. In his first general statement, Rotter (1966) described a continuum of beliefs about the source of events and their control ranging from "internal" to "external." The most succinct statement of this dimension is part of a recent historical assessment of this variable: "Internal versus external control refers to the degree to which persons expect that a reinforcement or an outcome of their behavior is contingent on their own behavior or personal characteristics, versus the degree to which persons expect that the reinforcement or outcome is a function of chance, luck, or fate, is under the control of powerful others, or is simply unpredictable" (Rotter, 1990, p. 489).

Rotter's 1966 monograph has stimulated vast amounts of research in what is now known as locus of control (LOC), much of it summarized by Lefcourt (1981). The most significant area of research examines the behavioral implications of an individual's position on the internal-external (IE) scale (e.g., Strickland, 1989). To avoid the problem of unwanted and unwarranted denotations of "internal," I use the word "personal," which in any case corresponds more closely to Rotter's original sense of personal control.

In behavior analytic terms, an individual's beliefs regarding locus of control are essentially sets of rules about the linkage between one's behavior and later events. Individuals at the personal pole of the LOC continuum believe that they can exert considerable control over the events that befall them; positive events can be produced if one performs the proper activities well, in the right situation, and at the appropriate time, whereas negative events can be avoided in similar fashion. These beliefs establish a strong linkage between a person's behavior and its positive/negative consequences—and one's world is filled with complete behavior lattices as in Figure 12-2. The major rules to which such individuals subscribe include: (1) My actions have certain definite and predictable consequences; (2) I can perform the appropriate behavior quite well; and (3) I can exert considerable power over future events. Observers are likely to describe the resulting activities as "responsible."

Conversely, people who are at the external pole of the IE dimension believe that their activities have little if anything to do with later events, which are seen as results of chance, luck, fate, or random processes. One cannot produce positive consequences or avoid negative events by acting "appropriately" in the "right" situations; one's world contains few complete behavior lattices as shown in Figure 12-2. Indeed the words in quotation marks do not make sense. In behavior analytic terms, there are few if any linkages between activities and their consequences. Actually, there are no "consequences" as such, because this very terms implies a distinct relationship to earlier events. The major rules to which such individuals subscribe state: (1) My actions have no predictable or definite consequences; (2) I have no power over events that befall me. In the face of such rules, "irresponsible" actions and apathy are not so senseless, after all.

Over the years, much research had been devoted to the relationship between an individual's position along the IE dimension and a great variety of activities. For example, people who believe that they can control events through their actions tend to be more independent and optimistic, have higher self-esteem, show greater resistance to external influences, are more trusting of other people, and have higher expectations of success (Strickland, 1989).

Research also indicates, however, that locus of control is only one of several factors that determine behavior. A typical example of such complexities is the question of persistence after failure. The reason people repeat successful actions is simple enough; success is reinforcing. But why do some people reduce their actions after failing, whereas others repeat or even increase their activities after they have failed? Part of the answer lies in the nature of the behavior: externally oriented individuals show greater persistence at tasks whose outcomes involve chance, whereas personally oriented individuals show greater persistence when the outcomes depend on activities that require skills (Gilmor, 1978). Another part of the answer reflects a person's attribution of negative events. If failure is ascribed to personal factors that are presumably constant, then the activity is less likely to be repeated. But if failure is attributed to external factors that might change, then a person is likely to persist (Kernis, Zuckerman, Cohen, & Spadafora, 1982).

The locus-of-control factor in people's attributions of their past successes and failures—and expectations of future events—is learned in childhood and has significant implications from then on. One recent study showed that popular fifth graders see their social world as controllable, and they explain social success mainly in terms of individual characteristics and effort. Their less popular peers see the world as much less controllable and attribute social success and failure mainly to luck (Earn & Sobol, 1990). The two very different rules "I can work at becoming popular" and "popularity is a matter of luck" are presumably learned through experience, but once formulated lead to the (in)activities and outcomes that eventually support the rules. There is growing consensus among LOC researchers that *controllability of the world* is the crucial variable of attribution, which influences a wide range of behaviors far beyond academic success and the probability of dropping out of school (e.g., Lefcourt, 1981; Parker & Asher, 1987; Weiner, 1986).

The (Un)just World

A fascinating component of attribution is the individual's view of the larger world in which activities, events, and possible behavior consequence linkages are

APATHY AND IRRESPONSIBILITY

embedded. In recent years, social psychologists have analyzed people's different perceptions of the physical world and the social system in which they live; two perceptions are especially important, each implying its own set of operating principles (Lerner, 1980). These principles, in turn, are the major foundation of the rules that govern the behaviors of an individual's daily life.

One set of principles has been called the "just world hypothesis." Individuals who hold this perception of the social and physical systems in which they live assume that the world as a whole is just. Two significant components of this perception are: (1) the world is a coherent system of interrelated elements, and (2) events and relations among them are regular, predictable, and can be discovered. The major practical implications of this view are: (1) there are "right" or "appropriate" actions (by the individual and other people) that lead to success or are rewarded; (2) there are "wrong" or "inappropriate" actions that lead to failure or are punished. Hence, it makes sense for the individual to study the world, to discover what actions are appropriate, and to learn and perform them while avoiding other acts—in short, to behave "responsibly."

The second major set of principles has been called the "unjust world hypothesis." Individuals who share this perception of the social and physical systems in which they live assume that the world as a whole is unjust. Two significant components of this view are: (1) the world is a loose collection of independent elements, and (2) events occur randomly and cannot be predicted, and much of the world cannot be understood. The major implications of this view are: (1) positive and negative events are randomly distributed in the world and have no necessary linkage to human actions; (2) there are no "right" or "wrong," "appropriate," or "inappropriate" actions. A culture may define some actions as "good" or "appropriate" (and the opposite), of course, but the culturally designated consequences of such behaviors often do not occur and are difficult to predict. "Good" and "wrong" actions are equally likely to be rewarded and punished—at least in this world. Hence, there is little point in trying to understand the world or to discover "appropriate" and "effective" actions—indeed, all of these adjectives are meaningless and irrelevant. Consequently, it makes little sense to learn or prepare, even to try—anything. The result may well be (in)actions that an observer would label "apathy" and "irresponsibility."

Once again, behavior analysts see clear and definite implications for activities of daily life. An individual's description of the world as (un)just determines the presumed linkage (if any) between actions and their consequences—and thus the rules that govern one's behavior. For example, the large class of activities called "hard work" makes sense to those who believe that the world is just, for in such a world hard work will be rewarded. Conversely, low rates of behavior and even apathy are reasonable courses of (in)action for those who believe that the world is unjust: no matter how much or what a person does, positive and negative consequences are equally likely. In an unjust world there are few complete behavior lattices (Figure 12-2).

An example of research in this area concerns the attribution of problems and accidents (Burger, 1981). Most people believe that minor problems, mishaps, and small accidents are usually the result of bad luck or chance, perhaps of "probabilities catching up with me." Major problems and severe accidents, on the other hand, are usually considered to be the responsibility—even the fault—of the individual, who was careless, did not do the "right" thing, or performed the appropriate action inadequately. Blaming the victim is a common procedure and a reflection of one's perception of the world as just (e.g., Ryan, 1971).

The just-world hypothesis is another example of defensive attributions that make life in dynamic urban industrial societies bearable. Individuals can now explain to their own satisfaction why major problems happen to some people but are not likely to happen to themselves. If great difficulties and severe accidents are the results of ineffective or inappropriate actions, major problems can be avoided through the "right" behaviors—and people can therefore protect themselves.

The origin of these perceptions of the world has not been examined in detail, largely because long-term longitudinal studies would be required. However, there are indications that the number and proportion of positive events in a person's life, and the frequency of behavior-reward events one experiences, help shape one's view of the world (e.g., Scheier, Weintraub, & Carter, 1986). In this connection it is interesting to note that the just-world hypothesis has received considerably more research attention than the unjust-world hypothesis. Could this be a reflection of the fact that most social psychologists are members of the middle class and thus probably enjoy a good life?

Unique Invulnerability

A major variant of the (un)just world hypothesis is a perception of one's behavior called the "illusion of unique invulnerability." People who share this illusion believe that minor problems are randomly distributed in the population (e.g., the proverb: "into every life a little rain must fall"), but major problems inevitably affect only other people, and especially those who are very dissimilar (e.g., Shaver, 1970; Walster, 1966). The basic rule that arises from this illusion is: "this action of mine is not followed by aversive consequences." Whereas in a "just world" one has to behave appropriately to avoid problems, such avoidance is here automatic.

In a study with interesting implications, researchers discovered that sexually active college women varied greatly in their use of contraceptives (Burger & Burns, 1988). On one extreme, some women systematically used several effective methods; on the other pole, some women used poor contraceptives haphazardly, and some used nothing at all. One might wonder why this is so, especially in these days of widespread knowledge and the easy availability of the necessary means.

When the subjects were asked about the probabilities of various women becoming pregnant during the next year, their answers were quite unusual. The women believed that they themselves faced a 9% probability of unwanted pregnancy, whereas "other college women" were thought to a face a 27% probability and "other women my age" a 43% chance of unwanted pregnancy. Interestingly, many women who used the least effective methods were also certain that they themselves would not become pregnant. Most important, the sexually active women who were convinced that "other women" were likely to become pregnant, whereas they themselves would not, did not take precautions—precisely because they did not believe that they needed to! Finally, contrary experiences (such as a friend's actual pregnancy) did not weaken the conviction.

These behaviors and beliefs are counterintuitive and at first glance appear to be quite illogical. But they make sense to individuals whose behavior is governed by the rules implied by the illusion of unique invulnerability.

Other studies have shown the operation of this illusion in such areas as driving. For example, many people believe that although "fender benders" are randomly distributed and can happen to anyone, serious accidents happen mainly to other people (e.g., Schneider et al., 1979). It is only a short step from here to the conclusion that "I don't need to wear a seat belt, but you should buckle up." The implications for drunk driving and fatal accidents, and sexual activities and AIDS, are obvious.

Some indirect evidence of this illusion is provided by the fact that poor drivers and people who have many accidents also have the lowest rate of seat belt use (Evans & Wasielewski, 1983)—just as one might expect that sexually active women who do not use contraceptives are most likely to become pregnant. After all, the illusion of unique invulnerability does not bestow actual immunity from disaster.

The significance of this illusion for behavioral analysis lies in the fact that it contains rules (e.g., "bad things don't happen to me"), that reduce and/or eliminate the major consequences of certain activities. A crucial aversive contingency disappears—not using seat belts (or contraceptives) no longer has anything to do with probable injury, death, (or pregnancy). A major reinforcer for using seat belts (or contraceptives)—avoiding injury, death, (or pregnancy)—also disappears. Hence, one would predict that such behaviors, even when they are very simple, will be both difficult to establish and hard to maintain. Conversely, people who do not suffer from the illusion of unique invulnerability will be quite ready and perhaps eager to buckle up or use contraceptives. Activities that an observer would label "irresponsible" become at least reasonable by virtue of this illusion.

Social psychologists do not contend that everyone shares this illusion or that it covers all activities of daily life. Hence, not everyone who disdains the use of seat belts, for example, can be assumed to hold this illusion. Malott (1988) is no doubt correct when he hypothesizes that some people do not use seat belts because they consider the consequences of their neglect as being highly improbable. Behavior analysts who study complex, dynamic societies with heterogeneous populations must be ready to consider a range of determinants for any one activity.

The illusion of unique invulnerability turns out to be rather different from the usual mentalistic chimera. This "illusion," which behavior analysts at first glance may deem to be alien and useless, on close examination turns out to be an interesting set of rules—about the lack of major contingencies—that has crucial implications for a person's daily affairs.

The world of reality, which includes the actual probabilities of accidents and pregnancies, is one thing; the world of unique invulnerability is something quite different. Not everyone lives in the first world. Could it be that far fewer than half of the people do? For the others, it would be reasonable to buckle up only if forced to do so or when prompted in various ways (e.g., Williams, Thyer, Bailey, & Harrison, 1989).

CONCLUSION

Much of the work done by anthropologists, sociologists, and social psychologists has immediate relevance for behavior analysts because it is congruent with, and often derived from, behavioral principles. Indeed, social systems can be understood only if we analyze their operations in terms of individuals' rule-governed behaviors. When we analyze cultural norms that give rise to such rules—in a tribe, community, or urban industrial society—we examine what behavior analysts call metacontingencies. Yet there is great variability in a population's adherence to norms (see Chapter 3). Not everyone is equally affected by metacontingencies.

This chapter has reviewed two problematic aspects of metacontingencies in dynamic, urban industrial societies based on social psychological research:

1. The complex social structures in which individuals are enmeshed produce a large proportion of indirect and often convoluted links between a person's behavior and the ultimate outcome. The greater the number of people and actions involved in the chain, the greater the chance of (deliberate or random) error, and the longer the time scale. Hence, the linkage between many behaviors and their consequences is weakened and becomes nebulous. This makes the outcomes of many actions unpredictable and uncontrollable, leading to apathy and irresponsibility. Those who analyze social systems would argue that these problems, being a function of system size and complexity, are to a considerable extent endemic to modern society.

2. The metacontingencies that supposedly guide people's actions do not exist only in a society's norms. An equally important aspect of metacontingencies is people's perceptions of them. Indeed, attribution research by social psychologists leads to the conclusion that such perceptions are crucial for many activities: by ascribing causes to events that befall us, we perceive or deny a linkage between behavior and its outcome—and act accordingly. When attribution reflects reality, all is well—individuals learn, for example, that appropriate actions lead to positive outcomes whereas negative consequences can be avoided. But as social psychologists have discovered, many people make more or less systematic errors in their attributions. All too often, human beings construct behavior-outcome linkages that do not exist, do not recognize linkages that are there, and then behave according to erroneous rules.

It is comforting to live in a just world one can control and to believe in one's unique invulnerability. Perhaps that is why these assumptions and the consonant rules are so widely shared. But the behaviors that reflect those rules are not likely to be as effective in daily life as other actions one has learned in the real world. Apathy and irresponsible behaviors are all too frequent consequences of indirect linkages and misperceived relationships of activities and their outcomes. It remains to be seen whether these linkage problems are inevitable aspects of life in a complex, dynamic, urban-industrial society. Perhaps behavior analysts can discover a solution.

REFERENCES

Abramson, L. Y., Seligman, M. E. P., & Teasdale, J. (1978). Learned helplessness in humans: Critique and reformulation. *Journal of Abnormal Psychology, 87,* 49–74.

Banfield, E. C. (1970). *The unheavenly city: The nature and the future of our urban crisis.* Boston: Little, Brown.

Blake, J., & Davis, K. (1974). Norms, values, and sanctions. In R. E. L. Faris (Ed.), *Handbook of modern sociology* (pp. 456–484). Chicago: Rand McNally.

Brickner, M. A., Harkins, S. G., & Ostrom, T. M. (1986). Effects of personal involvement: Thought-provoking implications for social loafing. *Journal of Personality and Social Psychology, 51,* 763–769.

Burger, J. M. (1981). Motivational biases in the attribution of responsibility for an accident: A meta-analysis of the defensive attribution hypothesis. *Psychological Bulletin, 90,* 496–512.

Burger, J. M., & Burns, L. (1988). The illusion of unique invulnerability and the use of effective contraception. *Personality and Social Psychology Bulletin, 14,* 264–270.

Dobyns, H. F., Doughty, P. L., & Lasswell, H. (1971). *Peasants, power, and applied social change: Vicos as a model.* Beverly Hills: Sage.

Earn, B. M., & Sobol, M. P. (1990). A categorical analysis of children's attributions for social success and failure. *The Psychological Record, 40,* 173–185.

Evans, L., & Wasielewski, P. (1983). Risky driving related to driver and vehicle characteristics. *Accident Analysis and Prevention, 15,* 121–136.

Feshbach, M. (1982). The Soviet Union: Population trends and dilemmas. *Population Bulletin, 37*(2). Washington: Population Reference Bureau.

Geller, E. S., Rudd, J. R., Kalsher, M. J., Streff, F. M., & Lehman, G. R. (1987). Employer-based programs to motivate safety belt use: A review of short-term and long-term effects. *Journal of Safety Research, 18,* 1–17.

Gilmor, T. (1978). Locus of control as a mediator of adaptive behavior in children and adolescents. *Canadian Psychological Review, 19,* 1–26.

Harkins, S. G. (1987). Social loafing and social facilitation. *Journal of Experimental Social Psychology, 23,* 1–18.

Harkins, S. G., & Jackson, J. (1985). The role of evaluation in eliminating social loafing. *Personality and Social Psychology Bulletin, 11,* 457–465.

Harkins, S. G., & Petty, R. (1982). Effects of task difficulty and task uniqueness on social loafing. *Journal of Personality and Social Psychology, 43,* 1214–1229.

Harkins, S. G., & Szymanski, K. (1989). Social loafing and group evaluation. *Journal of Personality and Social Psychology, 56,* 934–941.

Hayes, S. C. (Ed.). (1989). *Rule-governed behavior: Cognition, contingencies, and instructional control.* New York: Plenum.

Heider, F. (1958). *The psychology of interpersonal relations.* New York: Wiley.

Hilton, D. J., & Slugoski, B. R. (1986). Knowledge-based causal attribution: The abnormal condition focus model. *Psychological Review, 93,* 75–88.

Ingham, A. G., Levinger, G., Graves, J., & Peckham, V. (1974). The Ringelmann effect: Studies of group size and group performance. *Journal of Experimental Social Psychology, 10,* 371–384.

Jackson, J., & Harkins, S. G. (1985). Equity in effort: An explanation of the social loafing effect. *Journal of Personality and Social Psychology, 49,* 1199–1206.

Jackson, J., & Williams, K. (1985). Social loafing on difficult tasks: Working collectively can improve performance. *Journal of Personality and Social Psychology, 49,* 937–942.

Kelley, H. H. (1973). The process of causal attribution. *American Psychologist, 28,* 107–128.

Kernis, M. H., Zuckerman, M., Cohen, A., & Spadafora, S. (1982). Persistence following failure: The interactive role of self-awareness and the attributional basis for negative expectancies. *Journal of Personality and Social Psychology, 43,* 1184–1191.

Kerr, N. L. (1983). Motivational losses in small groups: A social dilemma analysis. *Journal of Personality and Social Psychology, 45,* 819–828.

Kerr, N. L., & Bruun, S. E. (1981). Ringelmann revisited: Alternative explanations of the social loafing effect. *Personality and Social Psychology Bulletin, 7,* 224–231.

Kravitz, D. A., & Martin, B. (1986). Ringelmann rediscovered: The original article. *Journal of Personality and Social Psychology, 50,* 936–941.

Kunkel, J. H. (1975). *Behavior, social problems, and change.* Englewood Cliffs, NJ: Prentice-Hall.

Kunkel, J. H. (1986). The Vicos Project: A cross-cultural test of psychological propositions. *The Psychological Record, 36,* 451–466.

Latané, B., Williams, K., & Harkins, S. G. (1979). Many hands make light the work: The causes and consequences of social loafing. *Journal of Personality and Social Psychology, 37,* 822–832.

Lefcourt, H. M. (Ed.). (1981). *Research with the locus of control construct.* New York: Academic Press.

Lerner, M. J. (1980). *The belief in a just world: A fundamental illusion.* New York: Plenum.

Lewis, O. (1961). *Five families.* New York: Random House.

Lewis, O. (1964). *Pedro Martinez.* New York: Random House.

Lewis, O. (1966). *La vida.* New York: Random House.

Malenfant, J. E. L., & Van Houten, R. (1988). The effects of nighttime seat belt enforcement. *Journal of Applied Behavior Analysis, 21,* 271–276.

Malott, R. W. (1988). Rule-governed behavior and behavioral anthropology. *The Behavior Analyst, 11*, 181–203.

Malott, R. W. (1989). The achievement of evasive goals. In S. C. Hayes (Ed.), *Rule-governed behavior: Cognitions, contingencies, and instructional control* (pp. 269–322). New York: Plenum.

Metalsky, G. I., Abramson, L. Y., Seligman, M. E. P., Semmel, A., & Peterson, C. (1982). Attributional styles and life events in the classroom: Vulnerability and invulnerability to depressive mood reactions. *Journal of Personality and Social Psychology, 43*, 612–617.

Parker, J. G., & Asher, S. R. (1987). Peer relations and later personal adjustment: Are low-accepted children at risk? *Psychological Bulletin, 102*, 357–389.

Pedersen, D. M., Keithly, S., & Brady, K. (1986). Effects of an observer on conformity to handwashing norm. *Perceptual and Motor Skills, 62*, 169–170.

Peterson, C., & Barrett, L. C. (1987). Explanatory style and academic performance among university freshmen. *Journal of Personality and Social Psychology, 53*, 603–607.

Peterson, C., & Seligman, M. E. P. (1984). Causal explanations as a risk factor for depression: Theory and evidence. *Psychological Review, 91*, 347–374.

Peterson, C., Villanova, P., & Raps, C. S. (1985). Depression and attributions: Factors responsible for inconsistent results in the published literature. *Journal of Abnormal Psychology, 94*, 165–168.

Reese, H. W. (1989). Rules and rule-governance: Cognitive and behavioristic views. In S. C. Hayes, (Ed.), *Rule-governed behavior: Cognition, contingencies, and instructional control* (pp. 3–84). New York: Plenum.

Rotter, J. B. (1966). Generalized expectancies for internal versus external control of reinforcement. *Psychological Monographs, 80* (Whole No. 609).

Rotter, J. B. (1990). Internal versus external control of reinforcement: A case history of a variable. *American Psychologist, 45*, 489–493.

Ryan, W. (1971). *Blaming the victim.* New York: Vintage.

Scheier, M. F., Weintraub, J. K., & Carver, C. S. (1986). Coping with stress: Divergent strategies of optimists and pessimists. *Journal of Personality and Social Psychology, 51*, 1257–1264.

Schneider, D. J., Hastorf, A. H., & Ellsworth, P. C. (1979). *Person perception* (2nd ed.). Reading, MA: Addison Wesley.

Shaver, K. G. (1970). Defensive attribution: Effects of severity and relevance on the responsibility assigned for an accident. *Journal of Personality and Social Psychology, 14*, 101–113.

Steiner, I. (1972). *Group processes and productivity.* New York: Academic Press.

Strickland, B. R. (1990). Internal-external control expectancies: From contingency to creativity. *American Psychologist, 45*, 1–12.

Sweeney, P. D., Anderson, K., & Bailey, S. (1986). Attributional style in depression: A meta-analytic review. *Journal of Personality and Social Psychology, 50*, 974–991.

Szymanski, K., & Harkins, S. G. (1987). Social loafing and self-evaluation with a social standard. *Journal of Personality and Social Psychology, 53*, 891–897.

Turnbull, C. M. (1972). *The mountain people.* New York: Simon & Schuster.

Walster, E. (1966). Assignment of responsibility for important events. *Journal of Personality and Social Psychology, 3*, 73–79.

Weiner, B. (1986). *An attributional theory of emotions and motivation.* New York: Springer.

Williams, K., Harkins, S. G., & Latane, B. (1981). Identifiability as a deterrent to social loafing: Two cheering experiments. *Journal of Personality and Social Psychology, 40*, 303–311.

Williams, M., Thyer, B. A., Bailey, J. S., & Harrison, D. F. (1989). Promoting safety belt use with traffic signs and prompters. *Journal of Applied Behavior Analysis, 22*, 71–76.

Williams, R. M. (1968). The concept of norms. *International encyclopaedia of the social sciences: Vol. 2*, pp. 204–208. New York: Macmillan.

Zettle, R. D. (1990). Rule-governed behavior: A radical behavioral answer to the cognitive challenge. *The Psychological Record, 40*, 41–49.

Zuckerman, M. (1979). Attribution of success and failure revisited. *Journal of Personality, 47*, 245–287.

III

THE FUTURE

13

The Road Ahead

J. H. Kunkel and P. A. Lamal

INTRODUCTION

This final chapter draws together several major themes that have emerged in the foregoing pages and outlines the future to which these point. The discussion begins with a sketch of the roots that nurtured behavior analysis in the early years and gave the field its present content and form. The chapter then describes the present state of behavior analysis, and, finally, considers the future course of behavior analysis, with an emphasis on social structures and processes and on social problems and their solutions. The preceding chapters bear eloquent testimony to the possibilities that lie in that direction.

THE EARLY YEARS

The major roots of modern behavior analysis lie in animal experiments of the 1940s and 1950s that were designed to elucidate the principles of operant conditioning. This tradition is still vigorous today, as is evident in the *Journal of the Experimental Analysis of Behavior* (JEAB). The last 40 years have witnessed an increasing emphasis on human beings, and today there are several publications in that area (e.g., the *Journal of Applied Behavior Analysis,* and *Behavior Modification,* and JEAB also publishing human studies).

In the early years of human behavior analysis, most experiments and field studies focused on single individuals, relatively simple activities, and restricted settings over which experimenters could exert considerable control. The classroom behavior of children and the activities of patients in (mental) hospitals were favorite topics, in large part because researchers encountered minimal problems of measurement and control (Kunkel, 1987). These problems were important concerns because the operation of learning principles in the complex activities of daily life had yet to be demonstrated—both to a skeptical public and to psychologists of other theoretical persuasions.

Within a few years, hundreds of human studies had demonstrated beyond a doubt that operant conditioning principles underlie a wide range of human activities. Once the nature and workings of operant principles in daily affairs had been well established, behavior analysts were free to venture beyond the confines of their earlier work. Complex behaviors, normal adults, and the free settings of ordinary life have become increasingly frequent aspects of behavior analysts' work. (Examples of this work can be found in Chapters 6 and 7.) Yet the strength of that early tradition has made it difficult to break new ground.

BEHAVIOR ANALYSIS TODAY

Behavior analysts have been especially reluctant to venture beyond the time-honored traditions of "single subject analysis" and "controlled settings." Were those traditions to continue, behavior analysts would be limited to little more than remedial and preventive work centering on individuals' behavior problems. Furthermore, those traditions would exclude behavior analysts from the study of social phenomena and prevent them from contributing to our understanding of larger societal issues.

B. F. Skinner was never reluctant to comment on social problems and often proposed that operant conditioning principles should become the basis of cultural design. Yet so far only a few behavior analysts have ventured into communities—or beyond—and few social scientists have taken behavioral principles seriously. The facets of social engineering have not become popular (for a related point, see Lamal, 1989), and flaws have been all too evident—beginning with *Walden Two*.

However, in recent years an increasing number of behavior analysts have shown a deepening interest in the study of large-scale social phenomena. We cite four major reasons for this shift in interest. First, the study of individuals' problems naturally led to contextual determinants that are embedded in the larger social world. Second, a broadening of vision allowed younger behavior analysts to venture beyond the boundaries that the first generation had originally defined. Encouraged, perhaps, by greater self-confidence, behavior analysts ventured beyond experiments, discovered new legitimate areas of study, and relaxed the rigid standards of "proper experiments." Third, new theoretical tools have enabled behavior analysts to venture with confidence beyond single individuals and small groups. Among these tools are the acceptance of rule-governed behavior and meta-contingencies as both legitimate concepts and appropriate foci of research. Finally, it is likely that new research opportunities were sought because there was not enough work in the traditional pursuits—just as anthropologists have turned to the study of modern cities as exotic tribes have become scarce.

THE ROAD AHEAD

The route that behavior analysts are about to take is not a trail that must be laboriously hacked through the dangerous jungles of an inhospitable social science. Instead, we can follow a winding path that others have already cleared—and on which we can now greatly improve. Theorists, as well as researchers with practical interests such as economic development, have for some time employed the principles of behavior analysis though not, perhaps, by name.

For example, more than 30 years ago the anthropologist Charles Erasmus (1961) described several effective community development projects whose success was mainly a result of the wise use of operant principles. Erasmus advocated what is today called behavior analysis and argued that the essence of economic development is large-scale behavior modification. Kunkel (1970) described the technical details of that position based on operant principles and drawing on case material from around the world. Whyte and Williams (1968) outlined an "integrated theory of development" that also had behavior analysis as its major foundation—necessarily unacknowledged. Although most sociologists focus on the analysis of large-scale phenomena, there has been a strong theoretical undercurrent that emphasizes the role of individuals' activities. Beginning in the early 1960s, researchers as diverse as Homans (1961) and Blau (1964) demonstrated the utility of learning principles for the analysis of social behavior, and Kunkel (1967) showed that human ecology is essentially the large-scale manifestation of operant principles.

In short, there is a 30-year history of receptivity to principles that are now part of behavior analysis. In the future, the social sciences will no doubt continue this tradition of intellectual hospitality. Many researchers in several disciplines are likely to consider behavior analysts as potential colleagues—if we practice some humility while we donate proven principles and effective methods.

The present state of behavior analysis offers its practitioners ample opportunities to chart a wide and variegated future. As the preceding chapters have demonstrated, this future includes a host of novel research topics, the exploration of new variables, and the discovery of new explanatory propositions. Equally important, there are growing possibilities of mutually beneficial relations with other areas of psychology and promises of effective cooperation with other disciplines (e.g., Chapter 12). The several developments that have been outlined in this book indicate that the coming years will be as exciting as the past. Researchers who are interested in behavioral analysis of societies and cultural practices are likely to focus their attention on the following four areas.

Theory

It is generally agreed that theories that account for a wide range of phenomena are more useful than theories of more limited scope (for an example of theory appraisal and radical behaviorism, see Lamal, 1988). Hence the extension of behavior analysis to societies and cultural practices is a positive development for both theory and practice. This theoretical broadening is made possible—and encouraged—by the appearance of such conceptual tools as rule-governed behavior and metacontingencies (Chapters 1, 2, and 3), and by the recent exploration of contextualism. The subject matter itself will introduce new and fascinating dimensions (such as longer time frames) into researchers' analyses. The next 20 years will no doubt witness the discovery and development of additional concepts and principles as investigators study more complex social phenomena and face new questions. As Lamal noted in Chapter 1, the formulations that appear in this volume are tentative, not canonical.

Methods

In Chapter 1 Lamal also maintained that the behavioral analysis of societies and cultural practices requires a variety of methods—some borrowed from the social sciences long experienced in the area, and others derived from the classic behavior analytic perspective. A major change will be the move away from high degrees of experimental control and short time frames that heretofore have been the hallmark of applied behavior analysis. Instead, quasiexperiments and observational studies will have to be carried out, as suggested by Pierce (Chapter 2) and Kunkel (Chapter 12). Equally important, the new emphasis on societal processes will require that researchers be open to new sources of information and data collected over longer periods of time—such as the effects of legislation and the course of political reforms and economic policies.

Relations with Psychology and Other Disciplines

Behavior analysis will no longer be able to retain its present rather insular position. As investigators shift their attention to societal processes and cultural phenomena, they will increasingly rely on researchers in adjacent disciplines. Chapters 1 and 12 have demonstrated that the work of social psychologists and anthropologists can—and should—become valuable sources of new data and methods, not to mention interesting hypotheses. Indeed, the behavioral analysis of societies may not be possible without new colleagues. For example, the anthropologist Marvin Harris has investigated several hypotheses that fit directly into the behavior analytic paradigm (cf. Chapters 2 and 3).

However, at the same time behavior analysts should not overestimate the potential contributions of other perspectives and disciplines. Some of these differ significantly from radical behaviorism and may not be compatible with the behavioral analysis of societies.

Applications

The behavioral analysis of societies provides a firm empirical foundation for designing social programs and implementing procedures that have a high probability of success. During the last few years numerous effective projects in organizations and communities have been described in the *Journal of Organizational Behavior Management.* In the future, further large-scale applications will be discussed in the new publication *Behavior and Social Issues.*

Policy Issues

Several chapters in Part II analyze the failures that result from widespread ignorance of behavioral principles. Pierce (Chapter 2) points out that for many years economists and other social scientists have provided policy makers with general advice and specific programs that lacked valid foundations. Lamal (Chapter 4) and Rakos (Chapter 5) outline some of the behaviorally deficient practices in socialist countries. Greenspoon (Chapter 8) and Ellis (Chapter 11) discuss several practices in higher education and penology, respectively, that are generally ineffective and would greatly benefit from rigorous applications of the behavioral perspective. In Chapter 10, Hovell, Kaplan, and Hovell draw a similar picture of the preventive medical services in the United States. Redmon and Wilke (Chapter 6) and Redmon and Agnew (Chapter 7) provide numerous examples of successful behavioral interventions in the public and private sectors of the economy.

In spite of frequent and notable failures policy makers and politicians in many countries continue to seek advice from the same old sources. In large part this loyalty reflects an ignorance of viable alternatives—in terms of both empirically grounded theories and successful, effective applications. The behavioral analysis of societies and cultural practices described in this book offers a proven alternative.

REFERENCES

Blau, P. M. (1964). *Exchange and power in social life.* New York: Wiley.

Erasmus, C. J. (1961). *Man takes control.* Minneapolis: University of Minnesota Press.

Homans, G. C. (1961). *Social behavior: Its elementary forms.* New York: Harcourt Brace.

Kunkel, J. H. (1967). Some behavioral aspects of the ecological approach to social organization. *American Journal of Sociology, 73,* 12–29.

Kunkel, J. H. (1970). *Society and economic growth: A behavioral perspective of social change.* New York: Oxford University Press.

Kunkel, J. H. (1987). The future of *JABA*: A comment. *Journal of Applied Behavior Analysis, 20,* 329–333.

Lamal, P. A. (1988). Radical behaviorism and selected theses concerning theory appraisal. *The Psychological Record, 38,* 175–185.

Lamal, P. A. (1989). The impact of behaviorism on our culture: Some evidence and conjectures. *The Psychological Record, 39,* 529–535.

Whyte, W. F., & Williams, L. K. (1968). *Toward an integrated theory of development.* Ithaca: Cornell University Press.

Index

Gillmore, M. R., 19, 20
Glass, G. V., 22, 23
Glenn, S. S., 3, 10, 28, 56, 59, 60, 62, 70,
    88, 89, 92, 115, 120, 125, 142, 169,
    170, 176, 201, 203, 204, 205, 208,
    213, 215
Glenwick, D., 4, 31
Goetz, E. M., 50
Golden, K. M., 211
Goldstein, M. K., 8
Gomulka, S., 87, 88, 90, 99, 102
Gorbachev, M., 87, 88, 91
Gortmaker, S., 190
Gottman, J. M., 22
Gould, S. J., 43
Graves, J., 222
Gray, L., 148
Gray, L. N., 19, 23
Green, C. W., 112
Green, L., 95
Greenway, D. E., 95
Gregory, D., 172
Gross, A. E., 26
Guevremont, D. C., 166
Gunkler, J. W., 133, 134

Haas, J. R., 95
Hake, D. F., 17
Hall, R. V., 114
Hamblin, R. L., 17
Hannah, G. T., 110
Harkins, S. G., 222, 223
Harlow, H. F., 17
Harnad, S., 170
Harrington, W. A., 206
Harris, M., 3, 8, 28, 29, 40, 57, 59, 60, 63,
    64, 66, 67, 68, 70, 71, 125, 142, 169,
    170
Harrison, D. F., 237
Hart, J. M., 144
Hartnagel, D., 112
Hartstone, E., 172
Harwood, I., 185
Harzem, P., 170, 174
Hastorf, R. H., 25
Hause, J. D., 21
Hawkins, R., 203, 204, 209, 214
Hayes, S. C., 4, 54, 77, 95, 175, 228
Haynes, S. N., 174
Heider, F., 231
Heinrich, H. G., 87, 88, 91, 92, 96, 97, 98,
    99, 100, 101, 102
Henderson, R. J., 129

Hendricks, C. G., 4, 170, 174, 175
Henney, J. S., 172
Hensch, S. A., 22
Herman, K., 212
Hernandez, D., 32
Herrnstein, R. J., 15, 19, 51, 66, 92, 172,
    174, 202
Hersen, M., 167
Hershey, C., 190
Heth, D. C., 22
Hewett, E. A., 80, 81
Higher education:
    administrator contingencies, 159–164
    consequences, 154–159
    faculty contingencies, 142–154
Hillson, J., 103
Hilton, D. J., 233
Himelein, M. J., 201
Hineline, P. N., 44, 48
Hinrichs, J. R., 134
Hobbs, T. R., 206
Hockenos, P., 87
Hofstadter, R., 143
Hokanson, J. E., 167
Holburn, C. S., 204
Holland, J. G., 10, 31
Holt, M. M., 206
Homans, G. C., 3, 245
Hopkins, B. L., 109, 125, 132, 133
Hoppe, C., 205, 214
Hovell, M., 181, 182, 183, 185, 186, 194
Howell, W. C., 135
Hsiao, W., 188
Hughes, D., 192
Hull, D., 46
Hurley, J., 190
Hutchison, E., 205, 213, 215
Hyten, C., 17

Ingham, A. G., 222, 223
Ingram, D., 192
Institute of Medicine, 192
Irresponsibility:
    behavioral principles and social structure,
        225–227
    definition of, 220, 221
    norms and rule-governed behavior,
        227–230
    personal rules and attribution, 230–237
        general attribution, 230–233
        just/unjust world, 234–236